D0945522

Beans, Greens & Sweet Georgia Peaches

SECOND EDITION

THE SOUTHERN WAY OF COOKING FRUITS AND VEGETABLES

Damon Lee Fowler

Guilford, Connecticut

ST. JOHN THE BAPTIST PARISH LIBRARY
2920 NEW HIGHWAY 51
LAPLACE, LOUISIANA 70068

To buy books in quantity for corporate use
or incentives, call **(800) 962-0973**
or e-mail **premiums@GlobePequot.com**.

Copyright © 2014 Damon Lee Fowler

ALL RIGHTS RESERVED. No part of this book may
be reproduced or transmitted in any form by any
means, electronic or mechanical, including photo-
copying and recording, or by any information storage
and retrieval system, except as may be expressly
permitted in writing from the publisher. Requests
for permission should be addressed to Globe Pequot
Press, Attn: Rights and Permissions Department, 246
Goose Lane, Suite 200, Guilford, CT 06437.

Photos by Damon Lee Fowler: pages 13, 18, 24, 34, 57,
59, 63 (left), 69, 73, 81, 85, 87 (right), 69,73, 81, 85, 87
(right), 89, 91, 95, 100, 101, 105, 107, 126, 130, 132, 134,
142, 155, 157, 199, 200, 201, 202, 203, 220, 222, 224,
226, 243, 249, 259, 264, 271, 272, 276.
Photos licensed by Shutterstock.com: pages ii–iii, 1,
2, 4, 5, 6, 7, 8, 10, 11, 15, 17, 20, 27, 30, 33, 36, 40, 43, 45,
49, 50, 52, 54, 62, 63 (right), 65, 66, 67, 70, 75, 80, 83,
87 (left), 90, 93, 97, 98, 102, 119, 120, 122, 125, 129, 135,
147, 164, 165, 166, 167, 168, 171, 172, 174, 175, 177, 182,
186, 188, 193, 195, 196, 197, 206, 210, 212, 221, 227, 228,
230, 232, 252, 254, 260, 268, 275, 278, 283.
Photo by John Carrington: page 151.

Editor: Amy Lyons
Project Editor: Meredith Dias
Text Design & Layout Artist: Nancy Freeborn
Map by Alena Pearce © Morris Book Publishing, LLC

Library of Congress Cataloging-in-Publication Data
is available on file.

ISBN 978-0-7627-9212-2

Printed in the United States of America

IN LOVING MEMORY OF MY AUNT, ALICE HOLMES VERMILLION,

THE BEST VEGETABLE COOK I'VE EVER KNOWN

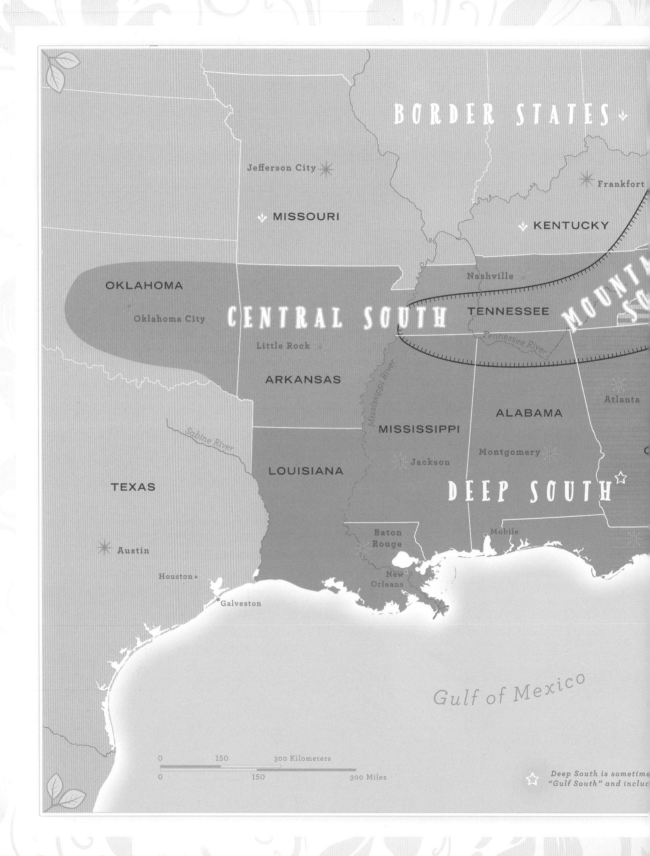

BORDER STATES

Jefferson City ✳

⌄ MISSOURI

✳ Frankfort

⌄ KENTUCKY

Nashville

MOUNTAIN
SO

OKLAHOMA

CENTRAL SOUTH

TENNESSEE

Oklahoma City ✳

Tennessee River

Little Rock ✳

ARKANSAS

Mississippi River

ALABAMA

Atlanta ✳

MISSISSIPPI

Sabine River

Montgomery ✳

LOUISIANA

Jackson ✳

DEEP SOUTH ☆

TEXAS

Baton
Rouge

Mobile ●

✳ Austin

Houston ●

New
Orleans

● Galveston

Gulf of Mexico

| 0 | 150 | 300 Kilometers |

| 0 | 150 | 300 Miles |

☆ Deep South is sometime
"Gulf South" and includ

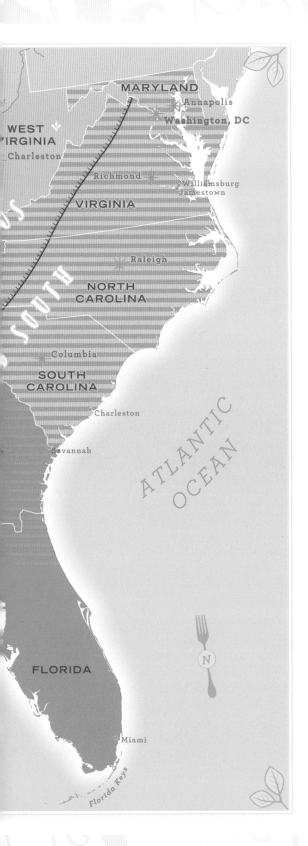

Contents

Acknowledgments

Southerners only sound as if their mouths are full of grits all the time; usually, they aren't. But our mouths really are open most of the time where food is concerned. We're either eating or, the next best thing to it, talking about eating. This is a lucky break for any writer interested in Southern food.

In order to get the essential character of the Southern way with produce, I talked to as many good Southern cooks as I could find. Getting them to talk wasn't difficult; getting them to hush was. Fortunately, they tend to be generous souls; I often got recipes without asking for them. Many recipes came from friends and relatives, and even from people who were complete strangers to me when I asked for their help. I have a file of twice as many recipes as follow on these pages, a testament to their generous spirit. Those who gave me recipes are credited in the text. Space prevents my listing you all here, but I thank y'all with all my heart.

The first people I must thank are the ones who will protest that they were only doing their jobs—my agents, Elise and Arnold Goodman. Without their believing in me, the idea for the book would never have blossomed, much less sold. My original editor, Harriet Bell, with her keen eye, keener taste buds, and enthusiasm for good food and writing—not to mention her friendship—made this book great fun to put together. And my new editor, Amy Lyons, who believed in this book, did not believe it was finished and rescued it from the dusty shelf where it had been lying fallow for the better part of two decades.

The late Marcella Hazan and her husband, Victor, continue to be my inspiration and the rule by which I measure my own work. They have touched every aspect of my life and career with a generosity that still fills me with awe. Without them, I would never have had the courage to make the fateful leap into a new career and it is their unflinching fidelity to the universal principles of good cooking that have kept me on the straight and narrow.

Karen Hess was my friend, teacher, counselor, and moral guide in one. She was never too busy to help me with a problem in research or cooking technique, or to just lend me her ear when my spirits were lagging. I miss so much about her, but I think what I miss most is her raucous laugh. Such merit as my work has owes her a large debt.

John Martin Taylor has been constant with his friendship and professional support. His friendship and, through him, that of his sister Sue Highfield and partner, Mikel Herrington, have been a continuous joy and inspiration.

While I was working on the original edition of this book, Jackie Mills, Andria Hurst, and Judy Bess Feagin were at *Southern Living* magazine, and generously provided great technical and moral support. Jackie gave me recipes, and Judy (then head of the magazine's legendary test kitchen) talked me though recipe-testing problems.

When I am lax about staying in touch with her, I'll get a call out of the blue from my drill sergeant, Nathalie Dupree, to catch up on gossip, see what I'm up to, and to make sure that I'm staying as busy as she thinks I ought to be. She gave me several recipes for this collection, but her contribution, through her friendship, has been much larger than that.

As only Southerners can, Ruth Adams Bronz and I became very close friends in a short period of time. When we were barely acquainted, she carted me all over New England with no more recommendation than that we were both Southern and loved food. She's my one-woman therapy group. And speaking of therapy, one phone call from my late friend Marie Rudisill (also known as the Fruitcake Lady) was known to get me through six months without going off the deep end. Her wit and wisdom have been both life preserver and compass, and I miss her every day.

Fellow writer Martha Giddens Nesbit has been an ever-present and reliable friend and technical support. When I think I can't go on, I would just watch Martha juggle a successful marriage, two growing boys, and two careers, and think I had it easy after all. Martha also introduced me to our mentor and Macon Mama, Clara Eschmann, who shared my creed: Thank God for Bourbon. Clara let me run off with some of her books without scolding me—much. She has passed on since the first edition of this book, but her spirit still informs and inspires my food writing.

"Jane's Canners," the brigade of women who make pickles, relishes, and chutneys for St. John's annual bazaar, were game to be invaded by a man and helped me test the canning recipes in this book. Headed up by the parish's capable (and first female) senior warden, Jane Pressly, and co-chair Betty Shepherd, they were Evelyn Birchall, Nancy Cope, Mary Ellen Greenwood, Cathy Jarman, Louise Mauer, Laurie Osteen, and Millie Summerell.

My former neighbor Tom Edenfield had nothing whatsoever to do with this book, but badgered me about not being mentioned in my first one until I promised to put his name in here. There you go, Tom. Yet another neighbor, Richard Galloway, gave me free access to modern office equipment and let me regularly raid his herb garden. Still another, Renee Zito, loaned me antique books. Virginia Scott lent me several cookbooks from her collection and let me keep them for a lot longer than most would. My friend and former architectural clients Susan and Rick Sontag have been a tremendous support—in both professions.

As always my parents have been generous in their support. They spent years and untold amounts of money helping me become an architect, but they also have thrown their unqualified support behind me as I drift into another career—and have been amazingly silent about the tremendous debt that I owe them. This time, they also actively helped with recipe research. I feel lucky that they are still around.

My late friend Jim King allowed me to subject him to test runs of every single recipe in this book and was generous and unflinchingly honest with his opinion, whether I wanted to hear it or not. Jim is no longer with us, but in the years since this book was first published, the role of unflinching critic has been amply filled by Timothy Hall, who keeps me grounded and centered.

Finally, my gratitude and love to all traditional Southern cooks everywhere, from Shreveport to Sri Lanka, who have never stopped believing that the Southern way with flavor is good and worth preserving, who have kept the faith in the face of culinary fads and packaged food—who remain steadfast in a world that is changing faster than a Southern belle's mind.

Thank God for every one of you.

The Essentials

The Soul of Southern Cooking

VEGETABLES AND FRUIT

The words "Southern cooking" inevitably have great conjuring power, though what they conjure may not always be very close to reality. The first thing that the words usually evoke, at least for most people, seems to be fried chicken; and, you might well wonder, why not? Celebrated the world over, there are surely few things to eat that can equal its perfection. I've heard fried chicken called the "soul" of Southern cooking, a point that surely few would argue.

And yet, if I were to choose one thing that characterizes the many diverse cuisines that make up what we call Southern cooking, what I would call its "soul," it would not be fried chicken—even though I wrote an entire book on the subject. What I would choose is produce. For the real heart and soul of a Southern table, whether that table is in Tidewater Virginia, the Carolina Lowcountry, or the depths of a Louisiana bayou, is not the meat in the middle of it but the vegetables and fruit that surround it.

Yet Southern vegetables have not—at least in our century—enjoyed much of a reputation. In fact, for years they've been maligned and subjected to much derision. One might almost say that Southern vegetables have made our foodways not famous but infamous. If you are persistent and finally pry people away from notions of fried chicken, the best they will probably do in recalling Southern vegetables is "slimy" okra, boiled collards, and green beans boiled to hell and back with a piece of bacon—a sad, and grossly mistaken, impression.

In direct contradiction of that impression, the South has often been called "America's garden," and not without justification. From the very beginning—even before heavy-duty European colonization—ours has been a mostly agrarian society and our economy has depended almost completely on growing things. Though every farm and plantation had the usual barnyard animals, animal husbandry was not a highly developed art until recent years. It's important to remember that whenever people live close to the land in this way, regardless of where they are, produce inevitably has a high profile in their diet. This is especially true of the South, even of today's urbanized, industrialized, and internationalized South.

Few modern Southerners would raise their own frying chickens, even if their local zoning laws would permit it, yet it isn't unusual to find a vegetable patch in the midst of urban Atlanta. In less urban settings, the most elegant of gardens in the most fashionable of suburbs will, at the very least, sport a few tomato plants. Southerners will put up with a lot, but don't mess with our fresh tomatoes and okra.

Now, there's no one vegetable or fruit that can be singled out as the most representative of a Southern garden. I would even hesitate over tomatoes and okra. For, while a single vegetable may figure prominently in the diet of a particular region or community of the South, as rice did for centuries in the Carolina Lowcountry, or as collard greens do even now among so many African-American families, what really characterizes the Southern table is not any single fruit or vegetable but the fact that there are so many. From early spring, when much of the rest of the

country is still frozen, until the late frosts of our relatively mild winters, literally hundreds of varieties of fruits and vegetables are to be found growing in Southern gardens and enjoyed on Southern tables. It's on the strength of this diversity that the once legendary reputation of Southern cooking was built.

The greatest obstacle to understanding Southern cooking is that which makes the region itself so difficult to grasp: the sheer size of it. Stretching from the Mason–Dixon line to Key West, from North Carolina's Outer Banks to the plains of western Texas, the South (including Arkansas, Oklahoma, and West Virginia) incorporates nearly a million square miles of land.

In short, the South is many places and has many faces—a land of felicitous harmonies and jarring contradictions. It is, at once, the earthiness of the rolling upcountry farmland, my home by birth, and the urbane elegance of my adopted home on the Colonial coast. It's the rugged wilderness of the Ozark Mountains and the electric wilderness of South Beach, Miami; the lush bottomland of South Georgia and the arid plains of West Texas. It's the forthright, earthy subsistence of mountaineers and genteel civility of coastal planter aristocrats. It's Mr. Jefferson's Monticello and Dori Sanders's produce stand in Filbert, South Carolina. It's string quartets in Charleston

and jazz in New Orleans, Jessye Norman at the opera and Patsy Cline at the Grand Old Opry, tent revivals and televangelists, Elvis and Charlie Daniels.

Obviously, Southern cooking can be—and is—as complex and varied as all that. From hoppin' John to fried rice, the variations are endless, for all these different elements have made their contributions to the Southern pot. But even with all these differences, one can distinguish a common thread—and that is the union of the English cooking practices, which came to dominate all other cuisines both native and immigrant, with the sensibility of the African cooks, which transformed it.

The most useful thing to know about all the different cuisines of the South is that their foundation is basically European. Legends of Native American cookery notwithstanding, the European settlers swept aside the indigenous cultures and brought their own culture—and cooking practices—with them. While the settlers did learn from the Native Americans, most particularly about the many plants that have become so intrinsically a part of our diet today, their fundamental cooking practices did not change; they simply adapted new ingredients to their old foodways. So, the basic structure of Southern cooking remained European—and,

since it was the English colonists who eventually dominated, mostly English.

Now, in other parts of the Anglo colonies, that's just about as far as it went. The basic structure survived little altered from what it had been in England. But the cooking of the South very quickly went in its own direction. The difference, of course, lay in who was doing most of the cooking—the African slaves, at least in the cooking of the upper-classes. For the better part of three centuries, African cooks dominated upper-class Southern kitchens. As those cooks established themselves, and gradually began to change the food that went on their white masters' tables, their cooking practices eventually changed those of the white mistress and even trickled down the social ladder to poor white families. Gradually, as generation upon generation adapted, the cooking of the entire region was transformed.

There are many clues that give away the African influence on Southern foodways. Most obvious are the many African ingredients that are so common in Southern food: rice, peanuts, okra, legumes such as black-eyed and cowpeas, and sesame seeds. (Ironically, peanuts are not native to Africa, and ultimately nor is okra, but both were already an established part of the African diet when slaves began to be imported into America.) It also seems pretty certain that we owe the popularity of such diverse vegetables as Asian eggplant, Central American tomatoes, American sweet potatoes, and European collard greens to the influence of those African cooks as well. While none of those vegetables are African in origin, they were either already known to African cooks before they were brought into America, or they resembled vegetables with which they were already familiar.

Aside from ingredients, there are a number of Southern specialties that are distinctly African—if not in origin, at least in sensibility. There are bean and rice dishes, including (and especially) the bean pilau we call "hoppin' John," those many pots of greens and gumbo, and fritters of all kinds. Another telling clue is that in the midst of all the radical changes that were happening in other areas, baking, which remained mostly the province of the white mistress, changed only nominally. And baking was something over which the African cook had the least control.

Now, the intention here is not to throw credit too far in one direction or the other. I have mentioned it because, historically, while African cooks have been given full credit for skill, they get very little credit for innovation. But even as we celebrate that innovation, we must keep in mind that it occurred within the framework of European cooking practices, in what were basically European kitchens, sometimes (though admittedly probably less often than not) hand-in-hand with the white mistress. The real magic of Southern cooking is not solely its European foundations or African innovations but the masterful union of the two traditions.

Nowhere is that union better displayed than in the way Southern cooks have with the produce of the garden. Whether it is a savory gumbo, or a sumptuous peach cobbler, or a fried apple or a green tomato pie, the Southern touch is subtle, carefully balanced, full of flavor, and yet never overblown. So perfect is the balance that one is sometimes hard-pressed to discern what's European, African, and Native.

The strength of the Southern way with produce has always lain in the freshness of its

ingredients. Even with our modern air freight, real just-picked freshness is only possible when the fruit or vegetable has been locally grown in its natural season.

In *Mrs. Hill's New Cook Book* (1867), Annabella Hill asserted that vegetables intended for dinner (which was at two o'clock in the afternoon) "should be gathered early in the morning. A few only can be kept twelve hours without detriment." I wouldn't want to hear that lady pronounce on the average supermarket produce section. Such sensibility has unfortunately been lost to most of us, but some of it can be recovered, even if you live in the middle of the city. With a little care, you can still find reasonably fresh produce for these recipes. All it requires is that you redevelop a seasonal mentality and take a little more time and care to seek out locally grown fruits and vegetables. A seasonal mentality simply means becoming more conscious of the rhythms of planting and harvest in the area where you live, learning to appreciate the fuller flavors of in-season produce.

Since the first edition of this book, urban farmers' markets have made a big comeback, and it's not only easier than ever for even city dwellers to get quality fresh produce, the selection of available produce has broadened enormously.

To that end, the recipes in this book are divided into seasons in accord with the time of year that they ripen *where I live*. These divisions aren't meant to be taken as gospel. Even in the South, the exact season for a fruit or vegetable can vary. I've put broccoli in the fall chapter, but in Savannah it remains seasonal through the winter and into spring. In other places, it's mainly a spring vegetable. But by organizing them in accordance with their distinctive seasons—at least in Southeast Georgia—a rhythm begins to develop. Once this rhythm is established in your kitchen, then you start to appreciate the fuller flavor of seasonal cooking.

You'll prefer spring asparagus and find yourself passing by the bland, out-of-season variety in the fall, because then fragrant new turnips are available, which you know are going to taste so much better.

ABOUT THE RECIPES

In sifting through the hundreds of recipes that came my way for this book, whether they arrived in written form or actually steaming on my plate, I had one primary aim—to paint as diverse a picture of the Southern kitchen as possible. To do so, I've painted with a very broad brush. Historian that I am, I have included a number of lovely historical dishes that had all but disappeared from our tables along with others that have only come to it in recent times. But unlike my first book, I am not interested in presenting you with a slice of history: the recipes included here reflect how modern Southerners are cooking right now. There are recipes from traditional African-American cooks who have hardly been out of their hometowns and from expatriate Southerners living as far away as Berkshire County, Massachusetts, and Rome, Italy. For example, there are a number of pasta recipes in this edition—not because I'm an Italophile (I am) but because today Southerners cook and eat a lot of pasta—and not necessarily in an Italian way. There are things that I learned from the most elemental country cooks to the most accomplished professional chefs.

The other factor is that the face of the South has changed drastically over the last half century. "Southern cook" is now a description that applies to cooks like my friend Sandra Gutierrez, who has gracefully melded the cuisine of her Guatemalan heritage with that of her adopted home in Chapel Hill, North Carolina, and to Vietnamese-American cooks who were born and raised in the South and have infused our old traditions with a refreshing new Asian sensibility.

What you will not find, however, is complicated restaurant cooking or a lot of what is nowadays fashionably referred to as "fusion" cooking. Though I've included recipes from professional chefs, they don't necessarily represent the cooking that those chefs do for their patrons but, rather, the kind of cooking that they do for themselves—at home. And as for so-called fusion cooking, in which concepts and ingredients are borrowed willy-nilly and dumped together in an abstract composition—well, you can probably guess what I think of that. I don't consider black-eyed pea–stuffed ravioli with a coulis of collard greens and a hot-sour mango sauce to be Southern; I consider it to be something Italian that got out of hand. It can be argued that traditional Southern food is "fusion" cooking, since it is to a large extent borrowed from Europe, Africa, the Caribbean, and Native America. Well, in that

sense, any of the world's great cuisines can be considered "fusion" cooking. But what is missing from the whole fusion concept is the two elements that are essential to the lasting success of a cuisine—foundation and balance.

So, what I looked for when I began to search out recipes, whether from old cookbooks or my neighbors down the street, was the traditional taste and aroma that sparked a keen sense of recognition on my palate. I did not want flavors that startled but, rather, those that enveloped and reassured me. In short, I looked for flavors that were distinctly Southern, that brought to my tongue and imagination the memory of the tables of my childhood—even if it was something I'd never had on that table.

Those flavors and aromas of the Southern table are difficult to pin down and describe. As our region is many different things, so is our cooking: The flavors are in part African, yes, but they are also in part English and French and Native American and Caribbean; they are full of high-flown elegance and down-home familiarity; they taste of crisp mountain air and of salty coastal breezes. But one thing is sure, whether served to you from a pine table in a rough mountain cabin or from a mahogany sideboard in the polished elegance of a Lowcountry town house, they are flavors and aromas that all of us recognize and share, flavors that define us to ourselves and identify us to the outside world.

Flavors and aromas that say "taste this— that's what it means to be Southern."

The Southern Kitchen

EQUIPMENT, METHODS, AND INGREDIENTS

EQUIPMENT

The most reassuring thing about Southern cooking is that for centuries it has been done by simple people using the simplest of tools. There are very few special pieces of equipment that you are likely to need to successfully turn out the recipes of this book. If I have a sharp knife and a cast-iron skillet, I can do just about anything. Nonetheless, there are a few items that you will find useful to have on hand. This is by no means a complete kitchen list; I'm taking for granted that you know you need things like pot holders, spoons, and dishrags.

Cast-Iron Pans: Despite the new super-engineered cookware that is available, South-ern cooks continue to prefer these durable pans for a number of reasons. Their low conductivity makes them retain heat well and provide that heat more evenly than other cookware. A well-seasoned cast-iron pan is indispensable for frying chicken (or anything else) or for baking cornbread, and a cast-iron Dutch oven makes the best gumbo imaginable. Most Southern-ers believe that these pans add to the flavor of the food that cooks in them. This may be imaginary, but I do think it makes a discern-ible difference. It's a good idea to have several sizes of cast-iron pans on hand: a large (12-inch), deep pan for frying and braising, a medium (8- to 10-inch) pan for smaller batches of food and cornbread, and a small (6-inch) pan for half-batches of cornbread. A 4- to 7-quart Dutch oven with a lid should answer for the stews, gumbos, and wilted greens.

To season a new iron pan, preheat the oven to 250°F. Wash the pan in soapy water, then rinse and dry it thoroughly. Rub the inside of the pan well with lard or olive oil and place it in the oven. Let it bake for an hour, turn off the oven, and let the pan sit in it overnight. The next day, wipe the pan out, rub it with more lard or oil, and repeat the baking. The pan is now ready for use.

To maintain cast-iron pans, never, ever put them in a dishwasher or wash them with soap. If anything sticks to the pan, scrub it loose with coarse salt, a plastic scrubber, or a natural bristle brush, thoroughly rinse and dry the pan, then rub the inside well with a cloth that has been dipped in fresh lard or olive oil.

It's also good to have several sizes of heavy-bottomed stainless and enameled cast-iron pots and kettles, at least one heavy-bottomed sauté pan with sloping sides, and an unglazed earth-enware baking dish. If you enjoy putting up your own conserves and pickles, a large canning pot with a jar rack is useful not only for that process, but for big batches of corn on the cob, artichokes, Lowcountry boil, or gumbo.

Scale: Wherever possible, I give weight mea-sures for vegetables so that it is simpler to shop for key ingredients in the market. It's still sensible to weigh ingredients for many recipes—especially when you are baking. For example, it's easier to know how many sweet potatoes you are going to need if the recipe says 3 pounds instead of "3 cups cooked, mashed." But be warned about scales; not all of them are created equal. Test the accuracy of your scale with 2 level cups (dry measure) of sugar; it should weigh exactly a pound. If the measurement is off, adjust its calibration until it's exact.

Knives: This is no place to be cheap; buy the best knives you can afford and keep them razor sharp. A heavy 8-, 10-, or 12-inch chef's knife, a 2½- to 3-inch paring knife, and a serrated knife (for slicing tomatoes and citrus fruit) will take care of just about any job in the kitchen. In general, the heavier the knife is, the easier it will be to use, because the weight of the knife does most of the work. Other indispensable cutting tools are a good sharp vegetable peeler and a pair of heavy-duty kitchen scissors.

Miscellaneous Tools: A large, fine-mesh wire strainer is useful for draining small vegetables, rinsing rice, or can be put to work pureeing vegetables when you are caught without a machine.

A food mill is also especially useful for pureeing and often does a better job than the food processor or blender. If you plan to can any of the preserves, pickles, or condiments in this book, you'll also need some of the things listed in the description of that process below.

THE HOME CANNING PROCESS

Most of the recipes in this book for pickles, relishes, and other conserves can be processed, or "canned" for prolonged storage. Canning is a sealing process by which heat builds steam in the top (or headroom) of a jar of conserve. As the steam escapes, it creates a vacuum, pulling the lid of the jar into a tight seal. Once properly sealed, the jar can be stored at room temperature for long periods of time.

Canning is not a difficult operation, but if you have never done it, there are a few key fundamentals that you should be familiar with before trying it.

Necessary Equipment

For all preserves, it is important to use the right jars and lids. Old commercial jelly and pickle jars are not designed for home use. Put the jars in the recycling bin and buy jars specifically made for home canning. For sealing them, use only new metal lids and rings that are free of rust. Never reuse old lids, as the sealing compound may be damaged. New jars are usually packed with lids, and replacements are available wherever the jars are sold. Don't use the old-fashioned glass-lidded jars with clamps and rubber rings. No matter how clean the jars and lids appear to be, they must be sterilized before using them.

There are two types of home canning processes: steam-pressure canning and water-bath canning. I prefer the water-bath canners, because the pot is more versatile and can be used for things other than canning. It is a deep enameled or stainless-steel pot fitted with a rack that keeps the jars from bouncing on the bottom or bumping into each other during processing. The rack also makes it easier to put the jars into the boiling bath and remove them when they're done.

Aside from the proper jars, lids, and processor, it is helpful to have a large pair of canning tongs for handling the jars, stainless-steel ladles, and a wide-mouthed canning funnel for filling them, and plenty of clean cotton or linen kitchen towels.

Processing Conserves

Before canning, everything that touches the pickle or preserve must be sterile. Sterilize jars covered in boiling water for at least 10 minutes; boil the lids for 1 minute in a stainless pan, then take them off the heat and let them remain in the water until you are ready to use them. Don't touch the insides of the jars or the lids with your hands after they're sterilized.

Use a wide-mouthed funnel to fill the jars, and don't touch pickles, fruit, or other conserves with your bare hands. Transfer the food to the jar

with clean stainless-steel tongs, ladles, spoons, or forks. For whole pickles and fruit preserves, leave no less than ½ inch of headroom at the top of the jar and cover them with the pickling or preserving syrup by at least ¼ inch, leaving an overall headroom of ¼ inch in the top of the jar (pack them tightly so they won't float). For jams, marmalades, relishes, and chutneys, leave ¼ inch of headroom. Once the jars are filled, place the canning lids on them with the tongs. (Avoid touching the inside of the lid with your bare hands.) Screw on the rings until they are just lightly tightened. Don't tighten the rings too much, or the air will not be able to escape, preventing a proper seal.

To process the conserve in the water bath, the jars are submerged in boiling water. The water must cover the jars by at least 1 inch. Don't worry that it will leak into the jar; steam builds up in the "headroom" and prevents this from happening. As this steam is forced out, it creates the vacuum that seals the jar. Different preserves require varying lengths of processing time in the bath, so refer to the individual recipes for times.

When the jars first come out of the bath, they are very hot and fragile and must not touch each other or any cool surface. As you take them from the bath (using the canning tongs), place them on clean, double-folded cotton or linen towels. Never allow them to touch one another or the bare counter, or they could crack. As the jars cool, the vacuum formed in the top will pull the domes of the lid inward, making a "popping" sound. Let the jars sit for at least 24 hours before storing them. Any that do not seal can be reprocessed, but jars that don't seal after the second try should be stored in the refrigerator and used as soon as possible.

A Few Precautions on Storage

All unprocessed conserves must be refrigerated. They should keep for up to 2 months *if packed in a sterile jar*. Processed conserves should be stored in a cool, dark cupboard or pantry. *Do not* eat any conserve with a bulging lid. I try to use canned goods within a year, though most will last a lot longer.

In any case, if you are ever in doubt about any conserve, *don't eat it*; throw it out. It's better to lose a little bit of work and material than to end up being poisoned.

INGREDIENTS

You will be relieved to know that a well-stocked Southern pantry is in many ways a well-stocked American one. Even if you're not from the South, if you are at all enthusiastic about cooking, most of the ingredients that are called for in this book will already be on your pantry shelves. Nonetheless, there are a few things that are specifically regional, which you may not already have on hand.

If you have any trouble finding these ingredients, listen around you at work, among your neighbors, or among the patrons of your local market for the soft drawl of a Southern accent. It

is axiomatic that you can take Southerners anywhere in the world and they don't change; they just keep right on being Southern. Chances are, they can tip you off about where to find good collards and okra, or where you can find grits, white cornmeal, and soft-wheat flour. Failing that, I have provided addresses and phone numbers of select mail-order sources for some of the essentials at the end of the book.

Dry Goods

Flour: Southern cooks prefer flour milled from soft wheat. This type of wheat has a lower protein and gluten content than the hard red-wheat flours that dominate markets outside the South. The lower gluten content is critical for producing tender pastry, fluffy biscuits, and light cakes with a delicate crumb. Widely marketed brands of soft-wheat flours include White Lily, Dixie Lily, and Martha White. If you live where the King Arthur Flour brand is sold, look for their unbleached soft-wheat pastry flour. If none of these are available where you live, some mail-order sources are listed in the Resources section at the end of the book.

All-purpose flour is the most commonplace and universally available type. It's a blend of both soft- and hard-wheat flours, often mixed with a little barley flour to enhance its workability. For most of the recipes in this book, all-purpose flour is fine unless the recipe says otherwise. I used to hear it said that the blends of these flours marketed in the South tended to be weighted on the soft-wheat side, but I've used flours from all over the country and frankly can't see any real difference. For baking, I've even made biscuits, pastry, and cakes with all-purpose flour and gotten good results. While soft-wheat flour is preferable and will make it easier for you to achieve success, every recipe in this book was tested using all-purpose flour.

Bread flour is blended to have an extremely high gluten content, which makes yeast dough stretch and allows for more air to be trapped so that the bread rises higher. Unfortunately, what makes this blend desirable for yeast dough makes it undesirable for baking-powder breads and pastries. High-gluten flour makes biscuits and pastries tough and heavy. Therefore, bread flour can't be substituted in any of the recipes, except as a thickener or for breading vegetables that are to be fried.

Cornmeal: In the South, you can take for granted that "meal" means cornmeal. What you can't take for granted is that it means white cornmeal. Though white meal is the preference in most places, there are pockets of the South where yellow meal takes precedence. Yellow meal has a more robust, slightly sweet flavor, but white meal is more delicate and, to some people, richer-tasting. The really important thing about cornmeal is freshness. I prefer white meal, but I have bought yellow meal when I could tell it was fresher. Use whichever you prefer, but choose freshness over type when you have a choice.

The other important thing about cornmeal is how it is made. Stone-ground meal has by far the best texture. Stone-ground means that the corn was milled on an old-fashioned millstone. The package may read "water stone-ground," which means that the mill was powered by running water. It doesn't really matter; the corn can't tell if it's a motor or a waterwheel that is making the stone turn. It gets crushed all the same. Unbolted meal has none of the bran removed, so it is more flavorful and interesting, but it is also more perishable, so if the meal is unbolted, make sure that it is fresh and not stale-smelling. Unbolted meal is almost always labeled as such. If the package doesn't say so, it is probably bolted meal.

Stone-ground meal is available in natural and health-food stores, specialty groceries, and some supermarkets. For mail-order retailers of stone-ground meal, see the end of the book.

Grits: There are two basic types of grits: hominy grits and whole-corn grits.

Hominy grits is the most universally available; it's made from dried corn from which the husk is removed. There are three types of hominy grits. Avoid instant grits like the plague, and pass over the "quick" grits if you can. Stick to regular hominy grits: The package cooking directions will say that it takes at least 20–30 minutes to cook. To be really good, the grits should be cooked for at least an hour.

Whole-corn grits is ground from the whole grain; none of the outer husk is removed. Mail-order sources for whole-corn grits are listed in the Resources section at the end of the book.

Before you write to me about my grammar, please read the discussion of the singularity of grits on page 38.

Salt: Most markets offer three types of salt: sea, kosher, and regular table salt. For all my cooking, I use only kosher and sea salt—the first for routine cooking and the latter for finishing at the table. They're more expensive than table salt, but if you can buy them in bulk, the difference in cost isn't enough to worry about. Larger cartons of kosher salt are often sold in the ethnic section of your market instead of the spice aisle and many natural or health-food stores sell refined

sea salt in bulk. For many cooks, the flakes of kosher salt make it easier to measure in their fingers. However, the reason to use kosher and sea salt is that they're pure and have a clean salt flavor, so you'll find that you actually use less of them than you are accustomed to with table salt.

Table salt, while common and inexpensive, has a harsh, chemical taste—and the cheaper it is, the more pronounced that aftertaste becomes. If you've always used it, chances are you don't notice that drawback. Try this little test: buy a little sea or kosher salt. First taste it directly on your tongue, then clean your palate and taste the table salt. You'll be surprised how sharp and chemical the table salt will taste by comparison.

Sugar: Our consumption of this innocent product has gotten way out of hand, in part due to all the soft drinks that the average American puts away every day. But I'll spare you the health lecture. My only problem with sugar is the way it has come to be overused in cooking, especially with vegetables. For most of the savory recipes in this book, sugar has no place.

However, when a recipe calls for sugar, the type to use for the most authentic Southern flavor is pure cane sugar. In some of the recipes, I specify turbinado or demerara sugar (sometimes labeled "raw" sugar), a partially refined cane-sugar product whose crystals are larger than those of regular white sugar. Its color is a lovely light brown, and the flavor is mellower than that of fully refined sugar. It isn't the same as modern brown sugar, which is merely refined sugar with some of the molasses added back. Since this book first came out, "raw" sugar has become more readily available, but if you can't find it in your area, regular brown sugar can be substituted. The reverse, however, is not always true. In the event that a recipe does call for brown sugar, it means commercial brown sugar; don't substitute turbinado or demerara unless the recipe states that it's all right to do so, because they react differently in cooking.

Miscellaneous Ingredients

Anchovies: Salt-packed whole anchovies are the finest quality. In larger cities, they are readily available in Italian and specialty markets. Elsewhere, they are not as easy to find. Next in quality are anchovy fillets packed in olive oil in glass jars. A distant third are oil-packed canned fillets. As convenient as it is, I don't care for anchovy paste that comes in a tube but if you have a small household and rarely use anchovies, it is probably the least wasteful way to keep it in stock in your refrigerator, and in the small quantities called for in this book, it should make very little difference.

Bread Crumbs: Don't throw out those old, dried-out loaves of French bread and yeast rolls; make your own bread crumbs with them in the food processor or with a box grater. Once you start making your own, you'll really appreciate how much better they taste than the commercially produced variety.

Capers: The pickled flower buds of a trailing plant, *Capparis spinosa,* that's native to the Mediterranean, capers have long been imported and used in Southern cooking. The finest are packed in salt; these are available at Italian groceries and specialty markets in larger cities but are difficult to come by in most places. Capers packed in brine, which are almost universally available, work just fine in these recipes.

Salt-packed capers must be well rinsed before they are used.

Olives: Use only imported Greek or Italian brine-cured black or green olives. Yes, they are traditional, especially in port cities like Charleston, Savannah, and New Orleans. The most economical way to buy them is at Italian, Greek, or other specialty groceries where they are sold in bulk. Today they're often sold in bulk in regular supermarkets as well. Look for them in the deli section of your market.

Tomato Paste: The imported variety that comes in a squeeze tube like toothpaste seems to have the best flavor and is the most convenient to use. There's never a half-used can of the stuff moldering in the back of your refrigerator. However, any all-natural tomato paste is suitable.

Cooking Fats

Butter: There is no substitute for good butter. Use unsalted butter, the best you can find.

Drippings: Drippings are the rendered fat from bacon or salt-cured pork. Whenever you make bacon, save the drippings. After they cool, pour them into a glass jar, seal it well, and store it in the refrigerator. You can also make the drippings as you need them. Fat levels differ, but an average slice of thick-cut bacon should give you about 1 tablespoon of drippings.

Lard: Lard is discussed in the section on pork products (page 20). Look for lard without preservatives (some butchers carry it), or render your own. If you buy lard, check the package. It should be dry, and the lard should be creamy white and have a clean, pleasant, faintly oily smell. If it is yellow and has a strong odor, the lard is rancid.

Oils

Vegetable Oils: Much touted these days as being a healthy alternative to animal fats, these oils do not have a long tradition in Southern kitchens. The oldest and most famous, olive oil, has always been known and used by upper-class Southern families, both for limited cooking (generally reserved for salads) and for medicinal uses. Most of the other oils, including the now-popular peanut oil, have come into common use only in the last century.

For most deep-fat frying, I still prefer lard, in spite of all the negative things that the nay-sayers have laid at its door. However, if you are avoiding animal fats, you can use filtered, refined vegetable oils for all your deep-fat frying. The best of them is peanut oil. Many Southern cooks also swear by cottonseed oil, but it's not easy to come by.

For sautéing, where only a small amount of fat is required, the most traditional Southern flavor is to be had from animal fats—rendered bacon drippings, lard, and butter. Their distinct advantage is flavor: A little of them goes a long way. The less flavor the fat has, the more of it we tend to use. With that in mind when searching for animal-fat substitutes to use in these recipes, what I looked for first was flavor. The best flavor to be had is from cold-pressed, unfiltered oils, such as an extra-virgin olive oil, unfiltered corn oil, or peanut oil. These oils are loaded with flavor, so a little of them adds big things to the pot. You generally won't find them in your supermarket; with the exception of olive oil, cold-pressed oils are usually available only at natural-food and specialty groceries. They cost more, but they are worth it.

If you are accustomed to working only with refined oils, there are a few things you should know about the cold-pressed, unfiltered variety. Because these oils are not filtered or refined, they still contain some of the flavorful solids of the vegetable or seed from which they are pressed. These solids spoil more easily; therefore, unfiltered oils are a lot more perishable than mass-produced refined oils. Buy them from a vendor that has high turnover and store them in a cool, dark place, well away from light and heat. If you don't use the oil very often and your house is warm all the time, the refrigerator is the better place to keep it. (Note: It'll cloud, but it will still be safe to use.)

Corn Oil: Corn oil is not especially traditional in Southern cooking, but if you are avoiding animal fats, it makes a good substitute for those fats in certain types of cooking. For deep frying, regular refined corn oil does an acceptable job, though it is not as good as peanut oil. It has very little flavor on its own, and it stands up fairly well to high heat. For sautéing, cold-pressed, unfiltered corn oil has a rich, almost buttery flavor that makes it a good substitute for butter or bacon fat, especially in dishes that contain corn. Look for it at natural-food or specialty groceries.

Olive Oil: As Southern cooks have begun to use more and more olive oil in their cooking, reasonably good extra-virgin olive oil has become more widely available in the South; even supermarkets are beginning to carry more than one brand at a time. If, however, your supermarket stocks the oil on a top shelf, unshielded from the fluorescent lights, don't buy it there. It's better to shop for it in specialty groceries, where the oil is given proper care and the selection is usually better.

For sautéing and salads, use only extra-virgin olive oil, the best you can afford. Later pressings, golden colored and very clear, are fine for sautéing when flavor is not important or for frying. Cheaper, lesser-grade oils are extracted from olive pulp that has already been pressed a number of times, using chemicals and heat. They have little or no flavor and are of no gastronomical interest whatsoever. Like good wine, extra-virgin oils differ in flavor and character from region to region—and even within regions. Experiment with the ones available to you, letting your own taste guide you in selecting one for your kitchen.

Peanut Oil: I once heard some patriotic Southern soul describe peanut oil as the olive oil of the South—an admirable bit of national loyalty but a thoroughly silly remark. That's not to say that peanut oil isn't important. Along with lard, it is unparalleled for deep-frying, lending a crispness of crust that no other vegetable fat can approach. Use a refined peanut oil. It should be clear but smell like fresh peanuts.

For sautéing without animal fat, a cold-pressed, unfiltered peanut oil is a great substitute for bacon drippings, lard, or butter. Of course, it does not taste like bacon, but it still provides a distinctive—and Southern—flavor. You'll find it only at natural-food and specialty groceries. The oil will be a little cloudy and may have residue on the bottom, but it should have a clean, fresh peanut aroma. If it smells like stale peanuts, the oil is rancid and shouldn't be used. If you don't use it often, store it in the refrigerator.

Dairy Products

Look for minimally processed dairy products from grass-fed, pastured cattle, preferably not homogenized. Homogenization is a process that suspends the cream in milk so that it no longer rises to the top. Almost all the milk Americans consume is homogenized, and it would seem a harmless thing. Unfortunately, the fat stays suspended because its molecular structure has been changed, and studies show that this may be doing us more harm than good. I get lovely whole milk, buttermilk, and cream from Southern Swiss Dairy, a local Georgia farm that is producing unhomogenized, minimally pasteurized milk from pastured, grass-fed cattle. The difference it makes in my cooking is significant, and I find that I never have a problem tolerating the milk and cream.

Buttermilk and Yogurt: Real buttermilk is the soured milk leftover from making butter. What passes for buttermilk nowadays is skimmed or whole milk treated with enzymes. Most commercial brands contain stabilizers, thickeners, and salt—and way too much of the latter. When I can't get buttermilk from Southern Swiss Dairy, I substitute an all-natural, organically produced plain yogurt, thinned to buttermilk consistency with a little plain milk. Look for organically produced (preferably from a biodynamic farm) yogurt at natural or health-food stores. Stonyfield Farm and Seven Stars are dairies whose products are nationally marketed, and they are both excellent.

Cheese: For the best results, use all-natural cheese. So-called American cheese, that lurid, elastic orange vinyl stuff that blankets most fast-food cheeseburgers, is beneath discussion, and its imitations are even worse. Their only claimed benefit is that they melt into a smooth emulsion. So does plastic. Think about that. Pass them by. Here's what you *do* want:

Cheddar: Use a sharp, all-natural cheddar, ideally an artisanal local cheddar. A good commercial Vermont or Canadian cheddar is also acceptable. Where commercial cheddar is concerned, there's a lot of hoopla about using "white" over the orange-dyed stuff; dyeing the cheddar in part covers up a truncated curing process and has been done for 200 years. If all you can find is orange-dyed cheddar, don't worry. All-natural cheeses are colored with vegetable dyes that are harmless.

Blue: During the late War of Northern Aggression, on land that was to become my old alma mater in the foothills of Carolina, Confederate workmen busied themselves digging tunnels into the hills for reasons that are now lost in time. Eventually the tunnels were abandoned, incomplete. It would be years before they were finally put to use—by the dairy school of Clemson University—as aging caves for an excellent, rich blue cheese. For many years, this cheese was available only through an outlet at the university and has always been as popular as it was scarce. Today it is being marketed commercially and has been picked up by a few national mail-order vendors, but production is still limited and it is sometimes hard to get. Good-quality Roquefort,

Gorgonzola, or Danish blue cheeses all make good substitutes. English Stilton, as good as it is in its way, is not an acceptable substitute.

Parmesan: Use only imported Parmigiano-Reggiano. The reason that it is the best for use in Italian cooking applies equally to Southern (or for that matter, any other) cooking.

Cream: Unless the recipe calls for "light" cream, look for cream with a minimum milk-fat content of at least 36 percent, preferably not ultra-pasteurized or homogenized. It's more perishable than commercial dairy cream, and therefore more expensive, but just close your eyes to the cost and buy it—it's well worth it. Because it's richer and more flavorful, you'll find yourself using less of it.

Sour Cream: All of the recipes in this book were tested with commercial sour cream—and it will work in all of them, but it isn't the best choice. Homemade sour cream, which usually goes by its romantic-sounding French name, *crème fraîche*, will give you much better results, and it's very easy to make.

Crème Fraîche   MAKES 1 PINT

2 tablespoons all-natural whole-milk yogurt
     or Greek yogurt
1 pint heavy cream (minimum 36 percent milk fat)

1. Line a wire sieve with a double layer of cheese-cloth or an undyed microwave-quality paper towel over a bowl. Put the yogurt into it and let it drain for 30 minutes. Discard the whey in the bowl. If using Greek yogurt, omit the draining step.

2. Either whisk the yogurt into the cream or put it and the cream in a clean glass jar, seal the jar tightly, and shake until the yogurt is dissolved into the cream. Set the cream aside, uncovered, at room temperature until it clots, about 4–8 hours, depending on the warmth of the room. When the clotting is complete, cover and store it in the refrigerator. It will keep for about 2 weeks.

The Ubiquitous Pig

The best-known, and perhaps most infamous, flavoring in Southern vegetable cookery is the salt-cured flesh and fat of that much-maligned barnyard animal, the pig. Poor thing; he spends his life minding his own business—and the best that he gets is a wallow in mud and a dinner of swill. When this rather prosaic life is ended, he provides the farmer not only with dinner but all manner of beneficial products. In return for this blameless life and sacrifice, he has been posthumously charged with killing the farmer off by clogging his arteries.

Pork is not, however, by any means as universal in our cookery as is widely supposed. Nita Dixon, a traditional chef in Savannah, explains that the reason her vegetables are so good is because she learned to cook them without using meat. Her family—as was true of so many Lowcountry black families—was poor; they couldn't afford to have meat often, so, she says, "I had to learn to make vegetables taste good some other way." That other way was with herbs, garlic, and cayenne pepper.

All the same, if porcine husbandry were brought to a halt, and pigs were to be banned from the South altogether, the blow to what we think of as a Southern flavor would not be fatal, but it would nonetheless be severe. It's widely supposed that salt-cured pork was first added to the pot by African-American cooks as a means of supplementing a meager, mostly vegetarian diet—and this is probably in part true, though there were families like Nita's that couldn't even afford that. What I've found, in fact, is that adding salt-cured pork to the pot was more a white thing than a black one, because the white settlers had long been using this seasoning in their native Europe, and pigs are not native to Africa.

Here are the pork products that every good Southern pantry is seldom without. For those who are not able to cook with them, I've suggested some alternatives, both here and in the applicable recipes. I only did this where it was possible to get at a recognizably Southern taste without using meat, and in looking for substitutes for pork, my aim was not to imitate meat by using another product, but to find another way of producing the same character and essential substance. My aim was not to find a substitute for the meat, but rather for what the meat did. So I won't coyly pretend that these suggestions are anything more than substitutes; naturally they will not taste the same as pork. However, they will still give you a taste of that traditional satisfying flavor.

Country or Dry-Cured Ham: These are hams that are cured with dry salt and air or smoke. The hind leg is first rubbed with salt and left to lie for a week or so. Then it is wiped dry, rubbed with more salt and sometimes spices and sugar, and hung up to air-dry just like prosciutto. Usually, though not always, country ham is finished with smoke, after which it goes through a final hanging to age the meat. A good country ham that has been smoked will have a distinct flavor of smoke to it, but it is subtle and never as heavy and pervasive as commercial water-cured hams. The longer the ham hangs and ages, the more concentrated and richer the flavor will be.

Lean country-ham meat is used when a dish calls for its salty, dusky depth of flavor but does not also need fat. You can use a good-quality prosciutto instead of country ham, but for meatless cooking, the only satisfactory substitutes I've found for it (believe it or not) are salt-cured anchovy fillets, a dash of Thai fish sauce (an anchovy-based condiment), or for strict vegetarians, a small dash of good-quality soy sauce. The secret to these substitutes is to use them in very small quantities; too much anchovy will make the dish taste fishy, and too much soy will overpower the other flavors.

Salt-Cured Pork or Salt Pork: This is the side or belly meat of the pig, which is heavily streaked with fat, pickled in dry salt but not smoked. When salt pork is called for in a recipe, never substitute a smoked product. It is used when a certain amount of fat is required in addition to flavor. Generally, you can use one of the substitutes suggested for country ham in conjunction with a mild-flavored fat such as peanut oil or butter.

When a recipe calls for a piece of salt pork or ham to be stewed with the vegetables, a well-scraped Parmesan cheese rind (preferably from a piece of Parmigiano-Reggiano) is a very good substitute for either meat. It lends a body and richness to the broth that is similar to that lent by the salt-cured meat. Scrape the inner side of the rind well to remove any soft bits of cheese before using it.

Bacon: When bacon is called for in this book, I mean smoked breakfast bacon. Historically, all salt-cured pork used to be called "bacon," regardless of the cut, and it was usually not smoked. In the historical recipes, I've used salt pork or ham in my version of the recipe and call for bacon only when the sweet-smoky taste of modern bacon is the desired flavor. I've never found a satisfactory substitute; smoked turkey and tofu are too harsh and smoky tasting, and the "bacon" made from soy products is beneath even mentioning. Therefore, the suggested substitutions were not aimed at imitating bacon, but at producing a distinctly Southern, albeit different, taste.

Fatback: This is the layer of pure fat on the back of the hog. It is salt-cured in the same way as salt pork, but it is not the same thing. The cheapest and crudest of the pork seasonings used in Southern cooking, it is not used anywhere in this book. If the salt pork in your market does not have a generous streak of lean meat, it's probably fatback. Pass it by and use country ham, prosciutto, or one of the suggested substitutes.

Lard: Here we go: pure, rendered pig fat—full of flavor and browning properties that cannot be imitated. I believe that lard is healthier than a fat that has been hydrogenated and treated with chemical hardeners and emulsifiers. As long as you do not have a medical condition that is aggravated by ingesting saturated fat, using limited amounts of lard wisely will not jeopardize your health. If you are not able to use pork fat, butter can be substituted for lard in pastries or for sautéing. If you do not use any animal products, substitute a flavorful vegetable fat such as peanut or olive oil for sautéing and peanut oil for frying.

Broth

A good broth or stock is often the sure foundation on which the flavors of so many vegetable dishes—and not only soups—are built. It is very little trouble to make, freezes beautifully, and adds a depth of flavor and body that makes the difference between a good dish and a great one. And yet so few cooks take this extra careful step. I tested many of the recipes in this book with canned broth, not because I prefer it or cook with it very often in my own kitchen, but because I wanted to be sure that the dish still tasted good when that shortcut was used. So

when the ingredients list says "or canned broth," it will work in the recipe, but it is not, and never will be, a recommendation. My preference, in all instances, is broth that I've made myself.

If you choose to use canned or commercially frozen broth, look for a brand that does not contain monosodium glutamate (good luck), and if it is canned broth, dilute it with equal parts water, even if the package directions say to use it full strength.

The only caution I have about homemade broth is that it is addictive. Once you make your own and taste the difference that it makes, you'll never again be satisfied with anything else.

Meat Broth   MAKES ABOUT 5 QUARTS

This is a sort of master recipe that can be used to make any sort of meat broth, since the kind of bones used determines the broth. The most usual is beef, though occasionally veal and even pork broth are used in traditional Southern

vegetable cookery. You can even mix up the bones for a more complex broth, but where pale color and subtlety of flavor are important, it's better to use only veal bones. If, on the other hand, you want a more intense color, brown the bones first in the oven. Position a rack in the upper third of the oven and preheat it to 400°F. Put the bones in a roasting pan and toss them with just enough oil to coat them. Bake them until they are nicely browned and fragrant, about half an hour. Be careful not to scorch them.

When a clear broth is important, careful skimming is critical, but when all that matters is flavor, you can happily ignore the pot. If the simmer is kept imperceptible, the broth will still be clear enough for most of the recipes of this book. If you want crystalline aspic, though, take the time to skim the broth.

6 pounds meaty bones, shank, neck, tail, knuckles, or feet

1 large yellow onion, peeled and stuck with 3 whole cloves

1 large carrot, peeled and thickly sliced

1 rib celery with leaves attached, thickly sliced

1 leek, split and washed (or the green part only)

1 Bouquet Garni (page 32), made with 2–3 sprigs parsley, 2–3 sprigs thyme, and 2 bay leaves

6–8 whole peppercorns

1 quarter-size ginger slice

Salt

1. Put the bones in a 10-quart soup kettle with 6 quarts of cold water. Place the kettle over very low heat, as low as you can get it, and let it come slowly to a simmer, which will take about three-quarters of an hour. As the scum begins rising to the top, skim it carefully away, and continue to do so as more forms on the top of the liquid. Do not stir the kettle, now or hereafter.

2. When the scum no longer forms, let the liquid simmer for half an hour. Raise the heat to medium low and add all the remaining ingredients and a large pinch of salt. Let the pot come

back to a simmer, again carefully skimming off the scum as it rises to the surface.

3. Reduce the heat, as low as you can get it, and cook the broth at a bare simmer, uncovered, for at least 1½ hours or even longer, checking it periodically. The longer the broth simmers, the more concentrated its flavor will be. Simmer it very slowly, the steam bubbles not quite breaking the surface; it should never boil. Turn off the heat and let the broth settle and cool. Carefully strain it from the solids into a lidded metal or ceramic container or glass jars. Let the broth cool, uncovered, then seal it with a tight lid and refrigerate. It will keep like this for 4 or 5 days. To store it longer, chill it, skim off the fat, then spoon it into freezable containers, seal tightly, and freeze. It will keep indefinitely.

Chicken Broth   MAKES ABOUT 5 QUARTS

Stewing hens or scrap chicken parts make excellent broth, and they are inexpensive.

1 whole stewing hen, about 6 pounds, or the same weight in necks, back, wings, and feet

1 large onion, peeled and stuck with 3 whole cloves

2–3 large carrots, peeled and thickly sliced

1 rib celery with leaves attached, thickly sliced

1 leek, split and washed (or the green part only)

1 Bouquet Garni (page 32), made with 2–3 sprigs parsley, 2–3 sprigs thyme, and 2 bay leaves

8–10 whole peppercorns

1 quarter-size slice fresh gingerroot

Salt

1. Put the hen or chicken parts in a 10-quart soup kettle with 6 quarts of cold water. Place the kettle over very low heat, as low as you can get it, and let it come slowly to a simmer, which will take about three-quarters of an hour. As the scum begins rising to the top, skim it carefully away, and continue to do so as more forms on the top of the liquid. Do not stir the kettle, now or hereafter.

2. When the scum no longer forms, let the broth simmer for half an hour. Raise the heat to medium low and add all the remaining ingredients and a large pinch of salt. Let the pot come back to a simmer, again carefully skimming off the scum as it rises to the surface.

3. Reduce the heat, as low as you can get it, and cook the broth at a bare simmer, uncovered, for at least 1½ hours or even longer, checking it periodically. The longer the broth simmers, the more concentrated its flavor will be. Simmer it very slowly, the steam bubbles not quite breaking the surface; it should never boil. Turn off the heat and let it settle and cool. Carefully strain it from the solids into a lidded metal or ceramic container or glass jars. Let the broth cool, uncovered, then seal it with a tight lid and refrigerate. It will keep like this for 4 or 5 days. To store it longer, chill it, skim off the fat, then spoon it into freezable containers, seal tightly, and freeze. It will keep indefinitely.

Ham Broth   MAKES ABOUT 3½ QUARTS

The rich aroma and subtle flavor of salt-cured pork is a characterizing element of so many Southern vegetable dishes, whether it's slow-simmered pole beans, collards, black-eyed peas, or old-time soup beans, but our modern paranoia about sodium and animal fat has led many traditional cooks to avoid this seasoning. There's no getting around the sodium, but ham broth is one way to get those traditional flavors without the fat. Don't trim away the fat from the scraps: It must be present during the cooking to give the broth its full depth of flavor. Once finished, the broth is chilled and the fat settles to the top and congeals. It's easily removed. Used judiciously, that fat is wonderful for sautéing.

If you are avoiding animal products altogether, there is of course no substitute for ham here: use the vegetable broth that follows instead.

1 leftover country ham bone, with some meat still attached, or 1½ pounds ham hocks

2 large yellow onions, peeled, 1 left whole and stuck with 4 cloves, the other thinly sliced

1 medium rib celery, thickly sliced

1 medium carrot, peeled and thickly sliced

8–10 whole black peppercorns

1 whole pod hot pepper such as cayenne, serrano, or jalapeño

1 large bay leaf

4 quarts water

Salt

1. Put all the ingredients except for salt into a 6- to 8-quart stockpot. Bring slowly to a simmer over medium heat, uncovered, about 30 minutes. As soon as bubbles begin breaking the surface, reduce the heat to low and simmer slowly for at least 1½ hours; 3 or 4 hours will be even better if you have the time.

2. Turn off the heat. Taste and add salt if it is needed, then let the broth cool. Strain it and refrigerate until the fat on top has solidified. Skim off the fat and discard it or save it to use for sautéing. The fat will keep in the refrigerator for several weeks, up to 3 months if frozen in a well-sealed container. The broth will keep for up to a week, refrigerated, or as long as 3 months frozen in small batches.

Vegetable Broth   MAKES ABOUT 4 QUARTS

Now that very few Southerners observe meatless fast days, few of us use vegetable broth anymore. But if you are cooking without meat, this aromatic broth will provide a welcome depth of flavor without adding meat to the pot. The flavor secret is the whole garlic. When garlic is slow-simmered in one piece as it is here, its taste is not pronounced, but it adds a subtle, almost meaty flavor to the broth.

3 tablespoons butter or extra-virgin olive oil

2 medium onions, peeled, 1 left whole and stuck
with 3 cloves, the other thinly sliced

2 large carrots, peeled and thickly sliced

2 ribs celery with leafy tops, thickly sliced

2 leeks, white and green parts, split, thoroughly
washed, and thickly sliced

6 quarts water

4 large cloves garlic, peeled but left whole

1 medium fresh tomato or one whole canned tomato

1 Bouquet Garni (page 32), made with 3 sprigs
parsley, 3 sprigs thyme, 1 sprig each oregano and
sage, and 2 bay leaves

2 quarter-size slices fresh gingerroot

6–8 whole peppercorns

Salt

1. Put the butter or oil, the sliced onion, carrots, celery, and leeks in a large kettle that will hold all the ingredients. Turn on the heat to medium and sauté, tossing frequently, until the vegetables are nicely browned but not scorched, about 10 minutes.

2. Add the remaining ingredients, a healthy pinch of salt, and reduce the heat to low. Bring the liquid slowly to a simmer, skimming it carefully of any scum that rises to the top.

3. Reduce the heat, as low as you can get it, and cook the broth at a bare simmer, uncovered, for at least 1½ hours or even longer, checking it periodically, or until the liquid is reduced by about a third. The longer the broth simmers, the more concentrated its flavor will be. It should simmer very slowly.

4. Turn off the heat and let the broth settle and cool. Carefully strain it from the solids into a lidded metal or ceramic container or glass jars. Let the broth cool completely, uncovered, then seal it with a tight lid and refrigerate. It will keep like this for 4 or 5 days. To store it longer, chill it, then spoon it into freezable containers, seal tightly, and freeze. It will keep indefinitely.

The Southern Spice Cabinet

One crisp winter day I spent the better part of a morning hashing over Southern cooking with two visitors from England, describing the many different cuisines that make it up, discussing its many regional differences, enumerating its characteristic elements. A good bit of that time went into trying to describe the real essence of the Lowcountry kitchen. Finally, famished from all that talk of food, we went over to Nita Dixon's cafe for lunch. Nita is a dynamic cook who is doing a lot to wake people up to real Lowcountry food. It isn't a crusade with her; she just cooks the way she learned to cook from her mama and grandmama—making people fall in love with both the cuisine and her. They keep coming back for more. We walked in and took a deep breath of the rich aroma that met us. I turned to my visitors—"Do you smell that? That aroma of okra and spice? That's the smell; that's the essence of the Lowcountry kitchen." Suddenly, they understood. Nita's cooking had accomplished in one deep breath what I hadn't been able to do in more than an hour of babbling.

There are kitchens that you can walk into blindfolded, and though you may not have been told where you were going, you nonetheless know where you are. The aroma of a particular spice—or of a blending of spices and herbs—is a culinary hallmark, defining a place more clearly than a road sign. That smell of spice defines so many of the world's cuisines, setting each distinctly apart from its neighbors.

These are the ones that define ours:

Cayenne, Chiles, and Other Hot Peppers:
The seedpods of the many varieties of *Capsicum frutescens*, what we know as hot or chile peppers, are perhaps the most pervasive of all spices in the Southern kitchen. They are a hallmark of all African-influenced cooking and are common in all the cuisines of the South—from Creole New Orleans to Tidewater Virginia. The reason that

these peppers—which by the way are not even remotely related to true pepper—have become so commonplace is simply that they were so cheap and readily available. True pepper was imported and, in the early days at least, very expensive. Naturally, peppercorns did not figure in the home cooking of Southern African Americans during the days of slavery—or even for many years after slavery ended. Even white families of average means had to be frugal in their use of this spice. But capsicum pepper plants were easy to grow; they flourished in practically any soil and in the South's milder climate; so it's easy to see how they became so common an element in Southern cooking.

The heat in capsicum peppers is generated by an oily acid that is contained in the inner flesh and (especially) the seeds of the pod. When you are working with the flesh and seeds, take care to protect your hands if you are especially sensitive to this acid, because it can actually cause blisters. And in all cases, always wash your hands well before touching anything else—especially your eyes or lips—after you've handled the cut pepper, or you will put yourself or someone else at risk of a cross-burn, which can cause a lot of discomfort at best and a serious blister at worst.

Cayenne is the most commonly used member of the vast family of capsicum peppers in our region, but any hot red pepper can be used in the recipes in this book. Be aware, however, that they can vary in pungency and in level of heat, from a relatively mild lightly-warm-your-tongue tingle to a blazing knock-the-top-of-your-head-off blister. If you are substituting a Scotch bonnet in a recipe that calls for a fresh pod of cayenne, for example, you will want to use substantially less of it than the recipe indicates.

And speaking of less, that's what you should keep in mind when using all hot peppers. The idea is to add flavor first and a warming lift second. I am so weary of the prodigal way that this spice is overused by modern cooks. They pour on

the hot pepper to the point that you can no longer taste anything, least of all the intriguing flavor that these peppers can actually lend to a dish.

Throughout this book, a whole pod of hot pepper, either fresh or dried, is frequently added to the pot in one piece, then removed and discarded when the dish is finished. This is an old Southern cook's trick for adding the flavor of the pepper without releasing the heat-generating acid. When the pod is left whole, the acid stays inside, but the flavor of the pepper is infused into the pot. Don't add part of a pepper, since the cut edge will release the hot acid into the food, and if you must substitute ground cayenne for the whole pod, use the smallest dose, since the dish is not intended to be hot.

Pepper Sherry   MAKES 1 CUP

Pepper sherry, made from the fiery little pea-size bird peppers that once upon a time grew in every almost downtown Savannah courtyard, was a standard condiment in the city's dining rooms, from the humblest creek-side dwellings to the most elegant of town houses in its historic downtown. It's not unique to Savannah, of course, but was common wherever British colonials settled in the subtropics. It was an indispensable seasoning, particularly for turtle, creamy crab, and okra soups, and was so commonplace that recipes for it were rare in old Savannah cookbooks. It's past time this lovely condiment was returned to Southern tables.

⅓ cup bird peppers or ½ cup other small hot
  peppers
1 cup medium-dry sherry (such as amontillado)

1. Rinse the peppers in cold water, drain, and put them in a heatproof bowl. Bring 1 cup of water to a rolling boil and pour it over the peppers. Let stand 1 minute and drain.

2. Put the peppers in a clean cruet, jar, or bottle that will hold at least 1½ cups. Pour the sherry over them, stop or seal it well, and steep for at least 24 hours before using. I find it helps distribute the peppery oils if you gently shake the cruet after 24 hours.

Pepper Vinegar   MAKES 1 PINT

Pickled peppers and the vinegar in which they are cured are important fixtures in a Southern kitchen, both in cooking, where they are used as a flavoring in countless vegetable and meat dishes, and at the table, where they are a condiment that accompanies everything from turnip greens to baked chicken. When a recipe calls for pepper vinegar, it means the vinegar from this pickle, and *not* hot pepper sauce, so don't substitute the latter for it. You can, however, use a few drops of hot sauce diluted in regular cider vinegar.

In the South, pickled peppers can be found in most markets, either in the pickle or bottled-sauce sections. Elsewhere, they can sometimes be found in West Indian or specialty markets. Or you can make your own; it isn't difficult.

6 ounces whole fresh hot peppers (see note)
About 1 cup cider vinegar

1. Sterilize a pint jar by boiling it in a water bath for 10 minutes. Wash the peppers well and dry them. Making sure that your hands are very clean, pack the peppers in the jar.

2. Bring the vinegar to a boil in a stainless-steel or enameled pan over medium heat. While it is still boiling hot, pour it over the peppers until they are completely covered. Seal the jar, let it cool, and store it in a cool, dark place (the fridge is okay) for 2–4 weeks before using. Use the peppers within 2 months.

3. For more prolonged storage, process the jar in a water bath for 10 minutes. Place the jar on a folded cloth so that it doesn't touch anything, and let it cool completely. If it doesn't seal, reprocess it. See page 10 for more detailed canning instructions.

Note: *You can use any green or red hot peppers to make pepper vinegar. Cayenne, tiny round bird peppers, and jalapeños are the most popular in the South. Each has its own distinct character, and some are much hotter than others, so take this into account when you are adding the peppers or pepper vinegar to a recipe.*

Some Southern cooks put their pickled peppers up in condiment bottles so that they are convenient to use at the table. If you like, you can use an old commercial catsup or Worcestershire sauce bottle, but make sure it is thoroughly cleaned and sterilized first. Also, never use a commercial bottle for canning purposes. Commercial bottles are not designed for the home canning process.

Ginger: The root, or more accurately, the bulb or rhizome of the perennial *Zingiber officinale* is a spice that has been popular in most Western cookery and medicine since antiquity. Originally native to Southeast Asia, ginger has been used in the West at least since the days of the Roman Empire. It was also widely used in English cooking by the beginning of American colonization, and so naturally it figures prominently in Southern cookery as well.

Ginger's popularity in the South is owed in part to the fact that, like capsicum peppers, the plant flourishes in our climate and is easy to grow. At one time, ginger was a common fixture in most Southern gardens; the fragrant flowers of the plants made them as ornamental as they were useful. Modern Southerners use ginger mostly to flavor pickles, preserves, and baked goods. The spice is less commonly found in meat or vegetable dishes, though historically that has not always been true.

Ginger is sold in several forms: fresh bulbs (or roots), dried powder, and preserved and candied ginger. Fresh gingerroot can be found in many vegetable markets and in the produce section of almost all supermarkets. Powdered ginger is universally available. Preserved gingerroot and stems—usually packed in syrup—can be found in specialty markets, as can the candied or crystallized variety. These last two types are used mostly in sweets and can't be substituted for fresh ginger is a savory dish.

Mustard: I don't mean that jar of turmeric-yellow condiment in your refrigerator, but those little round seeds in the jar of pickles. This spice has long been an important element of Southern cooking—flavoring those pickles, giving kick to a barbecue, putting the "devil" in anything that was called "deviled." Mustard doesn't figure as prominently in Southern vegetable cookery as it does in the preparation of meat, poultry, or fish, or as a seasoning in pickles and catsups or in spicy chow-chows and chutneys, but it does figure.

Historically, Southern cooks kept two kinds of mustard in the pantry: whole seeds and powdered mustard—or, as they called it, mustard flour. It was from the latter that the prepared condiment was made as needed. Cookbooks indicate that they knew and used both English (very hot and pungent) and French (much milder) mustards, depending on how hot the prepared condiment needed to be.

Today, most Southerners use a prepared mustard of one sort or another, but we do still use mustard powder. For the recipes in this book, keep a stock of three basic types of mustard in your pantry: dry powder (my own preference is English, but any dry mustard will do), a prepared Dijon mustard, and whole seeds. Many Southerners prefer an American-style salad mustard—that bright turmeric-yellow variety, which one clever manufacturer has labeled "classic yellow" in order to give it cachet. I never use it myself, because I find that turmeric is a spice that you cannot dress up and take everywhere. If you prefer, however, you may substitute American-style salad mustard in any recipe that calls for a prepared mustard.

Nutmeg and Mace: Once very common in the meat and vegetable cookery of the South, these spices have more recently been relegated mostly to the baker's pantry. Fortunately, however, they are making a comeback in the stewpot.

Nutmeg and mace are intimately related to one another, since they are different parts of the same fruit of a tropical evergreen tree, *Myristica fragrans*. The nutmeg is the kernel of the fruit, and mace is a lacy, netlike membrane that covers this kernel. Sometimes in Caribbean markets, whole nutmegs are sold with the mace still attached. Unfortunately, they are not sold this way in US markets. While whole nutmegs are readily available, whole-blade mace is hard to come by. Most of the mace available is pre-ground.

Avoid pre-ground nutmeg and mace like the plague. The flavor and aroma of these spices are due to the aromatic oils that they contain. As long as the spice is whole, these oils remain locked inside, but they are very volatile and evaporate rapidly once they are exposed to the

air, which is why pre-ground nutmeg and mace taste like old eraser dust after the jar has been opened a short time. Most of the oils have evaporated and, with them, most of the flavor. Keep a stock of whole nutmegs on hand and grate them with a nutmeg mill or grater only as needed.

When I don't have whole mace on hand, I usually substitute freshly grated nutmeg rather than resort to powdered mace. The spices have a similar flavor, though mace is the stronger and more assertive of the two. If powdered mace is all you can get and you prefer to use it, buy it in very small quantities and keep it in a small, tightly sealed jar, well away from light, air, and heat.

Pepper: True pepper—the black pepper that we use nowadays with such abandon—was once one of the rarest and most exotic of spices, the soul of the mysterious Eastern spice trade. Whether the peppercorns are the familiar black ones, or green, or white, all are the berries of a tropical vine native to India, *Piper nigrum.* Their color is determined by when they are harvested, and how they are treated after the fact.

When the berries first form, they are, like most fruit, bright green. If picked at this stage and dried or pickled, they retain their green color and have a more subtle, almost herbal flavor. Green peppercorns are seldom used in Southern cooking. As the berries ripen, the color develops,

first becoming pale yellow, then orange, then bright red. It is at these varying stages of ripeness that most of the berries are harvested. Green peppercorns are obviously the whole berries harvested before they begin to ripen. Black peppercorns are those harvested slightly underripe, then fermented and dried. The outer flesh turns black, producing the most common variety of peppercorn, with the most developed and complex flavor. White peppercorns are harvested when fully ripened. The outer skin is removed, leaving only the creamy, tan inner kernel. White peppercorns have the most assertive flavor and are often the hottest. They all taste a little different.

Like grapes and coffee beans, the terrain and climate in which peppercorns grow have a direct affect on the flavor of the pepper. Two of the world's most prized and celebrated peppers both come from India and are produced by the same plant: Tellicherry, from the mountains of the same name, and Malabar, from the Indian coast. Yet the flavors of the two have distinct differences.

The whole berries keep their flavor indefinitely, but once they are ground, they lose everything but the heat in pretty short order. Preground pepper may be convenient, but once you are accustomed to the fuller flavor of the freshly ground spice, you will appreciate why serious cooks never touch the pre-ground stuff. Get yourself a couple of peppermills, one for black and one for white pepper, and stock them with the best-quality whole peppercorns that you can find.

Spice Blends: In Southern kitchens, various blends of spices have long been used to flavor many different things, from the Sunday chicken to a seafood boil to the holiday fruitcake. Commercial versions of many of these blends are available, but the ones that are the most satisfying to use are always those that you have made yourself. The blends that follow are those called for in the recipes in this book. Please note that they are by no means definitive; there are many others that I haven't included, and individual cooks have their own variations.

All spice blends should be stored in well-sealed jars or tins, away from light, air, and heat for the best shelf life. Also, the jars should be small, so that there is as little air left at the top of the jar as possible.

Curry: There are cooks who think that "curry" is a single spice; and even those who should know better are often not aware that in India, where this family of spice blends originated, there is no such thing as "curry powder." Each cook blends, toasts, and grinds the spices as needed, and the precise blend will vary from cook to cook and dish to dish. The Madras blends that are exported from India were all designed for the Western market.

Well, regardless of their deviation from their origins, and of each cook's technical knowledge of what curry is, the blend is an important element in the Southern kitchen. All the early cookbooks included recipes for curry powder, and the blend has been frequently used to flavor many Southern dishes at least since the eighteenth century.

For meatless cooking, curry powder is especially valuable to achieve a traditional Southern flavor without adding animal products to the pot.

A small pinch added to a soup or pot of stewed vegetables lends a meaty richness and adds a fragrance and subtle flavor that is distinctively and satisfyingly Southern.

Curry Powder   MAKES ABOUT 1 CUP

This is not, by any stretch of the imagination, a Far Eastern blend, but a Southern adaptation, based on the traditional curries from early Southern and English cookbooks. Make curry powder in small quantities, since the spices don't hold their flavor once they are ground. Turmeric, the bright yellow spice that gives American-style mustard its characteristic color, is sometimes available whole. In ethnic markets it can be in a large chunk, but it's also found in small bits. The measurement given here is for small granules.

2 tablespoons whole allspice

2 tablespoons whole coriander

2 tablespoons powdered dried ginger

2 tablespoons whole white mustard seeds

2 tablespoons whole black peppercorns

2 tablespoons whole turmeric (or powdered turmeric)

1 tablespoon whole cumin seeds

1 tablespoon whole cardamom seeds

1 tablespoon whole fenugreek seeds

1. Grind the spices to a powder in a blender until they are finely ground and well blended, or in batches in a spice mill, combine them in a pint jar, and shake until they are evenly blended.

2. Spoon the powder into small containers (½-pint or ¼-pint canning jars or small spice jars), seal tightly, and store away from light, heat, and air.

Seafood Boiling Spice: This blend is so called because it is most often used to flavor the boiling liquid for crab, shrimp, or crawfish, or that wonderful one-pot feast—the Lowcountry boil.

However, this blend need not be limited to the boiling pot, nor to seafood. It's also frequently used to flavor stews, baked fish, deviled crab, and casserole-baked dishes. Good commercial boiling-spice blends are widely available in the South—Zatarain's, Old Bay, McCormick, and Savannah Spice Company are all good commercial blends. Even so, making your own boiling spice has distinct advantages. Not only will it be fresher and more flavorful, but you can tailor it to suit your and your family's individual tastes.

Hoppin' John's Seafood Boiling Spice   MAKES ABOUT 1 CUP

This is my favorite recipe for boiling spice, from John Taylor's classic *Hoppin' John's Lowcountry Cooking*. Notice that it contains salt. John says that this helps preserve the flavor of the blend and also makes it easier to use, since you won't have to add salt separately. For boiling shellfish, allow ½ tablespoon of boiling spice and half of a fresh lemon for every quart of water. For use in other dishes, refer to the individual recipes in this book. If a recipe from another book calls for a commercial mix, keep in mind that this has added salt, and cut back on, or even omit, the salt called for in the recipe.

¼ cup whole mustard seeds
2 tablespoons whole black peppercorns
2 tablespoons hot red pepper flakes
6 bay leaves
1 tablespoon whole celery seeds
1 tablespoon coriander seeds
1 tablespoon ground dried ginger
A few blades of mace or ¼ teaspoon powdered mace
¼ cup salt

1. Put all the ingredients except the salt into a blender, and process until they are evenly ground. Add the salt and pulse the blender until the salt is evenly mixed with the seasonings.

2. Spoon the spice mix into a ½-pint jar, seal tightly, and store away from light, heat, and air.

Note: *After making and using a couple of batches, you will know what you like and don't like, and can balance the blend to suit your own tastes. For example, if you prefer a milder boil, cut back on the cayenne pepper, and add a little sweet paprika for color and a more subtle flavor.*

Homemade Bourbon Vanilla
MAKES 1 CUP

Making your own vanilla extract may seem a little extreme, particularly since good-quality extracts are available to us, and commercial extracts can certainly be used in any recipe in this book. Once you taste the rich depth of flavor that bourbon lends to vanilla and understand the distinctive difference that so simple a preparation can make, you're sure to think the small effort required is well worth it. If you bake often, you can make this in larger batches: Just allow 1 vanilla bean for every ¼ cup of whiskey.

4 whole imported vanilla beans
1 cup bourbon

1. Split the vanilla beans in half lengthwise, then cut each half into quarters. Put the beans into a clean jar or bottle with a tight-fitting lid. Add the bourbon, tightly put on the lid, and give the jar a good shake.

2. Put it in a cool, dark cupboard that you use frequently. At least once a day for 2 weeks, give the jar a gentle shake. After 2 weeks, you no longer need to agitate the jar. Keep it in a cool place away from direct light.

3. Every time you use the vanilla, replace what you take out with an equal amount of bourbon. It will replenish itself for at least a year or two before the fragrance and flavor begin to fade.

I've kept one batch going for as long as 5 years. When the flavor begins to fade, stop replenishing and use up the extract. Then start a new batch with fresh beans, or strain the old extract, measure it, and use it as a base for your next batch.

The Southern Herb Garden

Every now and again, some folk historian pronounces with authority that Southerners have never had much use for herbs, and that—while the traditional cookery of the South may be aromatic with many spices—herbs, especially fresh ones, play only a nominal role in it. I wonder what South they are talking about, because it surely isn't this one. The old cookbooks and kitchen gardens of the South that I know tell a different—and compelling—story.

The fact is, herb gardens have always been important in the South, from the lush bed of mint that wreathed the front porch of countless plantations and farmhouses to the great laurel trees that still survive on Georgia's barrier islands. And if old cookbooks are any indication, those herbs weren't grown for their looks; they were used. It has only been during the last few generations—our living memory, in fact—that herbs, especially fresh ones, have fallen into disuse. Happily, they are being rediscovered all across the South. They figure prominently in the kitchens of our most notable regional chefs. And best of all, they have once again become important in home cooking.

Here are the herbs that are essential to a Southern garden and kitchen, with some notes on their use:

Basil (*Ocimum basilicum*): Though infrequently mentioned in historical Southern recipes, basil did turn up from time to time, especially as an ingredient for herb-scented vinegars. Today, it is widely used by Southern cooks.

Basil is a part of the large family of mints, and there are dozens of varieties within its own branch of the family, from the famous small-leaved Genoese basil to the spicy, purple Dark Opal variety. In between the exotic extremes is the common variety, usually labeled "sweet basil" at the nursery or garden shop.

Basil is of very little use once it is dried. I use it in my own herb blend (page 33), but that's about all. When the freeze kills off the last of the plants in my courtyard, I wait until the next basil season comes around and make use of other herbs that stand up better to drying in the meantime. The best plan is to grow your own; if you have a sunny, well-drained garden spot, or even a window that will accommodate a large pot, the plants are easy to grow and care for. Failing that, fresh basil is available in many markets. Look for firm leaves without any brown spots, especially at the center.

In vegetable cookery, basil has many uses. Pairing it with tomatoes is classic, and adding it to a pot of okra and tomatoes transforms something wonderful into something downright sublime. Basil is also lovely with squash, eggplant, and green beans.

Bay Laurel (*Laurus nobilis*): This is the herb of nobility in antiquity, revered by the ancient Greeks and used as a symbol of highest honor. The spicy aroma of bay laurel is a touchstone for all Southern cooking, from the Creole kitchen of New Orleans, to the rice kitchen of the Carolina and Georgia Lowcountry, to the soul kitchen of African Americans everywhere. Bay trees were imported into the Carolinas and Georgia very early on and still flourish in milder coastal climates.

Since the plants take to our climate so well, many Lowcountry cooks grow their own and use only fresh leaves. If you live in a temperate climate, you can grow your own in a sunny spot in the garden, or indoors in a pot. Dried bay leaves are, however, the most common form available. Buy them from a store that sells them in bulk. Look for whole, unbroken leaves with a clear, green color and a pungent scent. Keep the leaves in a tightly sealed jar away from light, air, and heat.

Bay, one of the essential herbs of a classic Bouquet Garni (page 32), is used to season most Southern soups and stews, especially gumbos.

Chives (*Allium schoenoprasum*): This delicate herb is actually a member of the pungent garlic branch of the lily family. Many's the wily Southern cook who has put its cousin, the common wild onion, to use and called it "chives." Actually, chives hardly figure at all in Southern cooking per se, yet they are an important herb in flavoring Southern vegetables. The seeming paradox is easily explained: The herb is never actually cooked; its fresh leaves are chopped or snipped and added at the end of the cooking, off the heat, so that the bright flavor is not blunted.

Use only freshly cut chives; the dried variety is of no gastronomical interest whatsoever. Chives grow well in a mild climate but wilt under the intense heat of a Southern midsummer, especially in a place like Savannah. Consequently, they are more commonly paired with delicate spring and hearty autumn produce.

Marjoram and Oregano (*Origanum*, mint family): These two closely related members of the enormous mint family are not commonly used in traditional Southern cooking. Oregano is frequently added to the pot if the cook is Creole, and marjoram is occasionally mentioned in some of the Anglo cooking of the Eastern Seaboard. Today, thanks in part to a national interest in all things Italian, a bottle of dried oregano can be found on most Southern pantry shelves. All members of the marjoram family stand up pretty well to drying. Oregano and marjoram are also fairly hearty perennials and are easy to grow in a sunny garden spot or in a pot on a sunny ledge.

Oregano is most often used to flavor gumbos, field peas, squash, and sometimes okra and tomatoes. Marjoram is lovely with green beans, squash, and all kinds of field peas and dried beans.

Mint (*Mentha* family): Along with sage and bay leaves, this family of herbs forms an herbal triumvirate, the foundation of all Southern herbal cookery. The most common member of the mint family in the South is spearmint (*Mentha spicata*), which flourishes in our warm, humid climate. You can grow your own fresh mint in a sunny garden spot or in a pot on a sunny window ledge. Fresh mint is also widely available in the market. If you go that route and your market doesn't have spearmint, don't panic; simply substitute peppermint for it. It's not quite the same, but it will still work in the recipe.

When dried, mint loses its warm, herbal quality and becomes more distinctly "minty." Dried mint is useful in stews and ragouts, but don't substitute it for fresh mint unless the recipe says that you can.

Mint is probably best known outside the South as the essential ingredient of a drink, but inside the South it is as frequently paired with lamb, mutton, and game as it is with bourbon. It is also used to season peas (both fresh green peas and field peas), new potatoes, fresh melons, and squash.

Parsley (*Petroselinum crispum*): Poor parsley: In every pot but seldom noticed—unless it happens to be sprinkled over the top of things as a garnish. Parsley may not have an assertive flavor, perhaps, but no other herb is as universally used or important. Its flavor does not dominate, but it is an important underpinning for virtually all soups, stews, and gumbos. Parsley is also one of the three essential herbs of a Bouquet Garni (this page).

Throughout this book, I never use the adjective "fresh" before parsley in the ingredients list, because this is one herb that must be fresh to be of any use at all. When dried, parsley loses all its flavor and is of absolutely no use to a cook. You could use it as a garnish, I suppose, but you might as well sprinkle hay all over your food.

Sage (*Salvia officinalis*): If I were asked to characterize, in a single smell or flavor, the essence of Southern cooking, my answer would probably be sage. Ever popular in English cookery, its universality in Southern cooking points straight back to Anglo roots.

Though better known in our region as a classic seasoning for poultry, pork, game, and dressing, sage has many uses in the vegetable pot. It is frequently paired with squash, both winter and summer varieties, okra and field peas, and is the flavoring of choice for onions.

Thyme (*Thymus*, mint family): Another member of the mint family; there are many varieties of thyme plants that are commonly grown, but the most familiar is *Thymus vulgaris*, or "common" thyme. This herb is one of the defining aromas and flavors of both Creole and Lowcountry cookery.

Thyme is one of the essential ingredients of a classic bouquet garni and a pot of Creole gumbo almost isn't gumbo without it. Thyme is also frequently paired with field peas and with both yellow crookneck and hearty winter squashes.

Bouquet Garni   MAKES 1 BOUQUET GARNI

You might think that this little bundle of flavoring herbs is used mostly in Creole cooking, since it still goes by its French name, but it's a common element of all Southern cooking, as important in a stockpot or Lowcountry pilau as it is in a pot of gumbo or étouffée.

The essential, classic core of a bouquet garni consists of a sprig of parsley, a sprig of thyme, and a bay leaf. Often the leafy part of a celery stalk is incorporated into it, and another herb may be used in addition to—or, depending on the dish, instead of—the thyme. When that's the case, I have so indicated in the individual recipe.

Note: *If you find yourself without any fresh thyme, you can use dried thyme in the bouquet garni. First, tie it up in a bit of muslin or a triple layer of cheesecloth, or place it into a stainless-steel tea ball. Tie it to the remaining ingredients so that you don't have to fish around for it at the end of the cooking.*

Fines Herbes   MAKES ABOUT 1½ CUPS

Another important herb combination with a French name, fines herbes is a classic potpourri of dried aromatic herbs that is a critical element in many cuisines. Use it to flavor a pot of okra and tomatoes, especially when the tomatoes are the canned variety, and your favorite vinaigrette; or fill a tea ball with it and put it in a stockpot or stewpot, or slip it into almost any stewed vegetable—from slow-cooked green beans to sweet potatoes.

I prefer to make this recipe in small batches, so that it stays fresh, but you can make it in larger quantities and either give away or freeze what you won't use right away.

3 tablespoons dried, crumbled basil

3 tablespoons dried, crumbled marjoram

3 tablespoons dried, crumbled rosemary

3 tablespoons dried, crumbled sage

3 tablespoons dried, crumbled savory
    (winter or summer)

3 tablespoons dried, crumbled thyme

1 tablespoon dried, crumbled bay leaves

1 tablespoon dried lavender flowers

Put all the herbs in a pint jar with a tight-fitting lid. Shake it vigorously until all the herbs are well mixed. Keep the jar tightly covered and store it away from light, air, and heat.

Make sure that the string you use to tie the bundle is cotton kitchen twine, and not a coated or synthetic material.

1 leafy celery-stalk top

1 large sprig parsley

1 (3-inch) sprig thyme (or 1 heaped teaspoon dried whole thyme leaves)

Optional: 1 (3-inch) sprig marjoram, sage, or oregano (or 1 teaspoon whole dried leaves)

2 fresh bay leaves or 1 dried bay leaf

1. If you're using all fresh herbs, wash the celery top and herbs, and pat dry. Gather them with the bay leaf into a bundle and tie them at the bottom with a 4- to 6-inch piece of kitchen twine. If the bay leaf is dried, tie the bundle gently so that the leaf doesn't crumble. Then, wrap the string up and around the bundle as you would the laces of a dancing slipper. Tie it securely at the top of the bundle.

2. You may also make the bouquet garni in a bundle of cheesecloth, (especially if you are using dried herbs). Lay a triple-folded square of cheesecloth on a work surface and put the herbs in the center. Then fold the cloth in around it on all sides, roll it up, and tied it the as directed in step 1.

Go-Withs and Other Necessaries

ACCOMPANIMENTS FOR UNDER, OVER, OR ON THE SIDE

Many Southern vegetable recipes are very simple, but they seldom find themselves going solo on the plate. There's always some kind of flavoring accompaniment, whether it's a splash of spicy Pepper Vinegar (page 25) or briny Old Sour (page 273), a dollop of sweet-sour relish or chutney or a garlicky okra pickle. And, more often than not, there's some kind of "go-with"—a bit of cornbread, a hoecake, or a bed of rice or

grits. The following go-with recipes are some of the classics that round out a Southern meal. Also included are recipes for basics, such as pie crust, used elsewhere in this book.

Recipes for essential condiments such as pepper vinegar, seasoning spices, and spice and herb blends are discussed in the chapter entitled The Southern Kitchen (pages 9–33), while a few others are scattered throughout the book along with the main ingredient for other recipes: Bill Neal's Pickled Okra (page 109), Dilly Beans (page 128), St. John's Golden Mango Chutney (page 176), John Egerton's Lemon Curd (page 272), and Purefoy Cranberry Relish (page 278).

Cornbread, Corn Sticks, and Skillet Bread   MAKES 14 CORN STICKS OR MUFFINS, OR ONE 9-INCH ROUND

Many a Southern vegetable dish is not considered complete without cornbread, whether it comes to the table in the form of a hoecake; a wedge of skillet bread, a crispy corn stick, or a dumpling floating among the greens. Originally, Southern cornbread was a simple, rough batter of meal, water, and salt. The combination evolved over the years, becoming softer and richer. Most modern recipes include buttermilk, eggs, and some kind of enriching fat—bacon grease, butter, or cracklings. They might also include other enrichments, such as fresh corn kernels or jalapeño peppers. Here is the basic recipe, with the classic taste and texture that Southerners have come to prize:

2 cups water stone-ground cornmeal

2 teaspoons baking powder, preferably single-acting (recipe follows)

½ teaspoon baking soda

1 teaspoon salt

2 large eggs, lightly beaten

1¾–2 cups buttermilk or all-natural whole-milk yogurt thinned with milk or water to buttermilk consistency

4 tablespoons rendered bacon fat, butter, or lard, melted

1. Position a rack in the center of the oven and preheat to 450°F. When it has reached that temperature, lightly but thoroughly grease the pan you plan to use and preheat it in the oven for at least 10 minutes.

2. In a large mixing bowl whisk together the meal, baking powder, soda, and salt. In a separate bowl, whisk together the eggs, 1¾ cups of the buttermilk, and 2 tablespoons of the melted fat.

3. When the pan is well heated, make a well in the center of the cornmeal and then pour in the milk and eggs and quickly stir together, using as few strokes as possible. If it seems dry, add a little more milk.

4. With a pot holder, remove the pan from the oven and add to it the remaining 2 tablespoons of melted fat. If you are using a corn-stick or muffin pan, drizzle the fat equally into each well. (When I use butter, I take a cold stick still wrapped in its paper and rub a little into each well. Butter will sizzle if the pan is hot enough. If it doesn't, put the pan back into the oven for about 5 minutes.)

5. Now, quickly pour the batter into the pan. Again, it must sizzle when it touches the pan. If you are using a corn-stick or muffin pan, fill each well level with the sides. Do it quickly so that each addition sizzles.

6. Bake in the upper third of the oven until nicely browned and firm, about 25 minutes for corn sticks or muffins and 35 minutes for a skillet cake. As soon as the bread comes out of the oven, invert the pan over a plate (for the cake) or a linen towel (for the corn sticks). The bread should fall right out of the pan.

Note: *If you are using a standard-size muffin or corn-stick pan, this batter will make two batches. I keep two pans on hand for the purpose, but you can make the bread in batches. As soon as you have removed the first batch from the pan, add more fat to the pan and repeat as above. Roll the first batch up in a tea towel to keep them warm while the second batch cooks. Don't use paper towels, foil, or an insulated mat, as they will trap the steam in the bread and soften the crust. Serve the cornbread warm with plenty of good butter.*

Single-Acting Baking Powder

MAKES ½ CUP

You can use commercial double-acting baking powder for the recipes in this book, but try to find one that is aluminum-free (such as Rumford). I prefer single-acting powder because many double-acting powders have a harsh chemical aftertaste. Single-acting powder isn't made commercially, but making your own is easy.

3 level tablespoons cream of tartar

2 level tablespoons baking soda

3 level tablespoons rice flour or unbleached all-purpose flour

Combine all ingredients in an airtight container and shake well. Shake the container well before each use, and use the powder up within a month.

Hoecakes   MAKES ABOUT A DOZEN CAKES

Hoecakes are supposed to have been so named because they were originally cooked on the blade of a hoe that was held over an open hearth. They're basically just cornmeal pancakes. Many Southern cooks today add wheat flour and sugar to their cakes, but I prefer the older version. They are especially good to make on hot days when you want cornbread but don't want to heat up the oven.

Hoecakes are the perfect accompaniment for any vegetable but are especially suited to a pot of spicy gumbo or slow-cooked greens.

2 cups fine stone-ground cornmeal

2 teaspoons baking powder, preferably single-acting (page 35)

½ teaspoon baking soda

1 teaspoon salt

2 large eggs, lightly beaten

2 cups whole milk, buttermilk, or yogurt

Oil, melted butter, or lard, for the griddle

1. Position a rack in the center of the oven and preheat to 150°F (or the warm setting). In a large mixing bowl, whisk together the meal, baking powder, soda, and salt. In a separate bowl, combine the eggs and buttermilk, and whisk until smooth. Stir this quickly into the dry ingredients, using as few strokes as possible.

2. Heat a griddle or cast-iron skillet over medium heat. When hot, brush it lightly with fat. Using a large, pointed kitchen spoon, take up about 2 tablespoons of the batter and pour it onto the griddle from the pointed end (this helps ensure that a round cake will form). Repeat until the griddle is full but not crowded.

3. Cook until the bottoms are nicely browned and air holes form in the tops, about 4 minutes. Turn, and cook until the second side is browned, about 3–4 minutes longer. Transfer the cakes to the warm oven and repeat with the remaining batter. Serve hot, with or without additional butter.

Buttered Croutons   MAKES 2 CUPS

These crispy, buttery morsels are the ideal accompaniment for just about any soup or salad. They are simple to make, much better than the store-bought variety, and are very economical, since they are best when made from stale bread. Freeze leftover baguettes and crusty rolls until you have enough. To cut them into croutons, use a serrated bread knife and cut the bread first into 1/2-inch slices and then cut the slices into cubes.

2 ounces (4 tablespoons or ½ stick) unsalted butter
2 cups crusty bread, cut into ½- to 1-inch cubes
    (depending on how you plan to use them)

1. Position a rack in the upper third of the oven and preheat to 300°F. Put the butter in a shallow pan (such as a rimmed baking sheet or sheet-cake pan) that will hold all the bread in a single layer. Put this in the oven until the butter is melted.

2. As soon as the butter is melted, add the bread and toss until it is thoroughly coated. Return the pan to the upper third of the oven and bake, tossing the croutons from time to time, until they are delicately browned and crisp, about ½ hour.

Note: *Though it requires more attention, you can prepare the croutons on top of the stove if you prefer not to heat up the oven. Put the butter in a large sauté pan or skillet over medium heat. When it is melted, add the cubed bread and toss until it is evenly coated with the fat. Sauté, tossing frequently, until they are brown and crisp, about 10-15 minutes.*

Carolina-Style Rice   MAKES 4 SERVINGS

Every rice-based cuisine in the world has its own way of cooking this daily staple. Where chopsticks are the tableware of choice, the rice tends to be a bit sticky so that it holds together when picked up. In northern Italy, it is creamy. If either one of these is what you are accustomed to, rice from the old rice-growing regions of South Carolina and Georgia will take some getting used to. When properly done, it almost rattles when it hits the plate: each grain is distinct, firm, and yet tender and fluffy. The only time it gets creamy is when cream gravy is poured over it.

There are two basic rules to remember when cooking rice by the Carolina method. First, the rice is always washed before it goes into the pot, even if the package says it is prewashed. Second, the rice should never be stirred while cooking. When it is cooked, fluff it with a fork that has widely spaced, narrow tines, such as a large dinner fork or carving fork.

1 cup raw, long-grain rice, preferably Basmati
2 scant cups water
Salt

1. Put the rice in a large bowl filled with water. Gently pick the rice up and rub it between your hands. Drain it over a wire-mesh sieve to catch stray grains, and repeat until the water runs mostly clear. Pour it into the sieve and rinse one last time under cold running water, and set it aside in the sink to drain.

2. Put the rice, water, and a healthy pinch of salt in a heavy-bottomed 2- to 3-quart pot. Bring it to a boil over medium-high heat. Stir it to make sure that the rice is not sticking, then put the spoon away.

3. Reduce the heat to medium low, and let the rice simmer for 11–12 minutes, or until there are clear, dry steam holes formed on the surface, and most if not all of the water should be absorbed. Gently fold the top rice under with a fork, "fluffing," not stirring it.

4. Put the lid on tight and let the pot sit over the heat for a minute more to rebuild the steam, then turn off the heat. Let it sit 12 minutes longer. It can be held like this for up to an hour without harm, but 12 minutes is the minimum.

When you are ready to serve the rice, fluff it by picking it with a fork, then turn it out into a serving bowl and serve at once.

Grits and Hominy Grits

Popularly known around here as "Georgia Ice Cream," grits is—with the possible exception of okra—perhaps the most infamous and misunderstood ingredient in all Southern cooking. (Now, let's just settle this singular/plural stuff right here: grits is singular and grits are plural—and that's that.) Once a staple on almost every Southern breakfast table, grits became a sort of culinary bogeyman in the South, equal to the nutty relative we kept hidden in the attic. We ate grits and still liked it, but some of us were pretty embarrassed about the whole thing. Grits began to disappear from breakfast menus, and hash-browned potatoes crept into their place. For grits-loving and otherwise patriotic Southerners who never did get embarrassed, it was a depressing state of affairs.

Then something even worse happened. Grits became trendy, the glitzy food star of every upscale Southern restaurant in the land. It went from unmentionable breakfast gruel to the one sure element of a nouvelle Southern menu. It got souffléed, caked and truffled, creamed and jalapeñoed, and infused with more garlic than a Genoa salami. It even got dumped into chocolate dessert. Today, grits is on the menu for practically every meal except, ironically, breakfast.

In short, it got nouvelled into culinary outer space.

However, there are those of us who haven't been impressed by all of this hoopla. Southern food preservationist Edna Lewis best summed up our take on the trend when she said simply, "They need to leave grits *alone*."

There are only two kinds of grits worth your notice: whole-corn grits (made with the whole grain) and hominy grits (made from hominy—corn with the outer hull removed). The former look speckled in their raw form, the latter are usually even white or yellow (depending on the kind of corn from which they're made). Despite the posturing of nouvelle cooks, whole-corn grits are not necessarily superior to hominy grits, and there are times when hominy grits are better because they don't compete with the food that they accompany.

Basic Boiled Grits   MAKES 4 SERVINGS

Here's the basic recipe for preparing both whole-corn and plain hominy grits. Exact measurements for the proportion of grits to water are difficult. The usual ratio is four to one, but the amount of water needed can vary, depending on the grits. The safest thing is to keep a teakettle of water simmering close at hand in case the grits need more water before they get tender. You should never add cold water to the pot; it just confuses the poor grits.

1 quart (4 cups) water
1 cup raw corn grits
Salt

1. Bring the water to a good boil in a stainless-steel or enameled pot, and stir in the grits. Bring the grits back to a boil, stirring frequently to prevent lumps from forming.

2. Reduce the heat to a bare simmer and cover the pot. Cook, stirring occasionally, until the grits absorb all the moisture and are the consistency of a thick cornmeal mush, about 1 hour. Season them with salt to taste and let simmer another minute or two to allow the salt to be absorbed. Taste and adjust the salt before serving.

Grits Squares   SERVES 9 AS AN APPETIZER, 4 TO 6 AS A SIDE DISH

These semi-traditional squares are from my friend Jackie Mills, who I met while she was a food editor with *Southern Living* magazine. Like her Grilled Okra Salad (page 106), this dish is at once rooted in Jackie's Kentucky childhood, where she was weaned on peas and grits, and enlivened by her forward-looking sensibility. Enriched with cream and cheese, the grits depart from tradition only in the way they are finished: Instead of the usual frying (see page 203), these cakes are baked.

The grits squares can be topped with a fresh vegetable sauté in summer or a hearty stew in winter. Jackie likes to top them with a light, elegant ragout of field peas.

4 cups Chicken Broth (page 21) or canned broth

1½ cups regular hominy grits (not quick-cooking or instant)

¼ cup heavy cream

1 cup freshly grated Pecorino Romano

Whole black pepper in a mill

1. Bring the chicken broth to a boil in a stainless or enamel-lined pan (this helps keep the grits from sticking). Pour in the grits, stirring constantly to keep them from lumping. Cook 35–60 minutes, or until they are very thick and tender, stirring occasionally at first and more frequently as they get thick. Stir in the cream and cook 2–3 minutes more. Turn off the heat.

2. Add the cheese and a few grindings of black pepper (about ¼ teaspoon) and stir until smooth. Rinse out an 8 x 8-inch baking dish with cold water and pour in the grits. Let cool and then refrigerate until the grits are very firm, about 4 hours.

3. Position a rack in the center of the oven and preheat the oven to 400°F. Lightly grease a

cookie sheet with butter or oil. Cut the grits into nine squares and put them on the cookie sheet. Bake for 7–10 minutes until the grits are just heated through. Don't overcook them or, as Jackie puts it, "they'll squash."

Basic Pastry for Pies and Tarts
MAKES TWO 9-INCH PIE SHELLS OR ONE 9-INCH PIE WITH TOP CRUST

This is my favorite all-purpose pie dough. It's perfect for just about any baked goods that need a pastry crust—from pecan pie to quiche. The secret to its flaky, tender crumb is lard, which helps tenderize the dough and lends a flakiness that even butter can't imitate. If you can't cook with lard, omit it and use an extra 2 tablespoons of butter in its stead. An all-butter pastry is still pretty good.

A lot of people are afraid of making their own pastry, which for the life of me I can't figure out. We're talking here about less than a dollar's worth of ingredients and a technique that is virtually artless. All it takes is a little caution and practice. Moreover, pastry is a cinch to make in the food processor; in fact, it's so easy that I seldom ever make it by hand. Alternate directions for the processor method are given at the end of the recipe.

10 ounces (about 2 cups) all-purpose, soft-wheat flour

½ teaspoon salt

¼ pound (8 tablespoons, 1 stick) chilled unsalted butter, cut into small bits

1 ounce (2 tablespoons) chilled lard (vegetable shortening may be substituted), cut into small bits

Ice water (⅓ cup or more)

1. Sift the flour and salt together into a metal or ceramic bowl. Add the butter and lard to the bowl, handling as little as possible to keep them from

softening. Work the fat into the flour with a pastry blender or two knives (not your hands) until it has the texture of coarse meal.

2. Add the ice water, starting with ⅓ cup, and lightly stir it into the flour until it is moistened. Stir in additional water by the tablespoon until the dough is soft and smooth but not sticky. Lightly dust the dough and your hands with flour, and gather it into a ball. Wrap it well with plastic wrap and let it rest in the refrigerator for half an hour.

3. Lightly flour a cool work surface (marble is ideal, but plastic laminate works, too) and roll out the pastry for use as directed in the individual recipe.

Food Processor Pie Dough: If you own a food processor, once you learn to make pie dough with it, you'll never do it any other way. The only tricky part is keeping the dough from being overworked and therefore overheated. The blade's speed causes it to heat up quickly, which can make the fat oily. To prevent this, chill the blade in the freezer for about 5 minutes before using it.

Fit the processor with the steel blade and put in the flour and salt. Pulse it a few times to sift it, then add the butter and lard. Pulse until the flour reaches the coarse meal stage. Add ⅓ cup of ice water and pulse again until mixed. Then add water in tablespoonfuls, pulsing to mix in each addition until the dough just gathers into a ball.

Sauces

FLAVORED BUTTERS, RICH CREAMS, AND OTHER ENHANCEMENTS

Judith Martin, better known as Miss Manners—the doyenne, not of food, but of good behavior—reminds us that books on decorum from the past give away some pretty hair-raising things about what was going on in the parlors and dining rooms of yesterday by way of their cautions about what one should *not* do. The very fact that they had to advise people *not* to pick their teeth with a knife or blow their noses on the edge of the tablecloth suggests that there were a lot of people who were actually doing it.

Similarly, a perusal of cookbooks used in nineteenth-century Southern kitchens paint a dim picture of the state of sauce making in those days. They are full of all sorts of alarming indictments, which I think was partly because Southern cooks have never been much for using elaborate sauces on their vegetables. Particularly in the agrarian nineteenth century, vegetables were gathered the day they were meant to be served. They were very fresh, intensely flavorful, and didn't need much enhancement to make them taste good. This has remained true even in our own industrial age, thanks to the renewed popularity of farmers' markets and backyard gardening.

All the same, there are sauces that most Southern cooks, both then and now, would be hard-pressed to do without. From elegant pecan butter, reserved for state occasions, to the homey bowl of mayonnaise on the family table, these sauces are subtle; their aim is to enhance flavor, not cover it up. So don't let their simplicity fool you; they won't let a careless cook off the hook.

Their preparation requires just as much care as an elaborate sauce and their subtlety leaves nothing for a badly prepared vegetable to hide behind.

Pecan Brown Butter
MAKES ABOUT 1 CUP

Nuts toasted in brown butter make a lovely sauce for all kinds of vegetables and fish. In Europe and other parts of the United States, almonds are the nut most usually put to use, but in the South, we prefer to use our native pecans. Their rich flavor is very distinctive. Try this sauce with the season's first asparagus, tender young French beans, or broiled fish—especially catfish.

For more on pecans, please see pages 208–13.

½ cup whole pecan halves
¼ pound (1 stick or ½ cup) unsalted butter
Salt (optional)

1. Pick over the nuts, removing any lingering bits of shell from their grooves and cut them lengthwise into thirds, using their grooves as guidelines. Prepare the food that will be sauced and have it ready on a serving platter or individual plates.

2. Put the butter into a heavy-bottomed skillet over medium-high heat. When it is melted, add the pecans and stir until they're well-coated. Cook, constantly but gently shaking the pan (or stirring), until both nuts and butter are golden brown. Remove the pan from the heat, swirl in a pinch of salt (depending on how it's used), and pour the pecan butter directly over the food that it is intended to sauce. Serve at once.

Note: *In some areas, growers sell imperfect, broken pecan pieces that are culled from the premium whole nuts. While they are much more economical than whole nuts, they often have bits of broken shell in them. You can use them for this recipe, but be careful to remove all those stray bits of shell.*

Drawn Butter   MAKES ABOUT ½ CUP

There is no vegetable sauce simpler or lovelier than this one, and yet it is seldom seen in modern American cookbooks. What usually turns up under the name nowadays is actually clarified butter, but in the nineteenth century, this thick sauce was what drawn butter originally described. Most old Southern versions followed eighteenth-century English practice, adding the smallest proportion of flour to aid in the thickening and lessen the risk of the butter separating. Later in the nineteenth century, the proportion of flour and liquid increased, and butter sauce degenerated into a pasty white sauce of flour and milk with hardly enough butter to justify the name.

The recipes that follow specify serving the butter sauce in a heated sauceboat. Don't warm the sauceboat too much or the residual heat could cause the sauce to separate. The sauceboat should be cool enough to handle with your bare hands.

The method I used in the first edition of this book was the old one from the nineteenth century, in which the butter was made in a pan that was gently shaken over another pan of simmering water. In those days, a good reliable whisk was rare. It was probably carrying fidelity to history a bit far: Today, I make these sauces using the same method as a classic beurre blanc.

It is important to have everything ready to serve before making this sauce; it won't wait while you finish cooking and cannot be reheated.

2 tablespoons water

Salt

4 ounces (1 stick or 8 tablespoons) cold unsalted butter, cut into ½-inch chunks

1. Put 2 tablespoons of water and a healthy pinch of salt in a small, heavy-bottomed saucepan. Bring it to a simmer over medium-low heat. Remove the saucepan from the heat and whisk in about 1 tablespoon of the butter chunks and continue whisking until it is almost melted.

2. Add another tablespoon of butter, return the pan to very low heat, and whisk until it's almost melted. Continue until all the butter has been added and is melted but still quite thick. Pour into a heated sauceboat or directly over the food to be sauced, and serve at once.

Lemon Butter   MAKES ABOUT ½ CUP

Melted butter is, by itself, just about the best possible sauce for fresh vegetables, and the fragrance of lemon enlivens even the most lackluster of them. Here, butter and lemon are brought together in an especially nice sauce for asparagus, artichokes, or broccoli, or for dipping shrimp and steamed crab.

1 lemon

¼ cup water

4 ounces (1 stick or 8 tablespoons) unsalted butter

1. Peel the zest from the lemon, scrape off any white pith, and cut the zest into fine julienne. Put the zest into a saucepan with the water and bring it to a boil. Boil until it is reduced by half and turn off the heat.

2. Cut the lemon in half and squeeze the juice from one of the halves into the saucepan with the zest and water. Put it over low heat and whisk in the butter as directed in the master recipe on the opposite page. Remove the pan from the heat, taste, and squeeze in more lemon juice as needed. Whisk it in, pour the sauce into a heated sauceboat or directly over the food it is to sauce, and serve at once.

Hollandaise, or Dutch Sauce

MAKES ABOUT 1 CUP

Every now and again a magazine article or cookbook will credit Fanny Farmer's edition of *The Boston Cooking School Cook Book* (1896) with the introduction of this popular sauce to American cooks. Actually, it was around long before Miss Farmer. Both Maria Parloa and Mary Lincoln, Miss Farmer's predecessors at the Boston Cooking School, gave recipes for it in their own cookbooks, and in the South it was already an integral part of *la cuisine Créole* when Miss Farmer was still in diapers. I suspect that some of the folk historians have forgotten that the word *Hollandaise* is just French for "Dutch." Recipes titled "Dutch sauce" were fairly common, and as for their being used in America, English writer Eliza Acton (*Modern Cookery for Private Families*, 1845) even called a variation of this sauce "Cold Dutch, or *American* Sauce."

Still popular here in the South, Hollandaise is just about the best sauce imaginable for almost any vegetable—from the season's first asparagus shoots to artichokes, broccoli, young green beans, and cauliflower.

3 large egg yolks

1 tablespoon water

Juice of 1 lemon

4 ounces (1 stick or ½ cup) unsalted butter, melted and kept hot (but not browned)

Salt and cayenne pepper

1. Have the bottom of a double boiler ready with simmering water. Combine the egg yolks and water in the top pan. Whisk until the mixture is smooth.

2. Place the upper pan on the lower half, over, but not touching, the simmering water. Whisk until the eggs have doubled in volume, about 2 minutes. Take the pan off the heat and whisk in the lemon juice.

3. Slowly whisk in the hot butter, a little at a time. The sauce should be quite thick and fluffy. Taste and beat in a pinch or so of salt and a bit of cayenne. Serve warm or at room temperature.

Homemade Mayonnaise

MAKES 1½ CUPS

This sauce has become so commonplace in the South that it seems to be on—or in—virtually everything we eat. This ubiquitousness has, perhaps justifiably, made it the brunt of not a few jokes. Maybe this wouldn't happen if more Southern cooks made their own mayonnaise and showed a little more restraint in its use.

Classic mayonnaise is made by hand, working oil and vinegar a drop at a time, into raw egg yolks, and it's still the way to get the best texture. If all that work seems too much for you, the food processor makes perfectly respectable mayonnaise. You can also make it in a blender, though you do have to stop the machine and keep scraping the sides down.

Because it is made with raw eggs, the sauce must be stored in the refrigerator and should not sit out at room temperature for any length of time.

2 large egg yolks or 1 whole large egg

1 teaspoon dry mustard or 1 tablespoon Dijon mustard

Salt and cayenne pepper

1 cup olive (or vegetable) oil

Juice of 1 lemon or 2 tablespoons wine vinegar

1. To make mayonnaise by the traditional hand method, put the egg yolks or egg in a mixing bowl with the mustard, a healthy pinch of salt, and a tiny pinch of cayenne, both to taste. With a wire whisk or pair of forks held together, beat everything together until the mixture is smooth.

2. Have the oil ready in a container that has a good pouring spout. Pour a teaspoon of oil into the yolk mixture and beat until it is incorporated. Begin adding the remaining oil a few drops at a time, whisking until each addition is thoroughly incorporated before adding more. Keep at it until you have used about half the oil.

3. Add a little of the lemon juice or vinegar and whisk it in, then alternate between adding vinegar and oil until both are completely incorporated into the sauce. Taste and adjust the seasonings. Keep the sauce cold until you are ready to serve it.

Food Processor Method

1. The sauce is less likely to break in this method if you use the whole egg instead of the yolks. Put the egg, mustard, a healthy pinch of salt, a tiny one of cayenne, and the lemon juice or vinegar in the bowl of a food processor fitted with a steel blade. Process until mixture is smooth, about 1 minute.

2. With the processor motor running, add the oil in a thin, steady stream. This should take about 2 minutes; if it takes less time, you are pouring the oil in too fast. When the oil is incorporated, let the machine run for a few seconds more. Stop the machine, taste and adjust the seasonings, and pulse it a couple of times to mix them in.

Note: *If you are cooking for someone with an immune deficiency disease such as HIV, or for a young child or elderly person whose immune system may be otherwise impaired, do not use homemade mayonnaise or make it with pasteurized eggs.*

Herb Mayonnaise   MAKES ABOUT 2 CUPS

The late Jim King, a longtime Savannahian who was born and raised in Talladega, Alabama, was a dear friend and long-suffering official recipe-testing guinea pig: he was subjected to pretty much everything I cooked for the first edition of this book—both the successes that made it into the book and the failures that didn't. Actually, he was a pretty good cook in his own right.

Jim was one of those Southerners who created that stereotype about our affection for mayonnaise: He was seriously addicted to the stuff. To feed his addiction, he made just about the best herb mayonnaise I ever tasted. You'll want to bury your face in it—it's that good. Use it with any cold cooked or raw vegetable, or with roasted meat or poultry, fish, boiled shrimp, or slather it on your next BLT.

1 large egg

1½ tablespoons lemon juice

1 tablespoon Dijon mustard

1 clove garlic, crushed and peeled

1 teaspoon salt

1 large sprig each fresh parsley, rosemary, and basil (do not used dried herbs), tough stems removed and discarded

¼ cup extra-virgin olive oil

1 cup vegetable oil

1. Put the egg, lemon juice, mustard, garlic, salt, herbs, and 1 tablespoon of the olive oil in the bowl of a food processor fitted with a steel blade. Turn on the machine and process for 1 minute.

2. If your processor feed-tube pusher has a pinhole in its bottom, put it in place, turn on the machine, and with the machine running, pour the olive oil into the pusher and let it dribble into the egg mixture. If you don't have such a contraption, add the olive oil in a slow, very thin stream through the feed tube. Add the other oil in a thin stream until it is all incorporated and emulsified.

3. Process for about 15 seconds more, or until the mayonnaise is quite stiff. Transfer it to a storage bowl, cover, and refrigerate it overnight, if possible, to allow the flavors to blend and mellow before using.

Savannah Sweet Red Pepper Sauce   MAKES ABOUT 1½ TO 2 CUPS

Southerners use green peppers so frequently that ripe red and yellow peppers became rare in our markets until they were recently rediscovered. Consequently, ripe peppers may not seem particularly Southern, except perhaps when they appear in that ubiquitous Southern spread, pimiento cheese. So it may surprise you to know that this recipe dates back at least a hundred years. Adapted from Harriet Ross Colquitt's *Savannah Cook Book* (1933), it almost certainly predates that publication by a generation.

Mrs. Colquitt used this sauce to stew shrimp, but it is also excellent on green beans (page 124), Maryland Squash Croquettes (page 162), and even on a baked potato. I've made a couple of changes: Mrs. Colquitt precooked the peppers by stewing them in a little water; I roast them. It makes them easier to peel and concentrates their flavor. I've also added a bit of shallot to bring out the peppers' sweetness.

4 medium red bell peppers or 12 ounces commercially packed roasted red peppers (not in vinegar; see note)

¼ cup minced shallot or yellow onion

2 tablespoons unsalted butter

Salt and ground cayenne pepper

Water

1. If you are using commercially packed peppers, skip to step 2. Position a rack in the upper third of the oven and preheat to 400°F. Remove any sticky labels from the peppers, wash them, and pat dry. Lay them on an ungreased baking sheet and roast in the upper third of the oven, turning periodically, until the skin is evenly blackened, about half an hour. (If you have a gas range, you can do this over a burner; see the note below.) Put the peppers in a paper bag, close it, and let stand 10 minutes.

2. Skin the peppers, split them lengthwise, and remove the seeds and stems. Rinse under cold running water. If you are using jarred peppers, they are already skinned, but you'll need to remove the seeds and rinse them. Cut them into wide strips.

3. Put the shallot or onion and butter in a lidded skillet that will comfortably hold all the peppers, and turn on the heat to medium. Sauté, uncovered, tossing frequently, until the shallot or onion is softened but not colored, about 5 minutes.

4. Add the peppers, a healthy pinch of salt (omit if using jarred peppers), a tiny pinch of cayenne, and about 2 tablespoons of water. Bring it to a boil, cover the pan, and reduce the heat to medium low. Simmer until the peppers are very tender, about 15 minutes. If they get too dry, add a spoonful or so more water, but only as much as is absolutely necessary. Puree through a food mill or in a blender or food processor fitted with a steel blade. Taste and correct the seasonings.

5. Before serving, reheat over medium-low heat, stirring often to prevent the sauce from scorching or sticking.

Note: *To roast the peppers on a gas range, insert a carving fork into the stem end of a pepper and hold it 4 inches above a high flame, turning constantly, until the skin blisters and blackens.*

This is at its best when made with fresh-roasted peppers, but commercially packed roasted peppers still make a very nice sauce. Look for peppers that have been packed in their own juices. Goya is one very good brand, which is sold in 6½-ounce jars. Do not use peppers that have been packed in vinegar.

To make Mrs. Colquitt's Stewed Shrimp and Peppers, add 1½ pounds (headless weight) peeled raw shrimp in step 5 and simmer until the shrimp are just cooked through, about 4 minutes. Serve over Carolina-Style Rice (page 37).

Cold Cream Sauce   MAKES 2 CUPS

Clotted with lemon juice, perfumed with nutmeg, this is one of the best all-purpose sweet sauces going. I can think of very few desserts or fruit dishes that it does not enhance. What makes it doubly appealing is that it is also very easy to make.

1 pint heavy cream (minimum 36 percent milk fat)
½ cup sugar
1 lemon
Whole nutmeg in a grater

1. Put the cream in a stainless-steel, glass, or other nonreactive bowl. Add the sugar and stir until dissolved. Grate the zest from the lemon and add it to the cream.

2. Cut the lemon in half and squeeze the juice from one half through a strainer into the cream. Stir until the cream begins to clot and thicken, then season it generously with a few gratings of nutmeg. Refrigerate until fully thickened, about 2 hours. Taste and adjust the lemon juice before serving cold.

Note: *This sauce benefits from being made at least 6–8 hours ahead of serving it. The longer it sits, the thicker it will be, up to a point. If you cannot make it ahead and it isn't thick enough when you are ready to serve it, whisk it lightly until it forms very soft peaks.*

Bourbon Custard Sauce, or Southern Boiled Custard
MAKES 2 CUPS

Called, more elegantly, *crème anglaise* ("English cream") by the French, this classic sauce has long been a standard in the South, both as a dessert sauce and as a dessert on its own. It's also, believe it or not, served as a holiday beverage on Christmas morning. The Southern moniker is dangerously misleading, since custard cannot be allowed to boil, or it'll curdle and end up a horrific mess like watered-down, sweetened scrambled eggs.

You needn't confine the flavoring to bourbon (unless you are using it in one of the recipes in this book). Boiled custard can be flavored with almost any kind of spice or liqueur that you like.

2 cups whole milk or 1½–1¾ cups milk
    and ½ or ¼ cup heavy cream

⅔ cup sugar

6 large egg yolks, lightly beaten

2 tablespoons bourbon

1. Choose a heavy-bottomed saucepan or prepare the bottom of a double boiler with water and bring it to a simmer over medium heat. Either in the heavy pan or top half of the double boiler bring the milk to a simmer over direct medium heat, stirring frequently. Add the sugar and stir until it dissolves.

2. If using a double boiler, put the pan over the simmering water in the bottom half. If using a heavy pan, lower the heat to medium low. Take up about ½ cup of the hot milk and slowly beat it into the egg yolks. Slowly add the eggs to the remaining hot liquid and cook, stirring constantly, until it coats the back of a metal spoon. It will be only lightly thickened; so don't overcook it. It will continue to thicken as it cools.

3. Remove the pan from the heat and stir until slightly cooled. Stir in the bourbon and keep stirring for another minute. Pour it into a glass or ceramic bowl and cool completely before serving. If you are making the sauce ahead, cover and refrigerate after it cools. Serve cold or at room temperature.

Mint Butter   MAKES ABOUT 1 CUP

When I came home after a semester of studying architecture in Genoa, Italy, pesto, that classic, fragrant Genoese sauce of basil, garlic, pine nuts, olive oil, and cheese, was almost unknown in our country. Since then, I've watched it become more popular than is good for it, and have seen it used in ways that would make a Genoese cook's hair stand on end.

Dearly as I love it, pesto is to Southern cooking what grits is to Chinese cooking, a foreign entity that does not belong. I have yet to see it used in a way that seemed logically Southern and can't help but wish that people would save it for pasta and Italian vegetables, and stop mucking up grits with it.

Having said all that, here's a similar idea that is right at home on a Southern table. It's based on a traditional English mint sauce, a blend of mint, vinegar, sugar, and sometimes melted butter, that has long been a favorite sauce for lamb, mutton, and game in the South. This one is a thicker, pesto-like version of that classic combination. It's our house sauce for Easter lamb but is also slap wonderful melting over a grilled lamb, mutton, venison, or pork chop. Here, it makes fresh steamed vegetables such as whole green beans, spring peas, baby summer squash, and tiny new potatoes positively sing.

6 ounces (1½ sticks) unsalted butter

1 cup (lightly packed) fresh mint leaves,
    preferably spearmint

1 large clove garlic or 2 small ones, crushed,
    peeled and chopped

Juice of 2 lemons (about ¼ cup)

Sugar

Salt

1. Melt the butter over low heat. When just melted, turn off the heat and set it aside to cool.

2. Put the mint, garlic, lemon juice, a large pinch of sugar and a small one of salt in the bowl of a food processor or blender fitted with a steel blade. Pulse until the leaves and garlic are finely chopped. Then, with the motor running, slowly pour in the butter in a thin stream, as if you were making mayonnaise. When all the butter is added and the sauce is smooth, turn off the machine, taste, and adjust the amount of sugar and salt to suit your taste. The sauce should not be sweet but should have just enough sugar to enhance the natural sweetness of the mint. Pulse to incorporate the seasonings and let it stand for at least 10 minutes. The butter will begin to solidify.

3. Just before serving, turn on the machine again and whip until fluffy and smooth.

Note: *Mint butter can be made ahead, but it is at its best when fresh. The sauce will keep for up to a week in the refrigerator. Let it stand at room temperature until softened, then before serving it whip it until fluffy with a whisk or fork.*

Spring

SPROUTS, NEW LEAVES, AND FRESH STRAWBERRIES

In spite of a milder climate—and contrary to what a lot of people think—even the deepest part of the Deep South has four distinct seasons. Yet spring is the one that is probably the best known and certainly the most beloved. A Southern spring is an explosion of color, beginning with the purple-pink redbud and wild plum blossoms as early as the beginning of February and lasting until the late azaleas drop their blooms and the magnolias begin to open up in May. Visitors flock to our region, drawn by the spectacular floral displays of countless azalea, dogwood, cherry blossom, and magnolia festivals.

As spectacular as these ornamental plants are, they aren't the only ones getting the Southern gardener's attention at this time of year. Summer gardens have to be planned, tilled, and seeded. And even before that summer garden goes into the ground, as much as two months earlier than other parts of the country, there are already fresh new vegetables to eat. Asparagus and poke shoots poke their way up through winter mulch and the ruin of last year's plants. Vidalia Sweet Onions, just beginning to form their bulbs, are pulled while still slender and bright green. Close behind are fragrant strawberries, a profusion of tender young lettuces, and fresh green peas.

Mint, lush and sweet, sprouts around countless porches, just in time to give its bright accent to peas, to the Easter lamb or ham, or to the year's first cooling juleps. Just as the earth renews itself, the sober colors and subtle smells of winter produce give way to fresh new greens and bright, herbal perfumes, making the Southern table as bright and fragrant as the air outside. Often the table is actually moved outside. While parts of the country are still digging their way out of snowdrifts, we're already eating alfresco—and thanking God that we are lucky enough to live where we can do it.

ASPARAGUS

Asparagus, at least the species known to us in America (*Asparagus officinalis*), is thought to be native to the Mediterranean region and has been enjoyed since antiquity. Imported into America by the early settlers, it was well established in the South by the time it began to appear in botanical records and cookbooks early in the eighteenth century. There are even places where it has so firmly established itself that it has gone wild.

People who have never had fresh-cut asparagus seem to think it is a great technological leap to have this quintessential whiff of spring shipped in from all parts of the globe and available in our markets year round, but I don't. And if you are ever lucky enough to find out how the freshly cut vegetable can taste, you won't either. The asparagus that appears in vegetable stalls during midwinter comes from somewhere considerably south of us. Even with modern shipping, that means it has been on the road and under refrigeration for days—if not weeks, to the irreparable damage of its flavor. It'll never be more than a ghost of what it once was. So I'd much rather wait for spring, watching for the price drop that signals locally grown asparagus—or, better still, schedule a visit home and gather it from Mama's asparagus bed only moments before it goes into the pot. However, most of us don't have that kind of luxury, and, with care, market asparagus can still be quite good. Here are a few tips on selecting and preparing it.

Look for tight, plump buds at the tips, clear, unblemished stalks, and a distinct fragrance of asparagus when you sniff it. The cut ends will be scarred over, but they should still look moist and full. As soon as you get it home, trim off half an inch of the base and stand the spears in a vase or basin of water for a couple of hours. If you can't cook the asparagus the same day, refrigerate it standing in water or with the stems well wrapped in moist paper towels. Take it out of the refrigerator several hours before cooking, change the water, and let the asparagus stand at room temperature.

Every time I read an article advising people just to break off the tough parts of the asparagus, I come pretty close to violence. What a shame to waste as much as a third of this vegetable, when even the toughest stem can be made edible by peeling it. It only takes a few extra minutes and is worth the extra trouble.

Have ready a basin of cold water. If you haven't already done so, trim the cut ends. Now, this isn't a complicated maneuver: arm yourself with a good, sharp vegetable peeler. Lay a stalk of asparagus on your work surface with the tip facing you. Put the peeler blade against the stalk just above the tough part, and using a light, quick stroke away from you, peel the base until the pale green center of the stalk is exposed, gradually rotating the stalk until all sides are evenly peeled. Drop it into the basin of water and repeat until all the asparagus is trimmed. Let the asparagus remain in the water until you are ready to cook it. It's preferable to wait until just before cooking the asparagus to peel it, but when this isn't feasible, you can prepare it up to 2 hours ahead. However, don't peel the asparagus a day ahead and then refrigerate it.

Boiled Asparagus   SERVES 4

In all the old recipes, the asparagus was trimmed and peeled as directed above, then tied into bundles and dropped into a large kettle of rapidly boiling salted water. The bundles made it easier to remove the asparagus from the pot. Unfortunately, they also made it cook unevenly. Here is the way I cook asparagus; it takes less time and doesn't require a special pot.

1½ pounds asparagus, refreshed, trimmed,
   and peeled as directed above
Salt

1. Choose a large, lidded skillet or sauté pan that will hold the asparagus in no more than two layers. Add enough water to come up the sides by an inch, cover, and bring it to a boil over high heat.

2. Uncover the pan and toss in a small handful of salt. Let the water come back to a rapid boil and add the asparagus, placing the stem ends first into the side of the pot nearest you. Let the asparagus drop away from you so that if the hot water should splatter, it won't do it in your direction. Cover and let the water come back to a boil. Uncover and cook until the asparagus is tender but still firm and bright green—as little as 2 minutes for some asparagus, but no more than 5 minutes.

3. Put on the lid slightly askew (to hold the asparagus in the pan) and carefully drain off all the water. Turn the asparagus out onto a serving platter and serve in any of the following ways.

Asparagus with Drawn Butter or Lemon Butter (page 42): Have all the ingredients for the butter sauce ready before cooking the asparagus. As soon as you turn it out onto the platter, make the sauce. Pour a little of it over the asparagus and serve the remaining sauce separately.

Asparagus with Hollandaise Sauce (page 43): Make the sauce just before cooking the asparagus and have it ready in a heated sauceboat. Pass the sauce separately.

Asparagus with Pecan Brown Butter (page 41): This is an unusual but very happy combination. Have all the ingredients for the butter sauce ready, but don't make the sauce until after you have cooked the asparagus. Pour all the sauce over the asparagus, distributing the pecans evenly over the vegetables, and serve at once.

Asparagus with Mayonnaise (page 44): The asparagus can be either hot or cold, but in either case make the mayonnaise first. Pass the sauce in a separate bowl.

Asparagus Vinaigrette: Traditionally, this salad was once served hot, but today we prefer it at room temperature. Let the asparagus cool. Use the following dressing: Combine ¼ cup of freshly squeezed lemon juice or red wine vinegar with a teaspoon of prepared Dijon mustard and a healthy pinch of salt. Gradually beat in ½ cup extra-virgin olive oil until it is emulsified. Stir in a tablespoon of chopped parsley or thyme and a liberal grinding of black pepper, and pour the sauce over the asparagus. Serve as soon as possible or the dressing will make the asparagus lose its color.

Cream of Asparagus Soup   SERVES 6

When it comes to asparagus soup, there is none in the world to equal Lettice Bryan's (*The Kentucky Housewife*, 1839), a lovely and simple triad of asparagus, broth, and cream, which I included in *Classical Southern Cooking*—so long as the asparagus is very young and of impeccable freshness. When your asparagus is not quite so impeccable, adding a leek to the pot does wonders.

1 large or 2 small young spring leeks

2 tablespoons unsalted butter

1 quart Meat Broth (page 20), made with veal bones, or Chicken Broth (page 21)

2 pounds asparagus, washed, trimmed, and peeled as directed on page 52

Salt and whole white pepper in a mill

1 cup heavy cream (minimum 36 percent milk fat), at room temperature

1 cup Buttered Croutons (page 37)

Reserved chopped raw asparagus tips

1 tablespoon chopped fresh chives

1. Trim off the root end, the tough, outer leaves, and any yellowed or withered leaf tips of the leek and split it lengthwise. Wash it carefully under cold, running water, gently folding back the layers to make sure that there is no lingering soil between them. Drain well and slice crosswise as thinly as possible.

2. Put the leek and butter in a 3- to 4-quart heavy-bottomed pot over medium-low heat. Cook, stirring frequently, until the leek is wilted but not colored, about 5 minutes. Add the broth, raise the heat to medium high, and bring to a boil.

3. Meanwhile, cut off the pointed tips of the asparagus, setting aside a dozen or so, and cut the stems crosswise into 1-inch long pieces. Drop the asparagus (except for the reserved tips) into the boiling broth. Cover and let the soup return to a boil. Reduce the heat to a simmer and cook until the asparagus is tender—about 5, and no more than 10, minutes. Season it to taste with the salt and pepper. While the soup simmers, coarsely chop the reserved tips and set them aside.

4. With a slotted spoon, take out and reserve about a cup and a half of the asparagus and leeks. Puree the remainder in batches in a blender or food processor, or by forcing them through a sieve or a food mill.

5. Return the soup to the pot and heat it through over medium heat. Stir in the reserved asparagus and leek and the cream. Simmer just long enough to heat it through, stir well, and turn off the heat.

6. Ladle it into individual heated soup plates and garnish the top with the buttered croutons and a sprinkling of the reserved chopped raw asparagus tips and chives.

Note: *There are no substitutes here for the butter and cream. However, a meatless version of the soup can be made using water instead of meat broth. Don't use vegetable broth; its flavor is too strong for this particular soup.*

This soup is very good served cold. Substitute half-and-half for the cream in the

recipe and omit the croutons. Let it cool to room temperature—uncovered—then cover and refrigerate until chilled. Let the soup sit for about 10-30 minutes at room temperature before serving it to knock off some of the tombstone chill of the refrigerator. Just before serving, whip 1 cup heavy cream until it holds soft peaks. Garnish each serving with a dollop of whipped cream and a sprinkling of reserved chopped tips and chives.

Asparagus with Leeks and New Potatoes SERVES 4

Here, leeks and asparagus are happily paired once again. When the asparagus is very young and fresh, the only respectable way to cook it is quickly and simply (as in Boiled Asparagus, page 53), so that its fresh flavor and texture is allowed to shine. When it isn't so fresh, pairing it with fresh leek greens and new potatoes and sautéing them both in butter is a lovely thing to do. The bright herbal flavor of the leeks revives the lagging flavor of older asparagus, and the pleasant hint of caramel adds another subtle dimension.

1½ pounds fresh asparagus, washed, peeled, and trimmed as directed on page 52

Green tops of 2 large leeks, washed and trimmed

½ pound small red new potatoes, cooked as directed on page 83 (step 1), but not peeled

4 tablespoons unsalted butter

Salt and whole black pepper in a mill

1. Cut the asparagus crosswise into 1-inch lengths, keeping the tips separate from the stems. Slice the leek greens crosswise about ¼-inch thick. Slice the potatoes into ¼-inch-thick rounds.

2. Melt the butter in a large skillet or sauté pan over medium-high heat. Add the potatoes and asparagus stems. Sauté, tossing frequently, until the potatoes are beginning to turn golden, about 3 minutes.

3. Add the leek greens and asparagus tips, a healthy pinch of salt, and a liberal grinding of pepper. Sauté, shaking the pan and tossing frequently, until the asparagus is tender and beginning to brown. It should still be firm and bright green. Turn off the heat. Taste and correct the seasonings, and serve at once.

Note: *There is no substitute for butter here. No other fat will caramelize the asparagus or give the dish that rich, buttery-brown flavor. Though the flavor would in no way be the same, the only substitutes that I could suggest might be extra-virgin olive or unfiltered peanut oil.*

Asparagus and New Potato Salad with Green Bell Pepper Vinaigrette

Here's another take on the asparagus and new potato from Savannah's award-winning chef, Elizabeth Terry. Since her restaurant, Elizabeth's on 37th, opened in 1981—in those days, as a modest dessert cafe—its transformation and rise to regional and then international fame has made Elizabeth one of the South's most celebrated chefs.

Elizabeth shares my passion for traditional Southern foodways, but we take slightly different approaches to preserving them. This and the foregoing recipe demonstrate our similarities and differences. Both of us begin with an idea that is firmly rooted in Southern tradition. But while I stay pretty close to traditional flavor combinations, she likes to mix them up in unexpected ways.

FOR THE DRESSING:

1 green bell pepper, cored, seeded, and cut into ½-inch dice

1 fresh poblano pepper, cored, seeded, and cut into ½-inch dice

¼ cup onion, cut into ½-inch dice

2 teaspoons cider vinegar

½ teaspoon salt

½ teaspoon freshly cracked black pepper

¼ cup extra-virgin olive oil

FOR THE SALAD:

6 medium (about 1½ pounds) new potatoes, scrubbed and cut into 1-inch dice

1 pound fresh asparagus, sliced crosswise into 1-inch lengths (tough stems peeled as directed on page 52)

1 bunch (about 6 small) scallions or other green onions, thinly sliced

½ cup minced parsley (preferably Italian)

1. To make the dressing: Combine the two peppers and onion with ¼ cup water in a saucepan. Bring it to a boil over high heat, cover, and lower the heat to medium low. Simmer until the peppers are quite soft, about 15 minutes. Transfer this to a blender or food processor, and puree until smooth. Add the vinegar, salt, and pepper, and turn on the motor. With the machine running, slowly drizzle in the olive oil until it is incorporated and emulsified. Set the dressing aside.

2. Bring enough water to cover the potatoes to a boil in a heavy-bottomed saucepan over high heat. Add the potatoes, bring it back to a boil, and reduce the heat to medium. Simmer until the potatoes are just tender, about 8–10 minutes. Drain and spread the potatoes on a platter to cool.

3. Prepare a large bowl of ice water. Wipe out the pan in which the potatoes cooked and add enough water to cover the asparagus. Bring it to a boil over high heat, drop in the asparagus, and blanch it for 30 seconds, or until it is bright green. Immediately drain and plunge it into the ice water to arrest the cooking. Drain and spread the asparagus on a platter to cool.

4. Just before serving, combine the potatoes, asparagus, green onions, and parsley in a bowl or platter. Pour the dressing over the salad and toss until it is uniformly mixed. Taste and

correct the seasoning, toss until blended, and serve.

Note: *The entire salad can be made ahead up through step 4, but don't add the dressing until you are ready to serve it. The dressing is improved by allowing it to sit for an hour after being made, but that's as far ahead as you can make it. Never refrigerate it. My own preference is for a milder dressing heat-wise, and I up the sweet bell pepper to about 1½ and cut the poblano by about half.*

ARTICHOKES

The artichoke (*Cynara scolymus*) may not seem like an especially Southern vegetable, but if old cookbooks are any indication, it has been enjoyed by Southerners for a lot longer than is widely supposed. Artichokes originally came from the Mediterranean. Their migration into our continent was gradual and convoluted. First they were introduced to England, where they were grown as early as the sixteenth century and, by the early colonial period, were popular enough in England to presume that the early settlers would have brought them along to America. At any rate, artichokes were growing in Virginia by the beginning of the eighteenth century. All the early Southern-cookery writers gave recipes for them and talked about them in an offhand way that suggests that they were more common than most people assume.

In spite of this history, today we treat artichokes as if they are relative newcomers to our tables. This is a sad indicator of how changed and misunderstood Southern vegetable cookery has become. Fortunately, artichokes have been rediscovered and are becoming commonplace in our markets and on our tables. I love once again seeing them in Savannah's gardens and finding them in our farmers' market. Southern chefs are doing some very interesting things with them, but the recipes that I offer here aren't new.

Basic Artichoke Preparation

The simplest and most effortless way (for the cook, at least) to serve artichokes is simply to wash them, trim off the dark discoloration, and boil them in well-salted water until tender. The artichoke is presented to each diner whole with a bowl of melted butter, Hollandaise Sauce (page 43), mayonnaise, or vinaigrette for dipping the leaves. The diner does all the work—and doesn't mind. For the recipes that follow, however, the artichoke must be trimmed before it goes into the pot. The cook is faced with a little extra work, but the diner is free to enjoy the dinner with no more effort than it takes to lift the fork.

Here is the Italian way of trimming artichokes, which I was lucky enough to learn firsthand from Marcella Hazan. It sounds like a lot of work, but after you've done it once or twice, the job goes quickly. When Marcella showed me, the whole operation took less than 5 minutes—even with the dull knives that she encountered in my kitchen.

For the job, you'll need a whole lemon, a sharp chef's knife, a small paring knife, and a scooping tool, such as a melon baller or a sharp-edged teaspoon.

Cut the lemon in half and have it close at hand on your work surface. Cover the work surface with newspaper. Don't cut off the stem of the artichoke; once peeled, it contains some of the sweetest and most delicate flesh. Pull off the small, tough leaves at the base of the artichoke (those close to the stem). Then begin snapping off the large outer leaves by bending them back until they snap. As you go, rub the cut surfaces well with the lemon to prevent them from turning brown. After a couple of rows of leaves, you'll find that they snap further and further away from the base. When this begins, put your thumb against the base of the leaf and pull down the top with your other hand so that the tough outer part strips away from the tender inner flesh. When you begin to see pale green about two-thirds of the way up the inner leaves, cut off the inner cone of leaves with a sharp knife. Rub the cut surface well with the lemon. Now pull back the leaves from the center and scoop out the fuzzy choke with the melon baller or spoon. Squeeze lemon juice into the cavity and rub it in with your fingers.

Finally, take a sharp paring knife and trim off any tough outer leaf parts that may be remaining on the base. Don't worry that you are wasting any of it; you'll be losing very little of the edible part of the vegetable. Rub all the cut surfaces well with the lemon. Then peel the stem, removing all the tough stringy skin, and again rub it well with the lemon. Set the artichoke aside and repeat the process with the remaining artichokes.

If you are preparing a lot of artichokes, or are cutting them into quarters, fill a basin with enough cold water to cover them, squeeze half the lemon into it, and drop in the spent rind. As you finish trimming an artichoke, drop it into the acidulated water to keep it from discoloring until you are finished with the others.

The artichokes are now ready to use in any of the following recipes.

Whole-Cooked Artichokes SERVES 4

This is the simplest way of preparing artichokes, and is the way to cook them when they will be used for Creole Artichoke and Oyster Soup (page 61) or when the bottoms will be scraped clean and stuffed or used as an edible base in dishes such as New Orleans' celebrated Eggs Sardou.

4 medium fresh artichokes
Salt
Hollandaise (page 43), Homemade Mayonnaise (page 44), or Lemon Butter (page 42), or about ½ cup melted butter, for serving (optional)

1. Bring enough water to completely cover the artichokes by 1 inch to a rolling boil in a large 8- to 12-quart pot. Meanwhile, thoroughly rinse the artichokes under cold running water, drain, and trim away the darkened cut end of the stems. Pull away the small, tough petals as a base.

2. When the water is boiling, stir in a small handful of salt and carefully add the artichokes. Cover and let it come back to a boil, then uncover, adjust the heat to a slow boil, and cook until an outer petal pulls away from the base of the artichoke when tugged. Drain and let cool briefly, then trim away the stem so that they will stand up on the plate, but don't discard the stems—the inner flesh is edible and delicious.

3. Serve with your favorite dipping sauce or simply with melted butter.

Artichokes in Cream SERVES 4

Artichokes take to cream like a duck to water, and I can think of no more luxurious or appropriate treatment for them than this recipe, which is adapted from Sarah Rutledge's classic, *The Carolina Housewife* (1847). It is just fine on its own but also is the foundation of a sauce for a wonderfully elegant veal main course given at the end of this recipe.

1 lemon
4 medium artichokes
2 tablespoons unsalted butter
Salt
1 cup heavy cream (minimum 36 percent milk fat)
1 tablespoon chopped parsley

1. Put enough water into a large stainless steel or glass bowl to cover the artichokes. Cut the lemon in half and squeeze the juice from one of the halves into the water. Drop in the spent rind. Trim the artichokes and remove the chokes as directed above. Cut them into quarters, rubbing well with the other half of the lemon and drop them into the acidulated water.

2. When all the artichokes are trimmed and quartered, drain and put them with the butter in a heavy-bottomed, lidded sauté pan or skillet that will hold them in one layer. Turn on the heat to medium high and sauté, tossing frequently, until the artichokes are hot and bright green but not browned, about 5 minutes.

3. Add a healthy pinch of salt and pour the cream over them. Bring it to a boil, then reduce the heat to low, cover the pan, and simmer, stirring occasionally, until the artichokes are tender, about half an hour.

4. Remove the lid and, if the cream is not thickened, raise the heat to medium high and let it boil until it is thickened, stirring frequently to prevent scorching. Turn off the heat. Pour the

artichokes into a warm serving bowl, sprinkle the parsley over them, and serve at once.

Note: *Obviously, there is no substitute for cream in this recipe. The entire dish can be made ahead up through step 3. Turn off the heat, set the lid askew, and let it cool. If you are making it more than an hour ahead, refrigerate it until you are ready to finish the dish. Reheat it gently over medium-low heat. Usually, the cream thickens up on its own when it sits, but if it is too thin when you reheat the artichokes, quickly boil it down as directed in step 4.*

VEAL SCALLOPS WITH ARTICHOKES AND OYSTERS, CREOLE STYLE:

To serve 6, you'll need a pound of veal scallops, 2 additional tablespoons of butter, 1 cup of shucked, drained oysters, and 2 scallions, trimmed and thinly sliced. Make the artichokes through step 4. Sauté the veal scallops in a separate pan with the additional butter over medium-high heat—about a minute per side. Transfer them to a warm platter. Add the oysters to the artichokes, and simmer over low heat until the oysters plump, about 2 minutes. Pour the artichokes and oysters over the veal and sprinkle the scallions over them.

Braised Artichokes with Onions

SERVES 4

As you can tell from this collection, I love to braise all kinds of vegetables, but it's an especially happy way of cooking artichokes. It concentrates their subtle flavor and makes them meltingly tender without making them mushy and dull. Here, they are combined with little onions, which add a touch of sweetness and yet another dimension to their flavor.

1 lemon

4 medium artichokes

8 very small boiling onions (about ½ pound)

3 tablespoons unsalted butter

Salt and whole black pepper in a mill

1 tablespoon chopped parsley

1 cup Chicken Broth (page 21) or water

1. Half-fill a heavy-bottomed 3- to 4-quart pot with water, cover, and bring to a boil over medium-high heat. Put enough water into a large glass or ceramic bowl to cover the artichokes. Cut the lemon in half and squeeze the juice from one of the halves into the water. Drop in the spent rind. Trim the artichokes and remove the chokes as directed on page 57 and cut them into quarters, rubbing them well with the other half of the lemon as you go. Drop them into the acidulated water.

2. When the pot of water is boiling, slip the onions into it, cover, and let it return to a boil. Boil for 1 minute, then drain quickly and rinse them in cold water. Trim off the root and stem ends, peel them, and cut a deep "X" into the root end.

3. Put 2 tablespoons of the butter into a large, heavy-bottomed, lidded skillet or sauté pan that

will hold all the ingredients in one layer and put it over medium-high heat. Thoroughly drain the artichokes and add them to the pan. Sauté, tossing often, until they are bright green, about 3 minutes. Add the onions and continue sautéing until the onions are beginning to color, about 3 minutes more.

4. Add a healthy pinch of salt, a liberal grinding of black pepper, the parsley, and the broth or water. Bring to a boil, reduce the heat to low, cover, and braise until the vegetables are tender, about half an hour. If the liquid gets reduced too much, add a few spoonfuls of water, but just enough to prevent scorching.

5. Uncover the pan. Raise the heat to medium high and boil away any remaining liquid. Add the remaining butter, shake the pan until it is melted, and serve at once.

Note: *A fine addition to this dish is a tablespoon of capers. Another one is 2 ounces of country ham, cut into julienne. Either should be added to the pan with the artichokes at the beginning of step 3.*

A completely vegetarian version of this dish can be made by substituting olive oil for the butter, but the flavor will be more Mediterranean than Southern.

Creole Artichoke Salad   SERVES 4

When I was growing up, we didn't grow artichokes in our garden, and they were nowhere to be found in the markets of the sleepy, rural towns where we lived, so I never had a fresh artichoke until I went away to college. The first of any sort that I ever tasted came out of a jar—marinated artichoke hearts, which my grandmother bought by the case when she visited my Aunt Alice in Florida. We used them to dress our salads and thought they were just wonderful, mainly I suppose because they seemed exotic.

In this salad, boiled fresh artichokes are marinated in a piquant lemon and olive oil

dressing, enlivened with a little garlic and green onion. It makes a fine salad on its own, but you can do what my grandmother did and use it to dress a larger mixed vegetable salad.

1 lemon
4 medium artichokes
Salt
1 clove garlic, crushed, peeled, and minced
Whole black pepper in a mill
¼ cup extra-virgin olive oil
1 tablespoon chopped parsley
2 scallions, trimmed and sliced thin (both white and green parts)
4 romaine or Boston lettuce leaves, washed and drained
1 large hard-cooked egg

1. Put enough water in a large heavy-bottomed pot to cover the artichokes completely, cover, and bring it to a boil over medium-high heat. Meanwhile, cut the lemon in half. Trim the artichokes and remove the chokes as directed on page 57, rubbing the cut edges well with half of the lemon as you go.

2. When the water is boiling, add a handful of salt and the artichokes. Cover until it is boiling again, then uncover and cook until the artichokes are just tender, about 25–30 minutes. Drain them thoroughly and let them cool slightly while you make the dressing.

3. Squeeze the juice from the lemon through a strainer into a mixing bowl. Add a small pinch of salt, the garlic, and a liberal grinding of pepper. Whisk until the salt is dissolved. Slowly whisk in the olive oil, a few drops at a time, until it is emulsified.

4. While the artichokes are still warm, cut them into wedges. If there is still any choke in the center or if some of the outer leaves seem tough, remove them. Put the artichokes in a stainless-steel or glass bowl, add the parsley and scallions, and pour the dressing over them. Toss until they are well coated, taste, and adjust the seasonings, then set the bowl aside and let the artichokes cool completely.

5. When you are ready to serve the salad, arrange the lettuce leaves on a serving platter or individual salad plates. Peel the egg and force the white and yolk separately through a coarse sieve. Spoon the artichokes over the lettuce leaves and sprinkle them with the egg white and yolk. Serve at room temperature.

Note: *If you are cooking for a vegan, omit the egg garnish. If you are one of those people who think that Creole food has to have cayenne pepper, and a lot of it, you can substitute it for the black pepper, but for heaven's sake don't overdo it. Artichokes have a delicate flavor that doesn't need a lot of heat.*

Creole Artichoke and Oyster Soup

SERVES 6

Here, the Creole pairing of artichokes and oysters really comes into its own in a classic soup that can still be found on the menu not only of such venerable New Orleans public dining rooms as Galatoire's and Antoine's, but in the city's best private dining rooms as well. It's a bit fussy to make, but well worth it for really special occasions.

6 medium fresh artichokes

2 pints oysters, preferably Apalachicola or Gulf oysters

½ cup finely chopped shallots

3 tablespoons unsalted butter

3 tablespoons all-purpose flour

4 cups whole milk

1 Bouquet Garni, made with 2 bay leaves, 2 large sprigs thyme, and 1 large sprig parsley

½ cup heavy cream

Salt and whole white pepper in a mill

Ground cayenne

6 thin slices lemon

3 tablespoons finely minced flat-leaf parsley

1. Trim and cook the artichokes as for Whole-Cooked Artichokes (page 58). Drain, cool, and break them down as follows: Remove the stems, split them in half lengthwise, and scrape out the tender inner pulp with the edge of a spoon; discard the tough outer fibers. Pull off the petals one at a time, scraping out the tender pulp from them and adding it to the stem pulp. When all the petals have been removed and scraped, scoop the choke from the artichoke bottoms and then cut the bottoms into ½-inch dice.

2. Set a large wire-mesh sieve over a glass or stainless-steel bowl and pour the oysters into it. Let them drain, stirring occasionally to help the liquor drain into the bowl. Pour the oysters into a separate bowl, cover, and refrigerate them until needed. Measure the liquor and add enough water to make 2 cups.

3. Sweat the shallots in the butter in a heavy-bottomed 3- to 4-quart pot over medium-low heat, stirring occasionally, until they are translucent and soft, but not in the least colored, about 8 minutes. Stir in the flour, raise the heat to medium, and cook until bubbly and smooth, about 1 minute. Slowly whisk in the oyster liquor and milk and add the bouquet garni. Bring it to a simmer, stirring constantly, and reduce the heat to medium low. Simmer 15–20 minutes, stirring occasionally.

4. Add the artichoke pulp and diced artichoke bottom and let it come back to a simmer. Season well with salt, white pepper, and cayenne to taste and simmer until the artichoke is heated through, about 5 minutes. The soup can be made ahead to this point. Turn off the heat and let it cool, then loosely cover. Remove and discard the bouquet garni.

5. When you are ready to serve it, bring the soup back to a simmer over medium-low heat. Add the oysters and simmer until they are plumped and their gills curl. Taste and adjust the seasonings, and immediately ladle the soup into soup plates or cream soup bowls. Garnish with lemon and parsley and serve immediately.

SPRING CARROTS

Like most other root vegetables (and come to think of it, like a lot of people), slender new spring carrots have a sweetness and delicacy that they lose as they mature and fatten. As they grow, their skins toughen and become bitter and must be peeled away, but spring carrots can be left whole, and the skins add a subtle flavor to them that it would be a shame to lose. The other part of carrots that we underappreciate is the green top, which (particularly in spring) have a bright flavor that is similar to the skins. Because they shorten the shelf-life of the carrots, the fronds are usually trimmed away before they go to market. But that is also the reason that you want the fronds to still be attached when you buy them: If they are still bright and freshly green, then the carrot from which they sprout will be fresh, too. But they're not just a freshness indicator: When young and tender the fronds are useful as a flavoring herb.

Spring Carrot and Leek Soup

SERVES 6 TO 8

This soup can be made at any time of the year, and is still good with fat, mature carrots and leeks, but in the spring, when all the ingredients are new and exceptionally sweet, is when it will be at its best. When that's the case, use water for the liquid. Once the carrots and leeks are older and their flavor is stronger, you may use chicken broth for the soup, but when they're really the season's first harvest, chicken and vegetable broth would overpower and blunt their flavor. If the carrots are more mature but still fresh

enough to have nice greens, put a couple of fronds into the pot while the soup simmers, then remove and discard them before pureeing it.

2 pounds young spring carrots, with tops attached

½ cup thinly sliced or chopped shallots

3 tablespoons unsalted butter

4 cups thinly sliced young spring leeks (preferably new baby leeks, both white parts and tender greens)

3 quarter-size slices fresh ginger

4 cups Vegetable Broth (page 22) or water

Salt and whole white pepper in a mill

6–8 tablespoons heavy cream

1 tablespoon thinly sliced chives, garlic chives, or green onion top

1. Scrub the carrots under cold running water and trim their tops, reserving a handful of the liveliest green fronds. If they're very young and sweet, don't peel them. Slice a little less than ⅛-inch thick. Put the shallots and butter in a 3-quart pot over medium-low heat, and sweat them, stirring often, until wilted and translucent but not colored, about 6–8 minutes. Add the leeks and ginger, stir well, and cook until the leeks are wilted but not colored, about 5 minutes.

2. Add the carrots, raise the heat to medium high, and toss until heated through, then pour in the broth. Bring to a boil and adjust the heat to a gentle simmer. Cook only until vegetables are tender, about 10–15 minutes. Take care not to overcook the carrots and leeks; they should be tender enough to puree, but their flavor should still be bright and fresh. Let it cool slightly, remove and discard the ginger, and puree in a blender or food processor fitted with steel blade or with a hand blender. (The smoothest puree will be with the regular blender, the coarsest with stick blender.)

3. Taste and season well with salt and white pepper. The soup can be made ahead to this point. Let it cool completely, cover, and refrigerate for up to 2 days. To serve it warm, gently bring it back to a simmer over medium-low heat, stirring often. To serve it cold, let it sit at room temperature for half an hour so that it loses the intense chill from the refrigerator. If necessary, thin it with a little water, then taste and correct the seasonings. Just before serving, chop enough of the reserved carrot fronds to make 1 tablespoon. Drizzle each serving with a tablespoon of cream and garnish with a sprinkling of carrot frond and chives.

Butter-Braised Spring Carrots

SERVES 6

One of the loveliest ways to cook any spring vegetable is to gently braise it in butter until it's a pale gold on the outside but just barely tender on the inside. When they're just pulled from the earth, they don't need anything more than a touch of salt to bring out their flavor, if that.

2 pounds spring carrots, preferably small "baby" carrots (3–4 dozen small or 6–8 long, slender ones), with green tops still attached

2 tablespoons unsalted butter

Salt

1. Scrub the carrots under cold running water and trim their tops, leaving a half inch or so of the green attached and reserving a handful of their liveliest green fronds. If they're really young and fresh, don't peel them, but if they're not as young as you'd like, lightly skin them with a vegetable

peeler. If using baby carrots (less than 4 inches long), leave them whole. If larger, cut them on the diagonal into 1½-inch lengths of as much same thickness as possible (leave slender parts whole, cut thicker pieces into halves or quarters).

2. Melt the butter in a lidded 3-quart sauté pan over medium-high heat, add the carrots, and sauté, tossing frequently, until they're beginning to color pale gold, about 4 minutes.

3. Add a large pinch of salt and a splash of water. Cover, reduce the heat to low, and braise until tender, about 10 to 15 minutes. If the pan gets too dry, add water by spoonfuls as necessary. Meanwhile, finely chop enough of the reserved green tops to make 2 tablespoons.

4. If, when the carrots are tender, there is liquid left in the pan, remove the lid, raise heat, and cook, gently tossing, until any excess liquid is evaporated. Taste and adjust the salt, sprinkle with the chopped carrot greens, give them one last toss, and serve warm.

Virginia's Honey Ginger Carrots

SERVES 4 TO 6

Though classically trained in France at no less than L'Academie de Cuisine and École de Cuisine La Varenne, Southern cooking teacher and author Virginia Willis's cooking has never strayed very far from her roots, but remains grounded by the solid foundation laid by her grandmother, Meme, and mother, Jenny. Her lovely first book, *Bon Appétit, Y'all*, celebrates the union between her classical training and the cooking that enriched her Deep South childhood. But it also reminds us that Southern and French cooking have always had lot more in common than La Cuisine Creole.

One overriding principle of both cuisines—despite the image that has been painted of haute cuisine by some of its more pretentious practitioners—is that nothing must be added that will cover up or take away from the flavor of the main ingredient. Its flavors are meant to ride on top of any additions, not underneath them. Nothing better illustrates that principle, and Virginia's genius at applying it, than the way she uses a handful of herbs, a whisper of honey, and a touch of ginger to bring out the best in a bundle of young spring carrots.

1 pound (about 3 bunches) small young spring
  carrots, well-scrubbed but not peeled

2 cups Chicken Broth (page 21) or reduced fat
  low-sodium chicken broth

1 Bouquet Garni (page 32), made up with
  2 sprigs parsley, 2 sprigs thyme and
  2 bay leaves (preferably fresh)

2 tablespoons unsalted butter

1 (2-inch) piece fresh ginger, peeled and
  cut into julienne

2 tablespoons mild honey

2 large sprigs fresh carrot fronds (washed and dried)
  or flat-leaf parsley, minced

Coarse salt and whole black pepper in a mill

1. Trim the tops and tips of the carrots, leaving half an inch of the sprouting top attached. Put the chicken broth and bouquet garni in a medium saucepan and bring them to a boil over high heat. Add the carrots, let it come back to a simmer, and reduce the heat to medium low. Simmer until the carrots are just tender, about 4 minutes. Remove and discard the bouquet garni and drain, reserving the broth if you like for another use such as the Spring Carrot Soup on page 62.

2. Melt the butter in a large sauté pan over medium-high heat, add the ginger, and sauté until tender, about 2 minutes. Add the carrots and honey and sauté, tossing often, until the carrots are glazed, about 5 minutes. Off the heat, sprinkle in the carrot fronds or parsley, season with salt and pepper to taste, and toss one last time. Serve warm.

FIDDLEHEADS, OR OSTRICH FERNS

The spring sprouts of our native ostrich fern (*Pteretis pensylvania*) can be found all over the eastern part of the country, from Maine to Georgia to the swamps of Louisiana. The common name, "fiddleheads," is peculiarly appropriate because that's precisely what the graceful, still-coiled fronds look like—the scroll head of a violin. They're not just pretty but also make very good eating. Popular with natural-food enthusiasts, they are usually gathered in the wild but in season can sometimes be found at farmers' markets or at natural-food and specialty groceries.

Fiddleheads can be eaten raw and make a fine addition to the salad bowl. When steamed, they may be served hot in any way that asparagus is, except for the cream soup (page 54), or cooled and tossed in a salad with spring lettuce and chopped spring onions. Dress the salad with salt, olive oil, and lemon juice to taste.

Camille Glenn's Fiddleheads
SERVES 4

Camille Glenn can arguably be called the "Grande Dame" of Southern cooking. A remarkable and irresistible lady, an incomparable cook, a generous and compulsive teacher—she personifies everything that is good about being both Southern and a cook. For decades, her graceful writing and lovely cooking enlivened the food pages of the *Louisville Courier*, and her grand opus, *The Heritage of Southern Cooking*, still sets a standard for youngsters like me to live up to.

No other recipe better encapsulates Mrs. Glenn's kitchen sensibility as does this one, in which local ingredients, selected at the peak of freshness, are handled with elegance, finesse, and forthright simplicity.

½ pound fiddlehead fern shoots
3 tablespoons unsalted butter
Salt
1 lemon, cut in 4 wedges

1. Wash the fiddleheads in cold water and drain them well. Put the butter into a skillet that will comfortably hold the ferns in one layer and place it over medium-high heat.

2. When the butter is melted and bubbling, add the fiddleheads and sauté, tossing them constantly, until they are just crisp tender—about 1, and no more than 2, minutes. Do not overcook them or they will go limp and unravel. Season liberally with a healthy pinch of salt, toss to mix it in, and serve at once with wedges of lemon.

Note: *Mrs. Glenn suggested using a good-quality peanut oil as a substitute for the butter. In the mountains, the fat was often rendered bacon or salt pork drippings. It's delicious, but not for the weak-hearted.*

SPRING LEEKS

Leeks are available almost year round in the South and make a welcome addition to the winter table, but it's in spring and fall—when they're new and sweet—that they are really at their best. Baby spring leeks are so delicate and sweet that they could be used in a salad just as you would scallions or other green onions. This heady member of the onion family is underappreciated and is seldom found on Southern tables by itself. Yet it is frequently used to flavor soups, stews, and, occasionally, other vegetable dishes. In the recipes that follow, however, leeks are allowed to shine all by themselves. For other recipes where spring leeks are a primary component, see also Asparagus with Leeks and New Potatoes (page 55) and English Peas with Leeks (page 79).

Braised Leeks   SERVES 4

Braising is a lovely treatment for tender young leeks because it brings out and concentrates their natural sweetness. It is also an exceptional way to cook spring onions, especially the season's first green Vidalia Sweet Onions.

4 medium leeks
½ cup water
Salt
2 tablespoons unsalted butter

1. Trim the roots and tough upper outer leaves and upper parts of the inner leaves of the leeks and partially split the green part lengthwise,

leaving the white part intact. Wash the leeks carefully under cold running water to remove all the grit and dirt.

2. Put the leeks into a lidded skillet that will comfortably hold them in one layer. Add the water and a healthy pinch of salt. Place the pan over medium-high heat and bring the liquid to a boil. Reduce the heat to medium low and cover the pan. Simmer until the leeks are almost tender, about 8–10 minutes.

3. Remove the lid and raise the heat to high, letting the liquid boil rapidly away until it is reduced to about 2 tablespoons. Turn off the heat and add the butter, swirling the pan until the butter has melted and thickened the juices. Serve at once.

Leek Spoonbread   SERVES 6 TO 8

North Carolina has been at the center of a renaissance of traditional Southern cooking in restaurants. One of the leaders and finest practitioners of the movement is Ben Barker, who, with his gifted pastry-chef wife, Karen, owned and operated the ground-breaking Magnolia Grill in Durham. Ben's cooking, while solidly traditional, always seems fresh and new. Here, for example, he gives a fresh lift to spoonbread, a traditional cornmeal soufflé, by folding in a slightly unorthodox puree of leeks.

Ben says that the batter will stand up to just about any addition: "quince, apple, sweet potato, winter squash, or Vidalia onion puree, herbs, pork products, the kitchen sink." I'll take his word for the latter.

2–3 leeks, split, washed, and with most
   of the green tops removed
2½ cups whole milk
2 cups half-and-half
1 tablespoon salt
3 teaspoons sugar

1 cup cornmeal

½ cup all-purpose flour

4 ounces (8 tablespoons or 1 stick) unsalted butter

6 large eggs, separated

¼ cup heavy cream

1. Put the leeks in a heavy-bottomed, lidded skillet with enough water to half-cover them. Cover and bring to a boil over medium-high heat. When it just starts to boil, reduce the heat and cook, tightly covered, until the leeks are wilted, about 8–10 minutes. Drain and puree the leeks in a food mill, blender, or food processor. You should have ¾ cup of puree.

2. Combine the milk, half-and-half, salt, and sugar in a heavy-bottomed saucepan. Scald over medium heat. When small bubbles begin to appear around the edges, gradually whisk in the cornmeal and flour. Continue whisking the mixture until it thickens. When it is smooth and creamy, remove it from the heat and stir in the butter until it is completely absorbed.

3. Beat the egg yolks with the cream until light and smooth. Gradually add them to the cornmeal mixture. Fold in the leek puree until it is evenly distributed. Set aside. (You can make the batter ahead up to this point. Cover and refrigerate, but bring it back to room temperature before baking it.)

4. Position a rack in the center of the oven and preheat to 350°F. In a stainless-steel, glass, or copper bowl, beat the egg whites until they are stiff but not dry. Fold them into the cornmeal batter. Lightly butter a large (3- to 4-quart) casserole dish and pour in the spoonbread batter, lightly smoothing the top with a spatula. Place the casserole in the center of the oven and bake until the spoonbread is puffy, golden brown on top, and just set, about 45 minutes. Serve at once from the dish in which it has baked.

MIRLITONS

Known also as chayotes (especially in the Southwest) and vegetable pears, mirlitons are actually a variety of American squash. Prized by Creole cooks, they are used in Louisiana more frequently than in any other part of the South. Creoles cook mirlitons in the same way that they do other squash and eggplants: they fry, braise, and bake them, and favor them as a vegetable casing for seafood fillings.

Mirlitons thrive year round in Louisiana but prefer a shady spot in the wilting heat of July and August. They make a welcome vegetable in spring, when other squash are not yet in season.

Mirlitons Étouffées or Smothered Mirlitons, Creole Style   SERVES 4

One of the most famous of Creole dishes is crawfish étouffée, in which those quintessential crustaceans are cooked in a spicy, roux-based sauce. However, there are many other étoufféed Creole dishes, including this one.

Étouffée, in French, simply means smothered, and that is exactly what happens here. The mirlitons braise gently in a covered pan, bathed in a classic combination of Creole flavors.

2 large or 3 small mirlitons

2 tablespoons extra-virgin olive oil

1 medium yellow onion, split, peeled, and chopped

1 clove garlic, peeled and minced fine

1 tablespoon chopped parsley

1 tablespoon chopped fresh thyme or 1 teaspoon dried thyme

1 large bay leaf

½ cup dry white wine

4 medium tomatoes, blanched, peeled, and seeded as directed on page 101, and chopped, or 1 cup canned Italian tomatoes, seeded and chopped

Salt and ground cayenne pepper or hot sauce such as Tabasco

1. Wash, peel, and split the mirlitons in half and remove the seeds. Cut them into bite-size cubes and set aside.

2. Put the olive oil and onion in a large, lidded skillet or sauté pan over medium-high heat. Sauté, tossing frequently, until the onion is translucent, about 4 minutes. Add the mirlitons and garlic, and sauté until the garlic is fragrant, about a minute more.

3. Add the parsley, thyme, bay leaf, and wine and let it come to a boil. Add the tomatoes, a healthy pinch of salt, a small pinch or so of cayenne, or a few dashes of hot sauce to taste. Stir, lower the heat to a slow simmer, and cover the pan. Simmer until the mirlitons are tender, about half an hour.

SEAFOOD-STUFFED MIRLITONS:

These are made in exactly the same way as Seafood Stuffed Eggplant (page 146). Prepare 4 mirlitons as follows: Put enough water to completely cover the mirlitons in a large pot, bring it to a boil over high heat, and add the mirlitons. Cook until they are tender when pierced with a fork or knife, about 15–20 minutes. Drain and cool them, then carefully split them and remove their seeds. Proceed with step 1 of the recipe for Seafood Stuffed Eggplant.

Pickled Mirlitons

MAKES 4 QUARTS OR 8 PINTS

Spicy pickled squash are a popular condiment in the South, but while people who live outside Louisiana use yellow summer squash for pickling, Creole cooks prefer mirlitons.

Mike and Shelly Sackett were for many years the proprietors of Kitchen Affairs, a cookware store in Evansville, Indiana, where I was privileged to teach for many years. The best part of teaching for them was the cooking we did afterwards, in their very eclectic home kitchen, where we did everything from Jewish to Southern cooking to Italian, Chinese, and classic French haute cuisine. Mike has Louisiana roots, and this recipe came from those roots by way of his aunt, Dot Fischer.

8–10 mirlitons

1 quart cider vinegar

1 scant cup kosher or pickling salt

Pinch alum

1 green bell pepper, seeded and sliced into ¼-inch strips

2 carrots, peeled and sliced

8 cloves garlic, peeled

8 whole jalapeño peppers

2 cups cauliflower florets (about 1 large cauliflower)

4 teaspoons dill seed

1. Wash, peel, split, and seed the mirlitons. Cut them into thin strips as you would potatoes for french fries. Put them in a stainless-steel or glass bowl, cover with ice water, and refrigerate for 24 hours.

2. The next day, drain them well. Put the vinegar in a stainless-steel kettle with 2 cups of water, a cup of salt, and a pinch of alum. Bring it to a boil over high heat and boil for 3 minutes. Turn off the heat.

3. Divide the bell pepper, carrots, garlic, jalapeño peppers, cauliflower, and dill seeds among 4 sterilized quart jars or 8 pint jars. Add the mirlitons, leaving about ½ inch of headroom at the top of each jar. Pour the hot vinegar solution over them until they are covered, leaving ¼ inch of headroom.

4. Seal with new lids and process the jars for 10 minutes in a boiling water bath (see page 11). Remove the jars with tongs and set them on folded towels so that they do not touch. Let them cool completely. Reprocess or refrigerate any that do not seal. (Refer to pages 10–12 for detailed canning instructions.) Age the pickles for at least 2 weeks before opening.

SPRING MORELS

As the dark earth of the South's Appalachian Mountains warms and moistens with the melting snows and spring rains, the gnarled caps of morel mushrooms begin to poke through, mainly in apple orchards, under elm trees, and near patches of wild sunflowers. There are several native variations within the morel family, their

honeycomb-pitted, conical caps ranging in color from light gray to deep chocolate brown. Though now successfully farmed, until recently they were harvested only in the wild during the spring, their natural growing season, and it is still mostly in the spring that fresh ones are available. For more on morels, see the mushroom section of the fall chapter (pages 199–201). Morels can be used in any of the mushroom recipes in this book, including those for chanterelles (pages 201–3). Another lovely way to cook them is Camille Glenn's Fiddleheads and Morels (page 65).

Ronni's Morels and Spring Greens

SERVES 2 AS A VEGETARIAN MAIN DISH, 4 AS AN APPETIZER

Kentucky food writer Ronni Lundy grew up in the city, but her heart belongs to the mountains around Corbin, where she was born. Like so many mountain folk who were forced into town to find work, her family's table stayed close to the country, following the rhythm of the seasons with produce sent to them by relatives back home. To this day, it's the simple, seasonal flavors of her native mountains that speak to her best, so while morels may seem exotic to many of us, for Ronni they are the essence of home, and the way she prepares them is as straightforward as her plainspoken and yet lyrical writing.

Here, they are quickly cooked with wild greens and a bit of green garlic, the aromatic bulb's first young spring shoots. Its flavor is similar to ramps, a wild, broad-leaved green onion (sometimes called "wild leek") that's highly prized by mountain folk in the spring. Green garlic has become a popular commodity at farmers' markets in the spring and early summer, but if you can't get such wonders, substitute a mix of green onion and half a clove of the youngest, freshest garlic you can find.

1 dozen small fresh morels
2 cups (lightly packed) arugula

Grits Squares (page 39), Pan-Fried Grits Cakes (page 203), or Hoecakes (page 36), made where indicated in the recipe

1 tablespoon unsalted butter

2 tablespoons minced green garlic (see previous page), garlic chives, or green onion mixed with ½ minced clove garlic

Salt and whole black pepper in a mill

1. Brush the morels clean with a soft brush or dry cloth. Wash the arugula in cold water, shake it gently to remove the excess water, and let it drain in a colander, but don't pat it dry. Cut it into ¼-inch-wide strips.

2. Prepare the grits square or cakes or hoecakes according to the recipe and divide them among two to four warm plates (depending on how you are serving it).

3. Melt the butter in a heavy-bottomed skillet or sauté pan over medium-high heat. When it is just melted, add the mushrooms and garlic and toss for 1 minute. Add the arugula and stir until it is coated with the butter and just wilted, about 2 minutes. Turn off the heat. Season to taste with salt and pepper, divide it among the prepared grits or hoecakes, and serve immediately.

VARIATION:

Pasta with Morels and Spring Greens—Increase the butter to 2 tablespoons and omit the grits or hoecakes. While you are prepping the morels and arugula, bring 4 quarts water to a rolling boil in a 6- to 8-quart pot over high heat. When it boils, throw in a small handful of salt, stir in ¾ pound of egg fettuccine or tagliatelle, and cook until al dente. While it cooks, prepare the morels and arugula, using a pan large enough to hold the pasta. When the pasta is done, drain and add it to the pan. Toss until the noodles are evenly coated and serve immediately.

SPRING ONIONS

Among the first and loveliest things to come from spring's garden are the fresh, new shoots of the onion family, generically known as "green onions." For most of us, the image those words conjure is that of a slender young scallion. But those are not the only members of the onion family that can be enjoyed as young sprouts. There are also leeks, chives, and the subtly different green shoots of the onions that are more commonly found in our pantry in their mature bulb form, from shallots and Vidalia Sweet Onions to red, yellow, and white onions.

Most of us have had our share of thinly sliced scallions and other green onions tossed in a salad or as a finishing garnish for a chilled soup or hot dish, but there's a lot more to spring onions than that. To use them only in the salad bowl or as a mere garnish is to miss out on what the full range of what they have to offer when they're stirred into the pot.

In season, really fresh scallions and green Vidalia Sweet Onions often turn up in the produce bins of regional supermarkets, but the best place to find fresh, young green onions is at a farmers' market or at a reliable produce vendor who specializes in local produce.

Spring Onions in Cream SERVES 4

Just to show that there's nothing really new under the sun, not even in spring, here's one of the loveliest recipes for spring onions that I know, adapted from Lettice Bryan's 1839 master-work, *The Kentucky Housewife*. I've made only one deviation from Mrs. Bryan's method: instead of thickening the cooking liquid with a beurre manié as she did, I let it reduce to a syrup before adding the cream for body and richness.

This should accompany a simple spring main dish such as roasted young poultry or leg of lamb, or perhaps grilled lamb or mutton chops. If you like, you may also cut the onions on the bias into short inch-long pieces and serve this as a seasonal sauce for any of those things, or as sublime topping for a simple omelet.

1½ pounds small green onions or scallions

Salt

1 cup heavy cream (minimum 36 percent milk fat)

Whole black pepper in a mill

1 small blade of mace, crushed with a mortar and pestle, or if still leathery and pliable, minced, or whole nutmeg in a grater

1. Trim the roots and any withered leaves from the onions. Cut off just enough of the green tops to make them all of a uniform length and drop the onions into a basin of cold water.

2. Over medium heat, bring a cup of water to a rolling boil in a wide, lidded skillet that will hold the onions in no more than two layers. Drain the onions and add them to the pan. Cover loosely and let it come back to a boil, then uncover, and add a healthy pinch of salt. Reduce the heat to medium, and cook, uncovered, until almost tender. This should take no more than 10 minutes, and may take as little as 5, so keep an eye on them. If they overcook, they will lose their color and much of their delicate flavor.

3. Raise the heat to high and reduce the cooking liquid until it's syrupy, stirring occasionally to be sure that the onions don't scorch, about 2–3 minutes.

4. Add the cream and let it come to a boil. Taste and adjust the salt, and add a liberal grinding of pepper and the mace or a few gratings of nutmeg. Simmer until the cream is thick and lightly coating the onions, about 2 minutes more. Transfer them to a warm platter or vegetable bowl, garnish with another light grinding of pepper, and serve at once.

Spring Onion Gratin SERVES 4

This is no mere variation on the previous recipe. The onions begin in exactly the same way, but finish in the oven under a golden blanket of grated cheese—and the flavor is completely different. You may use any of the cheeses given here or mix a couple of them together, but don't add more cheese than is called for altogether: This is onions with cheese, not cheese with onions.

20–24 small scallions or green onions

Salt and whole black pepper in a mill

3 tablespoons unsalted butter

Whole nutmeg in a grater

½ cup freshly grated Parmigiano-Reggiano, Gruyère, Comté, or very sharp white cheddar

1. Trim roots and withered leaves from onions. Cut off just enough of the green tops to make all of uniform length and drop the onions into a basin of cold water. When ready to cook, drain.

2. Over medium heat, bring 1 cup water to a rolling boil in a 3-quart sauté pan or lidded skillet. Add the onions. Cover and bring the liquid back to a boil; uncover, season with salt and reduce heat to medium. Cook the onions, turning them occasionally, until they're barely

tender and still bright green, about 5–10 minutes, depending on size. Take care not to overcook them, since they'll undergo further cooking.

3. Butter a 1½- to 2-quart gratin dish and transfer the onions to it. If the cooking liquid remaining in the pan is more than ¼ cup, boil until it's reduced, about 1–2 minutes. Remove it from the heat. Add the butter and shake the pan until it's melted and incorporated. Pour it over the onions and season them liberally with pepper and nutmeg. It can be made up to 2 hours ahead to this point. Let them cool and loosely cover.

4. When you're ready to finish them, position a rack in the upper third of the oven and preheat to 400°F. Uncover the gratin and sprinkle the cheese evenly over the onions. Bake until the cheese is melted and golden, about 15 minutes. Let it settle for 5 minutes before serving.

Spring Onions and Pasta

When I was growing up, we had only two pasta dishes on our table: Macaroni pie (baked macaroni and cheese) and spaghetti with meat sauce—and we did not call either one of them "pasta." In those days, to have considered "Southern-style" pasta, let alone to include it in a Southern cookbook, would have been pretentious and, at best, questionable—even as late as this book's original publication at the end of the last century. Over the last four decades, however, Southerners, like most other Americans, have adopted all kinds of pasta, Italian and otherwise, into our repertory and today it has become so commonplace on our tables that to exclude it from a Southern book would be equally questionable.

In every section of this book, you'll find several recipes for vegetables paired with pasta. What I've looked for is the narrow space where the logic, patterns, and flavors of Southern cooking overlap with the more traditional ways of using pasta on its native turf. They are not Italian: Like the celebrated tamales of Mississippi's African-American cooks, they are Southern dishes adapted from another culture. After all, that's what Southern cooking has been from the very beginning.

Pasta with Four Onions   SERVES 4 TO 6

This is only a little more involved than the two recipes that follow. The four members of the onion family that make up the sauce all bring something different to the bowl, and are all given different treatment. The shallots simmer in butter until they're golden; the leeks just until they're wilted; the scallions are merely warmed by the hot pasta; and the chives are added at the very end, so that their bright flavor is not in the least blunted.

2 young spring leeks

1 large shallot, peeled and minced

4 tablespoons unsalted butter

Salt and whole black pepper in a mill

4 small scallions or spring onions, trimmed and thinly sliced

1 pound thin spaghetti or angel hair

2 tablespoons thinly sliced chives

¼ cup freshly grated Parmigiano-Reggiano, plus more for serving

1. Trim the roots of leeks, remove tough, dark outer leaves, if any, and split them lengthwise. Holding them under cold running water with the root end up, fold back the layers and rinse away the dirt between them, rubbing it with your fingers if necessary. Cut them into 2-inch lengths and then cut each section into fine julienne.

2. Bring 4 quarts of water to a rolling boil in 6- to 8-quart pot. Meanwhile, sauté the shallots in 2 tablespoons butter in large skillet or sauté pan over medium heat until pale gold, about 4

minutes. Add the leeks and toss until wilted, about 3 minutes. Season with salt and pepper and turn off heat.

3. When water is boiling, add a small handful of salt and stir in pasta. Cook until al dente, and drain, reserving about ¼ cup cooking liquid.

4. Reheat shallots and leeks over medium heat, stirring to prevent scorching. Turn off heat and add pasta and scallions, tossing well. Add remaining butter in bits, adding pasta cooking liquid by spoonfuls if sauce is not creamy enough. Add chives and cheese and toss well. Serve at once, passing more cheese separately.

Thin Spaghetti with Butter and Scallions   SERVES 4 TO 6

One of the great treats of our childhood for my brothers and me was that each of us got to spend a couple of weeks each summer alone with our grandparents. Those visits were when I learned to love cooking. Dinner was still the midday meal in their house, and our daily routine included helping Ma Ma plan and cook that meal—a "chore" I loved better than playing in the yard. But at suppertime, she was on break: We were allowed to have anything we wanted, so long as we cooked it and cleaned up after ourselves. A lot of the time we were content with leftovers from dinner, but more often than not, my supper was macaroni or spaghetti simply tossed with butter and cheese. I had no way of knowing back then that it was one of the great classics of all Italian cooking. To this day, it is still one of my go-to comfort foods.

While making it for lunch one cold late winter day many years later, I came across a beautiful bundle of fresh, slim scallions that I'd brought home the day before. Now, toying with that simple duo of butter and cheese, even a little, risked upsetting one of the most perfectly balanced combinations in the world, not to mention the powerful tug of childhood nostalgia. But it seemed foolish to ignore those lovely scallions. It was a rare moment when foolishness was rewarded: The bright, herbal flavor of the still-crisp scallion, enrobed in silken butter and mellowed by the cheese, added a welcome hint of freshness, the first suggestion of spring on the breeze of a blustery late-winter afternoon.

4 small, thin scallions or very young, thin
  spring onions
Salt
1 pound thin spaghetti (or regular spaghetti
  or angel hair)
½ cup freshly grated Parmigiano-Reggiano cheese,
  plus more for serving
4–5 tablespoons best quality unsalted butter

1. Bring 4 quarts of water to a rolling boil in a 6-quart heavy-bottomed pot. Wash, thoroughly drain, and trim the scallions, removing any discolored leaves. Pat them dry and thinly slice both white and green parts. You'll have about ¼ cup—more or less.

2. When the water is boiling, throw in a handful of salt and stir in the pasta, separating the strands as they soften. Cook until al dente, firm to the bite, but without a trace of pasty rawness in the middle.

3. Have ready a warm serving bowl. Quickly drain the pasta, taking care not to over-drain it until it's dry and sticky, and immediately pour it into the warm bowl. Add the scallions and half the cheese and rapidly toss until the cheese is melted and forming a creamy coating on the pasta.

4. Add 2 tablespoons of butter and half the remaining cheese and toss until the butter is melted. Add 2 more tablespoons of butter, the rest of the cheese, and toss until the butter is melted and the pasta is evenly coated with the creamy butter and cheese mixture. If it looks a bit dry, add another spoonful of butter and toss until incorporated. Serve immediately, passing more cheese on the side.

Pasta with Spring Onions and Bacon SERVES 4 TO 6

This strays into more traditional Southern territory, but a cook from Italy's Emilia-Romagna would still feel completely at home with it.

12 small green onions or 2 bunches (about 24)
  thin scallions
4 slices thick-cut bacon, cut crosswise into
  ¼-inch-wide lardons
1 clove garlic, minced
Salt
1 pound penne or rotini
2 tablespoons chopped flat-leaf parsley
Whole black pepper in a mill
About ½ cup freshly grated Parmigiano-Reggiano
  cheese

1. Bring 4 quarts water to a boil in a 6-quart heavy-bottomed pot. Trim root ends and browned tops from onions and remove wilted or yellowed leaves. Slice on diagonal into 1-inch lengths.

2. Cook the bacon in a large, heavy-bottomed skillet over medium heat until it is browned

and its fat is rendered. Spoon off all but 1 tablespoon of the fat.

3. Add the onions and sauté, stirring often, until it's barely tender, about 2–3 minutes. Add the garlic and toss until fragrant, about half a minute. Turn off the heat.

4. When the pasta water is boiling, add a small handful of salt, stir in the pasta and cook, stirring occasionally, until al dente.

5. When the pasta is almost done, gently reheat the bacon and onions. Drain the pasta, put it in the pan with the bacon and onion, add the parsley, and toss well. Season with pepper, and taste and adjust salt as needed. Serve immediately, passing the cheese separately.

Jean's Scallion-Scrambled Eggs

SERVES 2

My dear friend Jean Anderson is the author of many award-winning cookbooks, from *The Doubleday Cookbook* to the definitive classic *The Food of Portugal*. But while she spent most of her career as a food journalist and cookbook author living in New York and traveling the world, her real love has been the cooking that she savored during her North Carolina childhood. Now living in Chapel Hill, North Carolina, a town that many consider to be the epicenter of the renaissance in classic Southern cooking, Jean has returned to her culinary roots and celebrated them in a lovely book, *A Love Affair with Southern Cooking*.

The thing that marks all of Jean's work, whether she's chronicling the ancient cuisine of Portugal or that of an energetic young chef down the street, is an exquisite simplicity and balance—as is illustrated in this lovely dish. It can be served all on its own as a simple brunch, supper, or impromptu lunch, or on toast as a last-minute first course to dress up dinner for unexpected company.

6–8 large scallions or small spring onions

1 small handful fresh, young arugula, washed and dried (optional)

5 large eggs

Salt and whole black pepper in a mill

2–3 tablespoons bacon drippings (preferred), olive oil, or unsalted butter

3–4 tablespoons freshly grated Parmigiano-Reggiano

1. Trim the root and any browned tops from the scallions and thinly slice both white and green parts. Roughly chop the arugula. In a medium mixing bowl, lightly beat the eggs to mix and season well with salt and pepper.

2. Warm the fat over medium heat in a nonstick skillet. Add the scallions and simmer until they're beginning to soften, about 1–2 minutes. Add the eggs and optional arugula and cook, stirring gently, until the eggs just begin to curd. Sprinkle the cheese over them and continue cooking, again stirring almost constantly, until eggs form soft curds. Serve immediately.

SORREL AND SPINACH

Sorrel is a sour herb that is not as widely used in this country as it is in France. But once it was common in Southern gardens, especially in the coastal regions of Carolina and Georgia. Spinach and sorrel are frequently mentioned together in the old cookbooks. Nowadays sorrel is rare in Southern markets and is expensive when you can find it at all. Unless you grow your own, using it in large quantities will be a luxury indeed. Consequently, the proportion of sorrel to spinach in the following recipes is smaller than was once possible.

Sautéed Sorrel and Spinach   SERVES 4

The traditional proportion of sorrel to spinach in this dish is one to one, and if you grow your own sorrel, or can afford prodigal quantities of it, you can adjust the proportions of this recipe accordingly.

1½ pounds fresh spinach (see note)

¾ pound fresh sorrel (about 3 bunches)

3 tablespoons unsalted butter

Salt and whole black pepper in a mill

4 buttered toast triangles, optional

1 large lemon, cut into 8 wedges

1. Wash the spinach and sorrel separately, and remove all the tough stems. Put the spinach in a large, heavy-bottomed pot without adding water. The water clinging to it will be sufficient. Cover and cook over medium-high heat until the spinach begins to wilt, about 3 minutes. Add the sorrel, cover, and cook until both greens are fully wilted, about 2 minutes more. Drain thoroughly in a colander.

2. Wipe out the pan and add the butter. Put it over medium-high heat and when the butter is melted and hot, but not browning, add the greens and sauté until tender and dry, about 3 minutes. Season lightly with salt (sorrel has a salty taste on its own and won't need much) and

a few grindings of pepper. If you like, arrange toast triangles on a platter or individual plates and top them with the greens, or just spread them on a platter. Garnish with the lemon and serve at once.

Note: *Served over crisped buttered toast with its classic accompaniment of poached eggs, this makes a very nice first course for any spring meal, or a main-course dish for supper or brunch.*

Spinach stands up fairly well to freezing; while it won't be quite as good, you may substitute two 10-ounce packages of frozen whole-leaf spinach for the fresh spinach.

Lenten Herb, or Spinach and Sorrel Soup   SERVES 6

Nowadays Lent seems to be little more than an excuse for the weeklong drunken blowout that precedes it in New Orleans's infamous Mardi Gras celebration. But actually Lent is a Christian religious observance—a solemn, introspective season of practiced restraint and abstinence. Historically, the blowout began as a final feast designed to get all the fat (and booze) out of the house before the season began on Ash Wednesday—hence the name "Fat Tuesday."

This lovely soup is to help you behave yourself after the big party; it sure makes doing without seem like no real hardship.

¼ pound sorrel leaves

¼ pound spinach

1 large leek

1 large yellow onion, split, peeled, and thinly sliced

2 tablespoons butter

1 clove garlic, peeled and minced

4 cups (1 quart) Vegetable Broth (page 22) or water

1 Bouquet Garni (page 32)

Salt and whole white pepper in a mill

4 large egg yolks

1 tablespoon freshly squeezed lemon juice
1 cup Buttered Croutons (page 37)

1. Wash the sorrel and spinach, and remove their tough stems. Put in a colander set in the sink and let them drain. Remove the tough outer leaves of the leek and trim off the upper part of its green shoots. Split it lengthwise and wash it under cold running water, being careful to remove all the grit and dirt between the layers. Thinly slice both the white and tender green parts.

2. Put the leek, onion, and butter in a heavy-bottomed 3- to 4-quart pot over medium heat. Sauté until wilted, about 8 minutes. Add the garlic and sauté until fragrant, about half a minute longer. Add the broth, bouquet garni, a healthy pinch of salt, and a liberal grinding of white pepper. Let it come to a boil.

3. Meanwhile, slice the sorrel and spinach into thin strips. Add them to the pot as soon as the broth is boiling, let it come back to a boil, and reduce the heat to medium low. Simmer until the vegetables are tender, about 15 minutes. Remove and discard the bouquet garni.

4. Puree the soup in batches in a blender or food processor, (or, if you want to be authentic, force it through a sieve or food mill). Return the soup to the kettle and bring it back to a simmer.

5. In a heatproof bowl, whisk the egg yolks and lemon juice together until smooth. Slowly whisk in a cup of the hot soup, then slow whisk this into the remaining soup. Serve at once with the buttered croutons.

Note: *To make a vegetarian soup, use olive oil to sauté the onion and leek, or omit the sautéing step altogether and simmer the onion and leek in the liquid until they are nearly tender before adding the other vegetables. To give the soup body without eggs, substitute a medium potato, peeled and sliced thin, in step 2. If abstention isn't your goal, you can also omit the egg yolks and enrich the soup with a cup of heavy cream* (minimum 36 percent milk fat) added before the final simmer in step 4.

ENGLISH, GARDEN, OR GREEN PEAS

Don't just ask for peas in the South unless you're in the mood for field peas—black-eye, butter, cow, crowder, lady, white-acre, or zipper peas—because that's what you'll get. If you want the green variety, you'd better ask for "English," "garden," or "sweet" peas. That's what we call them, though the latter two are probably more descriptive, since there's nothing exclusively English about them.

Like asparagus, fresh green peas were once a seasonal treat. Dried split peas were of course available year round, but only in the spring could one get tender, sweet fresh peas—so full of natural sugars that they are almost like candy. When I was growing up, the early peas were so sweet that we used to raid the garden and eat them raw. On the rare occasion that I get freshly gathered peas in late spring, I buy a lot more than I plan to serve because I know I'll eat more than my share while shelling them.

We've lost a lot of that sense of specialness. Canning and freezing have made green peas so commonplace (and ordinary) that the idea of this cafeteria standby as a rare treat seems perfectly ridiculous. Well, while nothing equals the sweetness and tenderness of freshly gathered peas, with care, even the frozen variety can be very satisfying to eat. They can be used in any of the recipes that follow.

Mary Randolph's Fresh English Peas

If you are lucky enough to find fresh peas in the market, or better yet, have a spot where you can gather your own, Mary Randolph's 1824 recipe is all you need—her instructions for gathering, keeping, and cooking the peas are lucid and still pertinent. Your only problem will be in finding peas that are really freshly gathered. Here's her recipe:

"To have them in perfection, they must be quite young, gathered early in the morning, kept in a cool place, and not shelled until they are to be dressed; put salt in the water, and when it boils, put in the peas; boil them quick twenty or thirty minutes, according to their age; just before they are taken up, add a little mint chopped very fine, drain all the water from the peas, put in a bit of butter, and serve them up quite hot."

—Mary Randolph, *The Virginia House-wife*, 1824

English Peas with Spring Onions SERVES 4

Contrary to the notion that ministers do nothing from Sunday to Sunday but write long, tedious sermons, when I was growing up my father was a very busy man. Aside from three services a week (unless someone died), Bible study groups, and not one, but three sermons to compose, there were visits to the sick, shut-in, worried, and grief-stricken and counseling sessions for troubled marriages and spirits. In short, he was running from early morning until supper, and did not have much time for cooking. When, on the rare occasion it fell to him to feed his three growing boys, his repertory was limited, and, like so many other busy fathers of his generation, included frozen TV dinners. Back then, the green vegetable in most all of those dinners was peas. Frozen peas were bad enough; baking them made them inedible, so, before the trays went into the oven, he'd fold back the foil, remove the peas, and cook them separately in barely enough water to cover. When they were tender but still bright green, he dressed them with butter, onion salt, and pepper. The rest of those meals was mercifully forgettable, but those peas were transformed into something that was not merely edible, but delicious.

Dad was on to something with that simple triad of peas, butter, and onion. When at last I had a kitchen of my own, I kept making his peas, substituting fresh green onions for the onion salt. The onion greens lend a sweetness and delicacy to older fresh peas, and give frozen ones an almost garden-fresh flavor.

2 small green onions or scallions

2 pounds (unshelled weight; 1 pound if shelled) young green peas or 1 pound frozen peas

Salt and whole black pepper in a mill

2–3 tablespoons unsalted butter, cut into bits

1. Wash the onions, drain well, and pat dry. Trim away the roots and any discolored leaves and finely mince them.

2. If you are using fresh peas, shell and wash them briefly in a basin of cold water. Transfer them to a colander or sieve, and set them aside to drain.

3. Bring about 2 cups of water to a boil in a heavy-bottomed saucepan over medium-high heat. Add the peas and a healthy pinch of salt and let it come back to a boil. Reduce the heat to a lively simmer and cook until the peas are just tender, about 15 minutes for fresh, or 8–10 minutes for frozen ones.

4. Remove the lid and raise the heat once more to medium high. Allow the liquid to boil away quickly until there are only a couple of tablespoons remaining in the pan. When the liquid is evaporated, add the minced onion, toss or stir well, and turn off the heat. Taste and adjust the salt and, if liked, a liberal grinding of pepper. Add the butter and shake the pan until it dissolves and coats the peas. Pour into a warm serving bowl and serve at once.

Note: *Unhappily for vegans, there is no substitute for the butter of this recipe. No other fat can enhance and complement the sweet flavor of the peas.*

English Peas with Leeks SERVES 4

Many recipes that contain leeks call only for the white parts, and yet the tender, pale greens are a lovely part of the vegetable. They can be set aside to add to the stockpot, but once you have tasted them, even that will seem like a waste. Here, their mild, fresh flavor is a perfect complement for the sweetness of the peas and, like the green onions of the previous recipe, gives the frozen variety back some of the freshness that they have lost.

Inner, pale green parts of 3 large leek tops

2 pounds (unshelled weight; 1 pound if shelled) young green peas or 1 pound frozen peas

2 tablespoons unsalted butter, divided

2 ounces lean salt pork, country ham, or prosciutto (about 3 thin slices salt pork, 2 slices of either ham), sliced about ⅛-inch thick and cut into julienne

½ cup Chicken Broth (page 21)

Salt

1. Carefully wash the leek greens to remove any lingering dirt. Most of the dirt is in the outer, dark leaves, but sometimes it gets into the inner shoot as well. Slice them crosswise as thinly as possible. If using fresh peas, shell and wash them briefly in a basin of cold water and let them drain in a colander. If using frozen ones, keep them frozen until you're ready to cook them.

2. Put 1 tablespoon of the butter and pork in a large, lidded skillet or sauté pan. Turn on the heat to medium high and sauté until the pork fat is beginning to color, about 2 minutes. Add the leek greens and shake the pan until they're glossy and coated with fat. Add the peas, and continue shaking the pan until they're coated (and the frozen peas are thawed). Add the broth; it should cover the peas. If it doesn't, add enough water to barely cover them. Bring it

quickly to a boil, then reduce the heat to medium low, cover, and simmer until the peas are just tender, about 15 minutes for fresh, or 8–10 minutes for frozen ones.

3. Remove the lid and raise the heat once more to medium high. Quickly boil the liquid away until there are only a couple of tablespoons remaining. Turn off the heat. Taste and adjust the salt, adding a pinch or so if needed. Add the remaining butter and shake the pan until it dissolves and coats the peas. Pour into a warm serving bowl and serve at once.

Note: *You may omit the salt pork or ham and use water instead of chicken broth, but as in the previous recipe, there is no substitute for the butter.*

Early English Pea Soup SERVES 6

This is an "early" recipe in both senses of the word. Not only is it best when made with the earliest and sweetest of green peas, the recipe itself is quite old, going back as far as the Middle Ages. The source of this soup's fine flavor is owed to first stewing the pea pods in the broth. This infuses the broth with a rich pea flavor while allowing the peas themselves to remain fresh and lightly cooked.

1 quart (4 cups) Chicken Broth (page 21)

3 cups (about 2 pounds) shelled young green peas, with hulls reserved

1 tablespoon unsalted butter

½ cup chopped onion

1 leek, split, washed, trimmed, and sliced

4 large sprigs fresh mint

1¼ cups heavy cream (minimum 36 percent milk fat)

Salt and whole white pepper in a mill

A dozen or so chive leaves, chopped

1. Put the broth and reserved pea hulls in a heavy-bottomed 3-quart pot over medium-high heat. Bring it to a boil, skim it carefully, and reduce the heat to a bare simmer. Cover loosely and let the broth simmer for about ½ hour.

2. Put the butter, onion, and leeks in a heavy-bottomed 3- to 4-quart pot, and turn on the heat to medium. Cook slowly until softened but not browned, about 10 minutes.

3. Strain the broth from the hulls and add it to the pot with the onion and leeks. Discard the hulls. Let the broth come to a boil, add the peas and two sprigs of mint, and reduce the heat to a simmer. Cook until the peas are tender, about 15–20 minutes.

4. Dip out a cup of the peas and set them aside. Puree the soup in a blender or food processor. Return the puree to the pot, stir in the reserved peas and 1 cup of the cream, and season to taste with the salt and pepper. Cook just long enough to heat the cream through. While the soup is heating, if you like, whip the remaining ¼ cup cream until it forms soft peaks. Chop the remaining mint and mix it with the chives.

5. When the soup is heated through, turn off the heat, remove the mint sprig, and serve at once, garnishing each serving with a dollop of whipped cream (or a drizzle of cream if you've not whipped it), and a sprinkling of the chopped herbs.

Note: *If you whip the garnishing cream, work quickly when serving the soup warm, because the cream will immediately begin to melt on contact with the warm soup. This is equally good served chilled. To do so, don't add the cream after pureeing it, but pour it into a bowl set in a basin of ice water and stir until it is cooled, then refrigerate until chilled. Don't cover until it is cold, otherwise you are inviting spoilage. The soup will be thicker cold than hot: add the cream when you're ready to serve it, and if you find it's*

too thick, thin it with a little water or half-and-half, but don't add more broth or heavy cream.

SUGAR SNAP PEA SOUP:

If you can't get fresh young peas still in their shells, you can make a very nice soup with sugar snap peas, which are becoming commonplace in many markets. You'll need 1½ pounds of sugar snaps. Top and tail them and be sure that all their strings have been stripped away. Slice them crosswise about ¼-inch thick. Omit step 1. Set aside a cup of the peas and proceed as directed in step 2. In step 3, the sugar snaps will be tender in about 10 minutes. After the soup is pureed, add the reserved peas and cook until they are just tender, about 4 minutes.

POKE SALLET

"Sallet" is the old English word for all leafy greens—a term that is still used in some rural parts of the South, especially when the greens are from our native wild pokeweed.

Pokeweed (*Phytolacca americana*) has long been relished as a vegetable in the South. While it was once grown in private vegetable gardens in the early nineteenth century, it has never been cultivated as a commercial crop. Those who eat it gather it in the wild. Fortunately, it's a hardy plant that can (and does) flourish nearly anywhere; I've even seen it growing in the median between street and sidewalk in downtown Savannah. Where I now live, I have pulled it from abandoned flowerpots and have several healthy plants that sprout up among the camellias in my backyard—a blessing since we can no longer safely harvest it from roadsides as my grandmother and I used to do. Today many public shoulders have been sprayed with chemicals, and many fields have been treated with pesticides.

Poke is a seasonal vegetable, in part because only the young shoots and early leaves are tender enough to eat, and in part because youth is the only stage at which they are thought to be edible. Poke contains a mild toxin that develops as the plant matures. There is a time of the year when the berries are supposed to be safe as well, but the seeds, roots, and mature stems are all poisonous, so don't gather any poke leaves or shoots that are tinged with red, and don't take a chance with the berries. As added insurance, many cooks blanch the sallet, which is supposed to remove any toxin that it may contain.

To prepare poke sallet, thoroughly wash the leaves in cold water, changing the water at least twice. Remove and discard any stems or red-tipped leaves. Half-fill a large kettle that will comfortably hold all the leaves with water. Bring this to a boil over high heat and add the leaves, pressing them below the surface of the water with a spoon. When they are wilted, but still bright green, drain them quickly and rinse under cold running water.

Ma Ma's Poke Sallet with Spring Onions   SERVES 4

My maternal grandmother, known to me as Ma Ma, was passionate about greens of any sort, so much so that they were the only thing that we ever knew to interfere with her favorite hobbies—traveling and eating out. If there was a pot of greens on the stove, you could rest assured that she would sharply veto any suggestion that we go out, even if we were going to her favorite restaurant.

My happiest and earliest memories of Ma Ma are of spring mornings spent in her old Chevrolet, driving down country roads with our eyes fixed on the shoulders, looking for signs of tender young poke shoots. Even when the trip wasn't a forage for greens, we'd throw a couple of grocery sacks in the backseat—just in case.

The best choice of green onions for this are spring shallots or very young, green Vidalia Sweet Onions, but even scallions will do nicely. If you can't get poke sallet where you live, Swiss chard makes an excellent substitute.

2 pounds tender poke sallet leaves or young
   swiss chard

2 ounces (about 2 thin slices) salt pork or country
   ham fat or 2 tablespoons unsalted butter

4 large green onions (or 6, if they are small)

Salt

Pepper Vinegar (page 25) or 1 lemon,
   cut into wedges

1. Wash the sallet or chard in at least two changes of water, making sure there is no lingering grit or dirt. Trim off any tough stems. (If you are using chard, remove all the stems and set them aside for another use. They make a delicious vegetable on their own.)

2. If you are using poke sallet, blanch it as directed on page 81. If you use chard, put it in a large heavy-bottomed pot without adding water. The water clinging to the leaves will be enough to wilt them. Cover and cook over medium-high heat until the greens are just wilted, about 3–5 minutes.

3. Drain the greens well and rinse them briefly under cold running water. Press them gently to remove the excess liquid and set aside.

4. Trim off the roots and any tough or defective outer leaves from the onions. Wash and slice them crosswise as thinly as possible.

5. If using salt pork or ham, put it in a large, heavy-bottomed skillet over medium heat. Sauté until the fat is rendered from it and the pork is crisp. Remove the pork with a slotted spoon and drain it on absorbent paper. Drain off all but 2 tablespoons of the fat. (If for some reason there isn't enough fat, supplement it with butter.) Alternatively, if you are omitting the pork, put 2 tablespoons of butter in the pan over medium-high heat. When the butter is almost melted, add the onions and sauté until they are softened but not colored, about 2 minutes. Add the greens and a pinch or so of salt. Sauté, stirring frequently, until they are tender and nearly dry, about 5–8 minutes. Taste and correct the

salt, then transfer the greens to a warm serving bowl. You may crumble the pork over them if you like. Serve at once, passing the pepper vinegar or lemon wedges separately.

Note: *Don't overcook poke sallet: After it has been blanched, it will only take a few minutes more cooking, and, as nineteenth-century author Lettice Bryan aptly noted, it isn't good when it has been boiled to mush. For a meatless version, substitute peanut oil for the salt pork or butter.*

NEW POTATOES

By "new" potatoes, I don't mean those small, red-skinned things that one finds loosely labeled as such in most supermarkets. I mean true new potatoes, freshly dug, smelling fragrantly of earth and tasting vaguely sweet, with waxy flesh and translucent, papery skins that are so thin and delicate that they rub right off when you roll the potato between the palms of your hands. At one time, they were the glory of every spring garden. Lightly steamed on top of the snap beans, or quickly boiled and shimmering with butter, they were also the glory of the spring dinner table. Sadly, few of us today have an opportunity to know such glories. The potatoes that are so frequently marketed as "new" seldom actually are. All that the name means now is that the potatoes were harvested before they were mature.

Luckily, regional farmers' markets are making all kinds of spring potatoes available to those of us who don't garden, and are reminding us that true new potatoes needn't be red by offering a rainbow variety from round whites, russets, and genuine red-skinned varieties to yellow ones such as Yukon Gold as well as pink, deep purple, red, and yellow fingerlings. Look for very small, thin-skinned potatoes, and be wary of bright red ones; some producers actually dye them. Even if you suspect that the potatoes have been around a while, you can still use them successfully in any of the recipes that follow.

Two other excellent recipes for new potatoes are Asparagus with Leeks and New Potatoes (page 55) and Asparagus and New Potato Salad (page 55).

Creole, Deviled New Potatoes, or Pommes de Terre à la Diable

SERVES 4

The legend behind the name of this dish may not be true but is typical of the Creole sense of humor. The story is that the dish was invented by a strong-willed Creole housewife to get back at her lazy no-count mari who spent most of his time—not to mention their limited income—on wine and cards. When he was especially surly and disobedient about being sent to the market for potatoes, and swore that the potatoes could go to the Devil, his wife in turn swore to make him eat potatoes à la diable for sure. In Creole and all Southern cooking, that means plenty of hot mustard: She dumped a healthy dose of it on the potatoes and added a big pinch of cayenne for good measure. She brought them angrily to the table and waited, arms folded, for her no-count mari to choke. But her revenge backfired: the potatoes were delicious; the lazy jerk actually liked them—and a new Creole dish was born.

Who cares if it's not true—how do you resist a story like that?

1½ pounds very small new potatoes

5 tablespoons unsalted butter, softened

1 tablespoon Creole mustard (see note) or 2 tablespoons Dijon mustard

Salt and cayenne pepper

1 tablespoon chopped parsley

1. Bring enough water to cover the potatoes to a boil in a heavy-bottomed 3- to 4-quart pan over high heat. Wash the potatoes under cold running water, and when the water reaches a rapid boil, add them to the pot. Cover and let it return to a boil, reduce the heat to medium, and cook until the potatoes are just tender, about 25 minutes. Drain well and put the pan, covered, back on the heat for half a minute, then turn off the heat, uncover, and let the potatoes sit until they are dry and cool enough to handle. Peel the potatoes and set them aside.

2. Blend 2 tablespoons of the butter with the mustard until it is smooth. Though this dish is best when the potatoes are finished right away, you may make it up to this point a couple of hours ahead. Keep the potatoes and butter-mustard mixture covered, but don't refrigerate them.

3. Put the remaining 3 tablespoons of butter in a large, heavy-bottomed skillet that will hold the potatoes in one layer over medium-high heat. When the butter is melted, add the potatoes, shaking the pan vigorously to coat them with the butter. Add a healthy pinch of salt and a small one of cayenne, and toss to distribute the seasonings. Sauté, tossing frequently, until the potatoes are lightly browned on all sides.

4. Add the butter-mustard paste and shake the pan until the potatoes are coated with it and it browns. Turn off the heat. Add the parsley and shake until it is evenly distributed. Turn out into a warm serving bowl and serve at once.

Note: *Creole mustard is very à la diable indeed; a little of it goes a long way. Exercise plenty of restraint if you use it. A larger amount of the milder Dijon mustard is necessary to give the potatoes their requisite kick.*

Sunday Dinner Herbed New Potatoes   SERVES 6

Sook Faulk, Truman Capote's eccentric great-aunt who was lovingly portrayed in *A Christmas Memory*, was one of many gifted cooks within the Faulk household, where Truman Capote spent much of his childhood. The cookery of that family was immortalized in a lovely culinary memoir *Sook's Cookbook* by another of the family's great cooks and characters, Mr. Capote's aunt Marie Rudisill, best remembered today as late-night television's "Fruitcake Lady." Gifts for cooking and storytelling seemed to run in the Faulk family; Marie inherited a goodly dose of each and *Sook's Cookbook* is a treasure.

These potatoes are just like one of Mrs. Rudisill's phone calls, which kept me sane right up until her death: they're light, fresh, and refined—yet homey and soul-nourishing all at once.

1½ pounds new potatoes
Salt
4 tablespoons unsalted butter
1 tablespoon lemon juice
3 tablespoons parsley, snipped
1 tablespoon fresh chives, snipped
2 head fresh dill, snipped (about 2 tablespoons)
Whole white pepper in a mill

1. Scrub the potatoes well with a coarse brush under cool running water. Pare a strip of the skin from around the middle of each potato, leaving the remaining skin intact.

2. Put enough water in a 3- to 4-quart heavy-bottomed pot to cover the potatoes. Cover and bring to a boil over medium-high heat. Add a small handful of salt and the potatoes and cover until the water comes back to a boil. Uncover and cook until just tender, about 25 minutes. Drain well, leaving them in the pan.

3. Melt the butter in a small skillet over low heat. Off the heat, add the lemon juice, parsley, chives, and dill. Pour this over the potatoes, season lightly with white pepper, and gently shake the pot (or stir very gently) until the potatoes are evenly coated. Turn out into a warm serving bowl and serve at once.

Butter-Braised Baby Spring Beets, Radishes, or Turnips   SERVES 6

Braising really brings out the sweetness of any vegetable, but especially fresh spring roots. Any small, round root can be cooked this way—baby beets or turnips or even young round radishes. We don't often think of cooking radishes, but they're particularly lovely braised. You can also mix them up, braising several kinds at once, and add a dozen or so small whole peeled shallots (choose round ones). Be sure to have plenty of crusty bread for dipping in the butter.

2 pounds small, round radishes, turnips, or beets, with their green tops still attached
4 tablespoons unsalted butter
Salt and whole black pepper in a mill
1 tablespoon whole small marjoram or oregano leaves, or chopped flat-leaf parsley

1. Scrub and trim the vegetables. Trim the leaves but leave some of the green stem attached. Set aside the nicest greens to wash and mix with other greens in a salad.

2. Melt the butter over medium heat in a lidded 3-quart sauté pan or large skillet. Add the roots

and shake the pan until they're coated with butter. Sauté, gently shaking the pan or tossing to keep the vegetables rolling, until they're beginning to color on all sides.

3. Season with salt and pepper and add about ¼ cup water. Cover and lower the heat to medium low. Braise until tender, about 8-15 minutes, shaking the pan occasionally and checking to make sure liquid doesn't completely evaporate. If it does, add water by spoonfuls as needed.

4. When the vegetables are tender, remove the lid and if any liquid remains, raise the heat and cook, shaking constantly, until the liquid is evaporated. Sprinkle in the herbs, shaking the pan to distribute them, then taste and adjust the salt and pepper. Give the pan one last shake to evenly distribute the seasoning and serve warm.

Roasted Spring Roots Vegetables   SERVES 6

Try to choose young vegetables of much the same size that can be left whole and don't peel them. If they're larger, cut them into halves or quarters. If beets are a part of the mix and are too large to leave whole, roast them in a separate pan and then mix them with the other vegetables just before serving. Otherwise, the juice from the cut beets will stain everything else bright pink.

2 pounds mixed small young root vegetables such as beets, carrots, radishes, and turnips

10–12 small round shallots or small green onions, trimmed

2–3 tablespoons rendered bacon drippings, melted, or extra-virgin olive oil

Salt and whole black pepper in a mill

1 tablespoon chopped fresh thyme

1 tablespoon chopped fresh parsley

1. Position rack in upper third of the oven and preheat to 400°F. Scrub the root vegetables under cold running water, trim, removing the root tendrils and most of the greens but leaving some green stem. The green tops can be set aside to mix with other greens in salads. If using carrots, reserve a handful of the freshest-looking green tops. Cut larger roots into halves or quarters, but leave small ones whole. If using shallots, trim and peel them; if using green onions, wash, drain, trim, and cut them into 2-inch lengths, reserving a few of the green tops.

2. Put the vegetables in a 3-quart metal gratin (lined copper or enameled iron) dish or medium-size roasting pan that will hold them in no more than two layers. Drizzle with the drippings or oil and toss to coat. Sprinkle with salt, pepper, and thyme. Roast, stirring occasionally, until the vegetables are golden and tender, about 30 minutes.

3. Meanwhile, if you have carrot tops, chop enough of them to make 1 generous tablespoon and mix them with the parsley. If you have green onion tops, thinly slice enough to make about 2 tablespoons. When the vegetables are done, remove them from the oven let them settle for 5 minutes before serving. Sprinkle them with the parsley (and carrot tops and green onion tops) and gently toss. Serve warm or at room temperature.

EDIBLE FLOWERS

393. Nasturtion.—The blooms are gay, and make a fine relish eaten with cold, light bread, buttered. They make a beautiful breakfast dish. This vegetable is seldom used, however, but for pickling; for this, gather the pods when fully grown. They were as a good substitute for capers in making sauce.

—Annabella Hill, *Mrs. Hill's New Cook Book*, 1867

We tend to think of edible flowers as a recent addition to America's culinary landscape, but here is dear Annabella Hill telling us how to use nasturtium blossoms as "a fine relish" and "beautiful breakfast dish"—more than a century before flower garnishes started turning up on nouvelle cuisine dinner plates.

Flowers have probably been a part of cooking ever since fire was applied to the hunt's kill; their use in European and Middle Eastern cookery was already ancient when Jesus was in diapers. If you think on it, once mankind figured out that ripened fruit was good to eat, why wouldn't they also have a go at the flowers that produced the fruit?

In the Old South, homemakers made flower-infused water both for fragrances and for flavoring such sweet confections as custards, teacakes, and pound cake. They also candied them and made them into sweet preserves and jellies. But flowers were also, as Mrs. Hill noted, eaten as a lovely relish for bread and butter, and as a delicate, edible garnish for meat dishes.

In those days, we could simply pluck lavender, nasturtium, orange, pansy, rose, and violet blossoms intended for the kitchen right from our own ornamental gardens. We can no longer do that today—and not just because ornamental plants are often treated with pesticides that are no better for us than they are for the bugs. Most commercially grown ornamental plants are started in treated soil with fertilizer that isn't intended for human consumption. Flowers that will be used at the table for more than just a decorative centerpiece must be started from seeds in clean soil using only plant food designed for vegetable gardening.

Fortunately, organically grown edible blossoms are becoming common at local farmers' markets and even some specialty grocers. All the same, buy them from a vendor you can trust, and if you aren't sure of a plant, assume its flowers aren't safe to eat. Here are a few notes on the most commonly used flowers in the South.

Lavender: Dried culinary lavender blossoms are becoming more widely available. It's the same flower that's used for its freshening fragrance, so when buying it, make sure you are purchasing culinary lavender (grown without spraying) and not dried flowers grown strictly for their fragrance. Lavender has a distinctive flavor and is used mostly for sweets, the most popular down South being lavender pound cake and ice cream, but it's also one of the key elements of classic Fines Herbes (page 33).

Nasturtium: These bright yellow to red-orange blossoms have a subtly peppery flavor, like a mild radish. In old cookery, however, it was the unopened buds and matured berries that were more commonly used, pickled in brine as a substitute for imported (and expensive) capers.

Orange Blossoms: Though used more often in fragrance, orange flowers are also infused in a flavoring water that was once common in sweet confections. Orange flower water intended for cooking is available at many specialty grocers. If you want to experiment with orange

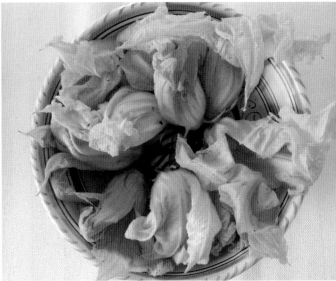

blossoms, be sure that the tree from which you gather them has not been sprayed.

Pansies and Violas: These lovely blossoms really have very little flavor, and are used mainly for their vivid color. Since they flourish in cooler weather, they're a popular ornamental flower in the South for winter gardens, and are seasonal in late autumn, winter, and spring. As a reminder, you can't just pluck them out of your ornamental beds. They must be grown from seeds in soil specifically for vegetables and not potting soil for strictly ornamental plants.

Roses: The flowers of most roses are technically edible, and their flavor is directly proportional to their fragrance. But because these showy plants can be temperamental and prone to disease, most are treated with all sorts of things that render their blossoms unsafe to eat. Sometimes untreated, organically grown rose petals turn up in the market and can be used raw in salads or to make culinary rosewater, preserves, jelly, and wine. They can also be candied. Culinary rosewater, candied petals, and rose petal preserves are commonly available in Middle Eastern markets and specialty groceries.

Squash Blossoms: In Italy, bundles of squash blossoms brighten every market in season, but until recently, they were rarely seen in our markets. Today, they're getting to be commonplace in most farmers' markets. If you garden and are gathering blossoms from your own plants, harvest only the male flowers (those with a single, pollen-capped stamen) or you will literally nip your squash crop in the bud.

Violets: Though most often candied, untreated violets can be used as a garnish and as a colorful addition to salad. Do not eat violets that have been grown as ornamental plants.

Mrs. Hill's Nasturtium Sandwiches

MAKES 12

12–24 nasturtium blossoms

3 thin slices firm, home-style sandwich bread

About 2–3 tablespoons Softened Nasturtium Butter (recipe follows) or unsalted butter

Salt and cayenne or whole white pepper in a mill (only if using plain butter)

1. Gently rinse the flowers in cold water and pat dry. Trim the crusts from the bread and cut each slice into four equal squares. Generously spread with Nasturtium Butter or plain butter. If using plain butter, lightly sprinkle with salt and cayenne or a grinding of white pepper.

2. Top with the nasturtium blossoms and serve within half an hour.

Nasturtium Butter   MAKES ABOUT ¾ CUP

1 cup (lightly packed) nasturtium blossoms

Salt

4 ounces (½ cup or 1 stick) best quality unsalted butter, softened

The grated zest and juice from ½ lemon

Ground cayenne or whole white pepper in a mill

1. Gently rinse the flowers in cold water and pat dry. To make the butter by hand, roughly chop and put them in a mortar with a small pinch of salt and crush them with the pestle. Work in the butter, lemon juice and zest, and season to taste with more salt and a small pinch of cayenne or, for a milder pepper flavor, a generous grinding of white pepper.

2. To make the butter in a food processor, put the washed and dried flowers, butter, zest, lemon juice, and a pinch each of salt and cayenne or white pepper. Process until smooth, taste, and adjust the seasoning, then pulse to mix.

3. Scoop the butter into a crock, cover, and refrigerate until needed. Or scoop it onto a sheet of wax paper, refrigerate until it's firm enough to shape (about half an hour), roll it into a cylinder, and wrap it well with the paper. Refrigerate until firm and then slice as needed.

Big Spring Salad with Meyer Lemon Lavender Vinaigrette

SERVES 6 AS A SALAD COURSE, 4 AS A MAIN DISH

There was a time when the first delicate leaves of lettuce were a more certain sign of spring than a red-breasted robin in the yard. The early crop could all too easily get nipped by a late frost, which made it that much more valuable. Even today, with bags of so-called "spring mix" filling every supermarket's vegetable bins year round, those first, new leaves of butter lettuce, lamb's tongue, frisée, spinach, and beet greens, freshly gathered and lightly dressed, bring wonder and a promise of summer's coming bounty to our tables.

Feel free to add things to this salad as they come into season: fresh-cut asparagus trimmed and cut into bite-size lengths, new baby artichokes trimmed and sliced thin, freshly gathered English peas or sugar snaps, sweet little baby squash, and blueberries.

10 ounces (about 6 lightly packed cups) mixed spring greens

3 medium young spring carrots (preferably "rainbow" carrots—1 each of purple, orange, and yellow), with greens still attached

4–6 small young red radishes, with greens still attached

6 small, thin scallions or other green onions

3–4 large sprigs flat-leaf parsley

½ cup slivered pecans

12–16 edible spring flowers such as violas, pansies, or nasturtiums

1 cup sliced strawberries, optional
Meyer Lemon Herb Vinaigrette (recipe follows)
2 cups Buttered Croutons (page 37), optional

1. Wash the greens and spin them dry with a salad spinner or roll in a large, clean kitchen towel and gently shake dry. Scrub the carrots and radishes under cold running water. Trim away the carrot fronds, reserving a handful each of the freshest-looking ones, and cut them into ⅛-inch julienne (matchsticks) about 1½ inches long. Trim the taproot and greens from the radishes and thinly slice them. If the greens are fresh and unblemished, pat them dry and reserve them. Wash and trim the scallions and slice them on the diagonal into 1-inch lengths.

Tear the reserved carrot fronds and parsley into small pieces.

2. Put the greens, carrot, radish, pecans, flowers, reserved carrot fronds, radish greens, parsley, and strawberries, if using, into a large salad bowl. Gently toss to mix. Spoon half the vinaigrette over the salad and gently toss to mix. Taste and add more dressing by spoonfuls until the salad is dressed to your taste. You may not need quite all of it. Add the croutons, gently toss one last time, and serve immediately.

Notes: *To make this a main-dish salad, add 2 cups of diced cooked chicken. A generous handful of sweetened dried cranberries would also make a nice, colorful addition.*

Meyer Lemon Lavender Vinaigrette   MAKES ABOUT ⅓ CUP

2 tablespoons freshly squeezed Meyer lemon juice (about ½ lemon) or other fresh lemon juice

2 teaspoons Dijon mustard

Salt

1 large clove garlic, crushed and peeled but left whole

½ teaspoon dried culinary lavender flowers (or 1 teaspoon fresh flowers)

4 tablespoons extra-virgin olive oil

1 tablespoon fresh herbs (thyme, marjoram, oregano, chives)

Whole black pepper in a mill

1. Whisk together the lemon juice, mustard, and a large pinch of salt. Add the garlic clove and lightly bruise it with the back of a spoon. Stir in the lavender and let stand 15–30 minutes.

2. Remove and discard the garlic. Slowly whisk in the olive oil until it is incorporated and emulsified. Add the herbs and a liberal grinding of pepper and lightly whisk to mix. Taste and adjust the seasonings. It can be made up to a day ahead, but hold back the herbs until you are ready to serve it.

Lavender Ice Cream   MAKES ABOUT 1½ QUARTS, SERVES 6

When I first taught the Provençal classic lavender-honey ice cream in cooking classes, it was met with reserved curiosity by my students. It has since become a new favorite for all Americans, but there is something about the whimsy of flower-scented ice cream that especially speaks to the Southern mindset, whispering as it does of dainty china and old lace. In Savannah, Stratton and Mary Leopold, proprietors of Leopold's Ice Cream, whose iconic tutti-frutti ice cream inspired songwriter Johnny Mercer, offer

their own house-made lavender and rose-petal ice cream seasonally, and both have become Savannah favorites.

The flowers won't change the color of the cream, so if you want it to look lavender, add a few drops of violet food coloring or a little blueberry juice to the custard after it comes off the heat.

1 rounded tablespoon dried culinary lavender

2 cups whole milk

1 cup heavy cream

7 egg yolks

1¾ cups sugar

½ teaspoon salt

Fresh mint and/or fresh lavender flowers (only if unsprayed) or candied violets

1. Tie the lavender in a tea ball or double layer of cheesecloth with kitchen twine. Prepare the

bottom pan of a double boiler with 1 inch of water and bring it to a simmer over medium heat, or choose a saucepan with a thick, heavy bottom.

2. Scald the milk, cream, and lavender in the heavy-bottomed pan or in the top pan of a double boiler over direct medium heat. Let simmer gently 3–4 minutes. Beat the egg yolks and sugar in a heatproof bowl until light and lemon colored. Beat 1 cup of the hot liquid into them and then slowly stir them into the remainder. Add the salt and cook, stirring almost constantly, until it coats the back of a metal spoon. Remove and discard the lavender.

3. Remove the custard from the heat and stir until slightly cooled. Pour it into a metal bowl, let cool to room temperature, and chill thoroughly in the refrigerator.

4. Freeze the custard in an ice cream maker following the manufacturer's directions. Pack it into a freezable container and put it in the freezer for at least 4 hours or overnight. Serve garnished with mint and/or lavender flowers or candied violets.

Mama's Fried Squash Blossoms   SERVES 3 TO 4

One of the great late spring delicacies of any garden, Southern or otherwise, is the delicate, butter-yellow bloom of the young summer squash plants. Picked early in the morning, the flowers are mixed into salads, minced and folded into compound butters, or, perhaps best of all, dipped in a simple fritter batter and fried, in almost exactly the same way that the Italians do. While Italians often stuff them with fresh ricotta or day-old mozzarella and a sliver of anchovy or prosciutto, they're usually not stuffed here in the South.

My grandmother's folks called them "poor man's fish"—she assumes because they were pan-fried in shallow fat, and ended up looking a bit like a flat fish fillet; otherwise, it made no sense because they lived at the headwaters of the Savannah River, where a mess of real fish cost a poor man nothing but time. But never mind: This is the South. Names that make no sense are part of our birthright.

1 dozen squash blossoms
4 ounces (1 light cup) all-purpose flour
Salt and whole black pepper in a mill
½ cup water or milk
1 large egg, separated

1. Gently clean the blossoms in water, drain well, carefully cut out the stamen. Set them aside while you make the batter.

2. Put the flour in a bowl with a pinch of salt and a light grinding of pepper. Lightly whisk to mix, then make a well in the center. Add about half a cup of water and the egg yolk and whisk until the batter is smooth. It should be fairly thin, but not too thin—like a good crepe batter

or rich heavy cream. If it seems too thick, whisk in a little more water.

3. Using a clean whisk and a copper or stainless-steel bowl, whisk the egg white until it forms soft peaks. Stir a little of it into the batter to soften it, then gradually fold in the remaining white.

4. Preheat the oven to 200°F. Put enough oil into an enameled Dutch oven or deep skillet to cover the bottom by at least an inch, but no more than halfway up the sides. Over medium heat bring it to 350–365°F. One at a time, dip the blossoms in the fritter batter and slip them into the fat. Fry, turning once or twice, until they are golden brown. Blot briefly on absorbent paper then transfer to a wire cooling rack set over a baking sheet. Keep them in the warm oven while you fry the remaining blossoms. Sprinkle lightly with salt and serve hot.

STRAWBERRIES

Strawberries, that fragrant, luscious herald of spring-time, have always figured prominently on the Southern table. Though commercially produced berries are available almost year round, the only ones really worth bothering about are the ones we pick ourselves, in season, from local fields, or from wild beds. For days afterward, our kitchens are fragrant with kettles of jam and preserves simmering on the back of the stove, but we always hold back some of the ripest and sweetest berries to smother with real cream or tuck into a rich, buttery shortcake.

You don't need a recipe to make the best strawberry dessert ever devised by men or gods: Just pick the sweetest and ripest berries, wash and core them, and put them into individual serving bowls; put some good cane sugar into a caster for each person to sprinkle over them to taste, and pass with it a pitcher of thick, heavy cream or a bowl of Crème Fraîche (page 18).

Strawberry Shortcake   SERVES 4

This quintessentially American dessert is usually made with shortcake, a biscuit-like quick cake, but here is another traditional version that uses a rich, buttery shortbread instead.

We Southern cooks are true believers in the power of pecans to lift a dish over the edge from good to incredible. They improve just about anything that they are added to. Here, they lend not only a crispy Southern twist, but nicely complement the subtle, tart-sweet flavor of the berries.

1 pint ripe strawberries
Sugar
8 (2½-inch) Pecan Shortbread cookies (next page)
1 cup Cold Cream Sauce (page 47) or 1 cup lightly sweetened cream, whipped to soft peaks
Whole nutmeg in a grater
1 tablespoon finely julienned lemon zest

1. Wash the strawberries, then stem and core them. If you are not serving the shortcake right away, pat the berries dry and set them aside. Just before you plan to serve the shortcake, thinly slice the strawberries and lightly sprinkle them with sugar. How much sugar you use will depend, of course, on how ripe and sweet the berries are.

2. Place four of the shortbread cookies on individual serving plates. Spoon a thick layer of strawberries over each cookie, reserving about ½ cup of berries. Spoon about 2 tablespoons of the cold cream sauce (or whipped cream) over each and top with the remaining four cookies. Spoon the remaining strawberries over the top cookies, top this with another spoonful of cold cream sauce or whipped cream. Sprinkle the tops with a few gratings of nutmeg or julienned lemon zest (or both) and serve at once.

Note: *You can make shortbread using any berries that are in season—raspberries,*

blackberries, or blueberries. In season, we Southerners love to make it with sliced ripe peaches, either by themselves or mixed with any of the above-mentioned berries.

Pecan Shortbread

MAKES ABOUT 20 COOKIES

Scotch shortbread has long been a favorite Southern confection, but when we mix our native pecans into the dough, it loses its Scottish brogue and takes on a real drawl. Not only does it make a great base for Strawberry Shortcake (previous page), it's superb just on its own.

⅔ cup demerara or turbinado sugar
10 ounces (2 cups) unbleached all-purpose flour
Salt
1 cup finely chopped pecans
½ pound (1 cup) unsalted butter, softened

1. Position a rack in the center of the oven and preheat the oven to 325°F. Pulverize the sugar until the granules are very fine, either in a mortar and pestle or in a blender or food processor fitted with a steel blade.

2. Sift the sugar, flour, and a small pinch of salt together into a mixing bowl. Mix in the pecans and then work the butter into the dry ingredients until a smooth dough is formed. You can do this in a food processor, pulsing until the dough just forms, but be careful not to overprocess it.

3. Pinch off a small handful of the dough and lightly roll it into a ball between your hands. Place the ball on an ungreased cookie sheet and lightly press it flat into a 2-inch-diameter round, either with the palm of your hand or with a patterned cookie stamp. Repeat with the remaining dough, spacing the cookies about 1 inch apart, until all the cookies are shaped.

Bake in the center of the oven until the cookies are lightly browned on the edges, about 25 minutes. Transfer the cookies to a rack to cool.

Fresh Strawberry Soup   SERVES 4 TO 6

At the Strawberry Street Cafe in Richmond, a seasonal favorite is a mildly sweet clear soup made from its namesake berry. Unlike most American strawberry soups, which are usually very thick with dairy products and have more in common with a smoothie than soup, it's light and refreshing and really allows the flavor of the berries to shine through. This is my own take on it.

2 large juice oranges
1¼ pounds fresh, ripe strawberries, washed
1¾ cups water
Salt
About ½ cup of sugar
1 teaspoon ground cinnamon
1–2 teaspoons freshly grated ginger (to taste, see step 2)
½ cup unsweetened heavy cream, whipped to firm peaks
4-6 small mint sprigs

1. Remove the zest from one of the oranges in fine julienne with a bar zester, or remove it with a vegetable peeler and then julienne it. Wrap eight to twelve strands in plastic wrap and refrigerate them to use as garnish. Put the remaining zest in the bowl of a blender or food processor fitted with a steel blade. Halve and juice both oranges through a strainer into the machine.

2. Set aside two to four of the smallest, nicest strawberries for garnish. Stem and core the remainder and add them to the machine. Add the water and a small pinch of salt, cover, and blend until smooth. Taste and add sugar as needed, the cinnamon, and 1 teaspoon of

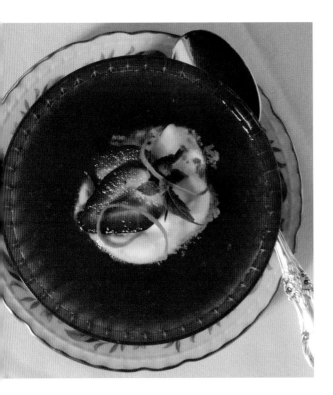

once popular on this side of the Atlantic, too, and ought to be popular again.

1 pint strawberries
Sugar
2 tablespoons bourbon
Freshly grated zest of one orange
1 cup heavy cream (minimum 36 percent milk fat)
4 sprigs fresh mint

1. Wash the berries and set aside four small, nicely shaped ones for garnish. Stem and core the remaining berries and cut them into thick slices. Sprinkle lightly with sugar—how much will depend on how sweet the berries are already—the bourbon, and the orange zest. Cover and set them aside to macerate for half an hour.

2. Mash the berries to a pulp with a potato masher. (Don't use a blender or food processor; both machines do too good a job and liquefy them.)

3. In a separate bowl, beat the cream until it forms soft peaks. Gently fold in the strawberries until the mixture is uniform. Spoon the fool into stemmed glasses. Thoroughly chill the fool for at least 1 hour. Just before serving them, garnish the tops with the sprigs of mint and reserved berries.

ginger. Pulse to blend, taste, and adjust the sugar and ginger. Transfer to a glass bowl, cover, and refrigerate for at least 4 hours.

3. To serve, halve or slice the reserved berries, leaving a little of their green tops attached. Ladle the soup into serving bowls, garnish with a dollop of whipped cream, the berries, reserved zest, and mint.

Strawberry Fool SERVES 4

This isn't what you're thinking it is: the word "fool" can actually mean several things other than one of your in-laws or a member of an opposing political party. In this case, it's an ancient English dessert—a simple, luscious confection of whipped cream and tart fruit similar in concept to a classic Bavarian cream. It was

Strawberry Ambrosia SERVES 6

This is an old Florida twist on the classic Southern fruit salad that Florida oranges have helped to make famous. Many people don't realize that oranges are seasonal in Florida—but they are. As their season wanes, vast fields of strawberries begin to ripen. Here, the berries replace the oranges, though the salad is doused with fresh orange juice to give it sweetness and zip.

The berries go mushy if they sit in sugar and acidic juice for very long, so the salad can't be made more than an hour ahead.

1 small fresh coconut (see note)

1 medium ripe pineapple (about 3½ pounds)

2 quarts (about 2 pounds) ripe strawberries

Sugar

2 cups fresh orange juice

Orange liqueur, such as Cointreau or Grand Marnier

1. Drain, crack open, and remove the meat from the coconut as directed on page 269 (step 1). Reserve any juice. Coarsely grate the coconut meat with a box grater and set aside. Peel, core, and cut the pineapple into bite-size pieces. Wash and core the strawberries.

2. Put a layer of strawberries in the bottom of a glass bowl that will comfortably hold all the ingredients. Lightly dust them with sugar and a thick layer of grated coconut. Cover the coconut with a layer of pineapple. Repeat with the berries, sugar, coconut, and pineapple until all of them are in the bowl.

3. Combine the orange juice and reserved coconut juice, if there is any. If you like, you may spike the juices with a few tablespoons of orange liqueur to taste—but don't overdo it; too much alcohol gives the salad a harsh aftertaste. Pour the juices over the ambrosia and let it macerate for 30 minutes to an hour. Serve cold.

Note: *You may use unsweetened frozen or unsulfured shredded coconut (available in natural-food stores), though the salad is at its optimum when you use fresh coconut. If the nut doesn't have any juice in it, make sure that it has a clean, fresh coconut smell before using it.*

Strawberry Salad with Spring Greens and Green Vidalia Onions with Warm Bacon Dressing SERVES 4

An unfortunately common element of the many community cookbooks in the South during the 1950s and '60s was molded gelatin "salad"—usually consisting of a slab of raw vegetables and or fruit encased in flavored gelatin plopped onto a lettuce leaf and topped with a dollop of mayonnaise. An especially popular spring version of these jellied wonders was made with strawberries. Fortunately, that's not the only way that strawberries turn up on a Southern salad plate.

Spring may come early to the South, but it can be just as unpredictable and changeable as it is in the rest of the country. This salad reflects that, blending the bright, refreshing flavors of spring berries, greens, and onions with the heartier, warming flavors of bacon dressing and cheese.

6 ounces (about 6 lightly packed cups) mixed spring greens (such as arugula, baby beet greens, baby lettuce, frisée, lamb's tongue, baby spinach and radish greens) or "spring mix"

16–20 ripe strawberries (depending on size)

2 medium green Vidalia Sweet Onions or other green onions

4 slices extra-thick cut bacon, cut crosswise into ¼-inch-wide lardons

½ cup pecans

2 teaspoons Dijon-style mustard

2 tablespoons late-harvest Riesling vinegar, sherry vinegar, or Raspberry Vinegar (page 169)

Salt and whole black pepper in a mill

About 1 teaspoon sugar (optional, only if using sherry or raspberry vinegar)

12–24 fresh mint leaves

1. Wash the greens and spinach and drain well. Pat them dry with a clean towel or dry in a salad spinner. Wash, stem, and thickly slice the strawberries. Wash and trim away the root and any withered greens from the onions and thinly slice them. Separate any larger slices into rings (sometimes green Vidalias have fat bulbs). Put the greens, berries, and onion in a large salad bowl and lightly toss to mix.

2. Cook the bacon in a heavy-bottomed skillet over medium heat until it is browned and its fat is rendered. Remove it with a slotted spoon and drain on paper towels. Add the pecans and toss until they are lightly toasted and beginning to color (they'll get darker as they cool, so take them off the heat before their color deepens too much). Remove them with a slotted spoon and drain on paper towels.

3. Turn off the heat and spoon off all but 2 tablespoons of the fat. Let the drippings cool slightly. While they're still quite warm, whisk in the mustard, vinegar, a large pinch of salt, and a liberal grinding of pepper. Taste and add sugar if needed: The dressing should be slightly sweet, but not syrupy. Pour the warm dressing over the greens, toss well, then tear the mint leaves into several pieces and add them. Sprinkle the pecans and bacon over the salad, gently toss, taste, and adjust the salt, pepper, and sugar.

4. Divide the salad among four salad plates or bowls and serve immediately.

Summer

TOMATOES, OKRA, AND RIPE GEORGIA PEACHES

Nothing equals a Southern summer. It arrives early, while spring is lingering in the rest of the country, and stays late, like a visiting relative who won't take the hint and go home. It comes to us full of fresh promise, so bright and bubbling with the happy memories of past fun that we forget its past indiscretions. But then it lingers, wearing out its welcome—and us in the process. Summer is our longest season, stretching from late April until well into October, and it is at once the South's blessing and curse.

For a while the long stretch of warm, moist weather means a prolonged growing season and plenty of easy, outdoor living, it turns ruthless with boiling heat and cloying humidity. When at long last the weather breaks, the cool air of autumn is welcomed with the hope that summer will never happen again. Yet, even as the season passes, we're already looking forward to it coming back again.

In a Southern summer, everything explodes with the intensity of the heat; the colors, smells, and flavors of summer are as brilliant as the sun that beats down on us. The gentle greens and subtle, fresh flavors of spring give way to richer, more dazzling colors and more voluptuous and complex flavors. It is the season when the Southern table truly comes into its own, for while the flavors and colors intensify and become more complex, the recipes become simpler and more direct, not only in response to the heat, but to the fact that it does not take much in the way of art to make things taste good.

It's probably not surprising, then, that summer is the time when vegetables take the forefront on Southern tables. A summer vegetable garden is still a fixture in many Southern households, including urban ones. Even Savannahians and Charlestonians grow tomatoes, herbs, and often a few hot peppers or beans in their courtyard gardens. Where there's a patch of land, no matter how poor and unpromising that land may be, a Southerner will plant things in it.

Often we Southerners become what I call accidental vegetarians; though the vegetables may be seasoned with salt pork or accented with butter, cream, or bacon fat, we may go for days without actually having a meat main dish on the table. We don't usually miss it, either—who would?—with all the sweet corn, fresh okra and tomatoes, succulent squash and eggplant, tender field peas and snap beans, spicy peppers, cooling cucumbers and mellow Vidalia onions, not to mention peaches, fresh blackberries and blueberries, watermelons, cantaloupes, and cherries.

The final ironic joke that summer plays on Southerners is that when the heat is its worst that we are forced inside to stand over steaming kettles, for when vegetables and fruit are most plentiful and flavorful is when they have to be put up for the winter—in relishes and pickles to give summer spice to winter meats, or in jams, jellies, and conserves to bring some of the taste and sunshine of summer to a cold, gray winter morning. It's a job we curse as the sweat rolls down our nose and back, but bless later on when we open that first jar of peach chutney or okra pickles.

TOMATOES AND OKRA

Perhaps nothing from Southern gardens speaks more of summer than does the union of fresh tomatoes with okra. The bright, sunny tartness of the tomatoes is at once underscored and mellowed by okra's more subtle, earthy musk. The combination is a classic and one of the essential pillars of Southern cooking; from it, dozens of dishes derive, from thick summer vegetable soups to Creole gumbos. However, the significance of the combination goes beyond its universality. It is an enduring symbol of the Southern culinary melting pot, in which okra, native to Africa, and tomatoes, which are native to Central America, are brought together in an essentially European kitchen by an African cook.

That it was an African hand and imagination that first put the two together there can be little doubt; many historians believe that tomatoes were introduced to West Africa by the Portuguese and were already assimilated into African cookery when the slaves were brought to North America. Well, regardless of who or how, the result is pure genius.

Stewed Tomatoes and Okra   SERVES 4

When okra and tomatoes are cooked together in the South, the okra is usually cut up into thick slices and stewed with the tomatoes for a very long time. The result is like a thick gumbo. Here, the tomatoes undergo a brief preliminary cooking, then young, tender okra pods are added whole to the pot and cooked briefly. Less of the mucilaginous juice escapes into the tomatoes, resulting in a lighter and fresher flavor and texture.

2 tablespoons bacon drippings, unsalted butter, or extra-virgin olive oil

1 small yellow onion, peeled and chopped

2 large cloves garlic, peeled and minced

2 pounds fresh tomatoes, blanched, peeled, and

seeded as directed on this page, and coarsely chopped, about 2 cups, or 2 cups Italian canned tomatoes, chopped

1 Bouquet Garni (page 32), made with thyme and parsley

1 pound whole young okra, each no more than 3 inches long

Salt, cayenne, and whole black pepper in a mill

6–8 fresh basil leaves

4 cups Carolina-Style Rice (page 37)

1. Put the fat and onion in a deep, lidded skillet, and turn on the stove to medium high. Sauté, tossing frequently, until the onion is translucent and softened, about 5 minutes. Add the garlic and continue cooking until it is fragrant, about a minute more. Add the tomatoes and bouquet garni, and bring to a boil. Reduce the heat to low, cover the pan, and simmer, stirring occasionally to prevent sticking and scorching, for 20 minutes.

2. Meanwhile, wash the okra under cold running water, rubbing the pods gently to remove their fuzz. When the tomatoes have simmered for 20 minutes, raise the heat to medium and

add the okra. Season with a healthy pinch of salt, a small one of cayenne, and a liberal grinding of black pepper. Stir well and let it simmer, uncovered, until the tomatoes are thick and the okra tender, about 20 minutes more. Turn off the heat, and remove and discard the bouquet garni. Taste and correct the seasonings. Tear the basil into small pieces and stir them into the tomatoes and okra. Serve at once over cooked rice.

TO BLANCH, PEEL, AND SEED TOMATOES:

here are two ways to blanch the tomatoes. The first is to half-fill a large (at least 8-quart) pot with water and bring it to a boil over high heat. Wash the tomatoes and slip them into the boiling water. Let them cook for exactly 1 minute, then immediately lift them out with a frying skimmer or slotted spoon and rinse in cold water (or drop them in a basin of ice water) both to arrest the cooking and to help shock them so that they'll peel more easily. The second does the least heat damage to the outer surface of the tomatoes when you won't be cooking them further: Bring a large teakettle of water to a boil; put the tomatoes in a heatproof bowl and pour the boiling water over them until they're covered. Let them sit 1 minute, then drain and rinse under cold running water or plunge them into the ice bath. Fit a wire-mesh sieve over a large bowl. Holding the tomatoes over this, cut out the core (stem scar) and slip off the peelings, then half them crosswise and scoop the seeds out into the sieve.

ST. JOHN THE BAPTIST PARISH LIBRARY
2920 NEW HIGHWAY 51
LAPLACE, LOUISIANA 70068

A Creole Gumbo SERVES 8 AS A FIRST COURSE, OR 4 AS A MAIN COURSE

Here is one spot where every Southern cook stakes out his or her own territory and dares anyone to cross it. Though the essential ingredients of a good gumbo are pretty universal, there are as many variations on the theme as there are Southern cooks.

This recipe is my own take, based mainly on *The Picayune's Creole Cook Book* (1901), which for most of this century has been the primary sourcebook for all things Creole. Nowadays, many Louisiana cooks use a spice mix to season gumbo, and usually add the so-called Trinity of the Creole kitchen—onion, celery, and bell pepper. I've included a healthy dose of the latter, but I find that the sausages provide all the spice the gumbo needs.

1 stewing hen or roasting chicken (about 4 pounds)

2 tablespoons bacon drippings or unsalted butter

8 ounces andouille sausage or other spicy smoked sausage, such as kielbasa, sliced into ½-inch rounds

1 small yellow onion, peeled and chopped

2 ribs celery, including the leafy green tops, washed, strung, and chopped

1 large green bell pepper, stemmed, cored, and seeds and membranes removed, chopped

2 large cloves garlic, lightly crushed, peeled, and minced

2 pounds fresh tomatoes, blanched, peeled, and seeded as directed on page 101, and coarsely chopped (about 2 cups), or 2 cups Italian canned tomatoes, seeded and chopped

1 quart (4 cups) Chicken Broth (page 21) or water

1 Bouquet Garni (page 32), made with thyme, parsley, and 2 bay leaves

1 whole pod cayenne or other hot pepper

1 pound whole young okra, each no more than 3 inches long

Salt

4 cups Carolina-Style Rice (page 37)

1. Wash the chicken under cold running water and pat it dry. Disjoint it as you would for frying. Warm the fat in a 7- to 8-quart, wide, heavy-bottomed stockpot or enameled iron Dutch oven over medium-high heat. Add the chicken and brown it on all sides. Remove it and add the sausage. Sauté, tossing frequently, until the sausage is browned. Remove the sausage and spoon off all but 3 tablespoons of the fat. Add the onion, celery, and bell pepper. Sauté until they are translucent and softened, about 5 minutes. Add the garlic and sauté until fragrant, about a minute more.

2. Add the tomatoes, broth or water, the bouquet garni, and the whole hot pepper pod. Bring to the boiling point and return the chicken and sausage to the pot.

3. Meanwhile, wash the okra under cold running water, rubbing gently to remove their fuzz. Cut off the stem ends and discard them. Slice the pods crosswise into ½-inch rounds and add them to the pot. When the liquids begin boiling, add a healthy pinch of salt.

4. Reduce the heat to low, stir well, and loosely cover. Let simmer until it is very thick and the chicken is tender, about 1½–2 hours.

5. Remove and discard the bouquet garni and whole pod of pepper. Remove the chicken, skin it, and take the meat off the bones. Roughly chop the meat and return it to the pot. Taste and correct the seasonings, and simmer until the chicken is heated through. Serve hot over cooked rice.

Note: *For meatless gumbo, omit the bacon fat, sausage, and chicken, and double the amount of onion, celery, and bell pepper. Begin by making a dark roux with ½ cup each flour and peanut oil. Put the oil and flour into a heavy-bottomed skillet (preferably cast iron) over medium heat. Cook, stirring frequently at first and constantly once it begins to color, until the flour turns a rich, dark red-brown. Take care not to scorch it (it will smell burned if this happens). Add the onion, celery, and bell pepper to the roux and stir until they are wilted, then add the garlic off the heat. Transfer the mixture to a soup kettle and proceed with step 2, adding 1 tablespoon of Seafood Boiling Spice (page 28) and a shot of Worcestershire sauce. You can also make a seafood-sausage gumbo by substituting 1 pound (headless weight) of shrimp and 1 pound of crab for the chicken. Peel the shrimp and make a stock with the shells by simmering them in a quart of water for about 1 hour. Strain, discarding the shells, and use this stock instead of chicken broth. Add the shelled shrimp and crab just before serving the gumbo, and simmer until the shrimp are pink and just cooked through, about 5 minutes.*

Ma Ma's Vegetable Soup   SERVES 8 TO 10 (ABOUT 6 QUARTS)

When the first pot of vegetable soup filled my grandmother's kitchen with the heady, mingled perfume of freshly gathered tomatoes, okra, butterbeans, and corn simmering together, I knew that summer was finally here. To this day, that smell brings on grateful memories of no school, bare feet, and lazy afternoons reading a good mystery.

If any one thing has marked my life as a cook, it has been the unfulfilled effort to reproduce that soup. My mother and I have both stood over Ma Ma as she cooked—and she has stood over us, telling us exactly what to do—and we still haven't been totally successful. Whatever it was that she brought to it—instinct, experience, or just vibrations—we never could imitate. My first printed attempt in *Classical Southern Cooking* only brought a smile to Ma Ma's lips and a gentle shake to her head. It was good; it was close even— but no, it wasn't right. Now that she is gone, the quest has become even more poignant.

4 ounces salt pork in 1 slice

2 pounds meaty beef shanks

3 quarts water

2 cups (about 2 medium) peeled, chopped onion

1 cup (about 3 ribs) thinly sliced celery

1 cup (about 2 large) peeled, chopped carrot

2½ pounds tomatoes, scalded, peeled, seeded, and chopped as directed on page 101, with their juice (about 4 cups)

2 cups fresh or frozen butterbeans, preferably speckled

1 pound potatoes, peeled and diced (about 2 cups)

2 cups (tightly packed) thinly sliced green cabbage

½ pound (about 1 cup) trimmed, strung, and sliced pole beans

3 cups thinly sliced okra (about 1½ pounds)

¾ pound turnips, peeled and diced (about 2 cups)

¾ pound yellow summer squash, washed and diced (about 2 cups)

Salt and whole black pepper in a mill

1 tablespoon sugar

2 cups corn kernels freshly cut from the cob (3 to 6 ears) or 2 cups good-quality frozen shoepeg corn

1. Put the salt pork in a heavy-bottomed 8-quart soup pot over medium-high heat. Sauté until the pork is well browned and most of the fat is rendered from it. Remove the pork and add the beef shanks. Brown them well on all sides and then slowly pour the water over them. Bring the liquid to a boil and then reduce the heat to a slow, steady simmer. Simmer, uncovered, for 2 hours. The liquid should be somewhat reduced—by about a quarter of its original volume. (This can be done 2-3 days ahead. Cool, cover, and refrigerate the broth until you are ready to finish the soup.)

2. Remove the beef and set it aside to cool. Raise the heat to medium high and bring the liquid to a boil. Add the onion and let the water return to the boiling point, then add the celery. Let the liquid come back to a boil, add the carrot, and let the water return to a boil again. Simmer for 10 minutes.

3. In the same manner add the tomatoes, butterbeans, potatoes, cabbage, pole beans, okra, turnips, and squash, allowing the liquid to come back to a boil between each addition. When all the vegetables are in the pot, remove the meat from the shank bones, chop it, and add it back to the soup. Season with a couple of healthy pinches of salt, a very generous grinding of black pepper, and the sugar. Reduce the heat to a very slow simmer and let the soup simmer, uncovered, for 2 hours; even longer won't hurt it.

4. Twenty minutes before serving, add the corn, taste and correct the seasonings, and simmer until the corn is tender, about 20 minutes longer. Serve hot with Corn Sticks (page 34).

Note: *The soup can be made in stages. Simmer the meat for the broth one day, do the vegetables the next day, and serve the soup several days later. It's a wonderful standby to have in the fridge for quick suppers. If you are making it ahead, however, especially in hot weather, note that the soup should be cooled and refrigerated*

as quickly as possible. Let it cool, uncovered, until you can touch the sides of the pot, then fill the sink with ice and water, set the pot in it, and stir until the soup is completely cooled. Cover and refrigerate promptly.

Fresh Okra and Tomato Salad

SERVES 4

One of my favorite summer snacks is a handful of small, raw okra pods—with nothing on them, not even salt and pepper. When very young, small, and tender, okra has a delicate flavor that is incomparable—and contrary to what you might expect if you've ever chopped or sliced this vegetable for a gumbo, they're not in the least gooey, but are crisp and as refreshing as a chilled cucumber. Whenever I'm shopping for them, I always buy more than I'll need because I know I'll end up eating a good bit of it before it can make it into the pot.

This affection for raw okra is nothing unique or new, and I got it honestly: Following an old family tradition, my mother used to mix cut raw okra into our summer salads. Raw okra also turns up on the table just about everywhere that this lovely vegetable is known and enjoyed.

Okra is also a great addition to a tray of crudités: Choose pods no longer than 2-3 inches long, wash, pat dry, and trim the stems but leave the caps intact. Serve them with your favorite dipping sauce as you would broccoli florets or carrot, celery, and cucumber sticks.

4 extra-thick-cut slices bacon, cut crosswise into ¼-inch-wide lardons

8 Romaine or Bibb lettuce leaves

4 small ripe heirloom tomatoes or 1 pint ripe cherry or grape tomatoes (see note)

16 small pods fresh okra, less than 3 inches long (red or green or a mix, see note)

½ small Vidalia Sweet or red onion, stem and root ends trimmed, split lengthwise and thinly sliced

10–12 large basil leaves or ⅓ cup (not packed)
   mint leaves

1 small clove garlic

Salt

1 tablespoon red wine vinegar

1 teaspoon Dijon mustard

2 tablespoons fruity extra-virgin olive oil

Whole black pepper in a mill

1. Cook the bacon lardons in a heavy-bottomed pan over medium-low heat until golden and crisp. Remove them with a slotted spoon and drain them on paper towels. Wash the lettuce leaves under cold running water and spin dry. Wash and dry the tomatoes; if using heirloom varieties, cut out the core (stem end) and quarter them (they shouldn't need to be peeled); if using cherry or grape tomatoes, cut them in half. Trim the stem end of the okra, wash it under cold running water, and pat dry.

2. Tear the leaves in bite-size pieces into a large salad bowl. Add the onion and tomatoes. Cut the okra in half lengthwise and add it to the bowl. Tear the large basil leaves into small bits; if using mint, tear only the large leaves, leaving smaller ones whole. Scatter the herbs over the salad. Add the bacon lardons.

3. Lightly crush the garlic clove with the side of a knife blade, peel, and chop it. Sprinkle a little salt over it and, with the edge of the knife blade, rub it to a puree. Scrape this into a small mixing bowl and add the vinegar and mustard to it. Whisk until smooth, then slowly whisk in the oil a few drops at a time. Taste and adjust the salt and seasoning with a generous grinding of pepper. Pour the dressing over the salad and toss until it is glossy and evenly coated. Divide among individual salad bowls and serve immediately.

Note: *When I was growing up, and even as late as this book's first publication in the 1990s, the only okra available to us was green. Now bright red and purple okra are turning up in local farmers' markets. Though they lose their vivid color when cooked, they're ideal for using raw in salads. Likewise, heirloom tomatoes are turning up in our gardens and markets in a rainbow of colors—purple, yellow, pink, and green; mixing them into this salad makes it as lovely to look at as it is to eat.*

Grilled Okra Salad with Tomato Vinaigrette SERVES 4

If you are put off by the idea of eating okra, this salad is a good way to warm up to this vegetable. The salad is a great side dish for a grilled main course, since the grill will already be fired up. The recipe comes from Jackie Mills, who I met while she was a food editor at *Southern Living* magazine. Jackie eventually moved north, but I'm happy to say that her accent and her cooking stayed down South.

Jackie brings to her work a forward-looking creativity that is tempered by a solid sense of tradition. Here, for example, the okra and tomato combination is given an unexpected and unconventional twist. First, each vegetable gets separate treatment: The okra is marinated and grilled; the uncooked tomato is tossed in a typically Southern mustardy and tart vinaigrette. Finally, the two are combined on a bed of mixed salad greens.

The tomato vinaigrette is good with other grilled vegetables, or cold boiled green beans, or asparagus. You can make it ahead, but don't add the basil until just before serving or it will turn dark and lose its fresh flavor.

1 large lemon

1 teaspoon minced garlic (1 large or 2 small cloves)

1 teaspoon salt

Whole black pepper in a mill

2 teaspoons Dijon mustard

¾ cup extra-virgin olive oil

2 dozen young pods of okra, each no more than 3 inches long

¼ cup fresh basil

¾ cup (1 large) tomato, peeled with a vegetable peeler, halved, seeded, and diced

8 cups mixed salad greens, washed and torn into small pieces

1. Grate the zest from the lemon and put it in a bowl along with the garlic, salt, a few liberal grindings of black pepper (to taste), and the mustard. Halve the lemon and squeeze the juice into the bowl through a strainer. Whisk until smooth and then slowly whisk in the oil a few drops at a time.

2. Wash the okra under cold running water. Make a slit down two sides of each pod without cutting all the way through either end. Put the okra in a shallow dish that will hold it in one layer. Pour ¼ cup of the vinaigrette over it, toss, and let it marinate for 1 hour.

3. Meanwhile, prepare a grill with coals. When they are ready, spread them and put the rack about 2 inches above the coals. Drain the okra and lay them on the rack. Grill them, turning frequently, until they are well browned on all sides, about 3–5 minutes.

4. While the okra is cooking, thinly slice the basil leaves and add them to the remaining vinaigrette base. If the emulsion has separated (this often happens), beat it until it is thick and smooth, then add the diced tomato. Remove the okra from the grill to a shallow bowl and toss it with ¼ cup of the vinaigrette.

5. Put the mixed greens in a salad bowl and pour half the remaining vinaigrette over them. Toss until they are coated and then divide them among individual salad plates, mounding them to one side. Arrange the okra pods in a fan pattern on the other side of the plate, overlapping the greens with them, and pour the rest of the vinaigrette over the okra. Serve at once.

GUMBS—A WEST INDIAN EVOLUTION

Cooking is an ever-evolving process; recipes are never static, but undergo subtle changes as each cook takes ingredient and method into the kitchen and makes them his own. Nowhere was this pointed out to me better than when Karen Hess, the eminent culinary historian who was my teacher and mentor, gave me a recipe for okra for this book. It was her own version of a recipe from Mary Randolph's *The Virginia House-wife* (1824). Though faithful to the method and intent of Mrs. Randolph's recipe, it was marked by Mrs. Hess's distinctive touch. When I started to work with the recipe, I realized that I was doing the same thing. Mrs. Hess understood, and told me, "You may attribute it, as you please, to this Yankee interloper. Whatever. It is now yours." The only way to demonstrate this evolution is to give you all three versions.

Gumbs—A West India Dish   SERVES 4

"Gather young pods of ocra, wash them clean, and put them in a pan with little water, salt and pepper, stew them until tender, and serve them with melted butter. They are very nutricious and easy of digestion."

—Mary Randolph, *The Virginia House-wife*, 1824

Mrs. Hess elaborates: "There may be other ways of fixing okra, but none simpler and none better than that. Mrs. Randolph's name for the dish would seem to reflect what was thought to be its origin; perhaps her cook had come as a slave by way of the West Indies. That it calls for butter indicates that it had already been adapted for the gentry.

"I have very little to add, except to emphasize that the okra must be of impeccable freshness, just gathered, as she says. No amount of cooking will make overgrown okra tender. Neither top nor tail them. My only departure from her recipe is to add a good splash of best olive oil along with very little water, and, of course, sea salt and several twists of the peppermill, both to taste. Cook them in a very heavy pot, covered, for no more than four or five minutes over a high flame. The result is lovely pods of okra that retain their shape and color, bathed in a light silken sauce of wonderfully subtle, haunting flavor, a flavor that is rarely permitted to star on its own.

"On no account should the sauce be allowed to dry up, although you do not want the okra to be swimming in it either. After a time or two, you will know exactly how you like it. Naturally, if

you prefer, you may serve them with melted butter, as Mrs. Randolph suggests, but we prefer the
olive oil, partly because we love them at room
temperature the next day, when the flavor has
deepened somewhat, and for that olive oil is best.
Nicely presented, it is a very pretty dish that
admirably illustrates what might be called the
elegance of simplicity and would grace any buffet, or serve as a first course." —Karen Hess, 1996.

1½ pounds very fresh okra pods, each no more
   than 2 inches long
1 large clove garlic, lightly crushed and peeled
   (optional)
2 tablespoons extra-virgin olive oil
Salt and whole black pepper in a mill

1. Wash the okra under cold running water, gently
rubbing it to remove the fuzz that coats the outside of the pod. Leave the pods whole; don't trim
off the tops or tips.

2. Put them into a heavy, lidded skillet or sauté
pan that will hold them all in one layer. Add ¼
cup of water, the optional garlic, 1 tablespoon of
oil, a liberal pinch of salt, and a few grindings
of black pepper. Cover the pan then turn on the
heat to high. Cook for 3 to 4, and no more than
5, minutes, until the okra pods are crisp-tender
but still bright green. Do not let the sauce dry
up or allow the okra to brown.

3. Pour the okra into a shallow serving bowl,
remove and discard the garlic, drizzle with the
remaining olive oil, toss well to coat it, and
serve warm or at room temperature.

Note: *Garlic with okra is consistent with the
dish's African roots. However, if garlic and
olive oil bother you, or you are being a strict
traditionalist, don't use the former and substitute
unsalted butter for the latter. Don't add the
butter until the end of step 3, when you've taken
the okra from the heat, shaking the pan until it is
just melted into the sauce. You can also just omit
the fat—the okra is still delicious without it.*

Fried Okra   SERVES 4 TO 5

If you want to make a homesick Southerner stop
whining, put a dish of hot fried okra in front of
him. This is a favorite in Savannah, not only at
the dinner table but in the parlor during cocktail
hour as well. There are many variations on the
basic theme, but this version is still my favorite.
It will work only if the okra pods are very fresh,
very young, and no more than 2 inches long.

5 dozen young okra pods, each no longer than
   2 inches
2 eggs
1 cup all-purpose flour
1 cup cornmeal or fine cracker crumbs
Lard or vegetable oil, for frying
Salt and whole black pepper in a mill

1. Fill a heavy-bottomed 4-quart pot with water
and bring it to a boil over high heat. Rinse the
okra, drain, and when the water is boiling, add
a small handful of salt and slip the okra into the
pan. Let it come back to a boil and cook 2 minutes; the okra should still be crisp and bright
green. Quickly drain it into a colander and refresh
it under cold running water. The okra can be
blanched a couple of hours ahead.

2. Fit a wire cooling rack into a rimmed baking sheet. Position a rack in the upper third
of the oven and preheat to 150–170°F (or
the "warm" setting). Break the eggs into a
wide, shallow bowl, and lightly beat until well
mixed. Put the flour in a similar bowl. Spread
the cornmeal or cracker crumbs out on a large
plate or piece of waxed paper. Put enough fat
in a deep iron skillet, enameled iron Dutch
oven, or a deep, nonstick pan to come up the
sides by at least ½ inch (but no more than
halfway up the sides) and turn on the heat to
medium high.

3. When the fat is very hot (about 375°F), a few pods at a time, roll the okra lightly in the flour, shake off the excess, and dip them in the eggs until coated. Lift out each pod, holding it over the bowl to allow the excess egg to flow back into the bowl and quickly roll it in the cornmeal or crumbs, making sure that it is thoroughly coated. Shake off the excess and slip the okra into the fat.

4. Fry quickly until golden on all sides, about 3–5 minutes, turning once if necessary. Lift them out of the fat with a frying skimmer, letting them drain until they no longer drip fat, lay them on the prepared cooling rack, and keep them in the warm oven while you repeat with the remaining okra. Sprinkle liberally with salt and a few grindings of black pepper, and serve at once.

Paulo's Okra   SERVES 4

South Georgia native Wendell Brock has covered a lot of territory over the course of more than three decades of writing as a news journalist, theater and restaurant critic, and global travel writer, but his real passion is cooking, especially that of his native South. While traveling in Brazil on assignment, he was delighted to find that Brazilian and Southern cooking had a lot in common, due in large part to a common link with West Africa. One of those parallels is a shared love of okra, which happens to be Wendell's favorite vegetable.

An old South Georgia way of cooking okra is to cut it crosswise, dust it with a little cornmeal, and brown it with bacon drippings in a hot, well-seasoned cast iron pan, a dish Wendell had cut his teeth on. So, when his Brazilian friend Paulo tossed sliced okra into a hot pan and browned it with a little garlic and olive oil, he felt right at home. To this day, it is still a favorite in his kitchen.

1 pound fresh young okra, each pod no more than 3 inches long

1 tablespoon olive oil

1 tablespoon finely chopped garlic

Salt and whole black pepper in a mill

1. Wash the okra, gently rubbing it under cold running water, and drain well. Have all the ingredients ready before proceeding. Trim the caps and slice the okra lengthwise.

2. Warm the olive oil in a heavy-bottomed skillet over medium-high heat. Add the okra and cook, tossing often, until it is beginning to color—about 2 minutes. Sprinkle in the garlic and continue cooking until the okra is browned and tender—about 2–3 minutes longer. Wendell likes to let the okra really caramelize to a handsome deep brown, and advises to watch the pan, not the clock. Season to taste with salt and pepper, toss well, and turn off the heat. Serve warm or at room temperature.

Bill Neal's Pickled Okra   MAKES 6 PINTS

Pickled okra isn't an especially old dish, but it has become a standard hors d'oeuvre at virtually every Southern cocktail party (try one in your next martini instead of an olive) and picnic. This is Bill Neal's recipe (from *Bill Neal's Southern Cooking*), which is easy to make, as typical of most pickled okra, and virtually identical to my mother's, with its healthy dose of garlic and dill.

My eldest niece, Erica, was literally weaned on Mama's okra pickles and became addicted to them as a toddler. Mama never failed to bring a jar when she came to visit, and Erica's mother soon learned that this offering couldn't be put out of her daughter's reach. No matter where she hid it, Erica would find it and usually have the jar half-empty before she was caught. Almost 20 years later, it warmed my heart to watch Erica's own daughter put pickled okra away with equal enthusiasm. Expect to have the same problem with your own pickles.

2½ pounds young okra pods, each no more than 3 inches long

6 cloves garlic

6 large sprigs fresh dill or 6 teaspoons dill seeds

12 whole small red pepper pods, preferably cayenne

3 teaspoons whole mustard seeds

48 black peppercorns

5⅓ cups distilled white vinegar

3¾ cups water

3 tablespoons sea salt, kosher salt, or pure pickling salt

1. Sterilize 6 pint-size canning jars and new canning lids (page 11) and let them air-dry. Don't touch the insides of the jars after you have sterilized them. Wash the okra under cold running water, rubbing it gently to remove the fuzz. Trim off most of the stems but leave the caps intact. Using clean tongs, pack the okra into the jars, first cap down and then caps up, so that they nest against one another. Add 1 clove garlic, 1 sprig of dill (or teaspoon of seeds), 2 pepper pods, ½ teaspoon mustard seeds, and 8 peppercorns to each jar.

2. Combine the vinegar, water, and salt in a stainless pan, and bring it to a boil over high heat. Divide the pickling brine among the jars, leaving a full ½ inch of headroom at the top of each jar. Discard any leftover vinegar-water solution. Don't overfill the jars.

3. Seal the jars with the lids and rings, and process in a boiling water bath for 5 minutes (see pages 10–12 for detailed canning instructions). Remove with tongs and set them—not touching—on folded kitchen towels. Cool completely and store for 6–8 weeks to allow the pickles to mature before using them. Store any jars that do not seal in the refrigerator and use them up within 2 months.

Tomato Aspic with Herb Mayonnaise   SERVES 6

When my first cookbook, *Classical Southern Cooking*, was published, I began to get letters listing things that I'd "forgotten" to include. Tomato aspic, a velvety congealed salad that is very popular in the South, was on every one of those lists. One woman wanted to know how I could even have thought of publishing a book on Southern food with so egregious an omission. The explanation that I had run out of space and had left it out on purpose because it didn't need rescuing, since it is still popular in the South, fell on deaf ears.

Tomato aspic is generally made with canned tomatoes or tomato juice, and is most popular during that in-between season when the weather is warm but fresh tomatoes are not yet ripe. We serve it as a first course for formal meals—traditionally, ladies' luncheons and that long-gone Southern institution, the midday dinner. To this day I think it looks a little out of place on anything but old floral china. Well, old-fashioned though it may be, it's still a fine starter for any luncheon, brunch, or formal dinner.

Fellow Southern cook and historian Marcie Ferris tells with combined mortification and amusement of the day she realized that despite spending a lifetime exploring and defending her native Southern foodways, she had partly failed her own children in their culinary education. It was at a wedding reception on a sultry summer afternoon when one of her children pointed to a tray of tomato aspic served in bite-size cubes on lettuce leaves and exclaimed "Look, Mom! Ahi tuna!"

Don't let that happen to you.

1 (28-ounce) can Italian tomatoes packed with basil or 4 cups canned tomato puree

2 tablespoons (2 envelopes) unflavored gelatin (see note)

¼ cup cold water

½ cup boiling water

¼ cup grated yellow or Vidalia onion

¼ cup finely minced celery

¼ cup chopped cucumber

1 tablespoon finely chopped celery leaves

1 tablespoon finely chopped fresh basil (do not use
  dried basil)

2 tablespoons fresh lemon juice or wine vinegar

Ground cayenne pepper or hot sauce

6 romaine or Boston lettuce leaves, washed and
  drained

½ cup Herb Mayonnaise (page 44)

2 tablespoons chopped fresh basil or chives, for
  garnish

1. If you are using whole tomatoes, seed them and strain their juice to catch any seeds that may be left behind. Put the strained juice and the tomatoes in the bowl of a blender or food processor fitted with a steel blade and puree until smooth.

2. Soften the gelatin in the cold water in a large mixing bowl for 10 minutes. Pour the boiling water over it and stir until the gelatin is completely dissolved. Stir in the tomato puree, making sure that the gelatin is completely mixed in. Add in the onion, celery, cucumber, celery leaves, basil, and lemon juice or vinegar. Season to taste with a pinch or two of cayenne or a few shots of hot sauce and mix well.

3. Rinse out 6 small molds or ramekins or one 2-quart mold with cold water and pour in the aspic. Cover the molds with plastic wrap and refrigerate until set, about 4–6 hours (keep in mind that the big mold will take longer) or overnight.

4. To serve the aspic, arrange lettuce leaves on individual serving plates or, if you are using a large mold, a platter. Unmold the aspic by dipping the mold in hot water for a few seconds. Slip a knife around the edge to break the vacuum in the mold and invert it over the lettuce leaves. Give the mold a gentile tap. The aspic

should slip right out. If it doesn't, dip it again in hot water. Top each serving with a dollop of mayonnaise and sprinkle with the chopped basil or chives, or if you've used a large mold, sprinkle the chopped herbs over the aspic and pass the mayonnaise separately.

Note: *Basil and tomatoes are a classic combination, but if you like, you can experiment with other herbs, or use chopped green onions instead of yellow ones. In that case, use canned tomatoes that don't have basil in them. As to other seasonings, I've given you free rein with the hot pepper, but don't overdo it. The idea here is to keep cool.*

Though there is no meat here, this is not a vegetarian dish, since commercial gelatin is made from animal products. If you are cooking for a conscientious vegetarian, agar flakes (a gelatin made from seaweed, available at health food stores and Asian markets) can be used instead of commercial gelatin, and, in fact, makes a more delicate aspic. Here's how: Place 3 tablespoons of agar flakes in a saucepan with the water and ½ cup of the tomato juice. Bring it to a boil over medium heat, stirring constantly, and cook until the flakes are completely dissolved, about 2-3 minutes.

Tomato Sherbet in Avocados

SERVES 6

Here are the ingredients of a classic tomato aspic again—but with a twist. Instead of setting the puree with gelatin, it's whirled together with seasonings and dressing and frozen into a luscious sherbet. It would be an appropriate first course for any meal but is especially nice with a fish or shellfish dish that doesn't contain tomatoes.

In case you are wondering, this isn't some clever nouvelle idea: the recipe that follows is based on one from Henrietta Stanley Dull's 1928 classic *Southern Cooking*.

2 cups tomato puree (see note)

¼ cup grated onion

¼ cup finely chopped celery, including a few leaves

2 cloves garlic, crushed, peeled, and finely minced

1 tablespoon finely chopped fresh basil, plus 6 whole sprigs for garnish

1 small cucumber, peeled and chopped fine

2 lemons, cut in half

Salt and cayenne pepper

1 tablespoon Worcestershire sauce

1 cup Homemade Mayonnaise (page 44)

3 ripe avocados

1. In a large mixing bowl, mix together the tomato puree, onion, celery, garlic, basil, cucumber, and the juice of one of the lemons. Season with a healthy pinch or so of salt, a pinch of cayenne to taste, and the Worcestershire sauce. Stir in the mayonnaise and beat until smooth. Cover and refrigerate until chilled, at least 2 hours or overnight.

2. You can freeze the sherbet in an ice-cream freezer, following the manufacturer's directions for your freezer. Or pour the mixture into a shallow pan, cover with plastic wrap, and put it in the freezer. When the mixture is frozen solid (about 4 hours), break it up and put it in the bowl of a food processor fitted with a steel blade. Whirl it until it is fluffy, but don't over-process it and let it get slushy. Pour it back into the freezing container and freeze until solid, about 1 hour more.

3. Chill individual serving plates for at least half an hour before you plan to serve the sherbet. Just before serving, split each avocado lengthwise and remove the pit. You can peel the avocados, if you like, but that isn't necessary. Slice off a little of the rounded side of each half avocado so that it lies flat. Squeeze a little lemon juice over them to prevent discoloration, and place them on the chilled plates, pit side up. Fill the pit cavity of each with a scoop of the sherbet, garnish with basil leaves, and serve at once.

Note: *You can use fresh tomatoes for the puree, but only when they are really good and truly vine ripened. You'll need 2 pounds of tomatoes (3 or 4 large ones) for 2 cups of puree. Blanch, peel, and seed them as directed on page 101, then puree them through a food mill or in a blender or food processor. If the fresh tomatoes at your disposal are not perfectly ripe and sweet, use canned tomatoes as for Tomato Aspic (page 110).*

Tomato and Vidalia Onion Salad SERVES 4

If you ask Savannahians for a recipe using Vidalia Sweet Onions, chances are they will give you a variation on one of two dishes—whole onions baked in a microwave and this salad. Both have become summer standards.

Savannah has long had a large and influential Greek community, so it is no real surprise that this salad should have a distinctly Greek flavor. It's rather substantial, almost a meal in itself, especially when served with crisp buttered toast triangles or, for a really Southern flavor, with hot Corn Sticks (page 34).

4 medium ripe tomatoes

2 medium Vidalia or other sweet onions

12 brine-cured black olives (Greek or Kalamata)

12–20 fresh basil leaves, depending on size

½ cup (2 ounces) crumbled feta cheese

Salt and whole black pepper in a mill

Wine vinegar or freshly squeezed lemon juice

Extra-virgin olive oil

8 buttered toast triangles or Corn Sticks (page 34), optional

1. Peel the tomatoes with a vegetable peeler, core them, and cut them into slices about ⅓-inch thick. Spread them on a platter or divide them among 4 individual salad plates.

2. Trim off the root and stem ends of the onions and peel them. Cut them crosswise into the thinnest possible slices and separate them into rings. Spread the rings over the tomatoes.

3. Pit the olives and slice them into thin strips. Tear all but the smallest of the basil leaves into several pieces. Scatter the olives, basil, and feta over the tomatoes and onions. Season with a liberal pinch of salt and several generous grindings of pepper. Sprinkle sparingly with vinegar or lemon juice, and then drizzle olive oil generously over all. Serve at once with toast points or corn sticks, if you like.

BLT (and O) Salad   SERVES 4

When I was a very small boy, my grandmother and I would get all dressed up—she in high-heeled pumps, hat, and gloves, I in Sunday shorts and oxfords—and go downtown to shop. An invariable part of these adventures was lunch at the Woolworth's lunch counter. I, who at the time lived in a place called Grassy Pond, thought we were being so sophisticated. I no longer remember what my grandmother ordered on those occasions, but my choice never varied: A BLT on toast. I loved it then and unapologetically love it now.

It's not without reason that the BLT became a diner standard: It's easy and good. Since basically a BLT is a salad between two slices of toast, I didn't see why my old favorite, with its classic combination of flavors and textures, would not be just as good on a salad plate, especially with a bit of Vidalia onion thrown in.

4 medium ripe tomatoes

2 medium Vidalia or other sweet onions

8–12 romaine lettuce leaves, washed and well drained

½ cup Homemade Mayonnaise (page 44)

Salt and whole black pepper in a mill

1 cup Buttered Croutons (page 37)

8 slices bacon, fried crisp

1 tablespoon chopped fresh chives or parsley

1. Peel the tomatoes with a vegetable peeler, core them, and cut them into ½-inch slices. Cut the slices into dice and put them in a salad bowl. Split the onions lengthwise. Trim off the root and stem ends, peel them, split each half lengthwise, and then slice into thin strips. Cut 4 of the lettuce leaves into bite-size pieces. Add the lettuce and onions to the tomatoes.

2. Add the mayonnaise to the salad bowl along with a generous pinch or so of salt and a few liberal grindings of pepper. Toss until the vegetables are evenly coated. Taste and correct the seasoning, but don't overdo the salt, as there's still a salty element that will be added by the bacon.

3. Line four individual salad plates with the remaining lettuce leaves. Add the croutons to the salad, give it one last toss, and divide it among the prepared plates. Crumble the bacon evenly over the top of each, sprinkle with herbs, and serve at once.

Southern Minted Gazpacho   SERVES 8

With an abundance of tomatoes and hot weather, it was inevitable that the South should heartily embrace this cool, uncooked Spanish salad-soup. It has been a summer standby at least since Mary Randolph, who probably learned of it from a sister who lived, for a time, in Gibraltar, first published a recipe for it in *The Virginia House-wife* in 1824.

A good gazpacho should have plenty of texture. Those baby-food versions where everything is ground up in a blender are never as interesting as one in which the ingredients are cut by hand. It does take time, but you have to peel the vegetables anyway and cut them into manageable chunks before you can puree them in a machine. It's worth the extra few minutes it takes to finish cutting them down to size by hand.

This is a basic recipe; you can go in all kinds of directions from here. Dress it up with sour cream, spice it up with fresh hot pepper, or take it uptown with chopped boiled shrimp and crabmeat. What you cannot do is use canned tomatoes.

4 pounds fresh, ripe tomatoes

1 large yellow onion, preferably Vidalia Sweet

2 medium cucumbers

2 medium green bell peppers

2 limes or lemons or ¼ cup red wine vinegar

½ cup extra-virgin olive oil

Salt and whole black pepper in a mill

Hot sauce or ground cayenne pepper or 1 fresh green hot pepper

1 cup firm white bread, cut into small cubes, or crumbled hard biscuits (see note)

2 tablespoons chopped fresh mint or basil

½ cup sour cream, optional

1. Holding a knife blade perpendicular to the skin of each tomato, scrape the entire surface of the fruit until the skin begins to wrinkle. Core the tomato and pull the skin off with your fingers. It should slip right off. Position a wire sieve over a bowl. Cut the tomatoes in half, holding them over the sieve to catch all their juices. Scoop out the seeds into the sieve and let the juice drain into the bowl. Roughly chop half the tomatoes and put them in a large glass or ceramic bowl. Put the remaining tomatoes and their reserved juice in a blender or food processor fitted with a steel blade, and puree them to the consistency of bottled tomato juice. Add this to the chopped tomatoes.

2. Trim the root and stem ends of the onion, halve it lengthwise, and peel it. Cut it into very small dice and add them to the tomatoes. Lightly peel the cucumbers and cut them into dice the same size as the onion. Add them to the tomato and onions. Slice off the top (stem end) and bottom of the bell peppers, remove the core and seeds, and trim off the membranes. Cut the peppers in half and lay them flat on a cutting board, then slice them into thin strips and cross-cut the strips into dice. Add them to the bowl.

3. Squeeze the juice from the limes or lemons through a strainer and add it (or the vinegar) to the bowl along with the olive oil, a healthy pinch or so of salt, a few liberal grindings of pepper, and a shot or so of hot sauce (or a small pinch of cayenne or the fresh hot pepper, seeded, and chopped). Stir until well blended. Cover and let it stand at room temperature for at least 2 hours or refrigerate it overnight.

4. If it has been refrigerated, an hour before serving take it out and let it sit at room temperature. Just before serving, taste and correct the seasonings. To serve it, put a few of the bread cubes or crumbled hard biscuits in each soup bowl. Ladle the gazpacho over it and let it stand for a few minutes to allow the bread or biscuits to soften. Garnish each serving with the herbs and, if you like, a dollop of sour cream.

Note: *In Latin America, the traditional herb for gazpacho is cilantro, and you could substitute it for the mint, but add it before marinating rather than at the end. Now that Uneeda Biscuits are no longer made, you may have trouble finding hard crackers like them. Look for Latin American or Italian hard crackers such as gallette del marinaio.*

Stewed Tomatoes à la Creole

SERVES 4 TO 6

Stewed tomatoes have been a Southern classic for more than two hundred years. Here, they get the full Creole treatment—with lots of fragrant herbs and a healthy dose of garlic.

Southern stewed tomatoes are often thickened with soft bread crumbs, usually crumbled stale breakfast biscuits. In the Lowcountry, they're usually served over rice instead. If you prefer the bread-crumb approach, add ½ cup (about 2 small biscuits) crumbled stale biscuits or homemade-type white bread in step 3 after the tomatoes have simmered for 15 minutes.

2 pounds fresh, ripe tomatoes (don't use canned tomatoes)

2 tablespoons bacon drippings or unsalted butter (see note)

1 medium yellow onion, peeled and chopped

2 large cloves garlic, peeled and minced

1 tablespoon chopped fresh thyme or 1 teaspoon dried thyme

1 tablespoon chopped parsley

1 whole pod hot red pepper

Salt

8–10 whole fresh basil leaves

1. Blanch, core, and peel the tomatoes as directed on page 101. Cut them into quarters. Over a sieve set in a bowl to catch all the juices, seed them and then add them to the bowl with their juices.

2. Put the bacon drippings (or butter) and chopped onion in a deep, heavy-bottomed pan (preferably cast iron) over medium heat. Sauté, tossing often, until the onion is translucent, about 5–8 minutes. Add the minced garlic and continue sautéing until fragrant, about half a minute more.

3. Add the tomatoes and their juices, thyme, parsley, hot pepper pod (left whole), and a healthy pinch of salt. Bring the tomatoes to a boil, reduce the heat to medium low, and loosely cover. Simmer, stirring occasionally, until the tomatoes are tender and beginning to fall apart, about 30 minutes.

4. If there is still a lot of liquid in the pan, uncover and raise the heat to medium high. Let it boil rapidly until the excess liquid has evaporated and the tomatoes are thick. This should take no more than 2 minutes, so don't turn up the heat and/or get distracted by something else. Turn off the heat and stir in the basil. Taste and correct the seasonings, and serve hot.

Note: *Bacon drippings lend this the most authentic taste, but many old recipes called for butter, so you can substitute butter and still be within the bounds of history. But if you don't care about that, you may, as I often do, use a fruity extra-virgin olive oil.*

Spanish Tomatoes   SERVES 4 TO 6

How and why this traditional mélange of tomato, pepper, and onion came to be called "Spanish" is lost in time, although it bears more than a passing resemblance to the *salsa criolla* that is found throughout the Spanish-settled Caribbean and North and Central America. In the South, it goes back at least to the mid-nineteenth century, and Savannah's celebrated Leila Habersham taught it in the cooking school that she opened just after the War Between the States. In the old recipes, everything was sautéed in batches, and the whole thing was baked. Today, the preparation is more streamlined, and the flavor, while not as concentrated, is fresher. Its secret is to use only good, ripe tomatoes and fresh, seasonal bell peppers.

In Savannah, it was served with rice, but it also makes a fine side dish for just about any poultry, pork, or fish.

2 pounds fresh ripe tomatoes

2 tablespoons bacon drippings, unsalted butter, or olive oil

1 large or 2 medium green bell peppers, stem, core, seeds, and membranes removed, thinly sliced

1 large Bermuda or yellow onion, trimmed, split lengthwise, peeled, and thinly sliced

Salt and ground cayenne pepper

Sugar

1. Blanch, core, and peel the tomatoes as directed on page 101. Over a sieve set in a bowl to catch the juices, cut them into thick wedges and scoop out the seeds. Add them to the bowl with their juices.

2. Warm the fat in a large frying pan over medium heat. Add the peppers and onions and sauté, tossing, until the onion is translucent and softened and the pepper is bright green, about 4 minutes. Add the tomatoes and their collected juices and bring to a boil. Sprinkle lightly with salt, and a dash of cayenne. Cook until the juices are evaporated and thick and the tomatoes are tender, about 20 minutes. Taste and adjust the seasonings, adding a pinch or so of sugar if needed to bring up the natural sweetness. Let it simmer half a minute longer, and turn off the heat. Serve warm.

Savannah Stuffed Tomatoes   SERVES 4

In our part of Georgia, late tomato plants are often producing fruit right into December, so our tomato recipes will sometimes have an autumnal touch, as does this one with its pairing of late tomatoes with the season's first pecans. It comes from *The Savannah Cook Book* (1909), an early charity cookbook produced by the ladies of Westminster Presbyterian Church.

4 medium ripe tomatoes (about 2 pounds)

Salt

½ cup bread crumbs

½ cup chopped Roasted Pecans (page 209)

1 tablespoon chopped parsley

Whole black pepper in a mill

1 large egg

Unsalted butter, for greasing

1. Position a rack in the center of the oven and preheat it to 350°F. Wash the tomatoes and slice off the stem ends so that all the seed cavities are exposed. Set the stem ends aside. Carefully scoop out the seeds and discard them. Lightly salt the tomatoes and invert them in a colander to drain.

2. Put the crumbs, pecans, and parsley in a mixing bowl. Season with a healthy pinch of salt, a few generous grindings of pepper, and toss until the ingredients are uniformly mixed. Break the egg into a separate bowl and lightly beat it until the yolk and white are well mixed. Add it to the crumb-and-nut mixture and stir until the egg has been absorbed into the crumbs.

3. Pat the tomatoes dry and fill the seed cavities with the crumb mixture (if there is a little excess, mound it on top). Replace the reserved stem ends over the top of each tomato like a lid. Lightly butter a 9-inch square casserole or a pie plate and put the tomatoes into it. Put the dish on the center rack of the oven. Bake until the tomatoes are tender and the tops are beginning to wrinkle and brown, about 45 minutes.

Note: *This is an ideal accompaniment for any game dish that does not contain tomatoes and is also good with pork and roasted chicken or turkey. The whole secret is to use good tomatoes and fresh pecans. Unfortunately, the latter aren't universally available. If the pecans available where you live taste heavy and a touch rancid, don't use them. English walnuts or pine nuts make an acceptable substitute.*

Though the original recipe didn't call for it, 1/4 cup chopped country ham is a welcome addition to the stuffing.

Fried Green Tomatoes   SERVES 6

There was a time when a certain so-called progressive element of Southern society was embarrassed by the whole idea of fried green tomatoes. Breaded in cornmeal and fried in bacon drippings, they were considered too countrified, folksy, and unsophisticated, and were relegated to the backwoods. Mind you, smart Southerners weren't bothered by all that and kept right on eating them. But ever since Fanny Flagg's lovely Fried Green Tomatoes at the Whistlestop Cafe was made into a motion picture, fried green tomatoes are not only fashionable, they are the one Southern vegetable dish that everyone knows about. It's not a bad dish to be known by, either.

In some parts of the United States, fried green tomatoes are made only in the fall with the last of the crop, plucked from the vines before the first frost kills them off. However, throughout the South, we start frying as soon as the vines produce the first fruit.

4–6 medium very green tomatoes

Sugar

Salt and whole black pepper in a mill

2 large eggs, lightly beaten in a shallow bowl

1 cup all-purpose flour

1 cup fine-ground white cornmeal

1 cup bacon drippings or a mixture of vegetable oil and drippings

1. Cut out the stems of the tomatoes and cut them crosswise into slices at least ⅜-inch thick. Don't peel them. Sprinkle them very lightly with sugar and salt, and lay them flat in one layer on a platter or rimmed baking sheet for at least half an hour. Meanwhile, break the eggs into a shallow bowl and beat them lightly until well mixed, spread the flour and meal in similar bowls, and have them all ready by the stove.

2. Wipe the tomatoes well with a cotton kitchen towel or paper towels. There should be no sugar remaining on them at all. Season them lightly with salt and a few grindings of pepper. Roll each slice one at a time in flour, shake off the excess, and dip both sides in the eggs, letting the excess drain back into the bowl. Roll them quickly in the meal, gently shake off the excess, and lay them on a clean plate or wire cooling rack. Let them sit for at least 15 minutes so that the breading can set.

3. Preheat the oven to 150–170°F (or the "warm" setting), and fit a wire cooling rack into a rimmed baking sheet. Put the fat into a well-seasoned deep iron (or nonstick) skillet and turn on the heat to medium. When it is hot but not smoking (around 365°F), slip the tomato slices into the pan. Fry until golden on the bottom, about 3 minutes, then gently turn with a spatula and continue cooking until both sides are golden. Lift them out with tongs or a frying skimmer, letting them drain until they no longer drip, then lay them on the prepared cooling rack and keep them in the warm oven while you cook the next batch. Repeat until all the tomatoes are fried. The tomatoes cannot be reheated so serve them at once.

Note: *The classic taste can only be had with bacon drippings, but vegetarians can use peanut oil instead, as it comes closest to producing the right crispness, though of course the flavor is in no way the same.*

The sugar is not intended to add sweetness to the tomatoes, but only to help remove the bitterness that some green tomatoes have. It should in no way interfere with the tartness of the tomatoes or make them taste sweet, so use only the very lightest sprinkling, and be sure you wipe it thoroughly from the slices before breading them.

Braised Green Tomatoes SERVES 4

Braising may not be as traditional a cooking method for green tomatoes as frying them, but it's a lovely way to prepare them. Their bright tartness is mellowed in the process, but it doesn't go completely away, so they are especially nice with just about any fish, and are also lovely with roasted or grilled meat or poultry.

2 pounds medium green tomatoes (about 5–6)

4 extra-thick slices bacon, preferably applewood smoked, cut crosswise into ¼-inch-wide lardons

1 large yellow onion, trimmed, split lengthwise, peeled, and thinly sliced

1 large clove garlic, lightly crushed, peeled, and minced

1 tablespoon chopped fresh thyme leaves, or chopped summer savory or sage (don't use dried)

Salt and whole black pepper in a mill

1. Wash the tomatoes under cold, running water, cut out the stem, and cut them vertically into thick wedges. Pat dry.

2. Fry the bacon in a large sauté pan or lidded skillet over medium heat, tossing often, until it is browned but not crisp and its fat is rendered. Remove it with a slotted spoon. Spoon off all but 2 tablespoons of the fat and add the onion. Sauté, tossing often, until pale gold, about 5 minutes.

3. Add the tomatoes and sauté, tossing often, until they are lightly browned, about 4 minutes. Sprinkle the garlic and herbs over them, return the bacon to the pan, and season lightly with salt and liberally with pepper. Cover, reduce the heat to medium, and braise, shaking the pan occasionally to prevent scorching, until the tomatoes are tender but still in distinct wedges, about 10–15 minutes. Taste and adjust the seasoning, toss once more, and turn off the heat. Serve hot or at room temperature.

Note: *There really is no substitute for bacon in this recipe, so for a meatless version, go for a brighter, fresher flavor and don't even try to imitate the bacon. Substitute 2 tablespoons of olive oil for the bacon drippings and add a dash or so of Worcestershire, Thai fish sauce, or for vegans, omit the salt and season with soy sauce.*

Grilled Green Tomatoes SERVES 4

Ripe tomatoes are an old favorite to put on the grill, and they are a classic accompaniment to grilled beef. Green tomatoes also take well to grilling, and their bright, tart flavor lends a pleasant accent to any grilled meat, poultry, or fish. You can also do this recipe under an oven broiler, though it will not have as much flavor.

2 large green tomatoes

Salt and sugar

2 tablespoons bacon drippings, melted, or olive oil

Ground cayenne pepper and whole black pepper in a mill

1. Wash the tomatoes and split them in half crosswise. Sprinkle them lightly with salt and the tiniest pinch of sugar. Invert them in a colander and let them stand in the sink for 30 minutes.

2. Prepare a charcoal fire (preferably hardwood) or preheat the broiler. When the fire is ready, wipe the tomatoes thoroughly and brush them with the bacon drippings or oil. Sprinkle with a little more salt, a small pinch of cayenne, and a few grindings of black pepper.

3. Put the tomatoes on the grill, cut side down (or under the broiler cut side up), and grill until the cut side begins to brown, about 5–8 minutes. Turn them cut side up and brush with more drippings or oil (if you are using the broiler, turning them won't be necessary, but watch to make sure they don't get too brown). Grill until tender, another 8–12 minutes, and serve hot.

Green Tomato Pie

MAKES ONE 9-INCH PIE (ABOUT 6 SERVINGS)

In the nineteenth century, when a tariff was levied on vegetables, a heated debate arose over whether tomatoes were a vegetable or a fruit—until a federal judge silenced the debate by ruling that they were a vegetable. Well, federal decrees notwithstanding, tomatoes are botanically speaking a fruit, and at one time they were frequently used as such in American cooking.

This typical, very old Southern favorite comes from a little-known, early postbellum cookbook, *Verstille's Southern Cookery* (1866), by Mrs. Ellen J. Verstille. Green tomato pies could be as simple as this one, or as elaborate as a mincemeat pie.

1 full recipe Basic Pastry (page 39)
4–6 medium green tomatoes
1 cup sugar
2 tablespoons cornstarch
1 lemon

1. Position a rack in the center of the oven and preheat the oven to 375°F. Divide the pastry into two equal parts. Roll out one half to a thickness of about ⅛ inch. Line a 9-inch pie plate with the pastry, prick it in several places with a fork, and let it rest in the refrigerator for half an hour.

2. Meanwhile, thoroughly wash the tomatoes, core them, and cut them crosswise into thin slices. Put them into a colander set in the sink for half an hour or so to drain. Put the sugar and cornstarch in a medium-size bowl and whisk them until they're evenly mixed.

3. Grate the zest from the lemon, then cut the lemon in half and squeeze out the juice into a separate bowl through a strainer. Gently press the tomatoes to remove their excess moisture; otherwise they will make a very soupy filling.

4. Sprinkle the prepared pastry shell generously with the sugar and cornstarch and put a layer of tomatoes over it, completely covering the pastry. Sprinkle the tomatoes with the sugar and cornstarch, lemon zest, and a little of the lemon juice. Repeat with another layer of tomatoes, sugar, zest, and juice until they are all used up.

5. Roll out the remaining pastry dough and lay it over the pie. Trim off the excess pastry, seal the edges by crimping or fluting them, and make several slashes in the top pastry. Put the pie onto a large, rimmed baking sheet and bake in the center of the oven until the pastry is evenly browned and the filling bubbly, about 45 minutes.

THREE SOUTHERN TOMATO SAUCES

We tend to think of tomato sauce as Italian, but rare is the Southern kitchen without some variation of it. It's a common theme in all the different cuisines of the South—not just our South, but the whole geographical area, from Maryland to the Southwest, the Caribbean, and the whole of Latin America.

Tomato Sauce   MAKES ABOUT 2 CUPS

This sauce was originally intended mainly to dress up breaded veal or pork cutlets, though occasionally it was poured over poached eggs and omelets. Old cooks seldom used it to sauce vegetables, but modern Southern cooks know no such restrictions. This is a fine sauce for Quick-Cooked Young Green Beans (page 126), Fried Summer Squash (page 161), or Braised Leeks (page 66). It's also spectacular over pasta or Carolina-Style Rice (page 37).

The whole point of this sauce is the mellow flavor and aroma of fresh tomatoes, but it is good even when made with canned Italian plum tomatoes. When choosing fresh ones, the best for all sauces are the small, meaty Roma or plum tomatoes, but the heftier, juicier garden varieties, such as Beefsteaks or Better Boys, will also work fine, though they may take a little longer to thicken.

2 tablespoons unsalted butter

3–4 shallots or 1 medium yellow onion, peeled and chopped

1 small carrot, peeled and chopped

2 cloves garlic, peeled and minced

1¾ pounds fresh tomatoes, preferably Roma or plum, blanched, cored, peeled, and seeded as directed on page 101, and coarsely chopped, about 2 cups with their juices, or 2 cups canned Italian plum tomatoes, seeded and chopped

1 Bouquet Garni (page 32), made of celery, parsley, thyme, and 1 bay leaf

1 whole pod cayenne or chile pepper

Salt (optional, see step 2)

2 ounces lean salt pork or country ham in one piece
(¼-inch slice about 4 inches long, optional)

1. Put the butter, shallots or onion, and carrot in a saucepan that will comfortably hold all the ingredients and turn on the heat to medium. Sauté until the vegetables are softened but not browned, about 5 minutes. Stir in the garlic and cook until it is fragrant but not the least colored, about half a minute longer.

2. Add the tomatoes, bouquet garni, the cayenne pepper pod, and a small pinch of salt, or the salt pork or ham (omit the salt if using either). Bring the tomatoes to a boil and reduce the heat to medium low. Simmer, uncovered, until the sauce is very thick, about 1 hour (depending on how juicy the tomatoes are), stirring occasionally to be sure that the bottom doesn't scorch.

3. Turn off the heat. Remove and discard the bouquet garni, pepper pod, and meat, if you have used it. If you like, you can puree the sauce through the food mill (or in the blender), as was done in the old recipes, or you can leave it as it is. Serve warm.

SAUCE CREOLE:

Make the Tomato Sauce as directed above, adding a medium green bell pepper, stemmed, cored, seeds and membranes removed, and chopped, along with the onions and carrots in step 1. After the sauce has simmered for about 1 hour you may also stir in ¼ cup sherry and simmer until the sauce is thick again, about 10 minutes more. Just before serving, thinly slice 2 scallions or small green onions, stir them in, and let it simmer about 2 minutes longer.

Raw Creole Sauce (*Salsa Criolla Cruda*)   MAKES ABOUT 2 CUPS

There is a strong link between the old coastal cities of the American South and the islands of the Caribbean West Indies that goes back to the early days of the slave trade right through to the slave uprisings of the late eighteenth century that forced French Huguenot planters to flee the islands for Charleston, Savannah, Mobile, and New Orleans. Perhaps nowhere is that link better felt than in the kitchen, and in none more so than in the Carolina and Georgia Lowcountry.

This sauce is just one of many suggestive elements that are common to the whole region. It is the ubiquitous *salsa cruda* of the Caribbean and of all Latin America, and a close cousin to the spicy salsas of our own Southwest. In the Deep South, we used to call it Creole sauce. But as Southwestern cooking spreads eastward from Texas, and as Cuban-Floridian cookery heads north, the Spanish name is nowadays falling from the most Southern of lips.

1 large or 2 small to medium ripe tomatoes
(see step 1)

1 medium yellow onion or small Vidalia Sweet Onion

2 large cloves garlic

1 fresh hot green pepper (banana, jalapeño, or serrano)

1 tablespoon chopped fresh cilantro or parsley

¼ cup freshly squeezed lime juice or red wine vinegar

½ cup extra-virgin olive oil

Salt

1. Peel the tomatoes with a vegetable peeler, core, and split them in half crosswise. Remove and discard the seeds and chop the pulp. You should have ¾ cup. Put it into a large glass or stainless-steel bowl.

2. Trim the root and stem ends of the onion, split lengthwise, and peel it. Chop it fine and add it to the tomatoes. Crush, peel, and mince the garlic. Cut off the stem end of the hot pepper and split it lengthwise. Remove and discard the seeds and connective membranes, and mince the hot pepper. Add it and the garlic to the tomato mixture. Add the herbs, lime juice or vinegar, and olive oil and toss until well mixed.

3. Let the sauce stand at room temperature for at least 15 minutes or as much as an hour, if you have time. Taste and add a pinch of salt—not too much, just enough to bring up the flavor. Toss well and serve at room temperature over fish, chicken, shrimp, or cold cooked green beans. It can also be used as a seasoning for cooked dishes. Spread it over raw vegetables (such as broccoli, leeks, squash, sliced sweet potatoes), or over fish steaks, filleted chicken breasts, or peeled raw shrimp, and steam them.

Note: *The flavor of fresh cilantro is an important element in Caribbean and Latin American cooking. Though less common in the South (at least, east of Texas and north of Florida), it is not completely unknown to traditional Southern cooking. Down here, people either love it a lot or think it tastes like soap. My advice is to use cilantro sparingly—too much really does taste like soap.*

In spite of the presence of chiles, this is not an especially hot sauce. Still, if you or someone in your family can't tolerate hot pepper, it is probably because of an allergy to the acid that makes the heat. Substitute ½ green bell pepper. If, on the other hand, the hot stuff really turns you on, you can double the amount of chiles, or use one of the really hot chiles such as habañeros or Scotch bonnets.

SUMMER BEETS

Beets are one of the nicest and loveliest of root vegetables—though not as prepared in all too many Southern households, boiled and embalmed as they all too often are in heavy sweet-sour pickling or, worse yet, doused with sugar and vinegar or dumped into molded salads. With such indifferent treatment, the wonder isn't that they aren't better liked, but that they are liked at all. Their earthy-sweet flavor is at its simple best baked and served with butter, salt, and pepper passed separately.

The green, leafy tops of beets are regretfully neglected in America, but when cooked just as their cousins chard and spinach are, they make a delicious green and are plain wonderful when substituted for poke sallet in Ma Ma's Poke Sallet with Spring Onions (page 81).

Nick's Beet and Orange Salad

SERVES 6 TO 8

Although we eat other root vegetables raw, we don't usually think of beets as a salad vegetable, except when they are cooked. But when young and tender, their crisp, sweet flesh is a lovely accent in mixed vegetable salads, and in this one, they're the main event. It's a perfect first course for a summer supper alfresco, or as a refreshing palate cleanser at the end of the meal.

The recipe is from Chef Nick Mueller, a born and bred Savannahian who is one of the city's most gifted and brilliant caterers. He's also one of its best kept secrets, because he doesn't have a restaurant in the city and never advertises. He doesn't have to: His brilliant cooking has made him one of Savannah's most sought-after cooks.

2 medium shallots

4 medium red beets

1 large navel orange

¼ cup orange juice reserved from sectioning the orange (see step 1)

2 tablespoons rice wine vinegar

1 tablespoon freshly grated ginger

Salt and whole black pepper in a mill

½ cup canola oil

1 tablespoon orange blossom honey (optional)

6–8 lettuce leaves

6–8 small sprigs mint

1. Peel and thinly slice the shallots. Put them in a small bowl, cover with ice water, and add a couple of lumps of ice. Scrub the beets under cold running water and, wearing latex gloves to protect your hands from the staining juice, peel them with a vegetable peeler and cut into thin julienne with a mandoline. Put them in a large glass serving bowl. Holding the orange over a glass bowl to catch the juice, peel and section it with a sharp knife as directed on page 269 (step 3). Add the orange segments to the beets.

2. Whisk together ¼ cup of the orange juice, the rice vinegar, ginger, and a pinch of salt. Gradually whisk in the oil, taste and season with pepper and add the honey if it doesn't seem quite sweet enough.

3. Drain and add the shallots to the beets and orange. Pour the dressing over the salad and toss until well mixed. Line six to eight salad plates with lettuce leaves. Toss the salad one last time and divide it among the plates. Garnish with mint and serve immediately.

VARIATION:

Golden Beet and Blood Orange Salad—In late spring, when blood oranges are still available and the golden beets are new and sweet, Nick likes to use them in this salad. They make a beautiful salad and the flavor is brighter and more distinctive. If you can get them where you live, by all means give them a try.

Baked Beets   SERVES 4

When the new beets are just coming in and are at their sweetest and juiciest, this is hands-down the best way to prepare them. Baking concentrates their natural sweetness and keeps all the flavorful juices inside the vegetable, where they belong.

4 medium beets, about 2 pounds
Unsalted butter
Salt and whole black pepper in a mill

1. Position a rack in the upper third of the oven and preheat the oven to 400°F. If the greens are still attached to the beets, cut them off but leave a little of their stems on. Set the greens aside to cook separately either as a vegetable on their own as for spinach, or mixed with spinach (page 76).

Scrub the beets well under cold running water, pat them dry, and trim off most of the taproot, leaving some of it attached to the beets. Do not peel them.

2. Rub each beet with a little butter and wrap each individually in foil. Place them on a cookie sheet or baking dish, and put them on the rack in the upper third of the oven. Bake, turning the beets occasionally, until they are tender, about 1 hour. They will yield slightly when pressed with your finger but will still be quite firm.

3. Unwrap the beets and quickly trim off the remaining stem and root ends. You can also slip off the skins if you like (wearing latex gloves to protect your hands from the staining juice), but the skins will be very tender and removing them isn't necessary. Serve the beets at once, passing more butter, salt, and freshly ground black pepper separately. Or let them cool completely and use them to make the following salad.

Baked Beet Salad   SERVES 4

As you can guess from the sharp words about them in the introduction to this section, I'm not crazy about most beet salads, which are often marinated in a dressing that's heavy with vinegar and sugar, but one bad salad shouldn't spoil the idea. The secret to a good beet salad is to keep the dressing light, and don't put it on the beets until you're ready to serve them.

4 Baked Beets (previous recipe)
1 large Vidalia or other sweet onion
1 large hard-cooked egg yolk
1 teaspoon Dijon mustard
2 tablespoons wine vinegar
Salt, sugar, and cayenne pepper
¼ cup extra-virgin olive oil

4–8 romaine or Boston lettuce leaves, washed and drained
1 tablespoon chopped parsley

1. When the beets have cooled completely, cut them crosswise into ¼-inch slices. Cut off the stem and root ends of the onion, peel it, and slice into the thinnest possible rings. Put the onion into a bowl of cold water with two or three ice cubes.

2. In a small mixing bowl, whisk together the hard-cooked egg yolk, mustard, vinegar, a large pinch of salt, and a small one of sugar until evenly mixed and smooth. Whisk in the oil, a drop at a time, until incorporated and emulsified. Taste for salt and sugar—keeping in mind that its flavor alone is more assertive than it will be when spread over the salad. Adjust the seasonings and add a small pinch or so of cayenne pepper. Whisk in the seasoning. The salad can be made to this point up to an hour ahead.

3. Just before serving, drain the onion and squeeze it dry. Line a platter or individual salad plates with the lettuce leaves and scatter the beets over them, then scatter the onions over the beets. Whisk the dressing again until it is smooth and pour it over the salad. Sprinkle with the chopped parsley and serve at once.

GREEN BEANS

Now here's a generic name to make you take to the bourbon. So-called green beans are the immature green pods of any member of the large family of legumes *Phaseolus vulgaris*, commonly known as kidney beans. There are many varieties, from French haricots and Italian cannellini to ordinary supermarket snap beans. Even though each variety has a distinctly different color, flavor, and texture, just as do their matured seeds, these distinctions are seldom marked when the beans come to market, let alone in recipes. They're just called "green beans."

this slop had no palate. Far from being offended by such culinary snobbery, Linda roared with laughter. Had she called it a "ragout" (which it essentially is) and compared it with its French cousin cassoulet, he'd probably have had a different attitude.

The only important point for success with this recipe is that you cannot slow-cook just any green bean. Use only broad, flat, thick-skinned pole beans for this recipe.

3 pounds pole beans

1 country ham hock or ½ pound country ham in 1 piece

1 small yellow onion, finely chopped

Salt and freshly ground black pepper

1 small Vidalia or other sweet onion, trimmed, split lengthwise, peeled, and diced, optional

Pepper Vinegar (page 25) or Pepper Sherry (page 24), optional

1. Wash the beans thoroughly in cold water and drain. Have ready a fresh basin of cool water. Top and tail the beans and strip off the woody "strings" that run down the seams of the pods. Be careful to remove all traces of these strings—they won't ever get tender. Break or cut the beans into 1-inch lengths and drop them into the basin of water.

2. Put the ham in a heavy-bottomed 4- to 6-quart pot over medium heat. Cook, turning frequently, until it has thrown off most of its fat. Add the onion and sauté until golden but not browned, about 5 minutes. Add about a pint of water and let it come to a boil. Lower the heat, cover, and simmer 30 minutes.

3. Raise the heat to high and bring the liquid back to a rolling boil. Drain and add the beans. If the water doesn't cover them, add more as needed. Let it come back to a boil, then reduce the heat to a bare simmer. Season with salt and pepper. Loosely cover and simmer for at least 1½ hours—longer won't hurt—until the beans are

Unfortunately, they are too often treated with indifference in the kitchen. This leads predictably to equally indifferent results—like skinny little snap beans slow-cooked to tasteless mush in salt-pork broth, or, conversely, tough pole beans (the slow-cooking variety) so underdone that you couldn't cut them with a chainsaw. The problem does not lie in the method but in its misapplication. There's nothing wrong with beans simmered slowly in an aromatic salt-pork broth; properly cooked, they are one of the South's culinary glories and perhaps the most satisfying vegetable dish on Southern tables. There will, however, be a lot wrong with this dish if you use the wrong kind of green beans. To that end, what follows are recipes that give each variety its appropriate treatment.

Southern Pole Beans SERVES 4 TO 6

This recipe has been largely misunderstood both without and within the South, making it the brunt of way too many rude jokes about Southern vegetables. When Linda Negro, a Southern-born colleague in Evansville, Indiana, was asked by an eminent chef to design an ideal menu, she included these beans. The chef turned up his elite nose and said that anyone who could down

1½ pounds young, thin, "stringless" green beans

Salt

2 tablespoons unsalted butter, softened

1. Wash the beans in several changes of water and drain well. Snap off the stem ends, but unless the individual recipe calls for them to be broken up, leave the beans whole.

2. Put 2 quarts of water in a heavy-bottomed 3- to 4-quart pot, cover, and bring to a boil over high heat. Add a small handful of salt and the beans. Cover until it comes back to a boil, then remove the lid and cook, uncovered, until barely tender, from 4–8 minutes, depending on the beans and your taste. Drain and toss with butter or serve in one of the following ways.

GREEN BEANS WITH SAVANNAH SWEET RED PEPPER SAUCE: As soon as the beans are cooked and drained, transfer them to a serving platter or divide them among individual plates. Spoon Savannah Sweet Red Pepper Sauce (page 46) over them and serve at once.

GREEN BEAN SALAD: Plunge the cooked, drained beans in ice water to arrest the cooking. Drain and serve with your favorite vinaigrette or the one for asparagus on page 53.

---

very tender. At this point, there should be very little liquid left. However, if there is, raise the heat to medium high and cook until most of the liquid has evaporated and been absorbed, stirring often to prevent scorching. Pour the beans into a warm vegetable dish.

4. I like these beans just as they are, but they're often served with chopped raw onion and pepper vinegar. Another once popular but now rare condiment for them is Pepper Sherry. If any of those appeal to you, pass them separately.

Quick-Cooked Young Green Beans

SERVES 4

Whether the beans are true French haricots verts or merely Blue Lakes (that ubiquitous supermarket variety), this is a good basic method of cooking them. Quick-boiled, young green beans can be served dozens of ways—from salads to savory gratins. The water must really boil—and hard—or the beans will lose their color and become flabby and uninteresting, especially if they are those generic supermarket beans.

Green Beans in Creole Sauce

SERVES 4

In this recipe the beans and the sauce cook together briefly, so that the sauce is absorbed into the beans and infuses them with flavor.

2 cups Raw Creole Sauce (1 full recipe, page 121)

1½ pounds Quick-Cooked Young Green Beans (page 126), cooked for 4 minutes (they should be very underdone)

Put the Creole sauce in a lidded skillet that will hold the beans in no more than two layers and turn on the heat to medium. When the sauce is bubbling, add the beans and toss well. Cover the pan and cook until the beans are just tender, about 4 minutes more. Remove the lid and raise the heat, allowing any excess liquid to boil quickly away. Turn off the heat, transfer the beans to a serving platter, and serve at once.

Creamed Green Beans   SERVES 4

This is a way of cooking green beans that gives new life to those that are not as fresh as you would like them to be. Before cooking the beans for this recipe, break them into bite-size lengths, which makes them easier to manage in the sautéing stage.

1½ pounds Quick-Cooked Young Green Beans (page 126), broken into bite-size lengths before cooking and cooked for only 2–3 minutes (they should be very underdone)

1 large shallot or small yellow onion, peeled and chopped

1 tablespoon unsalted butter, softened

1 cup heavy cream (minimum 36 percent milk fat)

Salt and whole white pepper in a mill

1. Rinse the cooked beans under cold running water to arrest the cooking and drain well.

2. Put the shallot or onion and butter in a large, heavy-bottomed pot over medium-high heat. Sauté, tossing frequently, until the onion is golden and beginning to brown, about 5 minutes.

3. Add the beans and toss until they're glossy. Pour the heavy cream over them, bring it to a simmer, and cook until the cream is thick and the beans are nicely coated with it, about 3–4 minutes more. Taste and add salt, if needed, and a few grindings of white pepper.

Young French Beans with Pecan Brown Butter   MAKES 4 SERVINGS

Pecans are nice to pair with green beans. Not only French haricots but any young, tender beans respond well to this recipe—even the ubiquitous supermarket variety.

1½ pounds Quick-Cooked Young Green Beans (page 126), cooked for about 4–5 minutes (they should still be quite underdone)

1 cup pecan halves

½ cup unsalted butter

Salt

2 tablespoons chopped parsley

1. The beans should still be underdone, so don't overcook them. Drain and plunge them in cold water to arrest the cooking. Let them rest while you slice the pecans lengthwise into three slivers per nut, using the natural grooves as a guide.

2. Melt the butter in a large cast-iron or heavy-bottomed nonstick skillet that will hold all the beans in a single layer over medium heat. Add the pecans and cook, swirling the pan constantly, until the pecans and butter are colored a uniform golden brown, about 3–4 minutes.

3. Add the beans and toss them with the butter until they are heated through, about 1 minute. Turn off the heat, taste, and add a pinch or so of salt, if needed. Add the parsley and toss once more to mix. Pour into a serving platter and serve at once.

Note: *There is no real substitute for the butter in this recipe, but if you are a strict vegetarian, try substituting ⅓ cup mild walnut or peanut oil. A tablespoon of marjoram, sage, or thyme can be substituted for the parsley to lend a brighter flavor, but be careful of strongly flavored herbs such as tarragon or rosemary. Basil also goes well with both beans and pecans, though the taste isn't traditionally Southern.*

New-Cut Plantation String Beans   MAKES 4 SERVINGS

This lovely recipe was first printed in the Charleston Junior League's now classic *Charleston Receipts* (1950). There is a bit of that notorious bacon here, yes, but the treatment the beans get is light and fresh—and delicious.

1 pound young "stringless" green beans or haricots verts
4 slices thick-cut bacon
6 small green onions, washed and thinly sliced
Salt and whole black pepper in a mill

1. Wash the beans in several changes of water and snap off the stem ends but leave them whole.

2. Put the bacon in a large, heavy-bottomed lidded skillet that will hold the beans in one layer. Over medium heat (uncovered), fry, turning frequently until it's crisp, about 10 minutes. Remove it from the pan and drain it on absorbent paper.

3. Add the onions to the pan and stir until they are just wilted. Add the beans and toss until they are glossy. Cook for 1 minute, then add a large pinch of salt and ¼ cup of water. Tightly cover and steam for 3 minutes. Uncover and cook until the moisture is evaporated and the beans are just tender, about 2-3 minutes more. Turn off the heat, taste, adjust the salt, and add a few grindings of pepper. Transfer to a warm serving plate and crumble the bacon over the top. Serve at once.

Dilly Beans   MAKES 6 PINTS

This old Southern favorite is prepared the same way as Bill Neal's Pickled Okra (page 109) and contains virtually the same ingredients.

If you like to make your own pickles, you'll love these. They are shamefully easy to make and even easier to eat. Try them on the relish tray at your next cocktail party, pass them as a cold relish with dinner, or mix them into a green salad.

3 pounds very young green beans (no more than 3 inches long)
6 cloves garlic
6 large sprigs of fresh dill or 6 teaspoons dill seeds
6 whole pods dried red pepper, preferably cayenne
48 black peppercorns
3¾ cups water
3¾ cups distilled white vinegar
3 tablespoons sea salt, kosher salt, or pure pickling salt

1. Prepare 6 pint canning jars and new canning lids by sterilizing them (page 11) and let them air-dry. Don't touch the insides of the jars after you have sterilized them. Wash the green beans in several changes of cold water. Trim off the stem ends but leave the beans whole. Using clean tongs, pack the beans vertically in the jars. Add 1 clove of garlic, 1 sprig of dill (or 1 teaspoon of seeds), 1 whole pepper pod, and 8 peppercorns to each jar.

2. Bring the vinegar, water, and salt to a boil in a stainless-steel or enameled pan over high heat. Divide the pickling brine between the jars, leaving a full ½ inch of headroom at the top of each.

3. Seal with the lids and rings, and process the pickles, completely covered, in a boiling water bath for 10 minutes (see pages 10–12 for detailed canning instructions). Remove with tongs and set them—not touching—on folded kitchen towels. Cool completely and store for 6-8 weeks to allow the pickles to mature before serving them. Refrigerate any jars that don't seal and use them up within 2 months.

BUTTERBEANS

Though many Southerners will vigorously protest the point, butterbeans, speckled butterbeans, butter peas, and the like are all varieties of lima beans, Phaseolus limensis, which are native to the Americas. The peculiarly Southern name for them—"butter" bean—appears to be a recent one; all the old cookbooks and reference books referred to them as either limas, civets, sievas, or occasionally, Carolina beans.

The most Southern of all the many varieties are speckled butterbeans, so called because their creamy-white skin is beautifully marbled with red and purple. The bright colors fade when they are exposed to heat, and the beans turn a rich coppery brown when cooked. Though once commonplace (they have been found growing wild in Florida), nowadays speckled butterbeans are not as easy to come by in the South, and they are almost unheard of in other parts of the country. Color isn't their only distinction; speckled butterbeans have a unique flavor for which there is no substitute. If you can't find them, any fresh or frozen lima beans can be used in any recipe calling for speckled butterbeans in this book. They won't taste the same, but they'll still work.

Butterbean Ragout   SERVES 4

Though not technically related, and don't really taste the same, butterbeans are similar to European fava or Windsor beans. Here, they are simmered with an aromatic combination of onion and salt-cured pork, a treatment similar to an Italian classic, *fave al guanciale* (or *alla romana*—fava cooked with cured pork cheeks in the Roman style), although in this instance the pork is not what Southerners call "hog jowls" but lean country ham.

1 small yellow onion, peeled and chopped

3 tablespoons butter, divided

4 ounces (one ⅛-inch slice) country ham or prosciutto, cut into julienne strips

16 ounces (3 cups) fresh shelled butterbeans (preferably speckled), or frozen limas such as Fordhooks, thawed

Whole black pepper in a mill

Salt

1 tablespoon chopped parsley

1. Warm the onion and 2 tablespoons of the butter in a large, heavy-bottomed lidded skillet or sauté pan over medium-high heat. Sauté, tossing often, until the onion is softened but not colored, about 3 minutes. Add the ham and sauté, tossing constantly, until it loses its raw, red color, about half a minute more.

2. Add the beans and toss well with the onion and ham. Season with a few liberal grindings of pepper, but do not add salt. Pour in just enough water to barely cover the beans and bring it to a boil. Let it boil for about 1 minute, then reduce the heat to a bare simmer, cover, and simmer until the beans are tender. Depending on the type of bean and its freshness, this could take as little as 20 minutes and as much as 45 minutes. Check from time to time to make sure they are not getting too dry. If the beans don't simmer in sufficient water, they will be mealy and tough.

3. Remove the lid and raise the heat to medium high. Rapidly boil until the cooking liquid is reduced and lightly thickened. Turn off the heat. Taste for salt and correct the seasoning, and swirl in the parsley and the remaining table-spoon of butter. Pour into a warm serving bowl and serve at once.

Note: *Like most stews, this ragout can not only be made ahead, but actually benefits from it. Stop at the end of step two, let cool, and then cover. Or if made more than a couple of hours ahead, transfer the beans to a storage container, cover, and refrigerate. When ready to serve them, gently reheat them, uncovered, over medium heat, and then proceed with step 3. Often their cooking liquid thickens after they cool, and may not need to be reduced much, if at all. If, in fact the liquid has gotten too thick, add a few spoonfuls of water before you reheat it.*

A traditional meatless version can be made by omitting the ham and adding ¼ cup of heavy cream (minimum 36 percent milk fat) before reducing the liquid in step 3. For strict vegetarians, omit the ham and substitute the same amount of peanut oil for the butter. Add five or six fresh chopped (or crumbled dry) sage leaves. The flavor won't be the same, but it will still taste Southern.

Buttery Butterbeans   SERVES 4

It is usually supposed that the name "butter-bean" derives from their distinctly buttery flavor, but my friend Clara Eschmann, a fine Southern lady who was for many years the food editor of the *Macon Telegraph*, said that when she was growing up, she thought they were so-called because they were always cooked with butter. As far as she was concerned, they ought never to be cooked any other way. Once you've tasted them done this way, you'll agree.

3 cups (about 1 pound shelled weight) fresh or good-quality frozen green butterbeans or butter peas

Salt

4 tablespoons unsalted butter, cut into small pieces

1. Put the beans in a colander and rinse them under cold running water. Put them in a heavy-bottomed 2-quart saucepan and barely cover them with cold water. Bring it to a boil over medium-high heat and reduce the heat to medium low. Loosely cover and simmer, stirring frequently, until the beans are nearly tender, about 15–20 minutes.

2. Uncover, add a healthy pinch of salt, stir, and cook, uncovered, until tender, about 5 minutes more.

3. Raise the heat to medium high and quickly reduce the cooking liquid until it is beginning to get thick, about 2 minutes longer. Turn off the heat and stir in the butter. The cooking liquid should be thick and creamy and coat the beans like a butter sauce. Serve at once.

Note: *You can make this several hours or even a day or two ahead and reheat them, but don't reduce the cooking liquid (it will thicken as it sits) or add the butter until you are ready to serve the beans. If, when you reheat it, the cooking liquid is too thick, add a few spoonfuls of water.*

Needless to say, there's no substitute for the butter here. No other fat—not even olive oil—will work. Don't even think about using margarine.

VARIATION: Butterbeans and Okra—Wash and trim the stem caps of a dozen very small okra pods (no more than 2–3 inches long), leaving the pods whole. When the beans are just barely done, lay the okra on top, cover, and steam until the okra is barely tender, about 4 minutes. Mix in the butter as directed, or, for a lighter, fresher flavor, you may omit it.

Pasta with Butterbeans and Ham

SERVES 4 TO 6

This is the same idea as the classic spring pasta of Emilia-Romagna, Italy's gastronomical center, made with fresh peas, prosciutto, and cream, except that the creamy texture here is provided by the butterbeans rather than dairy products.

4 tablespoons unsalted butter

1 tablespoon olive oil

1 small shallot, peeled and minced

1 ounce country ham or prosciutto cut from a ⅛-inch-thick slice into ⅛-inch julienne

2 generous cups cooked small green butterbeans, drained, but with liquid reserved

1 tablespoon fresh thyme leaves

Whole black pepper in a mill

Salt

1 pound fresh egg fettuccine, tagliatelle, or other egg noodles

½ cup freshly grated Parmigiano-Reggiano cheese

1 tablespoon minced flat leaf parsley

1. Bring 4 quarts of water to rolling boil in a heavy-bottomed 6-quart pot over high heat. Meanwhile, put 2 tablespoons of butter, the oil, and shallot in large skillet or sauté pan over medium heat. Sauté, tossing often, until colored pale gold; add the ham and toss until it loses its raw, red color.

2. Add the butterbeans and thyme and season with pepper to taste. Toss until the beans are hot. Add enough of their cooking liquid to barely cover them, bring to a boil, and cook, stirring often, until the liquid is thickened to the consistency of cream. Turn off the heat.

3. When the water is boiling, toss in small handful of salt and stir in the fettuccine. Cook until al dente and drain, reserving a few

spoonfuls of the cooking liquid. Add the pasta to the beans and return the pan to medium heat. Toss until hot and turn off the heat. Add ¼ cup of the cheese and toss well. If the sauce isn't creamy enough, add a few spoonfuls of reserved pasta water. Add the remaining parsley, toss, and serve immediately with remaining cheese passed separately.

Butterbean Puree   SERVES 4

When simmered with shallots and finished with herbs and green onions, butterbeans make a beautiful and delicious puree that I've seen called "Southern Hummus"— which is a bit silly, since this resembles hummus only in texture and not at all in color or flavor. It more closely resembles the old fava bean purees common to Italy and France, which occasionally appeared in old Southern cookbooks.

Though I prefer this as a side dish, it can in fact be served like hummus as a dip with crackers or toasted pita chips.

3 cups (about 1 pound shelled weight) green butterbeans

2 tablespoons unsalted butter

½ cup finely chopped shallot or yellow onion

1 large clove garlic, minced

Salt and whole white pepper in a mill

¼ cup heavy cream, optional

1 teaspoon minced fresh sage

1 teaspoon minced fresh thyme

¼ cup thin-sliced scallions or chopped green onion

1. Put the beans in a colander, rinse well under cold running water, and drain. Warm the butter and shallot in a large, heavy-bottomed skillet over medium heat. Sauté until translucent and softened, about 5 minutes, add the garlic, and sauté half a minute longer. Add the beans and stir until heated through.

2. Add enough water to cover the beans and bring to a boil, skimming off any foam that rises. Season generously with salt and pepper, reduce the heat to a slow simmer, cover, and cook, stirring occasionally, until beans are tender, about 20–30 minutes depending on size and maturity. Drain but reserve the liquid.

3. Puree the beans in a food processor fitted with steel blade, adding the cream, if using, and just enough cooking liquid to make it the consistency of mashed potatoes. Mix in the herbs and green onion. Taste and adjust the salt and pepper and serve warm or at room temperature.

Five-Bean Salad   SERVES 8 TO 10

During the 1950s and '60s, this mixed bean salad was a fixture in Southern picnic baskets and at church dinners-on-the-grounds— inevitably (and ironically) made with a collection of canned beans at a time when our gardens were producing a bumper crop. When the craze for salad bars swept the nation, this picnic standard went indoors, and became so commonplace and ordinary that the only time a "serious" recipe for it appeared, it was reinvented beyond recognition. If you go to the trouble of using fresh beans, however, and don't drown them in the dressing (which, get over it, is supposed to be sweet), you really don't need to reinvent a thing.

8 ounces haricots verts or other small, slender green beans, washed and trimmed

8 ounces yellow wax beans, washed and trimmed

Salt

1½ cups cooked fresh or frozen small green butterbeans or baby limas (such as Fordhook)

1½ cups cooked dark red kidney beans, drained and rinsed (1 15-ounce can)

1½ cups cooked black beans, drained and rinsed (1 15-ounce can)

1 cup thinly sliced green onions

1 rib celery, diced

1 clove garlic, smashed and peeled

½ cup sherry, red wine, or cider vinegar

2 teaspoons Dijon mustard

2–3 tablespoons sugar, to taste

Whole black pepper in a mill

½ cup olive or vegetable oil

1 tablespoon minced fresh thyme, marjoram, or oregano

1 tablespoon minced parsley

1. Cut or break the haricots verts in half. Cut the wax beans on the diagonal into 1-inch lengths. Bring 4 quarts water to a rolling boil in a heavy-bottomed 6-quart pot over high heat. Add a small handful of salt and the haricots verts. Boil rapidly for 2–4 minutes, or until crisp-tender. Lift them out with a mesh skimmer or slotted spoon and immediately rinse them under cold running water. Let completely cool, cover, and refrigerate.

2. Add the wax beans to the pot and cook until crisp-tender, about 4–6 minutes. Drain

and rinse under cold running water. Combine them with the butterbeans, kidney beans, black beans, green onions, and celery in large glass or stainless-steel bowl.

3. Sprinkle the smashed garlic with a pinch of salt and rub it to a puree with the edge of a knife blade. Scrape it into a small glass or stainless-steel mixing bowl. Add the vinegar, mustard, and sugar and pepper to taste and whisk until smooth. Slowly whisk in the oil and then fold in the herbs. Taste and adjust the salt, sugar, and pepper and whisk to mix.

4. Pour the dressing over the mixed beans and toss well. Cover and refrigerate at least 4 hours. Just before serving, add the haricots verts, toss well, taste and adjust seasonings, and toss one last time. Serve immediately so that the haricots don't lose their color.

Succotash   SERVES 6

This lovely mélange of beans and corn, usually credited to Native American cookery, has suffered much in the hands of the canned-food industry and lunchroom steam tables. Many people think they hate it, and small wonder: the fine flavor of fresh butterbeans and corn is killed when succotash is canned or is made from canned vegetables. Being allowed to sit indifferently on a steam table only nails the lid on its coffin.

The classic proportions are two parts beans to one part corn, though there are Southern cooks who mix the vegetables in equal portions. Let your taste guide you: The real secret to achieving the best flavor is seldom used nowadays, and that's the old practice of simmering the corn cobs with the beans.

3–6 large ears fresh corn (2 cups cut from the cob)

1 medium yellow onion, peeled and chopped

5 tablespoons unsalted butter, cut into small pieces
4 cups fresh butterbeans
Salt and whole white pepper in a mill

1. Shuck the corn from its husk and rub off all the silk with a vegetable brush. Cut 2 cups of kernels as close to the cob as possible, put them in a glass bowl, cover, and set aside. Break the cobs in half.

2. Sauté the onion in a tablespoon of the butter in a deep-lidded skillet over medium heat, tossing often, until it is translucent and softened, but not browned, about 5 minutes. Add the cobs and 2 cups of water, raise the heat to medium high, and bring to a boil.

3. Add the beans, let the liquids come back to a boil, then loosely cover and reduce the heat to a slow simmer. Simmer until the beans are just tender, about 20 minutes.

4. Stir in the corn kernels, season well with salt and a liberal grinding of white pepper, and raise the heat long enough to bring it back to a simmer. Lower it once again to a slow simmer and cook, uncovered, until the corn is just tender, about 10 minutes.

5. By this time the liquid should be somewhat reduced and creamy. If it isn't, raise the heat to medium high and quickly boil until it is, about 2-3 minutes. Turn off the heat. Remove and discard the cobs. Stir in the remaining butter, taste and correct the seasonings, and pour it into a warm serving bowl. Serve hot.

Note: *You can get away with using good-quality frozen butterbeans in this recipe, but don't use frozen corn. Not only does fresh corn taste better, but the cob provides an important flavoring agent.*

CORN

It would be hard to imagine any American table without corn, but most especially a Southern one. From grits at breakfast to pecan pie at supper, from a luncheon corn pudding to a creamy corn bisque on the formal dinner table, from a hunk of cornbread with a bowl of greens to the crackling-crisp crust of a fried green tomato, corn plays an important role. Used both as a grain and a vegetable, nothing has been as wholly integrated into our foodways as has this native American grass. Even our national alcoholic beverage is made with it.

Our weather may be hot and the trees may have been in full leaf for a month, but summer in the South doesn't really begin until the first local sweet corn appears in the market. In the very deep South, that may be as early as mid-June. In the northern reaches, it will not begin until July. Regardless, we consider that eating that first, early corn any way other than straight off the cob is almost a sacrilege. One of my favorite printed recipes for it directs the reader to put a large pot of water on to boil, go out to the garden to gather as many ears of corn as you will need, and, while running for the house, shuck it. If you should fall down on the way, throw that corn to the pigs because it will no longer be fresh enough, and go back for some more.

Well. We should all be so lucky as to get corn like that nowadays.

As summer comes on full force, fresh corn both on and off its cob begins to appear in dozens of different forms. Here are a few classics.

Corn Bisque   SERVES 4

This lovely soup was once very popular, but unfortunately it's seldom served anymore. Its fall from grace may have something to do with the fact that what was once a lovely balance of sweet fresh corn and cream had, by the middle of this century, degenerated into a conglomeration of several cans of things indifferently dumped together.

This recipe is the original delicate soup in which the fresh flavor of sweet corn is enriched with real cream and underscored by a suggestion of nutmeg and sherry.

3–6 ears fresh corn (2 cups cut from the cob)
  or 2 cups good-quality frozen cream-style corn

1 medium yellow onion, peeled and chopped fine

2 tablespoons unsalted butter

2 cups light cream

1 whole pod cayenne or other hot red pepper

Salt and whole nutmeg in a grater

¼ cup dry sherry

Whole milk, if needed

2 tablespoons chopped fresh chives (do not use dried chives)

1. Shuck the husks from the corn, rub off all the silk with a vegetable brush, and cut the kernels from the cob as follows: Over a large bowl, cut the outer half of the kernels from the ear with a sharp knife, leaving the other half of the kernels still attached to the cob. Thoroughly scrape the cob with the knife to force out all the milk into the bowl. Repeat with the remaining ears until all the corn is cut and scraped. Break one of the cobs into about 3 pieces. Discard the remaining cobs.

2. Sauté the onion in the butter in a heavy-bottomed 3- to 4-quart pot over medium heat, tossing often, until the onion is translucent but not in the least colored, about 5 minutes.

3. Add the corn and stir until it is heated through. Slowly add the cream, stirring constantly. Add the pepper pod (left whole), a small pinch of salt, and a few gratings of nutmeg and the reserved cob. Bring to a simmer and cook, stirring frequently, until thick, about 20 minutes.

4. Stir in the sherry and let the soup heat through. If you find that the soup is too thick, thin it with a little milk—don't add more cream—and let it heat through. Remove and discard the cob and pod of hot pepper. Taste and adjust the seasonings. Ladle the soup into individual soup plates and garnish with a light grating of nutmeg and sprinkling of the chopped chives.

Grill-Roasted Corn SERVES 4 HEALTHY
PEOPLE OR 8 DAINTY ONES

This is my favorite way of preparing fresh corn on the cob. It is practically effortless, since the ears need no preliminary cleaning and cook in their husks. The process also causes the pesky, sticky silks to loosen up and come right off with the husk when you shuck them.

The best way to do this is on the grill, but if you can't grill, the oven does a pretty good job of it. I've given both methods here.

8 large, fresh ears of corn in their husks
Unsalted butter, salt, and freshly ground black
  pepper

1. Prepare a grill with charcoal, light it, and when the coals are ready, spread them and position the grill rack about 3–4 inches above the coals. (Or position a rack in the upper third of the oven and preheat the oven to 400°F.) Meanwhile, put the corn in a basin filled with enough cold water to cover it and let it soak for 10 minutes. Lift it out and let it drain.

2. Put the whole ears on the grill and roast, turning them frequently, until the outer husk begins to brown and char and the kernels are tender, about 15–20 minutes, depending on the heat of your grill. (If you are using the oven, roast the corn—again turning it frequently—until it is just cooked through and tender when gently pressed, about 20 minutes.)

3. Wear a pair of insulated kitchen mitts, take the corn off the grill (or out of the oven), and quickly shuck it. The silks will pull right off along with the husks. Brush off any silks that remain, cut out any brown spots, and pile the ears onto a warm platter or serving bowl. Serve at once with fresh butter, salt, and freshly ground black pepper passed separately.

Grill-Roasted Corn Salad SERVES 4

When I'm roasting corn on the grill, I usually throw a couple of extra ears which will later be made into salad or relish.

3–6 large ears Grill-Roasted Corn (this page),
  see step 1
4 green onions or scallions, sliced thin,
  or 1 medium Vidalia or other sweet onion,
  peeled and diced
1 green bell pepper, seeded and diced
¼ cup red wine vinegar
Salt, ground cayenne, and whole black pepper
  in a mill
½ cup extra-virgin olive oil
1 tablespoon each chopped parsley and fresh basil
2 medium ripe tomatoes
1 bunch watercress

1. Cut enough corn kernels, cutting as close to the cob as possible to make 2 cups of corn. Put it, the green onions, and bell pepper in a glass or ceramic mixing bowl and toss to mix.

2. In a separate bowl, combine the vinegar, a large pinch of salt, a tiny one of cayenne, and a few liberal grindings of black pepper. Gradually whisk in the olive oil until it is emulsified. Whisk in the parsley and basil and pour the dressing over the corn. Cover and refrigerate for at least an hour. You can make the salad to this point up to 2 days ahead.

3. When you are ready to serve, wash, core, seed, and cut the tomatoes into ½-inch dice. Add them to the salad. Break the watercress into bite-size pieces and add it to the salad as well. Toss until the tomato and cress are evenly coated. Taste and correct the seasonings and serve.

Miss Ruby's Fresh Corn Relish

MAKES ABOUT 3½ CUPS, OR 4 TO 6 SERVINGS

Ruth Adams Bronz—Miss Ruby to her friends—is an expatriate Texan living in Berkshire County, Massachusetts. Eccentric, funny, and generous to a fault, Miss Ruby is living proof that you can plant Southerners anywhere in the world and they won't change: they'll just keep right on being Southern—whether they like it or not.

Nowhere is this tendency more evident than in Miss Ruby's kitchen, where her palate always wanders southward to the cooking of her native Texas. This corn relish is a case in point, exemplifying the almost schizophrenic character of Texas cookery—which is one part Deep South, one part Southwest, and one part Mexico.

This relish can stand alone as a salad, with thick slices of ripe tomato on the side, or can be served as a relish over grilled tuna steaks, pork chops, or chicken.

3–6 ears fresh corn (2 cups when cut from the cob)
½ cup red bell pepper, diced small
½ cup green bell pepper, diced small
1 small red onion, diced small
¼ cup celery, diced small
2 teaspoons cumin seeds, toasted and ground fine
1 tablespoon fresh chopped coriander (cilantro)
Salt
Tabasco or other red hot sauce
1 lime

1. Shuck the corn and rub away the silk with a vegetable brush. Cut 2 cups of kernels from the cob as close to the cob as possible. In a large glass bowl, toss together the corn, both bell peppers, onion, and celery until well mixed. Add the cumin, coriander, a large pinch of salt, and 2 long dashes of hot sauce.

2. Grate the zest from the lime, then cut the lime in half and squeeze the juice over the relish. Add the zest and toss until the seasonings are well blended. Cover and let stand in a cool place for at least 2 hours. Taste and correct the seasonings, and toss again before serving.

Fried Corn   SERVES ABOUT 4

Fried corn is a standard in the repertory of all Southern cooks. It isn't actually "fried" as we usually think of frying, but comes closer to stewing in its own milk and a little fat. The result is rich and creamy—not brown and crispy—and the natural sugars are marvelously concentrated and intensified.

My preferred choice of corn for this recipe is sweet white corn, such as Silver Queen, because that's what I was raised on, but you can use any sweet corn that is available to you.

8 young, tender ears sweet corn
2 tablespoons rendered bacon fat or unsalted butter

1 small yellow onion, peeled and minced (optional)

Salt and pepper in a peppermill to taste

1. Shuck the corn and rub away the silk with a vegetable brush. Over a large bowl, with a sharp knife cut the outer half of the kernels from an ear, leaving the inner half of the kernels still attached to the cob. Thoroughly scrape the cob with the knife to force out all the milk from the cut kernels into the bowl. Repeat this with the remaining ears until all the corn is cut and scraped.

2. Heat the bacon fat or butter and onion, if using, in a large, well-seasoned iron skillet over medium-high heat. If using onion, sauté it until it is colored, gold, about 4 minutes. Add the corn and all its milk. Bring it to a boil, stirring and scraping the pan to keep it from sticking, and turn the heat down to medium. Cook, stirring almost constantly, until the corn milk begins to thicken.

3. Reduce the heat once more to a slow simmer. Cook, stirring constantly and carefully scraping the bottom to keep it from scorching, until very thick and tender, about 5 minutes more. Turn off the heat, season to taste with a pinch of salt and a few grindings of pepper, and serve at once.

Note: *Bacon fat lends the taste that most Southerners are accustomed to today, but it's not necessarily the most traditional, as most of the old recipes called for butter. If you are not able to use animal or dairy fat, an acceptable substitute is corn oil—preferably an unrefined, cold-pressed oil that really tastes of corn. If you are omitting the animal fat, though, don't omit the onion.*

Creole Corn and Tomatoes   SERVES 4

Here's another traditional Southern favorite that takes full advantage of the full-blown summer flavors of vine-ripened tomatoes and fresh-picked corn.

2 tablespoons rendered bacon fat

1 medium yellow onion, peeled and chopped

4 large ripe tomatoes, scalded, peeled, and seeded as directed on page 101, chopped

1 tablespoon chopped parsley

1 tablespoon fresh thyme or 1 teaspoon dried thyme

1 bay leaf

3–6 ears fresh sweet corn (see step 2)

Salt, ground cayenne, and whole black pepper in a mill

1. Put the fat and onion in a large, deep cast-iron skillet or sauté pan and sauté over medium heat, tossing frequently, until the onion is translucent but not colored, about 5 minutes. Add the tomatoes, parsley, thyme, and bay leaf, and bring to a simmer. Cook, uncovered, for 10 minutes.

2. Meanwhile, shuck the corn and rub away the silk with a vegetable brush. Cut 2 cups of kernels from the cob as close to the cob as possible. Stir the corn into the tomatoes, add a healthy pinch of salt, a small one of cayenne, and a few grindings of black pepper. Let it come back to a simmer, cover, and reduce the heat to medium low. Cook, stirring occasionally, until the corn is tender, about 20 minutes. Uncover, raise the heat to medium, and cook until thick, about 5 minutes more. Turn off the heat. Remove and discard the bay leaf, taste and correct the seasonings, and serve hot.

Note: *The smoky flavor of the bacon fat is essential to the character of this dish, but if you are unable to use it, butter or corn oil would still make a reasonably good dish, though it will by no means taste the same. I would use sage instead of thyme, add a minced clove of garlic, and let the onion brown a little to compensate for the absence of the bacon flavor.*

Shrimp and Corn Pudding   SERVES 4

This traditional Lowcountry supper dish is an especially happy pairing of two summer staples of coastal Georgia and the Carolinas. The natural sweetness of fresh shrimp is both complemented and enhanced by the equal sweetness of freshly gathered corn. It is by no means an accident that in midsummer, when both shrimp and corn are at their peak, they frequently appear together on the table.

3–6 ears of sweet corn (see step 1)

4 green onions or scallions, washed, trimmed, and thinly sliced, or 1 medium yellow onion, stem and roots trimmed, split lengthwise, peeled and chopped

2 tablespoons unsalted butter

2 large eggs, lightly beaten

½ cup light cream or half-and-half

1 tablespoon each chopped fresh thyme and parsley

Salt, ground cayenne, and whole white pepper in a mill

Whole nutmeg in a grater

1½ pounds (headless weight) uncooked small shrimp, peeled

1. Position a rack in the center of the oven and preheat to 350°F. Put a teakettle full of water on to boil. Shuck the corn and rub away the silk with a vegetable brush. Cut 2 cups of kernels as close to the cob as possible. Put the onions and butter in a sauté pan and place it over medium-high heat. Sauté, tossing frequently, until the onions are softened but not colored, about 3–4 minutes. Turn off the heat.

2. Mix together the onion, corn, eggs, cream, and herbs in a large glass or ceramic mixing bowl. Season with a large pinch of salt, a small one of cayenne, a generous grinding of white pepper, and a liberal grating of nutmeg. Mix well and stir in the shrimp.

3. Lightly butter a 9-inch square or round ceramic casserole or soufflé dish and pour in the pudding batter. Put the casserole in the center of a wide, deep pan (such as a sheet-cake pan) and put it in the center of the oven. Carefully pour enough boiling water from the kettle into the larger pan until it comes about halfway up the sides of the casserole.

4. Bake until the pudding is set and the shrimp cooked through. Depending on the shape of your dish, it will take about 1 hour. The wider and shallower the pan, the quicker the pudding will cook, so keep an eye on it and be careful not to overcook it, or the eggs will separate and the shrimp will be tough. Serve hot or at room temperature.

CORN AND MUSHROOM PUDDING: The whole point of the preceding recipe is the flavor combination of shrimp and corn. However, a perfectly good corn pudding can be made without the shellfish by added a seeded and chopped red bell pepper and ½ pound sliced wild or cremini mushrooms to the mixture. Sauté the bell pepper with the onions in step 1, and when both are wilted, add the mushrooms and sauté until softened, and proceed with step 2, omitting the shrimp. Of course, if shellfish really turns you on, you can stretch the pudding to serve 6 by adding ½ pound (1 cup) of lump crabmeat, carefully picked over to remove any shell.

CUCUMBERS

There are two kinds of cucumbers that have played their part in Southern food, both native gherkins (*Cucumis anquria*) and imported European ones (*Cucumis sativus*)—which one record claims were growing in Haiti as early as 1494. However, the record of their cultivation, and exactly when and where each type was being used, is very confused. For our purposes, it's sufficient to say that cucumbers have always been on Southern tables.

In the summer they were, until recently, practically a permanent fixture on many tables, plucked from the garden that morning, cooled on ice, and bathed in a simple marinade of vinegar, salt, and black pepper. Naturally cooling and refreshing, they were a sort of culinary air-conditioning. Though modern technology has made the indoors cool throughout the summer, that simple salad is still how we like cucumbers best; indeed, *The Picayune's Creole Cook Book* (1901) asserted that this was the only way of serving them that the Creoles would tolerate—and that remains true to this day. But cooked cucumbers do turn up, from time to time, in Southern kitchens. One particularly nice way to cook them is to peel and cut them into thick wedges, then sauté them with onions in butter, following the variation for Sautéed Summer Squash and Onions on page 156.

Fried Cucumbers   SERVES 4

Yes, Southerners will fry just about anything. As a matter of fact, over the last two decades there has been a craze for—I am not making this up—fried dill pickles. Actually, fried cucumbers are an old European idea that the colonials brought with them to this country, but it gets a peculiarly Southern twist with cornmeal breading.

The cucumbers that you want for frying should be very young so that the seeds are still tender. Choose small to medium cucumbers that are quite green, not too fat, and very firm. If even after taking that precaution you find that the seeds have turned brown and woody, split

the cucumbers, remove the seeds, and slice them lengthwise into strips instead of rounds before cooking them.

1 pound young cucumbers (see headnote)

Salt

1 large egg

1 cup all-purpose flour

1 cup cornmeal, spread on a dinner plate

Lard or peanut oil for frying

Whole black pepper in a mill

1 lemon, cut into 8 wedges

1. Wash the cucumbers under cold running water. Lightly peel them with a vegetable peeler and cut them crosswise into rounds about ¼ inch thick. Spread them in one layer on a platter, sprinkle liberally with salt, and set them aside for half an hour.

2. Break the egg into a shallow bowl and beat it until it is smooth. Spread the flour and meal in similar bowls or plates and have all three within easy reach of the frying pan. Put enough lard or oil into the pan to come halfway up the sides. Turn on the heat to medium high.

3. Pat the excess moisture from the cucumbers and sprinkle them lightly with a few grindings of black pepper. Roll them a few at a time in the flour, shake off the excess, then dip one at a time in the beaten egg, let the excess flow back into the bowl, and roll them in the cornmeal. When the fat is hot but not smoking (about 375°F), add enough of the cucumbers to the pan to fill it without crowding. Fry until the bottoms are brown, about 3 minutes, turn, and continue frying until they are evenly browned, about 3 minutes more. Remove them to drain on absorbent paper and transfer them to a wire rack. Repeat with the remaining cucumber slices until they are all fried. Serve hot with lemon wedges.

Cucumbers in Sour Cream Dressing   SERVES 4

Here, the cool, mild flavor of cucumbers makes an inviting contrast to the sharp tang of soured cream. The luscious dressing is an old one, dating back well into the nineteenth century, but it still makes a great salad for any modern summer meal, tastes superb paired with barbecue when the meat is lamb or goat, and is tailor-made to serve with any kind of fish.

½ cup homemade Crème Fraîche (page 18) or sour cream

1 tablespoon freshly squeezed lemon juice

1 teaspoon Dijon mustard

2 tablespoons extra-virgin olive oil

Salt, ground cayenne, and whole black pepper in a mill

1 small Vidalia or other sweet onion

2 pounds (2 large or 4 small) cucumbers

4 large lettuce leaves, such as romaine or Boston

1 tablespoon chopped dill or chives and paprika (optional)

1. In a large glass or ceramic mixing bowl, stir together the crème fraîche or sour cream, lemon juice, and Dijon mustard, mixing until smooth. Whisk in the oil a little at a time. Season with a generous pinch of salt, a small one of cayenne, and a liberal grinding of pepper, and mix well.

2. Split the onion in half lengthwise. Peel it and slice each half as thinly as possible. Wash the cucumbers and if they have been waxed, lightly peel them with a vegetable peeler so that there is still a blush of bright green on them. Slice the cucumbers crosswise into rounds a little less than ¼ inch thick.

3. Add the onion and cucumbers to the dressing, and toss until everything is thoroughly coated. Put the lettuce leaves on individual salad plates and divide the cucumbers among them. If you like, you can sprinkle the top with chopped dill or chives and a light dusting of paprika. Serve at once, or the cucumbers will begin to throw off liquid and make the salad watery.

Cucumber and Fennel Salad

SERVES 4 TO 6

Fennel—that lovely vegetable that looks like a cross between celery and dill and tastes vaguely of licorice and sweet celery—is thankfully becoming commonplace in markets down South, though a lot of Southern cooks still look at it with wonder and puzzlement. Wonder no more.

This is a refreshing salad that goes nicely with all fish and shellfish dishes. It also perks up any roasted poultry or game.

1 large head fennel

1 large or 2 medium cucumbers

1 large Vidalia or other sweet onion, root and stem trimmed, split lengthwise, peeled, and thinly sliced

2 hard-cooked large egg yolks

1 tablespoon Dijon mustard

Salt, sugar, and whole black pepper in a mill

2 tablespoons fresh lemon juice

⅓ cup extra-virgin olive oil

1. Wash the fennel, trim the root end, and cut off the stalks. Clip enough of the nicest feathery fronds to make about ½ cup and chop them. Discard the stalks. Cut the fennel bulb lengthwise in half, cut out the core, and slice as thinly as you can manage. Put the fennel and chopped fronds in a salad bowl.

2. Wash the cucumbers and, only if they have been waxed or their skins are tough, lightly peel them; otherwise, peeling isn't necessary. Cut the cucumbers crosswise into thin rounds and add them to the fennel. Add the onion and toss until uniformly mixed.

3. In a separate bowl, mash the egg yolks with a fork, add the mustard, a pinch of salt, a small pinch of sugar, and a generous grinding of pepper. Mash them with the fork until smooth. Gradually whisk in the lemon juice, then, whisk in the oil a few drops at a time until it is incorporated and emulsified.

4. Pour the dressing over the salad and toss until the vegetables are evenly coated. Taste and correct the seasonings, and toss again to distribute them evenly. Serve at once.

EGGPLANT

What a strange name we have given this vegetable, or so it always seemed to me, having grown up with the type of large, deep-purple, pear-shaped fruit that resembles a chicken egg about as much as it does an artichoke. There are many varieties of eggplant, however, one of which is a small white oval, the variety from which the name is derived. This type was eventually eclipsed by its purple-skinned cousins, but it hasn't altogether disappeared; occasionally white and even yellow eggplants turn up in the markets. Still, in the South we continue to prefer the purple ones.

Originally native to the Far East, eggplant gradually migrated westward and was well known in the Mediterranean and Africa by the time the Americas were colonized. In some parts of the South, eggplants were once also known as "Guinea melons" or "Guinea squash," after the West African nation of that name, which suggests that they were probably introduced to our little corner of the globe by way of the African slave trade. At any rate, from the late eighteenth century forward, eggplant has been enjoyed on Southern tables. The recipes that follow have a long tradition.

Smothered Eggplant à la Creole

SERVES 6

A close cousin to the Provençal classic ratatouille, this Creole dish is usually served hot, but like ratatouille it is equally as good eaten cold the next day when the flavors have had time to settle in and marry with one another. It is an excellent side accompaniment to any seafood, fish, chicken, or lamb that does not contain tomato or cream.

1½ pounds eggplant (about 2 medium)

Salt

2 tablespoons unsalted butter or extra-virgin olive oil

2 medium onions, peeled and chopped

2 ribs celery, washed, strung, and chopped

2 green bell peppers, stemmed, seeded, and diced

2 large cloves garlic, minced

1¾ pounds ripe tomatoes (preferably plum), scalded, peeled, seeded, and chopped as directed on page 101, or 2 cups (28-ounce can) Italian canned tomatoes, seeded and chopped

2 ounces (a ⅛-inch-thick slice) country ham or prosciutto, chopped

Ground cayenne pepper and whole black pepper in a mill

1 tablespoon chopped fresh thyme or 1 teaspoon
   dried thyme

1 tablespoon chopped parsley

1. Peel and cut the eggplants into 1-inch dice. Put them in a colander, sprinkle liberally with salt, and toss to evenly coat. Set it in the sink and let stand for 30 minutes.

2. Meanwhile, put the fat, onion, celery, and green peppers in a large, heavy-bottomed, lidded skillet or sauté pan over medium-high heat and sauté, tossing often, until softened and beginning to color, about 4–6 minutes. Add the garlic and sauté until fragrant, about half a minute more. Add the tomatoes and their juices, ham, a pinch of cayenne, a generous grinding of black pepper, and thyme. Bring to a boil.

3. Wipe the eggplant dry, pressing it gently to remove any excess moisture, and add it to the pan. Bring back to a boil, cover, reduce the heat to low, and simmer gently, stirring frequently to prevent scorching, until the eggplant is tender, about 30 minutes. If, at the end of this time, there is a lot of excess liquid in the pan, raise the heat briefly and boil it away. Turn off the heat, stir in the parsley, taste and correct the seasonings, adding salt, if needed, and serve hot. You may also let it cool to room temperature, cover, and refrigerate overnight or for up to 3 days. Reheat it gently or serve at room temperature, taking from the refrigerator an hour before serving.

Fried Eggplant   SERVES 4 TO 6

One of the most satisfying things one can do with eggplant is to coat it with egg and crumbs and fry it. Nothing can quite equal that cracking-crisp, golden surface giving way to the contrastingly creamy, succulent flesh it conceals. In the South, they are sometimes simply cut into rounds, rolled in flour, and pan-fried in very little

fat—which has its own charms, but crispiness is not one of them. Here, I've broken with the traditional round cutlet and further cut each slice into sticks, so that each bite gives a mouthful of the crispy breading.

   The secrets to frying eggplant well are few and simple: The fat must, as for all frying, be clean and hot to keep it on the surface, where it belongs; the eggplant should always be salted and drained of some of its excess moisture before it's breaded and must rest after it's breaded so that it can set—otherwise the breading will likely fall right off when the eggplant hits the hot fat; and, finally, when the eggplant comes out of the fat, it must be lifted with a tool that won't trap the fat against it, and held over the pan until it no longer drips.

2 medium, firm eggplants (about 1½ pounds)

Salt

1–1½ cups cracker crumbs or panko

Whole black pepper in a mill

Ground cayenne

1 tablespoon crumbled Fines Herbes (page 33)

1 cup all-purpose flour

1 large egg

Lard or peanut oil, for frying

Tomato Sauce (page 120), Sauce Creole (page 121),
   or Raw Creole Sauce (page 121), or Savannah
   Sweet Red Pepper Sauce (page 46), and/or 2
   lemons cut into wedges, optional

1. Wash, stem, and peel the eggplants. Slice crosswise into rounds about ½-inch thick and cut each slice into ½-inch-thick sticks. Put them in a colander and sprinkle liberally with salt. Put the colander in the sink and let it sit for half an hour. Press them gently to squeeze out the excess moisture and pat dry, wiping away any salt that remains.

2. Meanwhile, fit two wire cooling racks into two rimmed baking sheets. Put the crumbs or panko in a wide, shallow bowl and season well with a large pinch of salt, liberal grinding of pepper, a dash or so of cayenne. Add the fines herbes and toss with a fork or whisk until well mixed. Spread the flour in a second shallow bowl. Break the egg into a third bowl and lightly beat until smooth. A few pieces at a time, toss the eggplant sticks in the flour, shake off the excess, and then roll them in the egg. Let the excess flow back into the bowl and drop them into the crumbs. Roll until they're coated and lay them on the prepared rack. Let them rest for at least 15 minutes; 30 will be better.

3. Position a rack in the upper third of the oven and preheat to 150–170°F. (the "warm" setting). Put enough fat in a heavy-bottomed, enameled iron or stainless-steel pot to come up the sides of the pot at least 1 inch but no more than halfway. Heat it to 375°F (very hot, but not smoking) over medium heat. Add enough of the eggplant sticks to fill the pan without crowding and fry until uniformly golden brown, about 4 minutes, turning once if necessary. Maintain a steady frying temperature between 355–365°F. If they begin to brown too quickly, the fat is getting too hot; adjust the heat accordingly. Lift them from the fat with a frying skimmer, holding them over the fat until they no longer drip oil, transfer them to the second cooling rack. Keep them in the warm oven while you fry the remaining eggplant. Put the eggplant on a warm platter or towel-lined basket and serve hot, passing any of the suggested sauces and/or lemon wedges separately.

Scalloped Eggplant SERVES 4

With not even a hint of the Mediterranean, the ingredients of this sumptuous casserole are not what one would expect to have paired with eggplant—cream, pecans, butter, and cheese. It is ridiculously rich and pure Deep South. It's also some kind of wonderful.

1½ pounds eggplant (about 2 medium)
1 large yellow onion, peeled and chopped
6 tablespoons unsalted butter
¼ cup all-purpose flour, spread on a dinner plate
1 cup heavy cream (minimum 36 percent milk fat)
1 cup freshly grated Parmigiano-Reggiano or extra-sharp cheddar
Salt and whole black pepper in a mill
¾ cup dry bread crumbs
1 cup chopped raw pecans

1. Peel and cut the eggplants into 1-inch dice. Put them in a colander, sprinkle liberally with salt and toss to coat evenly. Set them in the sink and let stand 30 minutes. Position a rack in the upper third of the oven and preheat to 375°F.

2. Gently squeeze the eggplant against the sides of the colander and pat it dry. Put the onion and 4 tablespoons of butter in a large, heavy-bottomed sauté pan over medium-high heat. Sauté, tossing often, until the onion is translucent and softened but not browned, about 4 minutes.

3. Quickly roll the eggplant in the flour, shake off the excess, and add it to the pan. Sauté, tossing almost constantly, until it is beginning to color, about 3 minutes. Turn off the heat.

4. Lightly butter a 2-quart casserole and transfer the eggplant to it. Pour over it the cream, add the cheese, a pinch of salt, a few grindings of pepper, and toss until well mixed.

5. Wipe out the pan in which the vegetables were sautéed. Put in the remaining 2 tablespoons of butter and place the pan over medium heat until the butter is just melted. Turn off the heat. Add the bread crumbs and pecans, and toss until the butter is evenly absorbed into the crumbs. Spread this over the top of the eggplant and bake it in the center of the oven until bubbling hot and golden brown on top, about 40 minutes. Let it settle for about 10 minutes before serving.

A Pair of Stuffed Eggplant Dishes

Stuffing eggplants with savory fillings is a wonderful way to cook and serve them. They make neat individual portions and—what's more important for most of us—can be assembled ahead of time to suit your schedule. Then all you will have to do is take them from the refrigerator, pop them in the oven, make a salad, and relax—dinner's ready.

To Prepare Eggplants for Stuffing: In the recipes that follow, the eggplants are parboiled before being stuffed. While this makes the pulp easier to scoop out, it also makes the shell a lot more fragile, so be careful not to break the skin or cut through it when you are removing the inner pulp.

Half-fill a large, heavy-bottomed stockpot with water and bring it to a boil on high heat. Meanwhile, wash the eggplants under cold running water. When the water is boiling briskly, add a small handful of salt to the pot and slip the eggplants into it. Cover and let it come back to a boil, then skew the lid and cook, frequently turning the eggplants over in the water, until they are softened, about 15 minutes. Drain and set aside to cool. They are now ready to use in the following recipes.

Stuffed Eggplant à la Creole SERVES 4

This fine meatless stuffed eggplant can be served as a side dish but is also substantial enough to stand on its own as a main course. The recipe is an old Creole one, though you don't have to be told that; the perfume of tomato, garlic, and thyme gives its origin away.

For a completely vegetarian version, substitute extra-virgin olive oil for the butter.

1 medium yellow onion, stem and roots trimmed, split lengthwise, peeled, and chopped fine

4 tablespoons unsalted butter

1 large clove garlic, lightly crushed and minced

2 medium eggplants (about ¾ pound each), parboiled whole as directed above

1 cup soft bread crumbs

1 medium ripe tomato, blanched, peeled, seeded, and chopped (page 101) or 2 canned tomatoes, drained, seeded, and chopped

1 tablespoon chopped fresh thyme or 1 teaspoon dried thyme

1 tablespoon chopped parsley

Salt, ground cayenne, and whole black pepper in a mill

¾ cup dry bread crumbs

1. Position a rack in the upper third of the oven and preheat to 375°F. Sauté the onion in 2 tablespoons of the butter in a heavy skillet over medium-high heat, tossing and stirring frequently, until translucent and softened, but not colored, about 4 minutes. Add the garlic and sauté fragrant but not in the least colored, about half a minute more. Turn off the heat.

2. Split the eggplants lengthwise and scoop out the inner flesh with a sharp-edged spoon or melon baller, leaving a shell about ½-inch thick on all sides. Chop the pulp and add it to the skillet with the onion and garlic. Add the soft crumbs, tomato, thyme, and parsley. Season with a large pinch of salt, a small one of cayenne, and generous of black pepper and gently toss until well-mixed.

3. Lightly butter a baking dish or heavy roasting pan that will hold the eggplant shells snugly without a lot of room around them. Put them into it and divide the stuffing evenly among them.

4. Wipe out the skillet and put in the remaining 2 tablespoons of butter. Melt it medium heat, turn off the heat, and add the bread crumbs, stirring until they evenly absorb the butter. Sprinkle them evenly over the eggplants, and bake the eggplants in the upper third of the oven until the crumbs are browned and the filling is heated through, about half an hour.

Seafood Stuffed Eggplant   SERVES 4

Shellfish has a happy affinity for eggplant, and their union in a dish is almost always a good idea. Here, fresh seafood is stuffed into eggplant shells and gently baked. This makes an especially nice luncheon dish but can be served as a first course for 6 persons at a formal dinner: Use 3 small eggplants (about ½ pound each) in place of the larger ones called for here.

2 medium eggplants (about ¾ pound each), parboiled as directed on page 145

1 large onion, peeled and chopped

2 ribs celery, strung and diced

1 red or green bell pepper, stemmed, cored, seeds and membranes removed, diced (or mix ½ red and ½ green pepper)

4 tablespoons unsalted butter

2 large cloves garlic, lightly crushed, peeled, and minced

2 tablespoons chopped parsley

4 ½-inch slices firm white bread, soaked in milk and squeezed dry

½ pound (1 cup) fresh lump crabmeat, picked over for bits of shell

½ pound (headless weight) small shrimp, peeled and, unless very small, cut in half

Salt, ground cayenne, and whole black pepper in a mill

Whole nutmeg in a grater

¾ cup crushed saltine cracker crumbs or dry bread crumbs

1. Position a rack in the center of the oven and preheat to 350°F. Split the eggplants lengthwise and scoop out the inner pulp, leaving a shell about ½-inch thick on all sides. Chop the pulp.

2. Sauté the onion, celery, and bell pepper in 2 tablespoons of the butter in a large, heavy-bottomed skillet over medium-high heat, tossing frequently, until the onion is translucent but not browned, about 5 minutes. Add the garlic and sauté until fragrant, about half a minute more. Turn off the heat.

3. Add the parsley and chopped eggplant pulp and crumble in the soaked bread. Add the crab and shrimp, season well with a large pinch or two of salt, a small one of cayenne, a liberal grinding of pepper, and generous grating of nutmeg. Gently toss until well mixed.

4. Lightly butter a baking dish or small, heavy roasting pan that will hold the eggplant shells snugly. Put in the shells and divide the stuffing among them, mounding it up in the center. Wipe out the skillet, put in the remaining 2 tablespoons of butter and melt it over medium-low heat. Turn off the heat and mix in the dry crumbs until the butter is evenly absorbed. Sprinkle them evenly over the eggplants and bake in the center of the oven until the shrimp is cooked through, about 40 minutes.

VIDALIA SWEET ONIONS

By now, most people know the history of Georgia's famous onion—how many years ago the farmers around the little central Georgia community of Vidalia discovered that their soil produced exceptionally sweet onions. Since that time, those onions have become so popular that a flood of pretenders and outright fakes prompted local growers to petition for legal protection. Today, the name "Vidalia Sweet Onion" is one of only a few regional American product names to be protected by law as French wines are.

The secret of the Vidalia onion's legendary sweetness lies in the region's soil—or, rather, in what isn't in the soil. A reporter from Atlanta, unfamiliar with the local dialect, was completely bemused when one farmer tried to explain the secret, telling her, "Ain gah no suffer inna soil." Sure that he was reciting some weird Druid incantation, she backed away and asked him to repeat it. After about three repetitions, the light finally dawned—it was no curse; he was only explaining that there was no sulfur in the soil.

Chemicals and incantations aside, the onions do tend to be milder than most, though the claim that they can be eaten raw—like an apple—is only carried out by people who want to prove the point. There are better ways of enjoying them. Patriotism and a sense of self-preservation dictates that I tell you to use only Vidalias, but there are other Southern sweet onions that will work as well in these recipes: Texas 1015s (so called because they are planted on October 15), Walla-Wallas, and Wadmalaw Sweets (from South Carolina's Wadmalaw Island) among them. I know, I'm in trouble now.

Baked Vidalia Onions SERVES 4

No wonder this way of cooking Vidalias has become a regional classic. It's easy to do, and no other way concentrates the natural sweetness of Vidalias as does slow baking. In the dead of summer, many local cooks bake them in a microwave to avoid the oven heat. Though I tend to view "microwave cooking" as an oxymoron, this is one of the few times that I have actually used a microwave. Still, this is at its best slow-baked.

4 large Vidalia or other sweet onions
4 tablespoons unsalted butter, plus more for greasing
½ cup freshly grated Parmigiano-Reggiano

1. Position a rack in the upper third of the oven and preheat to 375°F. Trim off the root tendrils of the onions, leaving all the layers attached to the root end, and cut out the stem ends with a short, sharp paring knife, leaving a shallow, funnel-shaped well in the top of each. Peel off the brown, papery outer skins and lightly rub the outsides of the onions with a little butter. Put them, stem side up, in a shallow baking dish that will just hold them and top each one with a tablespoon of butter.

2. Bake in the upper third of the oven, basting often with pan juices, until nearly tender, about 45 minutes.

3. Remove the dish from the oven, mound the grated Parmigiano in the cut well of each and baste with pan juices. Return it to the oven and bake until the cheese is melted and golden brown, about 15–20 minutes longer. Let them sit for 5 minutes or so to disperse some of the intense heat. Serve them directly from the baking dish, or if they are intended as a first course, put them in individual rimmed soup plates and pour their pan juices evenly over them.

Note: *To cook the onions in a microwave oven, prepare them as directed in step 1, using a microwave-safe baking dish. Cook at full power for 7 minutes. Baste, top with the cheese, and cook at full power until the cheese melts (it will never get as brown as it would in a regular oven) and the onions are tender, about 3–5 minutes more. Exact cooking times may vary depending on your oven and the size of the onions, so keep an eye on them.*

Vidalia Onions with Sausage and Pecans SERVES 4

Onions filled with sausage and baked are an old classic. Here, pecans enrich and give added depth to the filling, making for an especially luxurious—and wholly Southern-tasting—dish. They're comfortable in any social situation, as a first course at a formal dinner or luncheon, or as a main course, along with a green salad, at a casual family supper.

Though Vidalias stuffed with sausage can be found on many Georgia tables during the summer, the dish is also popular in early fall, before the last of the sweet onion crop disappears from the market.

4 large Vidalia or other sweet onions

Salt

½ pound bulk sausage meat, preferably seasoned with sage

½ cup soft bread crumbs

½ cup chopped Roasted Pecans (page 209)

1 tablespoon chopped parsley

1 teaspoon chopped fresh sage (or 1 tablespoon if sausage doesn't contain sage)

1 large egg

½ cup freshly grated Gruyère or sharp cheddar

1. Position a rack in the center of the oven and preheat to 375°F. Half fill an 8- to 12-quart heavy-bottomed stockpot with water and bring it to a boil over high heat. Add a small handful of salt and the onions, and let it come back to a boil. Reduce the heat to low and simmer 20 minutes. The onions will still be a little underdone. Drain and let them cool enough to handle.

2. Trim off the root tendrils, but leave all the layers attached to the root end, and cut out the stem end with a sharp, short-bladed paring knife, forming a shallow, funnel-shaped well in the top of each. Peel off the brown outer skins. With a melon baller or similar sharp instrument, carefully scoop out the center of each onion, without breaking the root end, leaving a ½-inch-thick shell (about three layers). Set the shells aside and chop the pulp fine.

3. Crumble the sausage into a skillet and sauté over medium heat, breaking it up with a spatula, until browned, about 5 minutes. Spoon off all but 1 tablespoon of fat and add the chopped pulp. Sauté, tossing often, until it is beginning to color, about 4 minutes. Turn off the heat.

4. Add the bread crumbs and pecans, a light pinch of salt, the parsley, and optional chopped sage. Toss well. Break the egg into a separate bowl and beat until the yolk and white are well mixed. Add it to the sausage mixture and stir until absorbed.

5. Lightly butter a baking dish that will hold the onions snugly and put them into it. Spoon the stuffing into them, mounding it up on top, and sprinkle the grated cheese over them. Bake in the center of the oven until the filling is set and the cheese is golden brown, about 40 minutes. Let them settle for 10 minutes to allow some of the intense heat to subside, and serve warm.

Scalloped Vidalia Onions

SERVES 6 TO 8

Here, pecans and onions are paired together again. Easy, rich, and oh-so-wonderful to eat, this dish is a fine accompaniment for just about any meat or fish that doesn't contain cream, and it can even stand on its own as a meatless main course. It makes a perfect addition to a buffet table, as it is simple to put together and forgiving of having been made ahead and reheated.

6 medium Vidalia or other sweet onions
  (about 3 pounds)
3 tablespoons unsalted butter
1 cup soft bread crumbs
Salt and whole white pepper in a mill
Nutmeg in a grater
2 cups heavy cream (minimum 36 percent milk fat)
1 cup dry bread crumbs
1 cup pecans, cut into slivers at the grooves

1. Position a rack in the upper third of the oven and preheat to 350°F. Cut off the root and stem ends of the onions, peel them, and cut them crosswise into ½-inch-thick rounds.

2. Lightly butter a 9 x 13-inch baking dish. Sprinkle the bottom with soft bread crumbs. Lay a row of onion rounds at one end of the dish, sprinkle a few soft crumbs over them, and season lightly with salt. Add another row of onion overlapping the first one. Sprinkle with more soft crumbs and a bit of salt, and continue until all the onions are in the dish in one layer of overlapping rows. Season with several generous grindings of white pepper and gratings of nutmeg, and pour the cream evenly over all.

3. Melt the butter in a 9- to 10-inch skillet and over medium-low heat. Turn off the heat and stir in the dry bread crumbs, stirring until they have evenly absorbed the butter. Add the pecans and toss to mix. Spread this evenly over the casserole and bake in the upper third of the oven until the onions are tender, the juices are thick, and the topping is nicely browned, about 1 hour. Let stand 10 minutes before serving.

FRESH FIELD PEAS

One of the great glories of a Southern summer is something that depressingly few people (including Southerners) are exposed to nowadays—fresh field peas. These peas get their name because they are grown in a field instead of the kitchen garden, as a rotation crop to refresh the soil with nitrogen and other nutrients after being planted with more demanding crops such as corn or cotton. From those ubiquitous black-eyes, to pink-eyes, white acres, cowpeas, lady peas, to nearly extinct types like Seminole peas, there are literally dozens of varieties, all with a wonderful subtlety of flavor that is partly lost when the peas are dried or even frozen.

Part of the charm and flavor of fresh field peas comes from mixing them with snaps—that is, whole, immature pea pods, so called because they literally snap in two when you bend them. Because the peas are fresh and the snaps are already pretty tender, they cook quickly and require very little additional seasoning to bring up their flavor.

One pound of any variety of whole peas will yield 2 cups of peas when shelled. Though many markets sell fresh field peas already shelled, it is worth the extra effort to seek out whole peas and shell them yourself, not only for those lovely snaps, but because their flavor is better preserved when they are left in their pods until they are ready to be cooked.

Fresh Field Peas with Snaps SERVES 4

When field peas are really fresh, just shelled, and have plenty of tender green pods mixed into them, there is no better way to cook them than quickly in plain water. Just season them with salt, pepper, and perhaps a lump of butter; they need nothing else. As the peas mature, their flavor diminishes and the complexity of the recipe's added flavorings increase proportionately.

Any fresh field peas are appropriate for this recipe: crowders, lady peas, white acres, pink-eyes, or even black-eyes, but crowder peas are my favorite.

Field peas are traditionally served with hot Corn-bread (page 34) and finely chopped raw sweet onions passed separately.

1½ pounds (unshelled weight) fresh field peas with snaps (3 cups shelled fresh peas)

2 ounces salt pork, well rinsed and patted dry

1 medium yellow onion, peeled and chopped

1 whole pod hot red pepper

Salt

1 small yellow or Vidalia Sweet Onion, stem and roots trimmed, split lengthwise, peeled, and finely diced, optional

1. Shell the peas and break the snaps into 1-inch lengths. Put them in a colander, thoroughly rinse under cold running water, and drain well.

2. Put the salt pork in a heavy-bottomed 3- to 3½-quart saucepan over medium heat. Fry, turning several times, until the fat is rendered and the pork is browned. Remove and drain it on absorbent paper. Add the onion to the pan and sauté, tossing frequently, until softened and translucent, about 5 minutes.

3. Add the peas, 2 cups of water, the pepper pod, and the salt pork, raise the heat to medium high, and bring to a boil. Do not add salt. Reduce the heat to a slow simmer, loosely cover, and simmer until the peas are tender, about 20 minutes. Don't overcook, or the snaps will be mushy and uninteresting. Taste and adjust the salt, adding a pinch or so if needed, and simmer until the peas have absorbed it, about 2 minutes more. Remove and discard the pepper pod and serve hot, passing the diced onion separately, if you like.

Note: *Though the peas should be as fresh as possible and kept in their pods until just before you cook them, they can be cooked up to 3 days ahead without losing flavor and are actually better warmed over the next day.*

For a meatless version, omit the pork and sauté the onion in 1 tablespoon of extra-virgin olive oil. Add a clove or two of garlic, lightly crushed, peeled, and minced, to boost the flavor, and pass a cruet of olive oil at the table so that each person can drizzle some over his or her portion to taste.

PEANUTS

Peanuts have long been an important crop in Georgia, but until a Georgia peanut farmer—James Earl Carter—was elected president in 1976, they were more often associated with Virginia. It took President Carter's high profile to make the country aware that the state has a venerable and thriving peanut industry.

Although peanuts are native to our hemisphere, specifically to South America, they most likely came into the South by way of Africa. Introduced to Africa by the Portuguese early in the sixteenth century, peanuts were so quickly and thoroughly assimilated into the African diet that by the time of the slave trade, many Europeans thought that peanuts were native to that continent.

Peanuts are really neither pea nor nut, but are, rather, subterranean legumes (*Arachis hypogaea leguminosae*), that is, beans that develop underground. The lion's share of peanuts are today used as nuts—toasted and salted or ground up into nut butter, and seldom see more than the top of a bar or the insides of two slices of white bread. Yet there was a time when they were better known as a vegetable.

Some of the recipes that follow call for "green" peanuts. That has nothing to do with color, but instead indicates immature peanuts that are freshly dug. Unfortunately, green peanuts are full of moisture and don't store or travel well, so they are only available within a short distance of their growing area. In some cases, cured peanuts can be used in place of green ones, though the cooking time will of course be longer, but where a recipe says to use only green peanuts, cured peanuts can't be substituted. The best sources for raw peanuts outside the South are vegetable markets that cater to African Americans and Caribbean immigrants.

Boiled Peanuts   MAKES ABOUT 8 CUPS

Because green peanuts don't travel well, boiled peanuts are a strictly regional specialty. When the weather turns warm, the roadsides all over Georgia, North Florida, Alabama, and the Carolinas sprout with vendors and produce stands selling this hot, salty confection out of steaming oil barrel–size kettles. They are the one sure appetizer at any Southern outdoor event, from ballgames to barbecues and Lowcountry boils (where shrimp and sometimes crab are cooked with smoked sausages, fresh corn on the cob, new potatoes, and spices). "Peanut boilings," outdoor parties that center around great vats of this salty treat, are still the way that the farmers around Americus and Plains celebrate the harvest.

Boiled peanuts are alleged to be an acquired taste, but if so, the people I serve them to acquire the taste quickly. When I put a bowl of boiled peanuts in front of fellow food writer and vegetable lover Faith Willinger and her very Italian husband, I did so with reservation, not being at all sure how their palates—conditioned as they were by Italian food—would react. I needn't have worried: those Tuscan bean lovers dug in with enthusiasm, and my only worry was whether or not I would have enough.

3 pounds whole (unshelled) green peanuts

3 quarts water (approximately, see step 1)

3 rounded tablespoons salt (approximately, see step 1)

1. Wash the peanuts briefly and drain them well. Put them into a heavy-bottomed 6-quart pot. Add the water in 1-quart batches until it covers them by about 1 inch: The nuts will float, so test the depth of the water by pressing them down. It will take about 3 quarts of water to cover them. Sprinkle in 1 rounded tablespoon of salt for each quart of water and stir until it is dissolved.

2. Bring to a good boil over medium-high heat. Reduce the heat to a simmer and cook until the peanuts are tender. This will take at least 1½ hours, and maybe as long as 2 hours, depending on the freshness of the peanuts and your own taste. Some people like them very soft, while others like them to fight back a little. Start testing after an hour and a half, and continue simmering until they're tender enough to suit you.

3. Turn off the heat and let the peanuts soak in the brine until they are salty enough, about 15–30 minutes, letting your own taste be your guide. When they reach the right stage of saltiness, drain off and discard the brine. (If you like your peanuts very salty, don't drain them at all.)

4. Serve the peanuts either warm or cold, providing a large bowl for castoff shells. If you accidentally serve them to a bunch of unrefined palates that hate them and you actually have leftovers, store them in the refrigerator. They'll keep for 4 or 5 days.

Note: *Southerners consider boiled peanuts a snack food, but you can shell them and eat them as a vegetable; either just as they are, enriched with a little butter or olive oil, or in the Peanut Ragout on page 154. If you plan to use them in any of these ways, don't let them sit in the brine after they're done or they will be too salty.*

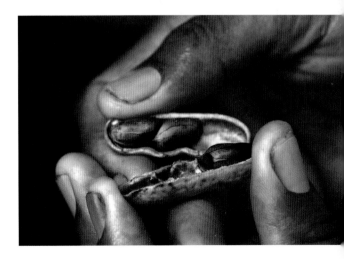

Roasted Peanuts   MAKES 4 TO 4½ CUPS, ABOUT 8 SERVINGS

Peanuts are commercially toasted by frying them in deep fat, but at home Southerners often roast or parch them in their shells. While it produces nuts that are a lot less fattening, they can be messy to serve. This method falls somewhere in between.

1 pound (4–4½ cups) shelled, raw peanuts
2 tablespoons peanut oil, preferably cold-pressed
Salt

1. Position a rack in the upper third of the oven and preheat to 275°F. Spread the peanuts on a rimmed baking sheet or 9- by 13-inch sheet-cake pan. Add the oil and toss until the nuts are coated.

2. Roast in the upper third of the oven until the nuts are crisp and are lightly colored to their centers, about 1 hour. Salt them liberally and toss until they are uniformly coated. Drain them briefly on absorbent paper and serve warm or at room temperature.

VARIATION: Parched Peanuts—To parch peanuts whole in the shells, allow 2 pounds of cured peanuts in shell and omit the oil and salt. Spread the nuts on a large, rimmed baking sheet and bake at 275°F until the nuts are lightly colored to their centers, which may take as little as an hour or as much as 1½ hours, depending on the nuts. Start checking them after an hour.

Verte's Goobers and Greens   SERVES 4

"Goober" and "goober pea" are just two of the dozens of folk names that have been given to peanuts. They are thought to derive from an African name for the legumes, and here they most definitely give away the African roots of this variation on that pot of greens common to all Southerners of African descent.

The recipe is from National Public Radio personality and culinary anthropologist Vertemae Grosvenor, whose memoir/cookbook *Vibration Cooking* has become a modern classic. Though Verte has lived all over the world, her mouth has never lost its Geechee lilt, nor its taste for the cooking of her native South Carolina Lowcountry. She says she was nearly grown before she found out that there were people in the world who did not eat rice every day. True to that tradition, rare is the day that she still does not eat rice. She even suggests adding shrimp to the greens and serving them over Carolina-Style Rice (page 37).

2 pounds fresh spinach, or spinach and beet greens, mixed (see note), or swiss chard
½ cup shelled Parched Peanuts (see this page, do not use dry-roasted, see note)
3 tablespoons extra-virgin olive oil
1 small yellow onion, split, peeled, and thinly sliced
1 clove garlic, crushed, peeled, and minced
Salt and whole black pepper in a mill
Whole nutmeg in a grater

1. Pick over the greens and remove any wilted or discolored leaves. Strip away and discard any tough stems (if you are using beet greens or chard, remove all the stems; see notes). Wash in several changes of water to remove all the grit. Drain, shake off the excess water, and coarsely chop the greens.

2. Grind the peanuts through a meat grinder or in a blender or food processor to the texture of coarse meal or raw grits; don't grind them too fine, or you'll release the oils and end up with peanut butter.

3. Put 2 tablespoons olive oil and onion in a heavy-bottomed 4-quart pot or lidded skillet over medium heat. Sauté until the onion is softened, about 3 minutes. Add the spinach (and greens) and sauté, stirring frequently, until wilted, about 5 minutes.

4. Sprinkle the garlic and peanuts over the greens and, if they appear to be too dry, a few spoonfuls of water. Cover, reduce the heat to medium low, and cook until the greens are tender, about 10 minutes. Check the pot about half way through to make sure that the moisture has not completely dried up and the greens are not sticking. If it has, sprinkle in a few more spoonfuls of water.

5. Uncover, add the remaining tablespoon of oil, a healthy pinch of salt, a few liberal grindings of pepper, and a generous grating of nutmeg to taste. Cook, uncovered and stirring frequently, until the excess moisture is evaporated, about 3 minutes more. Turn off the heat, taste and adjust the seasonings, and serve at once.

Peanut Sauce   MAKES ABOUT 3 CUPS

This sauce has African roots but has developed a distinctly Southern accent. It is the perfect mate for grilled chicken, fish, or meat kebabs and is good with roast poultry of almost any kind. It also makes a fine sauce for steamed or baked sweet potatoes, pumpkin or winter squash, or Carolina-Style Rice (page 37).

If you have access to a grocery or natural-food store that grinds peanut butter to order or sells an all-natural peanut butter with nothing added to it, you can substitute ½ cup of either of these for the peanuts. Just make sure that the peanut butter contains only peanuts.

¾ cup Roasted Peanuts (page 152)
½ cup water
2 tablespoons peanut oil
1 small onion, peeled and chopped fine
2–3 large cloves garlic, crushed, peeled, and minced
2 tablespoons tomato paste
2 cups Chicken Broth (page 21)
Salt, cayenne, and whole black pepper in a mill
2 tablespoons chopped parsley
½ teaspoon Worcestershire sauce
Juice of ½ lemon

1. Grind the peanuts, either with a mortar and pestle or in the food processor fitted with a stainless-steel blade. Gradually add the water until it is a smooth paste. Set it aside.

2. Put the oil and onion in a saucepan that will comfortably hold all the ingredients and turn on the heat to medium high. Sauté, tossing often, until the onion is softened and beginning to brown, about 5 minutes. Add the garlic and sauté until fragrant, about half a minute more. Stir in the peanut and tomato pastes. Gradually stir in the broth until it is incorporated and there are no lumps of either paste. Add a large pinch of salt, a small one of cayenne, and a few grindings of black pepper. Bring the liquid almost to a boil and lower the heat to a slow simmer. Simmer, stirring frequently, until the sauce is thick, about 15–30 minutes, depending on how thick you want it to be. Stir in the parsley, Worcestershire, and lemon juice, then taste and adjust the seasonings. Serve hot.

Note: *For a chunkier sauce, substitute ¾ cup (about 1 large) peeled, seeded, and chopped tomato for the tomato paste, and add a diced green bell pepper along with the onion in step 2. For a meatless sauce, use the chopped fresh tomato and diced bell pepper, and substitute Vegetable Broth (page 22) for the chicken broth.*

Peanut Ragout with Tomatoes and Country Ham   SERVES 4 TO 6

This stew may seem exotic to those unaccustomed to thinking of peanuts as beans, but there's really nothing new about it. This is the way that most Southern cooks would cook any kind of beans. It's an excellent accompaniment for any pork or poultry dish that does not already have tomatoes in it, or when served over rice, it makes a fine vegetarian main dish.

1½ pounds (4 cups, shelled) green peanuts or other acceptable legumes (see note, this page)

2 cups Chicken Broth (page 21) or canned broth

1 medium yellow onion, peeled and chopped

2 tablespoons bacon drippings or extra-virgin olive oil

2 large cloves garlic, peeled and minced

2 ounces (1 thick slice) julienned country ham or prosciutto

2 pounds ripe tomatoes, blanched, peeled, seeded, and chopped as directed on page 101, or 1 (28-ounce) can Italian plum tomatoes, seeded and chopped, with their juice

1 tablespoon chopped fresh thyme or 1 teaspoon dried thyme

1 tablespoon chopped parsley

1–2 bay leaves, depending on size

1 whole pod hot red pepper

Salt

1. Wash the peanuts, drain, and shell them. Put them in a pot with 2 cups of water and the broth. Bring to a boil over medium-high heat, skimming away the foam that rises. Reduce the heat to a slow simmer, loosely cover, and simmer until the peanuts are nearly tender, about 1 hour.

2. Sauté the onion in the drippings or olive oil in a heavy sauté pan over medium-high heat, tossing frequently, until softened and beginning to color, about 5–8 minutes. Add the garlic and ham, and sauté until the ham loses its raw, red color, about a minute more. Turn off the heat and add this to the peanuts.

3. Add the tomatoes, thyme, parsley, bay leaves, and pepper pod. Raise the heat to medium high and let bring it back to a boil, then reduce the heat to a slow simmer, loosely cover, and simmer until the peanuts are very tender, about an hour longer. If the liquid isn't thick, raise the heat and quickly boil it down. Taste and correct the salt, lower the heat, and let simmer another minute. Turn off the heat, remove and discard the pepper pod and bay leaves, and serve hot.

Note: *Any fresh beans, such as cranberry beans or field peas, work well in this recipe. Substitute 4 cups fresh beans or field peas, or 2 cups dried beans or peas. Soak the dried beans or peas for 6 hours or overnight in water to cover by at least 3 inches. Drain them and proceed with step 1. Fresh beans may take less time in the preliminary cooking in step 1; cured peanuts and dried beans will need more—as much as 2 hours. As a matter of fact, cooking times can vary a lot even with green peanuts. A lot depends on their freshness, size, and maturity. The younger and fresher they are, the quicker they'll cook, so don't take the cooking times as gospel, and keep an eye on the pot.*

For a meatless version, use all water or substitute Vegetable Broth (page 22) for the meat broth, omit the country ham, and add a small dash of soy sauce.

SUMMER SQUASH

The zucchini war. It strikes, in the South, in midsummer, late summer in the North. Overzealous gardeners, who cannot imagine that those tiny little seeds can possibly produce all that many squash, plant two hills too many. The plants flourish and mature and all at once start to produce—like nothing has ever produced before. Those gardeners go from being crazy for summer squash to just being crazed. They show up at your house, at church, at roadside stands, anywhere they think they have a prayer of unloading their surplus, with brown grocery sacks overloaded and splitting with glossy green things the size of baseball bats. The truly desperate drop them on your stoop like foundlings, ring your bell, and run.

Poor things, they've compounded the problem by letting the zucchini get too big. A squash the size of a baseball bat is not a gardener's pride; it ought to be a gardener's embarrassment. All summer squash—whether they are yellow crooknecks, cymlings (those little flying-saucer–like squash, also known as pattypan) or zucchini—are best when still quite immature. In fact, the name zucchini means "little squash." There's not much you can do with an overgrown one.

In spite of the annual war, we Southerners love summer squash, whether they are those Italian newcomers, zucchini, or our own yellow crooknecks. We steam them whole, mash them up with butter and cream, braise them with onions, fry them, stuff them, bake them in casseroles, and even turn them into pickles. Here is a sampling of some of our best recipes.

Yellow Summer Squash Soup with Sage and Thyme SERVES 4

Served hot or cold, this soup is the very essence of summer—from its bright, sunny color to its light, fresh flavor. Its secret lies in the youth and freshness of the main ingredient. Any variety of yellow summer squash will do; just make sure that they are very young, small, and impeccably fresh, with clear, taut skins and bright green stems.

1 pound yellow crookneck or yellow zucchini squash

1 medium leek

1 large yellow onion, stem and roots trimmed, split lengthwise, peeled, and thinly sliced

2 tablespoons unsalted butter

1 cup Chicken Broth (page 21), or ½ cup canned broth mixed with ½ cup water, or use all water

1 Bouquet Garni (page 32), made with a sprig each of thyme, parsley, and sage

Salt and whole white pepper in a mill

2 cups half-and-half

¼ cup heavy cream (optional)

4–5 fresh sage leaves, thinly sliced, or 1 tablespoon thinly sliced fresh chives

1. Scrub the squash under cold running water to remove any grit and sand that may be stuck to them. Trim off the blossom, and stem ends, and slice crosswise into ½-inch rounds. Split the leek lengthwise and holding it root end up, wash it well under running water, folding back the layers to remove the grit and sand from between them. Remove but reserve the greens of the leek and thinly slice the white part.

2. Put the leek, onion, and butter in a heavy-bottomed 3- to 4-quart pot over medium-low heat. Sweat until they are softened but not browned, about 10 minutes. Add the squash and toss well.

3. Add the broth or water and bouquet garni, raise the heat to medium high, and bring it to a boil. Add a pinch or so of salt (go easy on this if your broth is already salted; you can correct the seasonings later), and a liberal grinding of white pepper. Reduce the heat to medium low, cover, and simmer until the vegetables are tender, about 20 minutes. Turn off the heat.

4. With a slotted spoon, take up about 1 cup of the solids and set them aside. Remove and discard the bouquet garni. Puree the remainder of the soup through a food mill, or in batches in a food processor or blender. Return the puree to the pot. Thinly slice the inner light green leaves of the leek. Roughly chop the reserved solids and add them with the leek to the soup. Bring it back to a simmer over medium heat and simmer until the leek greens are just tender, about 5 minutes. The soup can be made several days in advance up to this point. If you've made it ahead or plan to serve it chilled, pour it into a bowl set in a basin of ice water. Stir until cold, then cover and refrigerate for up to four days.

5. To serve the soup hot, heat it gently over medium heat, stirring occasionally to prevent scorching. Add the half-and-half and let it come back to a simmer. Taste and correct the seasonings. Ladle the soup into heated soup plates. Garnish with a drizzle of cream and a sprinkling of the fresh sage or chives.

6. To serve the soup cold, stir the half-and-half into the chilled soup and taste and correct the seasonings. Garnish as you would the hot soup, or whip the cream until it forms soft peaks, put a dollop on each serving, and sprinkle with the herbs and a grinding of white pepper.

Note: *To make a meatless version of this soup, use water instead of broth and add a small pinch of Curry Powder (page 28). Keep the curry accent subtle; the idea isn't to make it a curried soup, but to compensate for the depth of flavor the chicken broth would have lent. Don't omit the half-and-half—the soup is lackluster without it, but don't add it until you are ready to serve.*

Sautéed Summer Squash with Onions SERVES 4

Summer squash stewed with onions and served up partially mashed with a big lump of butter is a classic summer staple on Southern tables throughout the summer. Here the same ingredients are sautéed instead, adding a light caramel element that we usually associate with cooler weather, but no less welcome when midsummer's heat blunts our appetites. It also generates a lot less heat.

1½ pounds very young yellow crookneck squash, cymlings (pattypan), or zucchini

2 small yellow onions or 4 large or 8 small green onions

2 tablespoons bacon drippings or unsalted butter

Salt and whole black pepper in a mill

1 tablespoon each chopped parsley and summer savory or chives

1. Scrub the squash under cold running water to remove any dirt and grit that may be clinging to them. Trim off the blossom and stem ends and slice them crosswise into ¼-inch-thick rounds. If using yellow onions, trim the root and stem ends, split lengthwise, peel and thinly slice them. If using green onions, wash, pat dry, trim, and slice them, keeping the white and green parts separate from one another.

2. Put the fat and sliced onion or white parts of the green onions in a large, heavy-bottomed skillet or sauté pan over medium heat. Sauté until the onions are translucent, but not colored, about 3–5 minutes. Add the squash and continue cooking, occasionally shaking the pan and turning the squash once or twice, until both vegetables are golden and tender, about 5 minutes.

3. Season liberally with salt and pepper, add the herbs, and, if you've used green onions, the green parts of those. Gently toss, taste

and adjust the seasonings, toss one last time, and turn off the heat. Transfer the squash to a warm serving bowl and serve at once.

Note: *For a vegetarian version, substitute peanut or olive oil for the fat and add a small pinch of Curry Powder (page 28) with the salt and pepper in step 2. The curry powder will lend the squash a dusky, meaty taste that it loses if you omit the bacon fat, yet will still be recognizably Southern in flavor and aroma.*

The flavor of fresh herbs is important, but if you don't have summer savory in your garden but have a nice stand of basil, use that. If you haven't any basil, but your sage is thriving, use it. Likewise, if you lack sage, use thyme.

VARIATION I: Braised Squash and Onions— When the squash are not as young and delicate as you'd like, a lovely way to bring them to their fullest potential is to braise them. When the squash are added to the pan in step 2, toss them just long enough to coat them with the fat, then season well with salt and pepper, tightly cover, and reduce the heat to medium low. Braise, shaking the pan occasionally and turning the squash after about 5 minutes, until the vegetables are tender and golden, about 10 minutes altogether. Remove the lid, and if any liquid remains, let it cook away, being careful not to scorch the vegetables. Taste and adjust the seasonings and finish the squash as directed in step 3.

VARIATION II: Sautéed Cucumbers and Onions—Substitute small, young cucumbers for the squash. Lightly peel them, split lengthwise, and if the seeds are large, scoop them out. Cut into wedges about 1½-inches long by ½-inch thick. Use butter rather than bacon fat to cook them.

Baked Stuffed Summer Squash

SERVES 4

Stuffed squash have traditionally been served as a side dish in the South. However, baked squash have a meaty flavor that allows them to hold their own as a main course, especially when reinforced, as they are here, with a bit of flavorful country ham. The neat, self-contained portions make it an appealing dish to serve at a luncheon or buffet.

4 medium yellow crookneck squash

3 tablespoons unsalted butter

½ cup minced green onions, green and white parts, or yellow onion

2 ounces country ham, chopped fine (a ⅛-inch-thick slice)

¾ cup soft bread crumbs

2 large eggs, well beaten

1 tablespoon chopped fresh thyme or 1 teaspoon dried thyme

Cream or milk

Salt and pepper

1. Position a rack in the center of the oven and preheat to 350°F. Half-fill a heavy-bottomed 4-quart pot with water and bring it to a boil over high heat. Meanwhile, scrub the squash under cold running water to remove any grit or dirt that may be clinging to them. Slip them into the boiling water, let it come back to a boil, and cook until the squash are nearly tender, about 10 minutes.

2. Lay the squash on a cutting board so that the crookneck allows it to lie flat without rolling. Slice off but reserve about ¼ inch of the side facing up. Using a melon baller or small spoon, carefully scoop out the center pulp of each squash, leaving about ¼ inch of the outer flesh intact, taking care not to puncture the shell. Chop the reserved top slices and pulp, and put it in a mixing bowl.

3. In a heavy frying pan over medium heat, sauté the onions in 2 tablespoons of the butter, stirring often, until it is translucent and softened but not colored, about 4-5 minutes. Add the ham and sauté until it loses its raw red color, about a minute more. Turn off the heat. Add the onions, ham, crumbs, beaten eggs, and thyme to the chopped pulp. Mix well, moistening it with a little cream or milk, if needed, keeping in mind that the filling should not be too wet. Season well with salt and a generous few grinding of pepper.

4. Lightly grease a shallow, flat pan (such as a rimmed baking sheet) or casserole, and arrange the hollowed-out squash open side up, not touching. Spoon the filling into each, carefully packing it in as you go to prevent air pockets, and mound it up on the top. Dot the tops with the remaining tablespoon of butter and bake in the center of the oven until the filling is set and the tops are browned, about 30 minutes. Let them rest for 10 minutes before serving hot or let them cool to room temperature.

Note: For a meatless stuffed squash, omit the ham and use a full cup of bread crumbs. Add a small pinch of Curry Powder (page 28) to the filling mixture along with the salt and pepper in step 3, to compensate for the depth of flavor that the ham lends.

Dinner-on-the-Grounds Squash Casserole   SERVES 4 TO 6

This casserole has for at least a century been a favorite of two venerable Southern social institutions, the church covered-dish supper and dinner-on-the-grounds. It's sometimes called squash soufflé, which veteran Southern food writer James Villas reminds us is what many Southerners call any casserole that contains eggs.

2 pounds yellow crooknecks or other yellow
    summer squash

2 medium yellow onions, split, peeled and
    diced small

3 tablespoons unsalted butter

½ cup soft bread crumbs

¾ cup coarsely grated aged sharp cheddar

Salt and whole black pepper in a mill

Ground cayenne pepper

2 large eggs, lightly beaten

1 cup light cream or evaporated milk

¼ cup finely crushed saltine crackers

¼ cup freshly grated Parmigiano-Reggiano

1. Scrub the squash well under cold running water, being sure to remove any grit that may be clinging to them. Bring 1 inch of water to a boil in a large, heavy-bottomed saucepan. Add the squash and onion, bring it back to a boil, then reduce the heat to medium, loosely cover, and simmer until the squash and onions are tender, about 10–15 minutes. Drain well, transfer them to a mixing bowl, and roughly crush them with a potato masher.

2. Position a rack in the center of the oven and preheat to 350°F. Mix in 2 tablespoons of the butter, the soft crumbs, and cheddar, and season well with salt, pepper, and cayenne. In a separate bowl, lightly whisk together the eggs and cream. Add this to the squash and mix well.

3. Butter a 9-inch square or 2-quart round casserole. Pour the squash batter into it and level the top. Wipe out the pan in which the squash cooked and put in the remaining butter. Melt it over medium-low heat and turn off the heat. Mix in the cracker crumbs, stirring until they're evenly coated with butter. Sprinkle the Parmigiano over the squash and top with the buttered crumbs.

4. Bake in the center of the oven until set and golden brown on top, about 30 minutes. Let stand 10 minutes and serve warm.

Uptown Squash Casserole or Gratin
SERVES 8

More complex and elegant than the old standby that precedes it here, this rich gratin is for really special occasions. Actually, come to think of it, its very presence on the table makes any meal a special occasion.

2½ pounds small summer squash, crooknecks or
    other yellow squash, yellow or green zucchini,
    or a mix of them all

2 medium yellow onions

5 tablespoons unsalted butter

Salt and whole black pepper in a mill

1 tablespoon fresh thyme leaves

1 tablespoon chopped fresh summer savory or sage
    (don't use dried)

2 cups heavy cream or Crème Fraîche (page 18)

1 cup finely crushed saltine crackers or dry bread
    crumbs

1. Scrub the squash well under cold running water, being sure to remove any grit that may be clinging to them. Trim the stem and blossom ends and slice crosswise into ¼-inch-thick slices. Position a rack in the center of the oven and preheat to 350°F, and lightly butter a 3-quart gratin dish or shallow 3-quart casserole.

2. Meanwhile, put the onion and 2 tablespoons of the butter in a large, heavy-bottomed skillet or sauté pan over medium-high heat. Sauté, tossing often, until the onions are golden brown, about 8–10 minutes. Remove them from the pan with a slotted spoon. Add another tablespoon of butter and half the squash. Sauté, turning them occasionally, until they are beginning to color, about 5 minutes. Take the pan from the heat and transfer the squash to the prepared casserole in a single layer. Season well with salt and pepper and scatter half the onions and herbs over them, then spoon half the cream evenly over them.

3. Return the skillet to the heat, add another tablespoon of butter, and sauté the remaining squash, then add them to the gratin dish, season with salt and pepper, and cover with the remaining onions, herbs, and cream.

4. Wipe out the skillet, put in the remaining tablespoon of butter, and melt it over low heat. Turn off the heat and stir in the crumbs, tossing until they are evenly coated. Sprinkle them evenly over the squash and bake in the center of the oven until bubbly at the center and golden brown on top, about 30 minutes. Let stand 10 minutes and serve warm.

Jo Bettoja's Georgia Pasta

SERVES 4 TO 5 (4 ITALIANS, 5 SOUTHERNERS)

Jo Bettoja is an extraordinary Italian author and cooking teacher, born and raised in a little town called Millen not too far from Rome—that's Rome, Georgia, not Italy. It was only after she married Angelo Bettoja that she found herself living in the Eternal City. Now when she comes back to Georgia, newspapers occasionally report, to her combined embarrassment and amusement, that "Contessa Bettoja" is in town, even though she is not really a contessa.

What happens when a fine Southern cook moves to Italy? She becomes a fine Italian cook, that's what happens, and two wonderful cuisines collide in her kitchen, getting happily muddled. There are many parallels between Italian and Southern cooking, and Jo has lived with them for nearly her entire career as a cook. Nothing illustrates the blend of traditions better than this dish, which is a cross between a Southern squash casserole and Italian pasta al forno. In Georgia she makes it with that most Southern of squash, yellow crooknecks, but in Rome, she says, she "made do" with zucchini. It's powerfully good no matter which squash you use.

2 pounds young, small zucchini or yellow crookneck squash

Salt and whole black pepper in a mill

4 tablespoons unsalted butter

Handful fresh basil leaves (about ¼ cup, tightly packed)

⅔ pound sedanini or pennette (small penne) or other small, tubular imported Italian pasta

¼ pound Parmigiano-Reggiano, freshly grated

1 large egg

2 tablespoons fresh dry bread crumbs

1. Thoroughly wash the squash under cold running water, trim them, and cut them into chunks. In a kettle that will comfortably hold the squash, bring enough water to just cover them to a boil over high heat. Add a large pinch of salt and the squash, bring it back to a boil, and cook the squash until they are tender, about 5 minutes. Drain them well and roughly mash them with a fork or potato masher. Add a liberal grinding of pepper and 2 tablespoons of the butter. Chop two-thirds of the basil and stir it into the squash. Set aside. (The squash can be prepared to this point a day ahead.)

2. Position a rack in the upper third of the oven and preheat to 350°F. Bring 3 quarts of water to a boil in a large, heavy pot. Add a small handful of salt and the pasta and cook for half the time indicated on the package (about 4–5 minutes—the pasta should be underdone). Thoroughly drain and spread it on a large platter. Add the remaining 2 tablespoons of butter and three-fourths of the Parmesan, mixing it in well, and spread the pasta to arrest the cooking.

3. Break the egg into a separate bowl and beat until smooth. Add it and the pasta to the squash and mix well. Lightly butter a 2½-quart baking dish and add in the pasta and squash.

4. Chop the remaining basil and mix it with the crumbs. (This can be done in a food processor: put both in the processor bowl fitted with a steel blade and pulse until the basil is finely chopped.) Mix the remaining Parmesan with the crumbs and sprinkle this over the top of the casserole. Bake in the upper third of the oven until the pasta is tender and the top nicely browned, about 30 minutes. Serve hot.

Note: *Jo advises that the squash can be prepared ahead of time, but don't mix it with the pasta until you are ready to bake it. If you make the squash a day ahead and refrigerate it, let it come back to room temperature before adding it to the pasta. The pasta cannot be made ahead, but since it only partially cooks before it goes into the casserole, it doesn't take long to get it ready.*

Fried Summer Squash   SERVES 4

Dyed-in-the-wool Southerner that I am, this is my favorite way of doing any young summer squash—whether yellow crooknecks, pattypans (cymlings), or zucchini. The secrets to success are two: the squash should be very fresh and still quite young (leave the more mature ones for the stewing pot), and the cornmeal should be fresh, clean-smelling, and really stone-ground.

1½ pounds young summer squash
1 cup fine stone-ground cornmeal
Lard or vegetable oil, for frying
Salt and whole black pepper in a mill

1. Position a rack in the upper third of the oven and preheat the oven to 150°F (or the "warm" setting). Scrub the squash under cold running water to remove any grit that may be clinging to them, dry them, trim off the stem and blossom ends, and cut them into slices a little more than ⅛-inch but less than ¼-inch thick—crosswise in rings if the squash are long and thick, or lengthwise if small.

2. Spread the meal on a dinner plate and have both squash and breading close by the cooking surface.

3. Put enough lard or oil in a wide, cast-iron or other heavy-bottomed skillet to come up the sides by at least ½ inch. Turn on the heat to medium high. When the melted fat is hot but not smoking (around 375°F), roll the squash slices in the meal until they are coated, and gently shake off the excess. Slip them into the hot fat as soon as they are coated, and keep adding more slices until the pan is full but not crowded.

4. Fry the squash until the bottoms are golden brown, about 3 minutes, then carefully turn them and let the other side brown. As soon as they have evenly browned, take them up with a slotted spatula or spoon and lay them on a wire rack set over a cookie sheet to drain. Keep them in the warm oven while the remaining squash cook. Add more squash to the pan as soon as there is space, until all the slices are cooked.

5. Season them lightly with salt and a few good grindings of pepper. Fold a cotton or linen napkin to fit and place it on a serving platter. Place the squash on the napkin in a single layer and serve hot. Never crowd or stack them or they will get soggy.

Note: *I find it best to drain all fried vegetables on a wire rack set on a cookie sheet rather than on the usual butcher paper or paper towels. The vegetables are full of moisture that seems to be naturally drawn to absorbent paper, making the bottom crusts limp and soggy.*

VARIATION: Mama's Fried Summer Squash in Parmesan Batter—My mother often fries summer squash in a Parmesan cheese breading. Substitute 1 cup finely grated Parmigiano-Reggiano for the cornmeal. Fry them in very little fat—use just enough to coat the pan. For a crisper texture, mix ½ cup Parmesan with ½ cup dry bread or cracker crumbs; dip the squash first in 1 beaten egg, then coat them with the crumb and cheese mixture, and deep-fry them as directed above.

Maryland Squash Croquettes

MAKES ABOUT 12 CROQUETTES, OR 6 SERVINGS

This old Maryland recipe is sometimes called "mock crab" because it is supposed to imitate the flavor of those famous Chesapeake Bay blue crabs. Well, I don't know that they really taste all that much like crab, but they taste pretty good, and the boiling spice blend, which was designed primarily as a seasoning for seafood, does give the croquettes a hint of the seacoast.

1 pound zucchini or yellow crookneck squash

1 small yellow onion

1 large clove garlic

1½ cups fine cracker crumbs

1 tablespoon Homemade Mayonnaise (page 44)

2 teaspoons Seafood Boiling Spice (page 28) or Old Bay brand seasoning and ½ teaspoon salt

1 large egg

½ pound (2 sticks) unsalted butter or ¼ pound (1 stick) butter and ½ cup peanut oil, mixed

1 lemon, cut into 8 wedges

Parsley sprigs, for garnish

1 recipe Savannah Sweet Red Pepper Sauce (page 46) or Herb Mayonnaise (page 44)

1. Position a rack in the upper third of the oven and preheat to 150°F (or the "warm" setting). Scrub the squash under cold running water to remove any grit that may be clinging to them. Cut off the stem and blossom ends and grate the squash through the large holes of a hand grater or food processor. Put the grated squash in a colander and let it stand in the sink for half an hour. Squeeze it to remove as much moisture as possible and transfer it to a mixing bowl.

2. Peel the onion and grate it to the same size as the squash. Crush, peel, and mince the garlic. Add both to the squash along with the cracker crumbs, mayonnaise, and spice blend. Break the egg into a separate bowl and beat lightly until the yolk and white are evenly mixed. Add it to the squash and mix well.

3. Heat the fat in a heavy-bottomed 10-inch skillet over medium heat. When the butter is melted and the foaming subsides, take up the squash batter by heaped 2-tablespoon-size scoops and slip them into the fat until the skillet is full but not crowded. Fry until the bottoms are golden brown, about 3 minutes, carefully turn, and fry until they are uniformly browned and their centers are set, about 3 minutes more.

4. Take them up with a slotted spatula and put them on absorbent paper, drain briefly, then transfer them to a rimmed baking sheet and put them in the warm oven. Fry the remaining croquette batter the same way. When they're all done, transfer them to a serving platter, garnish with lemon wedges and parsley, and serve at once, passing the sauce of your choice separately.

Note: *Draining the grated squash well is a critical step, as they throw off a lot of liquid that would otherwise make the batter too soupy. Even with the draining, they'll continue to throw off moisture, so don't let the batter sit once it is made, but cook it at once. Keep the croquettes fairly small as well, so you won't have trouble with them breaking up when you try to turn them.*

SWEET POTATOES IN SUMMER

There are many people who think that sweet potatoes are only for the fall and winter, who have never seen them without a thick covering of marshmallows, or brown sugar and pecans, or on a table that did not also have a turkey on it. In the South, sweet potatoes have never been confined solely to Thanksgiving dinner, but are a year-round staple. In the summer, we roast them on the grill or slice them and grill them directly over hot coals. We turn them into fries and salads—just like white potatoes—and serve them up in Sweet Potato Vichyssoise (page 215). They'll even put in an appearance at dessert.

Sweet Potato Salad   SERVES 6 TO 8

Southern sweet potato salads are often so full of sugar, apples, raisins, and marshmallows that they seem more like dessert than salad. So people meet this one with surprise, since it contains few ingredients besides potatoes, and none of them are sweet—green onions, red bell peppers, and a light vinaigrette. However, surprise usually turns into enthusiasm after the first bite.

This fits all my requirements for a great summer salad: It's nice to look at, simple to make, and, best of all, can be made on the morning before you plan to serve it, when the air is still fairly cool and you can deal with boiling potatoes. Its sweet-tangy flavor makes it a perfect accompaniment for grilled or barbecued meat of any sort.

Of course, the most appealing thing of all is that it also happens to be very, very good.

3 pounds sweet potatoes

2 medium red bell peppers, washed, stemmed, and cored, seeds and membranes removed

8 small scallions or other small green onions, washed and trimmed

Red wine vinegar

Salt and whole black pepper in a mill

Extra-virgin olive oil

2 tablespoons chopped parsley

1. Scrub the sweet potatoes under cold running water. Put them in a heavy 6- to 8-quart pot and add enough water to cover them by an inch. Lift out the potatoes, cover the pot, and bring it to a brisk boil over high heat. Return the potatoes to the pot, cover, and let it come back to a boil. Reduce the heat to medium, set the lid askew, and simmer until the potatoes are just tender and can be pierced through with a sharp knife. Drain and let them cool enough to handle.

2. Meanwhile, cut the bell peppers into small dice and thinly slice the scallions. When they're cool enough to handle, peel and cut the potatoes into ½-inch dice.

3. Put the potatoes, peppers, and scallions in a large serving bowl. Sprinkle generously with wine vinegar, salt, and pepper to taste, and gently toss to mix. Let stand for 5 minutes or so, then taste and adjust the seasonings. Drizzle lightly with olive oil—just enough to lightly coat the potatoes—and toss again. Let it cool completely before serving. (The salad can be made ahead and refrigerated, but take it out of the refrigerator at least half an hour before serving it to let it lose some of the chill.) Just before serving, sprinkle with the chopped parsley.

Grill-Roasted Sweet Potatoes

SERVES 4

These potatoes are an ideal accompaniment to barbecued spareribs, chicken, or any other meat that cooks slowly on the grill. You just put them on the back of the grill while the meat is cooking and give them an occasional turn—and when the meat is ready, so are they.

4 small sweet potatoes (about 8 ounces each)
Unsalted butter or peanut oil
Salt and whole black pepper in a mill

1. Prepare a grill with coals—preferably of natural hardwood—and ignite them. While the coals are burning down, scrub the potatoes under cold running water. Pat them dry and rub lightly with butter or peanut oil. Put them on a plate and set aside.

2. When the coals are ready, spread them so that there is a clear spot at the back of the grill without any coals. Put the potatoes over this bare spot, with no coals directly beneath them. Roast, turning frequently so that the skin browns evenly, until they are tender and yield

easily when pressed with your finger, about 45 minutes. Serve hot, passing more butter, salt, and the peppermill separately.

Sweet Potato Ice Cream   MAKES ABOUT ½ GALLON

This is really just a frozen version of a sweet potato custard pie. The flavorings are the same—lemon peel, nutmeg, and bourbon—and they are kept subtle so that the flavor of the sweet potatoes is allowed to come through. The pecan topping is a nice finish, but you can omit it and splash a spoonful of bourbon over each serving if you don't like chewy things in your ice cream.

There are several important secrets to ensure success in making this ice cream. The potatoes must be mature: New sweet potatoes that have not properly cured are often stringy and tend to "seize up" when frozen. Also make sure the potatoes are absolutely smooth and free of lumps before adding the cream: If you try to beat them smooth after the cream is added, the cream is likely to break and turn to butter, leaving hard little granules of fat in your base mixture.

1 pound (about 2 medium) sweet potatoes
1 cup sugar
3 cups half-and-half
1 cup heavy cream (minimum of 36 percent milk fat)
1 tablespoon bourbon
Grated zest of 1 lemon
Nutmeg in a grater
About 1 teaspoon ground cinnamon, optional
1 cup chopped toasted pecans or pralines (optional)

1. Position a rack in the center of the oven and preheat to 400°F. Scrub the sweet potatoes under cold running water, remove any root tendrils, and pat dry. Prick them in several places with a carving fork or paring knife, and put them on a

wrap directly on top of it, cover, and freeze until firm, about 2 hours more. If you like, you may serve this sprinkled with the chopped pecans or pralines.

Note: *Because of the rich, starchy qualities of the sweet potatoes, I've found that too much fat in the base mixture results in an unpleasant, waxy after-feel in the mouth, so don't be tempted to enrich the base with more cream: Trust me, I've tried it. If you have more than a cup of puree from the potatoes, don't worry about it—a little more shouldn't make much difference. A pound should produce about 1 cup of puree.*

SUMMER FRUIT

Southern summers may be muggy and hot, but they have always had their compensations—even before Coca-Cola came along and we all became imprisoned in our houses by air-conditioning. We iced our tea, we froze our cream, we juleped our bourbon, we moved the living room out onto the front porch and our parties out under the shade tree in the yard. And yes, we invented Coca-Cola.

The best and most satisfying compensation was always the plentitude of summer fruit that the hot climate made possible. A picnic without a sweet, crisp watermelon chilled in the nearest creek or spring is just not a Southern picnic; a church summer social that does not include peach ice cream is doomed to failure; a midday Sunday dinner without a bowl of sliced sweet cantaloupe is a dinner that is happening somewhere north of the Mason–Dixon line.

And a summer without a fresh fruit cobbler is a summer that is not worth living.

Blackberries and Other Cane Berries

In late summer, blackberry brambles grow wild all over the pastures and thickets of the South. As children, we ate them in prodigal quantities because they were plentiful and free for the picking. We would go out early and come home late

rimmed baking sheet. Bake in the center of the oven, turning once or twice, until tender and easily pierced with a carving fork, about 45 minutes. Let them cool enough to handle, peel them, and while they're still warm, put them through a potato ricer. You should have at least 1 cup of puree. Stir the sugar into the puree until it is dissolved, and let cool completely.

2. Gradually stir in the half-and-half and cream, stirring well after each addition until smooth. The mixture should be the consistency of a thick custard. Add the bourbon, lemon zest, and a few gratings of nutmeg and, if you like, the cinnamon, both to taste. Stir well until thoroughly blended, cover, and refrigerate until well chilled—2 hours or overnight.

3. Freeze the cream to the consistency of soft-serve ice cream in an ice-cream freezer, following the manufacturer's directions. Transfer it to a freezable container, lay a sheet of plastic with gallons of luscious deep-purple berries, our fingers stained and our stomachs as full as our buckets. Mama would be up late that night putting up countless jars of jam, because it was a family favorite, but she always saved enough berries for a cobbler or two. It would come to the table, its golden crust glistening with butter and oozing thick purple juice, the most beautiful thing, for the moment, that we'd ever seen. And then, in short order, it was gone.

Cane berries are so-called because the shrub grows in stiff canes. Botanically, they're a part of the rose family (*Rosaceae rubus*), a fact that's given away by their leaves and delicate blossoms, and are actually close relatives of strawberries. Varieties of this fruit can be found all over the world, but most of the blackberries we enjoy are native to America. True raspberries were imported from Europe by the early colonists, but they didn't do well south of Virginia until recently when heat-tolerant hybrid varieties were developed, and therefore figured only nominally in the traditional cookery of the Deep South.

Blackberry Cobbler   SERVES 4 TO 6

If you live in a place where the only fresh blackberries you ever see are sold in expensive little plastic packets, buy them anyway and make this; it's worth every penny. Out of season, individually quick-frozen berries make a very nice cobbler indeed, and bring a welcome whiff of summer to winter's table.

FOR THE CRUST:

2 cups unbleached all-purpose flour

2 teaspoons baking powder, preferably single-acting

½ teaspoon salt

¼ pound (1 stick) chilled unsalted butter, cut into bits

1 tablespoon chilled lard

⅔ cup buttermilk or ½ cup plain, all-natural yogurt mixed with enough skimmed milk to make ⅔ cup total

FOR THE FILLING:

Sugar

5 cups ripe blackberries, washed and drained

2 tablespoons flour

2 tablespoons bourbon

6 tablespoons unsalted butter, cut into bits

Vanilla ice cream, Sweet Potato Ice Cream (page 164), or 1 cup chilled heavy cream or Bourbon Custard (page 47), optional

1. Sift or whisk together the flour, baking powder, and salt together in a large mixing bowl. Add the butter and lard and cut it in with a pastry blender, fork, or two knives until it is the consistency of coarse meal. Make a well in the center and add ½ cup of buttermilk. Lightly but thoroughly mix it in. The dough should be fairly soft; if it's too crumbly or stiff, add the rest of the liquid by spoonfuls until you get the right consistency. Gather the dough into a ball and divide it into two parts—one slightly larger than the other.

2. Position a rack in the center of the oven and preheat to 375°F. Lightly flour a work surface and roll out the larger piece of dough to a thickness of about ⅛ inch. Line a deep dish, such as a 9-inch round casserole or soufflé dish with it and trim off the excess dough.

3. Sprinkle the bottom with a spoonful of sugar, and spread half the berries over it. Sprinkle them generously with sugar (how much will depend on how sweet the berries are), 1 tablespoon of flour, and 1 tablespoon of bourbon. Scatter 2 tablespoons of the butter bits over them and then lay the dough trimmings over them. Sprinkle the strips of dough with sugar and put in the rest of the berries, then sprinkle the berries with more sugar and the remaining tablespoons of flour and bourbon. Scatter another 2 tablespoons of butter over them.

4. Roll out the remaining dough to the same thickness as the bottom crust and lay it over the berries, seal the edges to the bottom crust by moistening them with a little water or milk.

Crimp the edges decoratively and cut several gashes in the top. If you like, you can also cut decorative shapes from any scraps of dough that remain, brush their backs with milk, and lay them decoratively over the top. Put the dish on a rimmed cookie sheet and bake in the center of the oven for 20 minutes.

5. Meanwhile melt the remaining 2 tablespoons of butter in a small pan over low heat. Remove the cobbler from the oven, brush the top with the melted butter and dust it well with sugar. Return it to the oven and bake until the top is golden and the filling is bubbling at the center about 40 more minutes more. Serve warm with vanilla ice cream, sweet potato ice cream, or a pitcher of very cold heavy cream or bourbon custard passed separately.

Blackberry (or Raspberry) Bourbon Sauce   MAKES 4 SERVINGS

The first time you make this sauce, especially if you're using delicate raspberries, you're going to suspect that I have been lying down with too many of those bottles of bourbon I keep talking about. The method is the same as Cherries Kentuckian (page 172), except that here the heat and flaming liquor are always applied behind the scenes in the kitchen and the berries lose their shape and are cooked until they disintegrate into a hopeless-looking mush. Don't give up: While they surrender their shape and texture, they're transformed into a silky sauce that, when strained, glides over ice cream like melted rubies.

This sauce is wonderful served over homemade peach or vanilla ice cream or, especially if you've made it with raspberries, over chocolate ice cream or your favorite chocolate mousse. Pooled underneath a slab of chocolate pound cake or a thick slice of chess pie, it will make your company roll over and play dead.

½ pound fresh blackberries or raspberries

2 tablespoons unsalted butter

3–4 tablespoons sugar, to taste

¼ cup warm bourbon

1. Gently rinse the berries under cold running water and drain them well. Warm the butter in a heavy-bottomed sauté pan over medium-high heat.

2. When the butter is melted and the foaming begins to subside, add the berries and sprinkle them with the sugar. Cook, shaking the pan constantly, until they are beginning to dissolve, about a minute (raspberries will do this right away; blackberries will take a little longer because of the center core—and will never completely come apart as raspberries will).

3. Add the bourbon, stir, and—leaning away from the pan—ignite it, either by tipping the pan toward the flame if you have a gas stove, or by putting a long lighted match near the surface. Continue cooking, shaking the pan and stirring after the flame subsides, until the flame goes out and the berries are collapsed.

4. Strain the sauce through a fine wire-mesh sieve set over a warm serving bowl, pressing well on the solids. Stir well and serve warm.

Raspberry Vinegar MAKES ABOUT 2½ CUPS

During the "gourmet" era of the 1980s, raspberry vinegar and tart-sweet vinaigrettes made from the stuff became the rage of practically every cafe and restaurant that had any ambition to fashion. By the time the trend finally ran its course, every salad dressing manufacturer in the land was making some version of raspberry vinaigrette and it could even be found among the individually packaged condiments of fast-food chains.

It was as if we had never seen the likes of it before. But we had.

In the eighteenth and nineteenth centuries, before the advent of carbonated soft drinks, berry-infused vinegars were commonplace. Mostly they were made into a sweet syrup and mixed with chilled water for a refreshing summertime drink, very much like lemonade. The big difference is that vinegar creates a subtle tingle at the back of the tongue that's close to the refreshing, cooling sensation created by carbonation. We'd do well to rediscover what this lovely vinegar can bring to a punch bowl, although nowadays we're more likely to use it in the salad bowl.

It's very easy to make, and homemade flavored vinegar never fails to impress company.

For most things, I would tell you that fresh fruit is the optimum, but fresh raspberries are always expensive, and it would be a shame to waste them on vinegar unless you just happened to grow your own and had a bumper crop. Good quality frozen berries are not only fine for this, they're preferable.

1 pound (4 cups) fresh or individually quick frozen raspberries

2 cups red wine vinegar

1. If using fresh berries, rinse them under cold running water and drain well. Put them into a stainless-steel or glass bowl and lightly crush them. If using frozen berries, put them in the bowl while still frozen. Crushing them is not necessary. Add the vinegar, stir, and cover with cheesecloth or wire mesh (a large mesh colander or frying splatter screen would be ideal) and let stand 48 hours.

2. Strain the vinegar through wire-mesh sieve (lined with cheesecloth if the mesh is not fine enough to catch all the solids). The vinegar can be bottled, sealed, and used as is, both as a base for beverages and as a condiment. To use it as a beverage, allow 2–3 tablespoons per 8 ounces of ice water and sweeten to taste.

Notes: *To make raspberry vinegar syrup for use in beverages, mix the vinegar with 1 cup of simple syrup made as follows: Stir 1 cup sugar and 1 cup water together in a heavy-bottomed saucepan. Bring it to a simmer over medium heat and simmer without stirring until it is reduced to the consistency of honey (230°F on a candy thermometer), about 1 cup. Take it from the heat and cool, then mix it with the vinegar, or add it to the beverage to taste.*

"Put 1 quart of ripe red raspberries in a bowl; pour on them a quart of strong well-flavored vinegar, let them stand 24 hours, strain them through a bag, put this liquid on another quart of fresh raspberries, which strain in the same manner, and then on a third quart; when this last is prepared, make it very sweet with pounded loaf sugar; refine and bottle it. It is a delicious beverage mixed with iced water."

—Mary Randolph, *The Virginia House-wife*, 1824

BLUEBERRIES

Ever since I was a small boy, blue has been my favorite color. It's no surprise, then, that a berry that was called blue would become one of my favorite fruits. Never mind that beneath its bluish skin, the juice and flesh were deep, red-purple—a color that the entire fruit takes on when it's cooked: Its name was "blue" and that was enough for me.

Blueberries are the fruit of a Native American shrub in the Vacciniaceae family that includes (among others) bilberries, deerberries, huckleberries, and whortleberries. Varieties of these shrubs grow from Canada to Mexico, and are even found in the Caribbean. They were once so profuse in the wild that they were not much cultivated until the late nineteenth century, but today, they're widely farmed and are a popular seasonal fruit at local farmers' markets.

Blueberries are associated with deep summer in the northeast, but down South they're seasonal from early spring in Florida, to late May and early June here in Southeast Georgia, to late June and July in the hill country of Carolina and Virginia. Though the best fruit will come from local farmers, these berries hold up well in shipping, and in season quite good ones can be found even in supermarkets. In fact, one can follow the progress of summer in its northward amble simply by watching where the blueberries in your market have originated.

Another delicious way to use blueberries is in Peach and Blueberry Compote (page 183). They can also be substituted for blackberries in Blackberry Cobbler (page 166) and make a lovely fruit sauce when substituted for cherries in Cherries Kentuckian (page 172). Follow the notes at the end of the recipe.

Blueberry Crumble   SERVES 6 TO 8

Crumbles, crisps, and cobblers may be homey and artless, but that's exactly what makes them so appealing: they're simply dumped together and baked. While all three of them can be made with any fruit, there's something about tart-sweet blueberries in a crumble that is as close to perfection as we ever get in this life. If someone

else has made it, I can enjoy a double-crusted blueberry pie, blueberry jam, or silken blueberry sauce spooned over pound cake or ice cream as well as anyone else, but in my own kitchen, a crumble is my favorite way to cook these berries, and may well be my favorite summer dessert.

3 pints blueberries

¾ cup sugar

Salt

1 tablespoon cornstarch

1 teaspoon ground cinnamon

½ teaspoon freshly grated nutmeg

1 lemon

1 tablespoon bourbon (don't use Bourbon Vanilla for this)

7 ounces (about 1½ cups) all-purpose flour

⅔ cup firmly packed light brown sugar

4 ounces (8 tablespoons or 1 stick) unsalted butter

Vanilla ice cream, heavy cream, or Bourbon Custard, for serving (optional)

1. Position a rack in the center of the oven and preheat it to 375°F. Lightly butter a shallow 2-quart casserole. Wash, drain, and pick over the berries to remove any stems and blemished fruit. Put it in a glass or stainless-steel mixing bowl and add the sugar, a small pinch of salt, cornstarch, cinnamon, and nutmeg. Grate in the zest from the lemon and add the bourbon. Toss well. Halve the lemon and add a squeeze of lemon juice, to taste—depending on the tartness of the berries.

2. Pour the berries into the prepared dish, scraping the bowl well. Wipe out, rinse, and dry the bowl and put the flour and brown sugar in it. Whisk until well mixed, then add the butter and cut it in until it resembles coarse meal, with lumps no bigger than very small peas. Sprinkle this over the fruit and bake in the center of the oven until golden brown and the filling is bubbly in the center, about 45 minutes. Let it settle for about 10 minutes before serving warm with, if you like, a small scoop of ice cream on each

portion or a pitcher of cream or custard passed separately.

Note: *When the berries are very tart, I'll often substitute the zest of half an orange and a little orange juice for the lemon. This recipe can also be made with any summer berries or fruit— blackberries, cherries (especially sour cherries), peaches, and mangoes—or for that matter, autumn apples and pears. Feel free to vary the spices, too—a whisper of freshly ground black pepper added with the cinnamon is lovely with blackberries or cherries, fragrant cardamom is fine with apples, a little fresh-grated ginger mates well with apples and pears.*

Nick's Lemon Cornmeal Cake with Rosemary Syrup and Blueberry Compote   SERVES 8 TO 10

This lovely lemon and rosemary scented corn-meal cake, from Savannah caterer Chef Nick Mueller (see also page 123), is the perfect end for just about any summer meal, but also transitions beautifully into autumn and is the ideal end for a hearty dinner of game or roasted pork. The compote is delicious on its own and can also be served with crisp shortbread cookies and whipped cream as a simple fruit dessert (this amount will serve about 4) or spooned over your favorite vanilla or *dulce de leche* ice cream.

FOR THE BLUEBERRY COMPOTE:

1 pint blueberries

¼ cup sugar

Salt

2 tablespoons sloe gin, blackberry brandy, or ruby port

6 fresh mint leaves, thinly sliced

½ teaspoon freshly squeezed lemon juice or cider vinegar

FOR THE ROSEMARY SYRUP:

¾ cup water

2 cups sugar

Salt

3 large sprigs fresh rosemary

FOR THE LEMON CORNMEAL CAKE:

1 cup fresh, stone-ground yellow cornmeal

½ cup cake flour or all-purpose flour

1¾ teaspoons baking powder

4 ounces (½ cup or 1 stick) unsalted butter

1 cup sugar

½ teaspoon Bourbon Vanilla (page 29) or pure vanilla extract

¼ teaspoon salt

Zest of 3 lemons

2 large eggs

¾ cup whole milk

1. Make the compote: Put the berries in a medium glass or ceramic mixing bowl. Add the sugar, a small pinch of salt, the sloe gin, brandy, or port, mint, and lemon juice, and gently stir until well mixed. Let it sit for at least 1 hour.

2. Make the syrup: Bring the water, sugar, and a small pinch of salt to a simmer and simmer until the sugar is completely dissolved. Add the rosemary and turn off the heat. Let it steep for at least 30 minutes.

3. Make the cake: Position a rack in the center of the oven and preheat to 350°F. Butter and flour a 10-inch cake or springform pan and line the bottom with a round of parchment. Whisk together the meal, flour, and baking powder in a medium mixing bowl. In a separate bowl, cream the butter and sugar with a mixer fitted with the paddle attachment until fluffy. Beat in the vanilla, salt, and lemon zest and continue beating until very fluffy and light.

4. Beat in the eggs one at a time. Alternating in four additions, beat in the dry ingredients and milk, mixing at medium speed until the batter is just smooth. Do not overmix it. Scrape the batter into the prepared pan and lightly tap it on the counter until level. Bake in the center of the oven until a cake tester or toothpick inserted into the center comes out clean, about 25 minutes. Remove the cake to a wire cooling rack and let it cool for 5 minutes or so.

5. Invert a large plate over the cake, then carefully turn the cake over onto it and remove the pan. Peel away the parchment, then invert a second plate over the cake and turn it over so that the cake is now top-side up. Puncture the cake at regular intervals with a skewer or the tip of a paring knife. Strain the syrup, discarding the rosemary, and return it to the pan. Warm it to blood heat over medium-low heat, turn off the heat, and spoon it over the cake.

6. To serve the cake, you may cut it into individual servings and spoon the blueberries over each serving, or top the entire cake with the compote before cutting it. Nick serves it with vanilla ice cream, but it's splendid just as it is.

Cherries Kentuckian SERVES 4

This is not just cherries jubilee with a Kentucky twist. There are a couple of important differences. First, the substitution of Kentucky's national beverage for the traditional brandy or cognac lends the fruit a smoother, richer flavor. And secondly, instead of pouring the cherry sauce over the ice cream while it is still flaming, it's cooked until the alcohol completely burns off, thereby eliminating the harsh aftertaste that the lingering alcohol often lends. It may not be as showy, but it tastes better—and that's what really matters.

The original cherries jubilee was always done tableside by a waiter, but I do enough cooking in front of people in my classes: At home, I put this together in the kitchen. You, of course, may do it tableside in a sauté pan or chafing dish over a portable burner if you want to show off.

10 ounces (about 3 dozen) Bing or other dark cherries

2–3 tablespoons sugar (see step 1)

2 tablespoons unsalted butter

⅓ cup bourbon, warmed but not hot

1 pint French vanilla ice cream, preferably homemade

1. Wash the cherries, pit with a cherry pitter, and then split them in half (or split them with a paring knife, twist them to loosen the pits, and then remove the pits). Sprinkle the cherries with 2–3 tablespoons of sugar—depending on how sweet the fruit is. Stir until the sugar is nearly dissolved. Chill four individual serving bowls for at least half an hour before you plan to serve this.

2. Put the butter in a large sauté pan over medium-high heat. When it's melted and hot, add the cherries and any juice that has accumulated and sauté until they are heated through, about 3 minutes.

3. Add the bourbon, stir, and—leaning away from the pan—ignite it, either by tipping the pan toward the flame if you have a gas stove, or by putting a long lighted match near the surface. Continue cooking, shaking the pan and stirring after the flame subsides, until the flame goes out and the juice is thick.

4. Quickly scoop the ice cream into the chilled serving bowls, divide the cherries among them, and serve at once.

PEACHES OR MANGOES KENTUCKIAN: Peaches and cherries are close kin to one another, and peaches are slap wonderful substituted in this recipe. So are mangoes. Allow 1 cup of peaches or mangoes (about 2 large ones), blanched, peeled, and pitted as directed in Georgia Peach Soup (page 181). Cut the peaches or mangoes into ½-inch chunks. If you do this ahead of time, squeeze a little lemon juice over them to keep them from discoloring.

BLUEBERRY BOURBON SAUCE: Substitute a pint of blueberries for the cherries and Cinnamon Sugar (1 tablespoon ground cinnamon mixed with 1 cup sugar in a covered jar) for the sugar. Add the grated zest of half an orange when you put the berries in the pan.

FIGS

An unproductive fig tree is the only inanimate object that Jesus was ever known to rebuke, and Southern gardeners fully understand his irritation. Imported with the European colonists, figs have been a common fruit tree in our gardens for more than four centuries. They're a late summer and even early autumn fruit in cooler climates, but down South they come into season early.

When they are at their absolute peak, you don't need a recipe to make one of the loveliest summer desserts possible. Wash ripe three to five ripe figs per serving, pat dry, and put them in a glass bowl. Refrigerate until they're lightly chilled—about an hour. When you're ready to serve them, cut one or two lemons into six wedges each. Halve the figs (or if they're small, just leave them whole), divide them among individual salad plates, and garnish each with two lemon wedges.

Another exquisitely simple and indulgent way to serve fresh figs is to wash, dry, and chill them in the same way, then just before serving, stem, quarter, and divide them among small compote dishes. Serve them with a pitcher of chilled heavy cream or Bourbon Custard (page 47) passed separately.

Figs and Country Ham   SERVES 4

Southern country ham and Italian prosciutto are dry-salt cured in exactly the same way and are very much alike. In the South, in season, country ham is sometimes served with fresh fruit, just as its Italian cousin is. Even out of season, a fruit conserve will be passed along with a Southern ham. Here it is happily paired with succulent, sweet, perfectly ripe figs. I like to also pass warm Corn Sticks (page 34) with this.

The ingredients are few, but the strength of this dish lies entirely in the quality of those few ingredients: The figs must be perfectly ripe, the ham of the best quality—not too salty with just an undertone of sweet smokiness—and the butter fresh and creamy.

4 large, ripe figs (or 8, if they are small)

2 lemons

16 paper-thin slices of raw (preferable) or cooked country ham

¼ pound best quality unsalted butter, softened

Whole black pepper in a mill

1. Cut the figs lengthwise into quarters and lemons into eight wedges.

2. Fold each ham slice double and arrange them on four salad plates, folded side out and centers overlapping. Arrange the figs and lemons in an alternating pinwheel pattern on top of the ham.

3. Whip the butter until fluffy and light, and put a large dollop in the center of each plate. Serve at once, passing the peppermill or a shaker of freshly ground pepper separately.

Note: *If the figs are really fresh and sweet, the combination of fig and ham will be rich enough all on its own, and the butter will be gilding the lily. Simply omit it.*

Fresh Fig Ice Cream

MAKES ABOUT 2 QUARTS

A few years back, fig ice cream made a big splash in the "foodie" community as the "new" frozen dessert sensation of the day. They little realized that there was nothing new about it: Fresh fig ice cream has long been a summer favorite, especially here in the South. In Charleston it had already been enjoyed for generations when the Junior League published a recipe in their 1950 classic, *Charleston Receipts*.

Many recipes call for the figs to be simmered into a jam before they're mixed with cream and frozen, much like Cinnamon Fig Ice Cream (page 226). Conversely, a few recipes require no cooking at all—the ingredients are simply whisked together and frozen. The flavors are lighter and fresher—and to my mind, that's the real point of fresh fig ice cream. This version, which owes much to that venerable *Charleston Receipts* recipe, falls halfway between, with the fresh, uncooked fig puree stirred into a rich custard base.

In her handsome book *A Love Affair with Southern Cooking*, Jean Anderson tops fig ice cream with a couple of spoonfuls of ruby port—a lovely idea.

1 pound (about 4 cups) ripe fresh figs

1 teaspoon freshly squeezed lemon juice

1 tablespoon bourbon

¼ to ⅓ cup sugar

1 cup milk

1 cup heavy cream

2 large egg yolks

1. Wash and stem the figs and put them in the bowl of a food processor fitted with a steel blade. Pulse until coarsely pureed. You may also puree them through a food mill into a glass mixing bowl. Add the lemon juice, bourbon, and sugar and pulse or stir until evenly blended.

2. Choose a 2- to 3-quart saucepan with a really thick, heavy bottom, or prepare the bottom of a double boiler with at least 1 inch of water and bring it to a simmer over medium heat. Either in the saucepan or the top pan of the double boiler, bring the milk and cream to a simmer over direct medium heat.

3. Whisk the egg yolks lightly in a heatproof bowl. Gradually beat in a cup of the hot liquid, then slowly stir them into the remaining liquid. If using the heavy saucepan, return it to medium-low heat; if using a double boiler, set it over the simmering water. Cook, stirring constantly, until the custard coats the back of the spoon. Remove it from the heat and stir until it's somewhat cooled. Stir in the fig puree, cover, and refrigerate until thoroughly chilled, at least 2 hours or overnight.

4. Prepare an ice cream churn following the manufacturer's directions, add the custard, and freeze to the consistency of soft-serve ice cream. Transfer to a freezable container, lay a sheet of plastic wrap directly on top of the ice cream, tightly cover the container, and freeze until firm.

Note: *If you'd like to try Jean's ruby port topping, spoon 2 tablespoons of port over each serving just before sending them to the table, or pass it in a cruet and let the diners do their own anointing.*

MANGOES

This tropical fruit, while not native to Florida, has long been a fixture in Florida gardens and kitchens. Floridians look forward to their mangoes ripening the way Georgians and Carolinians look forward to the season's first peaches. Throughout the Southern part of the state, the trees are so numerous and prolific that every other corner is staked out by a child selling the family's surplus from a little red wagon.

Aside from chutney, that Far Eastern condiment that Southerners have adopted and made their own, most Southern cooks prepare mangoes as they would peaches. The fruit can be substituted in any of the peach recipes on pages 180–85.

Mango or Peach Custard Tart (Kuchen)   SERVES 6 TO 8

After finishing graduate school, I worked through my architectural internship in West Palm Beach, Florida. There, I met up with tree-ripened mangoes and a brilliant teacher, painter, and interior designer named Wayne Jung. Both remain among my best memories of Florida, and here, they are combined in Wayne's favorite dessert.

A variation on that Southern classic custard pie, Wayne's kuchen is typical of the eclectic cookery of the Gold Coast, the southeastern arc of the Florida peninsula, where Southern and Caribbean flavors are blended and accented with the borrowed foodways of the region's diverse population. Here, the accent is German and Norwegian.

1 cup unbleached all-purpose flour

1 tablespoon sugar

Salt

¼ pound (1 stick) unsalted butter, softened

1 tablespoon cider vinegar

4 large eggs

1 cup light cream

1 cup sugar

1 heaping cup mangoes or peaches, peeled, pitted, and cut into cubes, or other fresh fruit (see note)

1. Position a rack in the center of the oven and preheat to 400°F. Whisk together the flour, sugar, and a small pinch of salt in a mixing bowl. Work in the butter until the mixture resembles cookie dough (you can do this with a pastry blender or your fingers). Work in the vinegar, then press the dough evenly over the bottom and up the sides of an 8-inch square casserole or 9-inch round pie plate. Bake in the center of the oven until it's beginning to color, about 10 minutes. Remove it and reduce the temperature to 375°F.

2. Prepare the bottom of a double boiler with 1 inch of water. Bring it to a simmer over medium heat. Break the eggs into the top pan and beat until they are smooth. Whisk in the cream until smooth, and then stir in the sugar and a tiny pinch of salt. Put the pan over the simmering water and cook, stirring constantly, until the custard is thick enough to coat the back of the spoon. Remove it from the heat.

3. Spread the fruit over the crust and pour the custard over it. Bake in the center of the oven until the custard is set and the crust lightly browned, about 40 minutes. Serve warm or at room temperature.

Note: *Though mangoes make a lovely kuchen, raspberries are actually my favorite fruit for this. You can also use fresh blackberries, blueberries, or sliced strawberries.*

If you enjoy gilding lilies, you may, as many Germans do, pass a pitcher of cold heavy cream along with the kuchen, but Wayne would say you were pushy.

St. John's Golden Mango (or Peach) Chutney   MAKES 7 TO 7½ PINTS

Every November the Episcopal churchwomen of St. John's Church, Savannah, hold a pre-holiday bazaar to raise money for various charities and for the maintenance of the church's parish house, the historic Green-Meldrim house, built in 1851–1853. One of the star attractions of these events is the sale of homemade baked goods, frozen foods, and preserves—especially the preserves.

The canning team, "Jane's Canners," spends the dog days of August over steaming kettles, making countless batches of chutneys, relishes, jellies, and pickles. Most of their effort goes into the chutneys, because it doesn't matter how much, or even what kind, they make, they're always a sellout.

This gorgeous chutney is the best of the lot, as golden in color as its name implies and of equally golden flavor. The ideal fruit to use for it is green mangoes, but underripe peaches or pears also work well.

8–10 green mangoes (12 cups when diced) or about 2 dozen underripe peaches

¾ cup chopped candied ginger

6 small red hot chile peppers, split, seeded, and chopped

4 large cloves garlic, peeled and minced

3 cups golden raisins

1 large onion, split, peeled, and chopped

2 tablespoons whole mustard seeds

1 tablespoon salt

3 cups cider vinegar

7 cups sugar

1. Peel the mangoes, cut the flesh from the seed, and then cut it into small dice until you have 12 cups (the exact number of mangoes you need will vary, depending on size). Mix in the ginger, hot peppers, garlic, raisins, onion, mustard seeds, and salt.

2. Put the vinegar and sugar in a large (at least 8-quart), heavy-bottomed, stainless-steel or enamel-lined pot that will comfortably hold all the ingredients, and stir until the sugar is dissolved. Bring it to a boil over medium-high heat and let it boil for 5 minutes.

3. Add the seasoned mangoes, stir well, and bring it back to the boiling point. Reduce the heat to a steady simmer, and simmer until the fruit is just tender and the chutney is thick, about an hour. Don't overcook it or the mangoes will go mushy on you. Pack the chutney in sterilized jars, leaving ¼ inch of headroom in the jar. Discard any leftover juice. Seal with sterilized new lids and process the jars in a boiling water bath (see pages 10–12 for detailed canning instructions) for 10 minutes.

MELONS

An enduring cliché of Southern culture is the image of a thick wedge of watermelon, its bright red, green-edged grin punctuated with impossibly regular rows of black seeds. From hand-painted produce stand signs to elaborate porcelain dinnerware, it's an image that never seems to go away. I even have a watermelon-wedge Christmas ornament. This is due, in part, to the fact that we Southerners really do love melons of all kinds. The vines thrive in our hot, humid summers, providing plenty of cooling fruit to refresh spirits that have wilted in the very heat that made the melon vines thrive.

Southern recipes for melons are few, because no one needs a recipe for the best way to prepare and eat them: Chill them in an obliging mountain-fed creek, cut them into wedges, and dig in. However, melons do occasionally get dressed up for the table.

Cantaloupe

One of my most vivid memories of my grandmother's summer table is a pink Depression-glass bowl filled with orange wedges of chilled cantaloupe. It was a better table decoration than any flower you can name, because it wasn't just pretty: We could eat it.

Choosing a ripe cantaloupe can be mysterious business for the uninitiated. Ripe ones are tan with blushes of yellow. Hard, green melons aren't ripe and were probably picked too green to have much flavor. The most important signal is aroma: the stem end should have a distinct melon fragrance. If it doesn't smell like ripe cantaloupe, it won't taste like it either. Press the stem scar gently with your thumb; it should yield slightly but not be mushy. If it gives too much, it's a sign that the melon is overripe.

Cantaloupe with Country Ham and Redeye Gravy   SERVES 4

An old favorite for breakfast (and sometimes supper) on many farms in the South is cantaloupe doused with milk or redeye gravy, and maybe served with ham or bacon, depending on what else there is on the table. Most people who weren't raised on it meet the idea with a wrinkle of the nose, yet they don't seem to have a problem pairing melon and prosciutto—which is exactly the same taste combination. Go figure.

Here, the contrast of the cool melon against the warm ham and gravy gives still another dimension to the salty-sweet flavor combination.

It would be appropriate served for breakfast, brunch, or even as a first course at dinner.

1 small ripe cantaloupe or honeydew melon
4 thin (⅛-inch-thick) slices of raw country ham (about 8 ounces)
¼ cup flour, spread on a dinner plate
½ cup freshly brewed coffee or tea
½ cup water
Salt and whole black pepper in a mill
Sprigs of mint (optional), for garnish

1. Cut the melon in half lengthwise, scoop out the seeds, cut it into eight even wedges, and slip the peeling from each wedge with a paring knife. Arrange two wedges per serving on individual serving plates.

2. Trim most of the fat from the ham and put it in a large, wide skillet that will hold the ham in a single layer without crowding. Cook it over medium-low heat until the fat is rendered and the crackling is brown and crisp. Meanwhile, cut the ham into medallions about 2 inches across, slashing the membranes around the edges to keep them from curling up when the ham is cooked. Lay the medallions on a flat work surface and lightly pound them with a mallet or the edge of a saucer.

3. When the fat is rendered, remove the browned cracklings and raise the heat to medium. Roll the ham medallions in flour, shake off the excess, and slip them into the pan. Cook for half a minute, turn, and cook until they are just heated through and beginning to brown, about half a minute longer. Take up the ham and divide it among the serving plates.

4. Raise the heat to medium high and deglaze the pan with the coffee or tea, stirring and scraping to loosen any bits of cooking residue that may be stuck to it. Add the water and let it come to a boil. Boil until the gravy is slightly

reduced and thickened, about 2–4 minutes. Turn off the heat. Taste and season with salt, if needed, and a liberal grinding of black pepper. Pour the gravy over the melon and ham, garnish with the optional mint, and serve at once.

Watermelons

If there is anything more satisfying or cooling on a hot summer day than a thick wedge of chilled watermelon, I've never found it. It's a fixture at virtually any outdoor event in the South from late June well into September. The genteel eat it with a knife and fork, but children happily bury their faces in it, and I'm not sure they don't have the best idea.

Occasionally, a host will cut a plug out of a melon and pump it full of rum, but don't count me as a fan; I think the harsh taste of alcohol does not do the clean, sweet flavor of this melon any favors.

A Watermelon Fruit Basket

SERVES 10 TO 12

A classic at dressy summer receptions, the basket itself can be as simple or as elaborate as your inclinations and carving skills allow. Don't feel bound by the fruits that are given here, either, but do taste them in combination with the melon to make sure they don't fight with one another before you dump them in.

The handle of the basket is only decorative; don't try to pick the melon up with it or it will break, especially after it is filled with fruit.

1 large watermelon, about 18 pounds

1 large cantaloupe

1 large honeydew

1 pint (2 cups, or 12 ounces) blueberries

½ cup chopped fresh mint leaves

5–6 sprigs of mint, for garnish

1. Wash the outside of the melon and pat it dry. With a long, sharp knife, make 2 parallel cuts halfway through the center of the melon on one side. This will create the "handle" of the basket. Now make a horizontal cut from each end until it meets the center cuts. Lift off the resulting 2 wedges, wrap in plastic wrap and refrigerate for another use. Cut the red inner flesh from the handle part, being careful not to cut through the rind. If you like, you can decorate the basket by fluting the edges, by carving designs into the rind, or anything that gets you excited.

2. Using a melon baller, scoop out the red part of the melon, leaving at least ½ inch of rind around the edges. Remove the seeds from the balls and put them in a separate bowl as you go. Strain the juice that remains in the melon basket through a sieve to catch the seeds, and pour it over the melon balls.

3. Split the other two melons lengthwise, scoop out and discard the seeds, and cut out the flesh with the melon baller. Add them to the bowl with the watermelon balls.

4. Wash the blueberries and drain well. Combine them with the melon balls, add the chopped mint, and toss gently to mix. Pour the fruit back into the basket and chill until you are ready to serve it. (The basket can be made several hours or even a day ahead. Cover it well with plastic wrap.)

5. When ready to serve, garnish with the mint sprigs, set it on a tray (in case the basket springs a leak or tips over), and serve, providing a slotted spoon for dipping out the fruit.

Note: *Some people add rum to the fruit. I don't care for it myself, but if it appeals to you, allow ½ cup rum and mix it when you add the mint leaves.*

Watermelon Salad   SERVES 6

Here, watermelon gives up its usual place at the table as a fruit and goes to work in a role that its cousin, the cucumber, usually occupies. The melon is a lovely foil for the salty feta, spicy onion, and tart vinegar. It makes a refreshing and unusual salad for any summer brunch, luncheon, or dinner.

When I first developed this recipe, watermelon salads were rare, and I was very smug about having come up with something clever and different—until a Greek-American friend here in Savannah burst my bubble by showing me that this was actually a very old Greek salad that had been brought to the South by twentieth century Greek immigrants and had been enjoyed in Savannah for decades. Many Southerners of Greek ancestry add a handful of brine-cured black olives, pitted and halved lengthwise.

½ small watermelon, about 5 pounds

1 medium Vidalia or other sweet onion, roots and stem trimmed, split lengthwise, peeled, and thinly sliced

¼ cup red wine vinegar

Salt and whole black pepper in a mill

½ cup extra-virgin olive oil

2 tablespoons chopped fresh mint

4 ounces feta cheese, crumbled

6 whole sprigs mint, for garnish

1. Cut the inner flesh from the melon and cut it into bite-size pieces, removing and discarding the seeds as you go and dropping them into a large glass bowl. Add the onion to the bowl.

2. Put the vinegar in a bowl and add a large pinch of salt, a few liberal grindings of pepper, and whisk until the salt is dissolved. Slowly whisk in the oil a few drops at a time. Stir in the chopped mint, taste and correct the seasonings, and set aside.

3. Crumble the feta over the melon and onion, pour the dressing over it, and toss gently until evenly mixed. Garnish with the sprigs of mint or divide the salad among individual salad plates and garnish each serving. Serve at once.

PEACHES

The only place that I could go through a summer without eating a single peach is Bonaventure Cemetery—because I'd have to be dead as a doornail. Peaches are the very essence of a Southern summer, lending their spicy, floral perfume and tart, yet mellow flavor to countless buttery cobblers, soothing ice creams, potent, bourbon-laced conserves, and spicy chutneys. But the best way to eat them is still the simplest—right out of your hand.

Ironically, peaches—at least the variety that we know and cultivate—are not native to the South or even to North America. They are one of the many imports that European settlers introduced to colonial America. They are thought to have originated in China, where they have been cultivated for at least ten thousand years. Their introduction to Europe is usually credited to the Persians, as suggested by their botanical name, *Prunus persica*. As that name also suggests, peaches are a part of the large botanical family of plums and are closely related not only to plums, but to apricots and cherries.

Perhaps even more ironic is the fact that Georgia, though officially known as the "Peach State," does not (and probably never has) led the country in peach production. We have long been outdistanced by California and South Carolina, but we Georgians don't care and continue to plaster pictures of peaches on everything from lottery tickets to license plates, and give the name "Peach State" to everything from fairs to our public-radio system.

Georgia Peach Soup   SERVES 8

Fruit soups are not intended to be sweet. They are served, not as a dessert, but as a first course in much the same way as a fruit salad. This particular one is popular in Georgia hotel dining rooms and in restaurants that cater to visitors. Though it is sometimes served warm, and I've given directions for serving it that way, it's more usually served well chilled, and is best that way.

6 medium, ripe yellow peaches (about 2 pounds)

1 lemon, cut in half

2 tablespoons unsalted butter

¼ cup chopped shallot or yellow onion

2 cups Chicken Broth (page 21) or 1 cup canned
broth mixed with 1 cup water

2½ cups heavy cream (minimum 36 percent
milk fat)

Nutmeg in a grater

1 tablespoon bourbon

1 tablespoon chopped fresh mint

1. Put the peaches in a large heatproof bowl or a stockpot. Bring a large teakettle of water to a boil and pour it over the peaches. Let them stand in the hot water for 30 seconds and then drain. Rinse them with cold water, slip off the peelings, and then halve them and remove their pits. Cut into thin wedges and put them into a glass bowl. Squeeze the lemon juice over them, then toss to coat them well.

2. Put the butter and shallot or onion in a heavy-bottomed 3½- to 4-quart saucepan over medium heat. Sauté, tossing often, until softened and transparent but not in the least colored, about 4 minutes. Add all but 1 cup of the peaches and stir until warmed through. Add the broth and let it come to a boil. Reduce the heat to low and simmer until the peaches are tender, about 10 minutes. Turn off the heat.

3. Puree the soup in batches in a blender or food processor, and return it to the pot. Cut the remaining peaches into small chunks and add them to the puree. The soup can be made several days in advance up to this point. Let it cool uncovered, and then cover and refrigerate it until needed.

4. To serve it cold, stir in 2 cups of the cream and season to taste with a few generous gratings of nutmeg. Stir until smooth. To serve it warm, gently reheat it over medium-low heat, stir in the cream, and just let the cream heat through. If it's too thick once it warms (which may happen because of the acid reacting with the cream), thin it with a little milk. Just before serving, stir in the bourbon.

5. If serving it cold, whip the remaining ½ cup cream until it forms soft peaks and garnish each serving with a spoonful. If serving it warm, don't bother to whip the cream, but simply drizzle a spoonful into each serving. Top with a sprinkling of mint and freshly grated nutmeg.

Georgia Peach Ice Cream

MAKES ABOUT 12 QUARTS, SERVING 6 TO 8

Rich, luscious, and tasting intensely of fresh peach, this ice cream is the essential ingredient of any Southern church ice-cream social in the summer. It also makes the perfect ending to a summer barbecue, and is the most graceful way I know to beat the heat of a Savannah summer.

4–6 ripe, juicy peaches

2 teaspoons lemon juice

½ pound (1 cup) sugar

1 quart heavy cream (minimum 36 percent milk fat)

Salt

1 tablespoon bourbon or 2 teaspoons vanilla extract

1 recipe Blackberry (or Raspberry) Bourbon Sauce (page 167, optional), or amaretto, or a dozen amaretti cookies

1. Peel the peaches over a large bowl to catch their juices. Halve them, remove the pits, and chop them roughly, almost pureeing some of the peaches and roughly chopping the rest to give added texture to the ice cream. Sprinkle them with the lemon juice and ¼ cup of the sugar. Let them macerate for at least half an hour.

2. Dissolve the remaining ¾ cup sugar in the cream, stirring carefully to make sure that no granules remain. Add a tiny pinch of salt and bourbon or vanilla and pour the cream over the prepared peaches. Stir well and thoroughly chill the cream in the refrigerator (about 2 hours, or you can make the cream a day ahead and let it chill overnight).

3. Prepare an ice-cream freezer with ice and rock salt according to the manufacturer's directions. Pour the cream into the freezing cylinder and freeze to the consistency of soft-serve ice cream, following the manufacturer's directions.

4. Pack the ice cream into a mold or freezable container and lay a sheet of plastic wrap directly on top of it. Put it in the freezer to completely solidify. When hardened, if you have molded it, dip the mold in a basin of hot water (or wrap it with a towel that has been heated in the clothes dryer for a few minutes). Invert the mold over a serving plate and lift off the mold. If it won't come off, dip the mold again or rewarm the towel and wrap it for a minute or two more.

If you like, serve the ice cream with the Blackberry (or Raspberry) Bourbon Sauce (page 167), or drizzle a tablespoon of amaretto liqueur, or crumble up a couple of amaretti cookies over each serving.

Peach and Blueberry Compote

SERVES 6

This recipe is the kind of happy creation that can happen when a hungry, curious young cook on a budget is gifted with free food. I was in graduate school at Clemson University, buried by a project deadline, and my mother had just left me with baskets of fragrant ripe peaches and blueberries. There was a jar of local sourwood honey in my pantry, so I tossed the fruit together, doused them with honey, and went back (literally) to my drawing board. When I checked in on the fruit an hour later, the three ingredients had become one, and the taste was pure magic. Not a single summer since has passed without my making this at least twice.

Peaches and blueberries have a great affinity for one another, and, when well doused with a good sourwood honey, they take on a subtle, spicy flavor that is hard to describe, but not at all hard to eat. The only problem you'll have is making enough.

6 medium, very ripe peaches, preferably freestones

1 tablespoon freshly squeezed lemon juice

2 cups (1 pint container, or 8 ounces) blueberries

½ cup (or to taste) honey, preferably sourwood (see note)

Cold Cream Sauce (page 49) or vanilla ice cream, optional

1. Wash the peaches and rub them well to remove all the fuzz. You don't actually need to peel them, but many object to the peels, so you can do so if you must. Halve them and remove the pits, then cut them lengthwise into thick wedges. Put them in a stainless or glass bowl that will hold all the ingredients, sprinkle with lemon juice to prevent them from discoloring, toss well, and set aside.

2. Wash the blueberries, drain, and pick through them to remove any stems and bad fruit. Add them to the peaches. Drizzle with honey to taste, and toss until the fruit is well coated. Cover and refrigerate for at least an hour. Serve cold—alone or with Cold Cream Sauce or vanilla ice cream.

Note: *Sourwood honey is a specialty of the mountain regions of the South, particularly the Carolinas, Georgia, and Tennessee. Its distinctive flavor comes from bees having gathered pollen from the blossoms of sourwood trees. It is available mostly from local vendors and occasionally from specialty groceries. So, while the flavor of this honey is preferable, you can substitute any good honey.*

Jessica Harris's Peach Fritters

SERVES 4 TO 6

Fellow culinary historian and Southern food lover Dr. Jessica Harris is not actually a Southerner by birth. But while she was born and raised in New York, her family roots go back to Virginia and, like most African Americans, her culinary roots are solidly grounded in the South. As she puts it, "We lived in New York, but we ate in the South."

Dr. Harris explains that African-American cooking developed from centuries of improvisation, which continues even today. Her peach fritters are a prime example. When she came South to do a cooking demonstration at Macon's Georgia on My Plate festival, she wanted to use Georgia products. Her solution? Her grandmother's banana fritters, but using Georgia peaches instead of bananas.

The recipe is also exemplary of the "fritter factor" of the African diaspora. While deep-fat frying cannot, by any stretch of the imagination, be called African, fritters turn up wherever there are African cooks in the Americas—from Brazil to Nova Scotia.

4 ripe, but firm, freestone peaches (about 1 pound)
½ lemon
Peanut oil, for frying

FOR THE FRITTER BATTER:

2 large eggs, lightly beaten
½ cup cold milk
3 tablespoons light brown sugar
1 cup flour
Pinch baking soda
2–3 tablespoons confectioners' sugar

1. Peel, halve, and pit the peaches and cut them into thin wedges (if they're too thick they won't cook evenly). Put the wedges in a bowl, squeeze the lemon juice over them, and toss to evenly coat them.

2. Put enough peanut oil in a deep skillet, enameled iron Dutch oven, or deep fryer to come halfway up the sides (if you are using a skillet, it should be deep enough to hold an inch of fat and still be only half-full). Turn on the heat to medium high and heat to around 375°F. (A small spoonful of batter should sizzle happily, but not start browning right away.)

3. While the oil is heating, put the eggs, milk, and sugar in a large mixing bowl. Lightly beat until well mixed, then gradually beat in the flour until the batter is smooth. Beat in the soda.

4. When the oil is hot, drop the peach wedges in the batter a few at a time, lift them out with a fork or slotted spoon, and slip them into the oil. Fry until golden brown, about 3 minutes, turning them halfway through the cooking. Drain briefly on absorbent paper and transfer them to a serving dish. Put the confectioners' sugar in a wire sieve, dust it over the fritters, and serve hot.

Alice's Gingered Peach Tart SERVES 6

My late aunt Alice Holmes Vermillion, in whose memory this book was dedicated, was a natural born cook and baker with a keen instinct for flavor that rarely failed her. Unhappily, like so many cooks who worked by instinct, most of her knowledge went with her to her grave. Mama and I have spent hours talking about remembered meals and flavors, wistfully prodding one another's memories in the hope of recapturing a forgotten secret. One thing that especially stood out in my memory was a fresh peach tart, the fruit laid in neat circles over a flaky, delicate shortbread crust, that once welcomed me home from a long and tiring business trip.

Circumstances may have figured into it, but that was simply the best peach pie I have ever tasted, before or since. Later, she could never remember how she had made it, and I've been left with only my memory to guide me.

About 10 ounces (about 2 cups) Southern soft-wheat flour or all-purpose flour

¼ cup white corn flour (superfine cornmeal, available at Latino markets and the ethnic food section of some supermarkets)

½ cup plus about 2 tablespoons sugar, divided

Salt

1 teaspoon ground ginger

½ pound (1 cup or 2 sticks) unsalted butter, cut into small bits

6–8 ripe peaches, preferably freestone

1 tablespoon freshly grated ginger

2 tablespoons bourbon

About 4 tablespoons turbinado ("raw") sugar

Whole nutmeg in a grater

Vanilla or *dulce de leche* ice cream (optional, for serving)

1. Position a rack in the center of the oven and preheat to 375°F. Whisk or sift together 10 ounces of flour, the corn flour, sugar, salt, and ground ginger. Add the butter and work it into the flour until it holds together but is not sticky. If it is, work in a little more flour. You may also do this in a food processor fitted with a steel blade. Put in the flour, sugar, and salt and several times pulse to sift. Add the butter and process until the mixture resembles coarse meal. Turn it out into a mixing bowl and finish blending the dough by hand, working in more flour as needed.

2. Turn the dough into a 12-inch round, removable-bottom tart pan and press it into a uniform layer over the entire surface and up the sides, pressing it into each flute. Prick it well with a fork and bake in the center of the oven for 10 minutes. Remove and let it cool.

3. Gently wash the peaches under cold running water. Peel, pit, and slice them into thick wedges. If the peelings are thin and delicate, you may, as I do, omit the peeling. Put them in a glass bowl and add the grated ginger and bourbon. Toss well. Sprinkle the crust lightly with turbinado sugar. Lift the peaches out of the bowl and arrange them on top of the crust in slightly overlapping concentric circles. Sprinkle well with the raw sugar and generously grate nutmeg over the top.

4. Bake until the peaches are tender and the crust is golden brown, about 40 minutes. Serve warm or at room temperature with a scoop of ice cream on the side.

Autumn

SWEET POTATOES, NUTS, AND CRISP MOUNTAIN APPLES

The line between summer and autumn in the South is never distinct; the autumnal equinox frequently comes and goes without a flicker on the heat index or a single leaf changing color and detaching itself. In many parts of the South, it stays warm and green right into October and sometimes November. In Savannah, the autumn leaves frequently reach their peak in December, so it's not unusual to have changing leaves and Christmas greenery all at once. Our clues that change is on the way are subtle ones: the trees begin to look heavy and tired; the light, though less direct, is brighter; the days begin to get shorter while, conversely, evening shadows get longer.

Even local produce stands are slow to change; in most places, they're still sporting voluptuous, deep purple eggplants, glossy zucchini, bright peppers, and the reddest tomatoes well past September. It isn't unusual to find fresh tomatoes right up to Thanksgiving. At home, my mother often has fresh tomatoes (picked from the freezing vines and stored in a cool room) at Christmas. It's often just sheer exhaustion, not the weather, that makes the plants stop bearing fruit.

Because of all this, autumn almost always takes us by surprise. One day, we realize with a start that summer is over. The lingering bright colors of its produce are gone, having given way to softer hues. Crisp, purple-topped turnips appear, bright orange pumpkins and winter squashes, dusky cabbages, collards, kale, and broccoli. Okra and tomatoes gradually dwindle and vanish, peaches and blueberries lose their place to apples and persimmons. And as the vegetables and fruits begin to whisper of cooler days to come, slowly, subtly, as if preparing us for the cold weather ahead, our palate begins to shift.

The cooking methods begin to change, too. Braising, roasting, gentle stewing, and slow baking, used less in the summer kitchen, dominate, replacing quicker, cooler methods. Dishes become richer, spicier, denser, and more complex. Even the produce that lingers from summer gets more complex treatment.

Autumn is the time of year when I am happiest in the kitchen. The abundance of produce can make summer cooking less monotonous, and the bright flavors certainly make it simpler, but the limited range of autumn produce makes the season's cooking more of a challenge. The summer kitchen is a bit like Carnival in Rio, an explosion of brilliant fruits and vegetables vibrating with intensity. The autumn palate is gentler, more like a subdued country fair, less excitable, perhaps, but lending a sense of comfort that exuberant summer produce can't.

APPLES

In the Appalachian mountains that stretch across western Virginia and the Carolinas, northern Georgia and Alabama, and eastern Tennessee and Kentucky, the cool nights, abundant moisture, and warm, sunny days of August and early September lead to two of the greatest miracles of autumn: a brilliant red, orange, yellow, and rust display of turning leaves and the mellowest, sweetest apples in the world. As the first blush of color touches the tips of the dogwoods and sweet gums, apple stands begin to sprout along the scenic roadside like mushrooms after a hard rain.

There are many varieties, each coming to market at different times as they ripen. First are the familiar Red and Gold Delicious apples, then the Romes, Yorks, McIntoshes, and Winesaps. My own favorites are the Arkansas Blacks (a Winesap variety that is so called because of its deep wine color, whose fruit is so hard that you can almost play baseball with them and still keep them over the winter. Unlike many varieties that are good either for eating out of hand or cooking, they are superb for both.

Naturally, some of these roadside vendors are scoundrels, selling Washington State apples and commercial cider to unsuspecting tourists, but plenty of good apples and real cider are there for the wily apple lover who knows where—and how—to look. When I was in college, I counted on the wiliness of Walhalla native Betty Hoadley, who was one of my surrogate Mamas while I was in college at nearby Clemson University. Betty could turn on her hill-country drawl and work a produce vendor like no one else. On a foray for fresh cider, for example, she had us pull over at a vendor that didn't sell it. When she slid back into the car with directions to a reliable cider maker, we asked why she'd stopped at a place that didn't sell what we wanted. Looking as if she doubted our mental faculties she drawled, "Well, you don't ask somebody who *sells* it, they'll just tell you to buy *theirs*, of *course!*" Long after I left school and moved to Savannah, I could still count on Betty's savvy without leaving town: Every October a box of the season's best apples would arrive from Walhalla—and with it, the barest suggestion of a mountain frost. Though the apples I cook today are no longer from Walhalla, I never take that first bite of the season's first, crisp apple without Betty in my heart.

Fried Apples   SERVES 4

Fried apples used to be a common breakfast dish, and an indispensable accompaniment for that luxurious hog-killing-time breakfast: biscuits stuffed with fried pork tenderloin. They still make a fine showing for breakfast or brunch but can serve as a side dish for any pork, game, or poultry that does not already have a sweet sauce. Needless to say, they also make a good dessert.

In most of the traditional recipes, apple rings or wedges were fried in bacon drippings without any kind of breading, but this is how my grandmother used to do them.

In choosing apples for frying, look for tart, firm fruit such as my favored Arkansas Blacks, Winesaps, or Granny Smiths. There is a very brief period in the beginning of apple season when Red and Gold Delicious apples will work, but they must be very firm. If they don't have a crisp snap when you bite into them raw, they'll only turn to mush when cooked. Leave them for making applesauce.

Lard, bacon drippings, clarified butter,
  or vegetable oil for frying
4 small, tart apples, or 2 if large
½ cup all-purpose flour
Confectioners' sugar in a shaker
Powdered cinnamon in a shaker
1 recipe Bourbon Custard Sauce (page 47), optional

1. Preheat the oven to 150°F. (or the "warm" setting) and line a rimmed baking sheet with a wire cooling rack. Put enough lard, drippings, butter, or oil in a skillet to completely coat the bottom by about ¼ inch.

2. Peel and cut out the stem and blossom ends of the apples, and slice them crosswise ¼-inch thick. Spread the flour on a diner plate and have it ready by the pan. Heat the skillet over medium-high heat until the fat is very hot, but not smoking (about 375°F.). Roll the apple slices in the flour one at a time, shake off the excess, and slip them into the hot fat until the pan is full but not crowded. Fry until the bottoms are nicely browned, about 3 minutes, turn, and fry until evenly brown, about 3 minutes more.

3. Blot on absorbent paper, transfer to the prepared baking sheet, and put in the warm oven while you fry the remainder.

4. Dust with confectioners' sugar and a sprinkling of cinnamon. If they're intended to accompany meat, omit the sugar. If you're serving them as dessert, film the bottoms of four dessert plates with the custard, tipping and turning the plates until they are evenly coated. Arrange the apples on the plates, drizzle a little more custard sauce over them, and serve at once.

Apples and Honey Mushrooms

SERVES 4

Bill Neal was a gifted North Carolina chef who fathered the renaissance of traditional Southern cooking in restaurants. His Chapel Hill restaurant, Crook's Corner, set a standard of excellence for a new generation of Southern chefs. When he published *Bill Neal's Southern Cooking* in 1986, it became a classic and set a standard for Southern cookbook authors as well. This was a cook who could write circles around the best. Unfortunately, his untimely death in 1991 robbed the South of one of its greatest champions.

Bill's cooking was always Southern to the bone, even when he used a seemingly unorthodox ingredient or technique, because it was so firmly rooted in Southern traditions and because he was never preoccupied with being clever or innovative (which was why his cooking usually seemed that way). This recipe illustrates that point. It takes advantage of two standard North Carolina ingredients—apples and local wild mushrooms—and pairs them in a way that seems fresh, new, and wholly unorthodox but is actually an adaptation of an old mountain recipe.

6 tablespoons bacon drippings, pan drippings from roast pork or poultry, or unsalted butter

1½ cups (about 2 medium) thinly sliced yellow onions

4 large, green (underripe) cooking apples (Granny Smiths are fine)

1 large clove garlic, peeled and minced

¼ cup sugar

1 cup (about 6 ounces) thinly sliced honey mushrooms or other wild mushrooms (see note)

Salt

1. Put 3 tablespoons of the fat in a lidded skillet or sauté pan that will comfortably hold all the ingredients. Turn on the heat to medium low. When the fat is melted, add the sliced onions and sauté until it is tender, shaking the pan from time to time.

2. While the onions cook, peel, core, and thinly slice the apples. When the onions are tender, add the apples to the pan and toss until they are well mixed. Add the garlic and sprinkle the sugar evenly over the mixture. Shake the pan to distribute the garlic and sugar, cover it, and steam until the apples are tender. Give the pan a vigorous shake from time to time to prevent sticking.

3. When the apples are tender, put the remaining 3 tablespoons of fat in a separate sauté pan and turn on the heat to high. When it is hot, add the mushrooms and sauté quickly, shaking and tossing until they are golden. Turn off the heat.

4. Add the mushrooms to the apples and onions, toss to mix, and raise the heat to medium high. Sauté, shaking the pan often, until the excess moisture has evaporated. Turn off the heat. Taste and adjust the seasoning with a pinch or two of salt (the amount of salt will depend on the kind of fat used). Serve warm with roasted pork or poultry, or with sautéed pork chops.

Note: *Honey mushrooms (*Armillariella mellea*), so called because of their yellow-brown color, are indigenous to the eastern portion of the country. But unless you know what you are looking for, don't go foraging for them, since they resemble certain poisonous varieties. Common field mushrooms, morels,* Boletus edulis *(porcini or cèpes), or shiitake can be substituted for them. Commercial champignons are a poor substitute, but cremini mushrooms as well as commercially cultivated "wild" varieties such as shiitakes, work well in this recipe.*

You can also substitute 1 ounce of dried porcini or cèpes. Soak them in a cup of hot water for half an hour, lift them gently out of the soaking water, dipping them in it to rinse off any sand that may be stuck to them. Filter the soaking water through a paper towel or coffee filter. Put the reconstituted mushrooms, their filtered liquid, and 3 tablespoons of the fat in a sauté pan over high heat. Cook, stirring frequently to prevent scorching, until the liquid is evaporated and absorbed into the mushrooms (this concentrates their flavor), then proceed as directed in step 4.

Baked Apples with Bourbon and Pecans   SERVES 4

There is nothing more old-fashioned and homey than baked apples—and also nothing better to warm up autumn's first cold night. No matter how sophisticated your company may be, they will meet them with murmurs of delight.

4 medium, firm apples (such as Arkansas Blacks or McIntoshes)

½ cup raw pecans, roughly chopped

¼ cup brown sugar

¼ cup bourbon

2 tablespoons unsalted butter, plus more, for greasing

1 recipe Bourbon Custard Sauce (page 47)

1. Position a rack in the center of the oven and preheat to 350°F. Wash the apples and pat dry. Cut out the stem ends and scoop out the cores with a melon baller, leaving the blossom ends intact. Lightly butter a 9-inch square baking dish or pie plate, and put in the apples, stem-side up.

2. In a separate bowl, combine the pecans and sugar until evenly mixed. Pack this into the core cavities of each apple, mounding it up on top. Spoon the bourbon over the filling and top each with ½ tablespoon of the butter.

3. Bake in the center of the oven, basting occasionally with pan juices, until tender, about 45 minutes to an hour. Let stand for a few minutes to dissipate some of the intense heat and serve warm or at room temperature, with a pitcher of bourbon custard passed separately.

Apple and Onion Bisque   SERVES 6

The savory combination of apples, onions, and sage has long been enjoyed in the South. Here, they're combined in a lovely soup that is the very essence of autumn in a bowl.

All onions, not just those famed Vidalia Sweets and their cousins, have a great deal of natural sweetness that's often overshadowed by their peppery bite. Because of this, they may seem unlikely companions for apples, but in fact they make a perfect foil for each other.

2 medium yellow onions, trimmed, split lengthwise, peeled, and thinly sliced

2 tablespoons unsalted butter

2 medium tart, firm apples, such as Granny Smiths

3 cups Chicken Broth (page 21)

1 teaspoon dried sage

White peppercorns in a peppermill

1 pint half-and-half

Salt

6 fresh sage leaves (optional)

6 tablespoons heavy cream

1. Put the onions and butter in a heavy-bottomed 4-quart pot over medium heat. Sauté until the onions have wilted, reduce the heat to medium low, and continue sautéing until they're pale gold, but not scorched, about 10 minutes.

2. Meanwhile, wash, peel, core, and cut the apples into thin slices or chunks (whichever is easiest for you). When the onions are colored and softened, raise the heat to medium and add the apples. Sauté until they begin to color. Add the broth and raise the heat to medium high. Bring it to a boil and reduce the heat to a simmer. Add the dried sage and a liberal grinding of white pepper but don't add salt yet. Loosely cover and simmer until the onions and apples are tender, about 20 minutes.

3. Puree in batches in a blender or food processor. Return it to the pot and stir in the half-and-half. Taste and correct the seasonings, adding salt as needed, and gently warm over medium low heat until it is heated through.

4. If using, slice the fresh sage leaves crosswise. Ladle the soup into individual soup plates, put a tablespoon of heavy cream in the center of each, garnish with the sage, and serve at once.

Note: *To make a meatless version, add the sliced white part of a leek and substitute Vegetable Broth (page 22) for the chicken broth. For strict vegetarians, sauté the apple and onion in peanut oil and substitute the vegetable broth for both the chicken broth and the half-and-half. Omit the cream and garnish the soup with chopped apple and sliced green onions.*

Apple, Pecan, and Clemson Blue Cheese Salad SERVES 4

For decades, the agriculture department of South Carolina's Clemson University has produced an admirable blue cheese, which was originally aged in nearby abandoned Confederate railway tunnels. It was (and still is) hard to come by, as supply always falls far short of demand, but when we could get it, Mama enlivened our winter salads by mixing tart apples, a handful of pecans, and a crumbling of this creamy, sharp cheese with the late fall lettuce from the garden. It became a traditional fall salad in our family.

Though Clemson blue cheese is now marketed nationally, and is available through a few mail-order catalogs, its supply is limited and its availability is still spotty. If you can't get it, Gorgonzola, Roquefort, or Danish blue all make acceptable substitutes.

My mother dressed this salad with homemade buttermilk ranch dressing, but in my own kitchen, I prefer a lighter dressing of oil and cider vinegar.

4 scallions or other green onions

1 small head romaine or large head Boston lettuce

1 tart, firm apple, such as Granny Smith or Arkansas Black

4 ounces Clemson or other blue cheese (see headnote), crumbled

½ cup whole Roasted Pecans (page 209)

2 tablespoons chopped parsley, or 1 tablespoon parsley and 1 tablespoon fresh sage or winter savory, chopped

Salt and black pepper in a peppermill

Extra-virgin olive oil

Cider vinegar

1. Wash the scallions, trim their roots and discolored leaves, and thinly slice them. Wash the lettuce, dry it, and break it into bite-size pieces. Peel (if you like—I usually don't), core, and cut the apple into small dice (see the note below).

2. Combine the onions, lettuce, apple, crumbled cheese, pecans, and chopped herbs in a salad bowl, and toss to mix. Add a pinch of salt and generously sprinkle with olive oil. Toss the salad until the greens are glossy and taste it to see if more oil and salt are needed (the taste of the oil should be pronounced, but not heavy or greasy). Lightly sprinkle on a little vinegar, toss, taste to see if it is tart enough to suit you, and adjust it as needed, but don't overdo it—the vinegar should enliven, not dominate. Add a liberal grinding of pepper and toss until mixed. Divide the salad between individual salad plates or bowls and serve at once.

TO CORE AND DICE OR SLICE APPLES:

This is the simplest way to get even slices or dice from an apple for use in an open-faced tart or in salads and such dishes as Braised Brussels Sprouts with Apples and Bacon (page 198). Stand the apple stem up on a cutting board and with a sharp knife, cut straight down on either side a little less than half an inch from the center. Lay each half-moon-shaped side that results flat-side down and either slice it thinly or cut it into thick slices and then cut those crosswise into dice. Now lay the center piece on one of its flat sides and cut straight down either side of the core. Turn them up and slice or dice them in the same way as the side pieces.

Applesauce   MAKES ABOUT 4 TO 5 CUPS

One of the great aromas of the autumns of my childhood is a pot of applesauce fragrantly simmering on the back of the stove. During apple season, my mother made it in large batches and froze it in smaller portions so we could enjoy it through the winter. But every now and again, she would make a panful for us as a bedtime treat. We ate it warm from teacups just like custard, and it was the perfect antidote to an autumn evening's chill.

It's so simple to make, because you don't even peel the apples, but just scrub them well to be sure they're completely clean. The peel adds both flavor and pectin for body, and will be removed when you put the apples through the food mill (which is why you can't use a food processor to puree the fruit). Since this isn't a conserve, the sugar's only job is to add sweetness, so it's added only after the fruit is cooked, since tasting the apples beforehand won't be a reliable gauge of how much sugar the sauce will need. You can make many lovely variations by adding a couple of 1- by 3-inch strips of orange or lemon zest, a healthy sprig of rosemary, or a couple

of slices of fresh ginger, but keep these things subtle; the whole point of a good applesauce is the pure, concentrated flavor of apples.

4 pounds apples
⅔ cup water or unsweetened apple juice
Sugar
1 lemon, halved
Ground cinnamon, whole nutmeg in a grater, or cardamom, to taste (optional)

1. Stem the apples and scrub well under cold running water with a vegetable brush. Don't peel or core them, but cut each apple into six wedges. Put them into a lidded heavy-bottomed enameled or stainless-steel saucepan and add the water. Cover and bring to boil over medium-high heat. Reduce the heat to low and simmer until apples are soft, about 20 minutes.

2. Put the apples through a food mill while still hot. Discard the peeling and seeds. Wipe out the pan and return the puree to it.

3. Taste and add sugar as needed and the juice from half the lemon. You may also add spices as you like. Taste and adjust the lemon juice and sugar again. Bring it back to a simmer over medium-low heat, and simmer 5 minutes. Remove it from the heat, let it cool completely, and transfer it to a sterilized glass jar or clean bowl. Store covered and refrigerated.

Apple Butter   MAKES ABOUT 5 CUPS

Though this thick fruit conserve begins as applesauce, it finishes as so much more: The slow simmer removes all the moisture so that the fruit pulp no longer runs but holds its shape when dipped from the jar and spread, exactly like softened butter. This is a conserve, so unlike applesauce, the sugar has a function aside from adding sweetness, and is added in exact proportions to the fruit. Most apple butters contain a mixture of spices that includes cloves, but I'm deeply allergic to that spice and can't abide the smell or taste, so this contains only cinnamon and nutmeg. You can always cut back half a teaspoon of cinnamon and add a quarter teaspoon each of ground cloves and allspice if you like them. If you use it quickly (within 4–6 weeks), you can store it in one large sterilized jar, well covered and refrigerated, but it's better to can it in smaller jars.

4 pounds apples

3 cups sugar

2 teaspoons ground cinnamon

½ teaspoon freshly grated nutmeg

1. Prepare the apples as for Applesauce (page 193) up through step 2. Rinse out the pan and return the apple puree to it.

2. Mix in the sugar and spices and bring it slowly to a simmer over medium-low heat, stirring frequently to prevent scorching. Adjust the heat to a bare simmer and cook, again stirring often so that it doesn't scorch, until it's very thick and the spoon leaves a distinct trail that doesn't close, there's no more apparent liquid, and the color is a deep russet, about an hour.

3. Divide it among hot sterilized canning jars. Cover with new lids and process in a water bath (page 11) for 10 minutes.

Nathalie's Quick Caramelized Apples SERVES 4

One blustery winter evening several years ago, Tim and I went up to Charleston to sing in a choral evening service at the Episcopal cathedral. We were staying with my friend and mentor Nathalie Dupree, and when we came back after an indifferent dinner that, to Tim's disappointment, had not included dessert, she exclaimed that this would not do at all, and immediately

bustled into her kitchen. Since there is always a dish of soft butter, a bowl of fruit, and heavy cream in her kitchen, we were sitting down to a warm dish of sautéed apples in caramel in less than ten minutes.

Nathalie says the trick to success is to use a nice hot pan that is slightly larger than the total amount of cut-up fruit, so the sugars in the fruit caramelize rather than turn to mush. She says you can dress it up by putting it over pancakes, crepes, a prebaked pie shell, or even vanilla ice cream if you omit the cream, but that night, we were happy with it just as it was, and hungrily scraped the plate for every drop of the caramel.

2 firm, ripe apples

2 tablespoons butter

2 tablespoons sugar, or to taste

½ cup heavy cream

1. Scrub the apples under cold running water and core and slice them as described on page 192.

2. Put the butter in a heavy-bottomed frying pan over medium-high heat. When it's hot and "singing" add the apples in one layer and cook for 1–2 minutes without turning, until the butter and the fruit begin to brown.

3. Sprinkle with sugar as desired and turn with a metal spatula. Cook on the second side until the fruit is lightly browned and caramelized. Sprinkle with more sugar, toss, and carefully pour the cream into the pan (it will bubble up), stirring and scraping the bottom of the pan to loosen any cooking residue. Continue to cook until the apples are tender and the cream has boiled down by half, about 5 minutes. (If the apples are already done when you are ready to add the cream, remove them first and add the cream, stirring up any cooking residue that may be stuck to the pan. Let it boil down and then pour the warm cream over the fruit.)

FALL BROCCOLI

Broccoli is not often thought of as an especially Southern vegetable, and yet it has been growing in the South at least since the eighteenth century, and was included in all the earliest Southern cookbooks, from Mary Randolph's iconic *Virginia House-wife* right through to the twentieth century. And it's in the South that this lovely vegetable enjoys not one, but two prime growing seasons—in spring and fall. Indeed, in part of our region it keeps on producing straight through the summer, though it's at its best in the seasons on either side of it. In spring, when broccoli is new and impeccably fresh, it really needs nothing more than a little salt and lemon juice, and is often so sweet and bright tasting that even that seems like gilding the lily. But in fall, when its flavor has deepened and mellowed, it lends itself well to richer concoctions and begs for those quintessential Southern vegetable accompaniments—bacon and cheese.

BASIC BROCCOLI PREPARATION

Trim the cut ends of the stems and rinse the broccoli well under cold running water. If it's not very fresh, prepare a basin of cool water and stand the stalks in it as you would flowers. Let it drink until it's taut and fresh looking (at least 15-20 minutes) and drain well. Peel the stems with a vegetable peeler until there are no stringy fibers visible. It's now ready to use in any of the recipes that follow.

Steamed Broccoli   SERVES 4

All the old Southern cookbooks, from Mary Randolph's *Virginia House-wife* onward, called for broccoli to be boiled quickly in abundant salted water to preserve its color and flavor. The trouble with that method is that the florets often overcook before the stems are tender. Steaming cooks everything more evenly, better preserves the flavor, and is a lot less trouble.

1¼ pounds fresh broccoli, trimmed, washed, and stems peeled as directed on this page

Salt

2–3 tablespoons melted unsalted butter, optional

1 lemon, halved, or, for state occasions, Lemon Butter (page 42) or Hollandaise (page 43), optional

1. Bring at least 1 inch of water to a boil over high heat in a heavy-bottomed pot fitted with a steamer insert. The water should not touch the bottom of the insert. Cut the thick stems from the broccoli and then cut them in half, lengthwise. Cut the tops into sections of two or three florets each, or one if the florets are large.

2. Put the stems in the steamer insert and arrange the florets over them. Cover and steam 2 minutes. Sprinkle generously with salt, cover, and steam until tender but still firm and bright green, about 4-6 minutes longer, depending on the freshness of the broccoli. Immediately transfer it to a warm platter or serving bowl, drizzle with butter and sprinkle with lemon juice, if using, or drizzle lightly with either sauce. Serve immediately or the lemon juice will damage the bright green color.

Broccoli Gratin SERVES 4

In the 1940s and '50s, casseroles made with chopped frozen broccoli, canned cream soup, and mild cheddar became inordinately popular all over America, but were especially so down South, where vegetable casseroles were (and still are) a mainstay of that revered institution, the church covered-dish supper. Fortunately, not all traditional cooks surrendered to convenience. This fresh gratin harkens back to some of the baked vegetable dishes of the late nineteenth century. It owes much to the late Camille Glenn, a lovely caterer and cookbook author who was Kentucky's premier culinary maven during the latter part of the twentieth century.

1¼ pounds broccoli cooked as for Steamed Broccoli (page 195, omitting the optional butter, lemon juice, and sauces), cooled

2 tablespoons unsalted butter

1 cup coarse saltine or butter cracker crumbs

Whole black or white pepper in a mill (your choice)

Pinch of dry mustard

1 cup coarsely grated extra-sharp cheddar or Gruyère

1½ cups heavy cream

1. Lightly butter a 9-inch shallow casserole or gratin dish. Roughly chop the broccoli, leaving small florets whole, and put it in the dish. Melt the butter in a small frying pan over medium-low heat. Add the cracker crumbs and toss until they evenly absorb the butter and are lightly toasted. Turn off the heat and sprinkle two-thirds of them over the broccoli.

2. Add a liberal grinding of pepper, the mustard, and half the cheese. Pour the cream over it and gently toss to mix, then gently level the broccoli with a spatula and sprinkle the remaining cheese over it. It can be made up to 4 hours ahead up to this point. Cool, loosely cover, and let it stand at room temperature.

3. When you're ready to bake the gratin, position a rack in the upper third of the oven and preheat to 375°F. Uncover the gratin, sprinkle the remaining crumbs over it, and bake in the upper third of the oven until bubbly and lightly browned on top, about 25–30 minutes. Let it settle for 5 minutes before serving, but serve hot.

Broccoli, Bacon, and Potato Soup

SERVES 6 AS A FIRST COURSE OR SOUP-AND-SANDWICH LUNCH, 3 TO 4 AS A MAIN DISH

I was very lucky that early in my career as a cooking teacher and food writer, the incomparable Marcella Hazan and her husband, Victor, became friends and mentors. Marcella's early books had long been my kitchen bibles, but all of her books have contained favorites that I go back to again and again. One particular favorite is an exquisitely simple broccoli and potato soup from *Marcella Cucina*, which was the inspiration for this one.

1 pound fresh broccoli, trimmed, washed, and stems peeled as directed on page 195

4 extra-thick cut slices bacon, preferably applewood smoked, diced

1 large yellow onion, peeled and thinly sliced

4 large waxy boiling potatoes, washed, peeled, and cut in small dice

2 cups Chicken Broth (page 21) or equal parts canned broth and water (even if the label reads "use full strength")

Salt and whole black pepper in a mill

2 cups whole milk or 1 cup whole milk and 1 cup heavy cream

1. Cut the florets from the stems of the broccoli and break them into bite-size pieces. Cut the stems into bite-size dice.

2. Sauté the bacon in a large, heavy-bottomed pot over medium heat until it is golden brown and its fat is rendered, but not crisp. Spoon off all but 2 tablespoons of the fat and add the onion. Sauté until golden, about 3–4 minutes.

3. Add the broccoli and sauté, tossing occasionally, until bright green, about 2 minutes, then add the potatoes and toss until heated through, about 2 minutes more. Add the broth, a large pinch of salt, and a liberal grinding of pepper. Bring to a boil, adjust the heat to a steady simmer, and cook until potatoes begin to come apart when stirred, about 10 minutes.

Note: *The soup can be made ahead to this point. Turn off the heat, cool completely, and cover well. If making it more than a couple of hours ahead, transfer it to a storage container and refrigerate it. Bring it back to a simmer over medium-low heat before proceeding.*

4. Stir in the milk and briefly raise the heat to bring it back to a simmer, stirring often and mashing a few of the potatoes against the sides of the pot. Adjust the heat to a gentle simmer and cook, stirring often and again mashing some of the potato until the soup is thick enough to suit you, another 4–5 minutes. Taste and adjust the salt and pepper and serve hot.

BRUSSELS SPROUTS

Brussels sprouts (*Brassica oleracea gemmifera*) are of course a relative of cabbage. But unlike their larger cousins, which form heads at the top of their stalks quite close to the ground, sprouts form in clusters on the sides of a tall, slender plant. Legend has it that they have been grown in Belgium since time immemorial, even though they aren't mentioned in botanical records until the nineteenth century. Sprouts are relatively new in Southern kitchens but have become very popular here as a staple green vegetable throughout the cold months of autumn and winter.

This is one vegetable which I mostly prefer steaming above any other cooking method. Even when I sauté them, they get a brief steambath first. One of the simplest and tastiest ways of preparing sprouts is to steam them until they are just tender—even large ones are done in under 10 minutes if they're halved before cooking. Sauce them lightly with a little unsalted butter or, for a really

sumptuous dinner, serve them with Hollandaise Sauce (page 43), Sauce Creole (page 121), or any of the drawn butter sauces on pages 41–43.

Brussels Sprouts with Pecans

SERVES 4

Brussels sprouts paired with chestnuts are a timeless classic. Here, the idea develops a Southern accent by combining the sprouts with that most Southern of nuts—pecans—which makes for an equally felicitous marriage.

2½ dozen small brussels sprouts (about 1 pound)
Salt
5 tablespoons unsalted butter
½ cup pecans

1. Fill a basin with cold water. Trim the sprouts at the base, rinse, and drop them into the water. Let them soak at least 30 minutes.

2. Put an inch of water in a large pot (or the bottom of a double-boiler-type steamer), fit it with a vegetable steamer basket, cover the pot, and turn on the heat to high. Bring the water to a rolling boil. Drain the sprouts and put them in the steamer basket. Sprinkle them with a liberal pinch or so of salt, cover, and reduce the heat to medium. Steam until the sprouts are tender but still bright green, about 10 minutes.

3. Turn off the heat, remove the sprouts and refresh them under cold running water to arrest the cooking. Drain well.

4. Put the butter in a large skillet over medium-high heat. When it's melted, add the pecans and sauté, tossing often, until they've barely begun to color, about 3 minutes. Add the sprouts and sauté, tossing constantly, until they're heated through and just beginning to color. Turn off the heat. Taste for salt and adjust it accordingly. Transfer to a warm serving dish and serve at once.

Note: *There's no substitute for the butter in this dish, since no other fat will react with the pecans and give the sprouts a lovely glaze.*

You can precook the sprouts several hours ahead up through step 3, but don't try to finish the dish completely and reheat it later, as the pecans will lose their crispness and get flabby. When the sprouts have steamed, drop them into a bath of ice water to arrest the cooking, drain them well, and keep them covered until you are ready to finish them.

Braised Brussels Sprouts with Apples and Bacon   SERVES 6

Across the hill country of the Carolinas, Tennessee, and Kentucky, settlers of German descent left a faint but definite imprint on the cooking and culture. One lingering reminder of those settlers is the classic pairing of local mountain apples with cabbage. Here, apples and savory bacon lend their sweet-savory richness to the cabbage family's smallest member. It's a delightful side dish for just about any autumnal pork or poultry dish, but is especially delicious with the Thanksgiving turkey.

1 large or 2 medium crisp, tart-sweet apples, such as Winesap or Honeycrisp
2 pounds fresh brussels sprouts
4 ounces extra-thick-sliced applewood smoked bacon, (about 3 slices) cut in ½-inch dice
1 small red onion, quartered, peeled, and thinly sliced
1 tablespoon chopped fresh or 1 teaspoon crumbled dried thyme
Salt and whole black pepper in a peppermill

1. Stem the apple and scrub it well under cold running water. Core and dice it as directed on page 192. Wash the sprouts under cold running water and drain well. Trim the stem end, remove the loose outer leaves, and split them in half lengthwise.

2. Sauté the bacon in a large, lidded sauté pan or skillet over medium heat, tossing often, until golden brown and its fat is rendered, about 4 minutes. Add the onion and sauté, tossing often, until golden, about 4 minutes. Add the apple and sprouts and toss until they're golden brown on the edges but the sprouts are still bright green, about 5–8 minutes.

3. Sprinkle in the thyme and season lightly with salt and generously with pepper. Pour in about ¼ cup of water, reduce heat to medium low, cover tightly, and braise until the sprouts and apples are tender but not mushy, about 8 minutes. The sprouts should still be a nice green and firm, but not crisp. Turn off the heat. Taste and adjust the seasonings, toss, and serve warm.

MUSHROOMS

Developments in the domestic cultivation of mushrooms over the last few decades have changed the face of American restaurant menus and created one of the most delicious of oxymorons in our modern culinary lexicography—the "cultivated wild" mushroom. Well, naturally any mushroom that is cultivated is no longer wild in any sense of the word. Indeed, the most commonplace, shiitake, had been cultivated in Japan for so long that it was as domesticated as button mushrooms when it was introduced to America. Yet "wild" does give a menu description a bit of cachet and daring.

Actually, mushroom agriculture in the West is a relatively recent development. Most of the fresh mushrooms available to early American markets were truly wild, though the most common—ordinary field mushrooms (*Agaricus campestris*)—are closely related to the cultivated variety. Field mushrooms are easily identified and are the least likely to be confused with poisonous fungi.

Except for Japanese enoki and shiitake, most cultivated mushrooms in America are still of the *Agaricus* family, but oyster mushrooms, chanterelles, and a few others have also been successfully cultivated.

Mushrooms are available in most supermarkets, but take the trouble to look for them in natural-food or specialty groceries that sell mushrooms in bulk; these vendors often buy from local growers, so the mushrooms are naturally fresher. Avoid any that have moist, dark spots. If you must buy plastic-wrapped mushrooms, remove the plastic as soon as you get them home, and, if you don't plan to cook them right away, cover the package with a dry paper towel and refrigerate it promptly. In any case, use the mushrooms as soon as possible.

Here are some notes on the most readily available mushrooms:

Common White Mushrooms or Champignons: The pearly white color of these mushrooms is owed in part to their cultivation in caves, cellars, or special "mushroom houses." They are closely related to common field mushrooms. The smaller these are, the better. Look for firm, creamy white, dry caps that are still closed on the underside, and gills that are a delicate brownish pink.

Common Brown (Cremini or Crimini) Mushrooms: Also marketed as "Baby Bella," and "Italian golden," these mushrooms are also in the *Agaricus* family. Look for the same qualities as you would for white mushrooms; the only difference in appearance is the golden-brown color of the cap. Because their flavor is more distinctive than that of white mushrooms, they are preferable when you can find them.

Portobello or Portabella: Resembling overgrown cremini mushrooms in color, texture, and flavor, these mushrooms are also in the *Agaricus* clan. They're always harvested when the caps are matured and open (between 4–6 inches in diameter) and the gills have darkened to a deep chocolate brown. They are often sold as "griller mushrooms," but don't confuse them with the creamy-white griller mushrooms, which are really just large champignons.

Morels: There are a number of varieties of morels, but true morels are supposed to be most plentiful in apple orchards, under elms, and near wild sunflowers. Their round, conical caps, ranging in color from light gray to deep chocolate brown, are gnarled and pitted, almost like a wrinkled honeycomb. Until the 1980s, these highly prized mushrooms defied all efforts to cultivate them. Therefore they were harvested exclusively in the wild during the spring, their natural growing season. Though today they're being successfully cultivated, they're still expensive and fresh ones remain a seasonal delicacy. Dried morels are available year round. Regardless of their origins, morels are not edible until they're cooked. See the recipe for Ronni's Morels and Spring Greens (pages 69–70).

Oyster Mushrooms: This fungus grows on trees in clusters. Wild oyster mushrooms can often be found in farmers' markets and at specialty grocers, but the ones that are most widely available in commercial groceries are cultivated. The same soft gray-brown of real oysters, their oblong caps do indeed resemble the bi-valve for which they are named. They're the most delicate of the many cultivated varieties, and must be very fresh or they'll cook up limp and flabby and have very little flavor. Look for clean, dry caps with absolutely no damp spots.

Shiitake: Indigenous to Asia, these forest mushrooms grow on fallen trees and limbs. Though also called Chinese and Black Forest mushrooms, nowadays we know them more by their Japanese name, which derives from the fact that in that country they are found in the wild in *shii* trees. Though genuinely wild mushrooms are beginning to turn up in restaurant kitchens, shiitake are still the "wild" mushroom you are most likely to find on your plate in a public dining room.

Wild Mushrooms: All along the eastern seaboard there are a number of highly prized indigenous mushrooms—the *Boletus edulis*, called *porcini* in Italian and cèpes in French, chanterelles, morels, chicken mushrooms, common field mushrooms, and puffballs. Foraging for edible mushrooms in the wild may seem romantic and it can be rewarding, but unless you are experienced at it, or can take someone along who is, you're better off forgoing the romance and sticking to cultivated mushrooms or to wild-gathered ones sold by a reputable vendor. The old caution was to make sure that you knew what you were gathering—and it's still valid—but nowadays it's equally important to know the pasture, lawn, or woodland where your crop is growing. Make sure the land hasn't been treated with pesticides and/or weed killer.

Chanterelles: These delicate, yellow-to-bright-orange mushrooms flourish in early autumn in shaded lawns and parks. They're indigenous to the Southeast, particularly the Carolina and Georgia Lowcountry. We use the French name, derived from a Latin word for "cup" and that's exactly what these mushrooms do. When mature, their caps cup in an inverted funnel shape. Their delicately fruity aroma and flavor have been likened to apricots. Though they've been successfully cultivated, the chanterelles available to most of us are harvested in the wild. Their season is brief and they're frightfully expensive, but worth it when they're really fresh.

Boletus edulis (porcini or cèpes): It's not widely known that a strain of the most famous of all wild mushrooms is actually native to America, and can be found in the woodlands of North Georgia and Carolina. They are not harvested and sold commercially.

Morels: like chanterelles, these mushrooms are also indigenous to the Carolina and Georgia Lowcountry and frequently turn up in our markets.

Miscellaneous Wild Mushrooms: Chicken-of-the-woods, sulfur shelf, puffballs, and common field mushrooms are found throughout the Southeast and have long been enjoyed by mushroom lovers.

Sautéed Chanterelles   SERVES 4

These luxurious but delicate mushrooms deserve simple, straightforward treatment. Here they're sautéed in butter with a spoonful of minced shallots and faint touch of garlic, and are finished with lemon juice, which really brings up their flavor. But if you are lucky enough to have a source where you can harvest and cook them within minutes, even the shallots and garlic are overkill.

3 tablespoons unsalted butter, plus more for toasting the bread

8 (½-inch-thick) slices baguette cut on the diagonal (or 4 slices if using a larger loaf)

¾ pound fresh chanterelle mushrooms, or chanterelles and shiitake or oyster mushrooms, mixed, cleaned as directed on page 199

1 medium shallot, split lengthwise, peeled, and minced (about ¼ cup)

1 medium clove garlic, lightly crushed, peeled, and minced

½ lemon

Salt and whole black pepper in a mill

2 tablespoons minced flat-leaf parsley

1. Heat a large, heavy-bottomed sauté pan or skillet over medium heat. Add about a tablespoon of butter to it and let it melt. Put the bread in the pan and quickly turn it to lightly coat it with the butter, then toast, turning once, until both sides are golden. Divide them among four serving plates.

2. Halve or thickly slice the larger chanterelles, but leave smaller ones whole. Wipe out the pan in which the bread toasted and put in 2 tablespoons of butter. Return the pan to medium heat and let the butter melt. Add the shallot and sauté, tossing often, until golden, about 4 minutes. Add the chanterelles and toss well. Sauté, tossing gently, until they start to collapse. Add the garlic and sauté half a minute longer. Season lightly with salt and liberally with pepper, then squeeze in a few drops of lemon juice. Toss, taste, and adjust the lemon juice, salt, and pepper. Continue cooking until the mushrooms are tender.

3. Add two-thirds of the parsley and remaining butter and remove the pan from the heat. Toss gently until the butter is melted. Divide the mushrooms among the toasts, sprinkle with the remaining parsley, and serve at once.

VARIATION: CHANTERELLES WITH PASTA

Omit the toast. Bring 4 quarts of water to a rolling boil in a 6-quart pot. Meanwhile, make the mushrooms through step 3 and turn off the heat. When the water begins boiling, stir in a small handful of salt, then stir in ¾ pound of pasta: good choices are fresh egg fettuccine or orecchiette, or dried factory pasta such as fusilli or penne. Cook the pasta until al dente, stirring occasionally. Just before it's done, gently reheat the mushrooms and finish as directed in step 3. Drain the pasta, toss it with the mushrooms, and serve at once.

Chanterelles with Country Ham and Thyme

SERVES 4 AS AN APPETIZER, 2 TO 3 AS A MAIN DISH

When you've not gathered chanterelles from an obliging field or yard, but from a bin in the market, adding a little country ham and thyme to the pan restores some of their woodsy depth of flavor. Served as they are here over warm sautéed grits cakes, they are substantial enough to suffice as a main dish for lunch or supper. They're also lovely spooned over an omelet or tossed with pasta as in the variation "Chanterelles with Pasta" for the previous recipe.

¾ pound chanterelle mushrooms

2 tablespoons unsalted butter

1 medium shallot, trimmed, peeled and minced (about ¼ cup)

1 ounce (¼ cup) julienned country ham

1 tablespoon chopped fresh thyme leaves

Whole black pepper in a mill

½ cup heavy cream or Crème Fraîche (page 18)

1 recipe Pan-Fried Grits Cakes (page 203), made ahead but not cooked

Salt

1. Brush the chanterelles clean with a soft brush or dry cloth and thickly slice them. Put the butter and shallot in a sauté pan or skillet over medium heat. Sauté, tossing often, until the shallot is pale gold. Add the ham and sauté, tossing constantly, until it just loses its raw, red color.

2. Raise the heat to medium high, add the chanterelles and thyme, and sauté, tossing almost constantly, until the mushrooms are collapsed but still firm and just beginning to color, about 3–4 minutes. Add a liberal grinding of pepper, toss, and pour in the cream. Bring it to a boil and cook, stirring constantly, until it is reduced and thick. Turn off the heat.

3. Quickly cook the grits cakes until they're golden brown as directed in the recipe below. Divide them among four warm salad plates. Return the chanterelles to medium heat and bring them back to a simmer. Taste and adjust the salt and divide them among the grits cakes. Serve immediately.

Pan-Fried Grits Cakes   SERVES 4

Grits cakes began as a supper dish, a practical way of using up leftover breakfast grits. But when shrimp and grits became the signature appetizer for restaurants dishing up "nouvelle" Southern cooking, this homey supper fare suddenly became fashionable haute cuisine. Classically, they're done two ways: The richer, showy version is dipped in an egg wash, coated with crumbs, and fried, but that's far too rich to pair with a cream-based sauce. The old recipes don't contain cheese, but I find that a little Parmigiano mixed into the grits helps hold the cakes together.

They actually don't need a sauce: They're lovely served just as they are, with perhaps a little freshly grated Parmigiano-Reggiano cheese sprinkled on top. But they're also an ideal carrier for sautéed vegetables and just about any ragout, from vegetables to meat or seafood.

4 cups water

1 cup raw grits (not quick-cooking)

1 cup freshly grated Parmigiano-Reggiano or aged, extra-sharp cheddar

Salt

1 tablespoon unsalted butter

1. Bring the water to a boil in a heavy-bottomed stainless-steel, enameled, or nonstick 3-quart saucepan. Stirring constantly, add the grits in a thin, steady stream. Bring to a boil, stirring constantly, until they begin to thicken slightly. Lower the heat to a simmer and cook, stirring occasionally, until very thick and tender, at least 45 minutes to 1 hour.

2. Off the heat stir in the cheese, taste, and adjust the salt. Choose a baking dish in which the grits will cover the bottom ½-inch deep or two straight-sided tumblers. Rinse out with water. Pour in the grits and spread them ½-inch deep in the dish, or fill the tumblers to no more than ½-inch from the top. Let cool, cover, and chill until quite firm.

3. If molded in the dish, loosen the edges, carefully unmold onto a plastic cutting board, and cut into eight ½-inch-thick rounds using a 2½-inch round biscuit cutter. If molded in tumblers, loosen the edges, unmold onto the board, and cut each cylinder crosswise into ½-inch-thick slices.

4. Melt the butter in a large nonstick pan over medium heat. Swirl the pan to film the bottom with the fat, raise the heat to medium high, and cook cakes until the bottom is golden brown, about 2 minutes. Carefully turn and cook until the second side is equally browned. Transfer to warm serving plates and top as directed in the individual recipe.

Broiled Mushrooms   SERVES 4

Today, we broil under a flame, but until gas and electric ovens came along, "broiling" was what we know today as grilling: The food was cooked over a bed of coals on the open hearth, exactly like the recipe for Grilled Mushrooms with Bourbon Herb Butter (recipe follows, this page). As gas and electricity made the old cast-iron ranges and open hearth obsolete, broiling under the flame became a favorite way to cook mushrooms—and not without reason. It really concentrates the flavor, creates a lovely sauce with the natural juices, and requires almost nothing from the cook but a watchful eye.

1 pound cremini or white champignon mushrooms, or a mixture of wild mushrooms

2–3 tablespoons softened unsalted butter

Salt and whole black pepper in a mill

1 lemon, halved

1 tablespoon chopped fresh parsley

1. Trim the mushroom stems and brush the caps clean with a soft brush or clean, dry cloth. Position a rack 6–8 inches from the heat source and preheat the broiler for at least 15 minutes.

2. Lightly butter a 9 x 13-inch roasting pan or rimmed baking sheet. Put in the mushrooms, stem-side up, in a single layer. Dot with butter and sprinkle lightly with salt and a few generous grindings of pepper. Broil until they are lightly browned and tender, about 5–6 minutes.

3. Pour the mushrooms into a warm serving bowl. They will have thrown off a lot of flavorful juice: Don't drain it away, but pour it over the mushrooms. Squeeze a few drops of lemon juice over them, toss, taste, and adjust the salt, pepper, and lemon juice. Add the parsley, toss one last time, and serve.

Grilled Mushrooms with Bourbon Herb Butter   SERVES 4

Grilling large mushrooms concentrates and enhances the earthy flavor of the wild ones and gives cultivated varieties such as portobellos a depth of flavor that they don't possess on their own. Here, they get an additional lift by bathing them with a sage-and-bourbon-scented herb butter.

The herb butter is also fine for other grilled vegetables that are compatible with sage—such as sweet potatoes or squash—and has a particular affinity for grilled pork (especially tenderloin), lamb, chicken, and virtually any game bird.

¼ pound unsalted butter, softened

1 tablespoon chopped fresh sage (do not use dried sage)

1 tablespoon chopped fresh parsley

1 medium shallot, peeled and finely minced

1 tablespoon bourbon

Salt and whole white peppercorns in a peppermill

4 large portobello, shiitake, or porcini mushrooms (about 2 pounds)

1. Knead together the butter, herbs, shallot, and bourbon. Season to taste with a healthy pinch of salt and a few liberal grindings of white pepper, and knead until the seasonings are well blended. Roll the butter into a log. This is easiest done by rinsing your hands with cold water, then gently rolling the butter on a flat surface covered with wax paper. (If the butter has gotten too soft, let it sit in the refrigerator until firm enough to handle.) Fold the wax paper around the butter and refrigerate it until firm.

2. Prepare a grill with lump hardwood coals (not briquettes) and light it. When the coals have burned down, carefully wipe the mushrooms with a dry cloth or paper towel to remove any dirt that may be clinging to them, and trim the stems so that the mushrooms will lie flat when turned stem-side down. (If you are using shiitakes, cut the stems off altogether and discard them.)

3. When the coals are ready, spread them and position the grill rack about 3 inches above the heat. Put on the mushrooms, stems down, and grill until they are hot and beginning to color around the edges of the gills, about 5 minutes. Meanwhile, cut the herb butter into tablespoon-size slices. Rub the tops of the caps with a piece of the herb butter and turn them over. Put a tablespoon-size slice of the herb butter into the center of each mushroom and continue grilling until the mushrooms are just cooked through and the caps are beginning to color, about 3–5 minutes more. Smear a serving platter with 2 tablespoons of the herb butter. Put the mushrooms on the platter, stems up. Sprinkle them lightly with a little salt, dot with a little more herb butter, and serve at once, passing salt and pepper separately.

Note: *The whole point of the herb butter is the flavor of fresh herbs, so don't used dried sage for this recipe. If fresh sage is unavailable, substitute another fresh herb that's compatible with mushrooms, such as thyme, marjoram, savory, or basil. And while we're on don'ts, don't be tempted to add more bourbon: Too much whiskey imparts a harsh alcoholic aftertaste.*

Wild Mushrooms in Cream   SERVES 4

When the mushrooms are impeccably fresh, there is nothing to equal this sumptuous dish, and no other way of doing them is more useful. Over toast points or puff pastry, they make the most elegant first course imaginable. When ladled over broiled fish or roasted poultry or an omelet, they turn a plain main course into a gastronomical event. They are also exceptional on

egg pastas, such as fettuccine, or short, sturdy factory pasta like *rotelle* or *penne rigati*.

And they are absolutely stellar all by themselves.

1 pound small wild mushrooms, or shiitake, cremini, or a blend of domestic mushrooms
4 tablespoons unsalted butter
Salt and whole white peppercorns in a peppermill
1 cup heavy cream (minimum 36 percent milk fat)

1. Trim the mushroom stems (remove them completely from shiitakes) and brush the caps clean with a soft brush or dry cloth. Halve or quarter large mushrooms, but leave the rest whole.

2. Put the butter in a large sauté pan that will hold all the mushrooms in one layer without crowding and turn on the heat to medium high. Add the mushrooms and sauté, tossing often, until they begin to color. Add a healthy pinch of salt and a grinding or two of white pepper, and pour in the cream. Toss until the mushrooms are coated and cook, tossing often, until the cream is beginning to thicken (it becomes even thicker after coming off the heat, so don't let it get too thick). Turn off the heat, pour into a warm serving dish, and serve hot.

Cream of Mushroom Soup   SERVES 6

One of my first insane acts as a cook occurred while I was in graduate school in Genoa: I decided to cook a five-course dinner for my fellow students, our cook, Ilda, and the rest of the school staff, and their spouses—some thirty-odd people. Somehow (and how, I don't know) it all came together and the meal was a success. This soup led the way, and Ilda asked for the recipe, even though it was she who had made it a success by coaching me to used dried mushrooms.

The original was thickened with flour, but over the years the pasty quality that flour

thickening often lends to food began to bother me, and I learned to use purees and real cream instead.

1 ounce dried porcini mushrooms

1 cup boiling water

12 ounces (¾ pound) cremini (brown or golden) mushrooms

¼ cup minced shallot or yellow onion

3 tablespoons unsalted butter

2 cups Chicken Broth (page 21)

Salt and whole white peppercorns in a peppermill

2 cups heavy cream (minimum 36 percent milk fat)

3 tablespoons chopped fresh chives or parsley

1. Put the dried mushrooms in a heatproof bowl and pour the boiling water over them. Let soak for 30 minutes. Meanwhile, trim the stems of the fresh mushrooms and brush the caps clean with a soft brush or dry cloth. Thinly slice the caps and roughly chop the stems. Set them aside separately.

2. Put the shallot and butter in a 3-quart soup pot. Turn on the heat to medium low and sauté until softened, about 8 minutes.

3. Meanwhile lift the dried mushrooms from their soaking liquid, dipping several times to remove any sand that may be stuck to them. Roughly chop them and when the shallots are softened, add them to the pot along with the chopped mushroom stems. Stir until the stems wilt, about 4 minutes. Meanwhile, strain the reserved soaking liquid through a coffee filter or undyed paper towel. Add it to the soup pot along with the chicken broth, a large pinch of salt, a few grindings of white pepper, and bring to a boil. Reduce the heat to low and simmer until the vegetables are tender, about 20 minutes. Turn off the heat.

4. Puree the soup in a blender or in batches in the food processor. Return it to the pot, add the cream, and turn on the heat to medium. Bring the soup back to a simmer, add the sliced

mushroom caps, and simmer until they are tender and the cream is lightly thickened, about 10 minutes more. Taste and correct the seasonings, and ladle the soup into a heated tureen or soup plates. Garnish with the chives or parsley and serve at once.

Note: *For a meatless soup, substitute Vegetable Broth (page 22) for the chicken broth. However, there is no substitute for the cream. The character of the soup depends on the silkiness of mushrooms and cream in combination. If you must avoid dairy products, you can make a respectable clear soup using all broth. Just omit the puree step and garnish the soup with the chives, parsley, and a few croutons (page 37) toasted in oil instead of butter.*

Mushrooms Stuffed with Country Ham SERVES 4

Stuffed mushrooms are so popular at Savannah parties that I've always wished that I could be more enthusiastic about them. Yet the first bite usually leaves me feeling vaguely disappointed. The mushrooms seldom have any real flavor and the filling, inevitably, has too much. The problem is that the cook is using the wrong mushroom and a filling that fights with it. All the same, I didn't think there was anything wrong with the basic idea, so I went to work looking for a stuffing that was flavorful on its own without dominating the mushrooms. And here it is, enlivened with a touch of garlic and a splash of bourbon.

½ ounce dried porcini mushrooms

½ cup boiling water

4 large portobello or shiitake, or 1 dozen small shiitake or large cremini mushrooms (see note)

5 tablespoons unsalted butter

2 large cloves garlic, crushed, peeled, and minced

¼ cup (about 1 ounce) minced country ham or prosciutto

2 tablespoons chopped parsley

½ cup dry bread crumbs

Salt and black pepper in a peppermill

3 tablespoons bourbon

1. Put the dried porcini in a heatproof bowl and pour the boiling water over them. Set them aside to soak for 30 minutes.

2. Position a rack in the upper third of the oven and preheat to 375°F. Brush away any dirt that may be clinging to the mushrooms with a clean, dry cloth or soft brush. Remove the stems and chop them fine (if using shiitake, discard the stems and chop a couple of extra caps for the stuffing—see note). Set both stems and whole caps aside.

3. Lift the reconstituted dried porcini out of their soaking water, dipping to remove any sand that may be clinging to them, and put them in a 10-inch skillet or sauté pan. Strain their soaking liquid through a coffee filter or paper towel and add it to the pan. Bring to a boil over medium-high heat and cook, stirring often, until all the liquid is absorbed and evaporated. Turn off the heat. Remove the mushrooms and chop them fine.

4. Add 3 tablespoons of the butter to the pan and melt it over medium heat. Add the garlic and sauté, tossing often, until fragrant and golden. Add the chopped stems and sauté until they're wilted and their moisture is mostly evaporated. Add the ham and parsley, toss, and turn off the heat.

5. Add the crumbs to the stem mixture, toss until well mixed, and season well with a pinch of salt (go easy on this if the ham is especially salty) and a few grindings of black pepper. Toss to blend the seasonings.

6. Lightly butter a baking dish that will hold all the mushrooms without touching and put in the caps, stem-side up. Sprinkle lightly with salt, and divide the stuffing among them, mounding it up in the center. Sprinkle the bourbon over them, dot them with the remaining 2 tablespoons of butter, and bake until they are lightly browned and the caps are tender, about 20 minutes. (Shiitake often take less time; start checking them after 10 minutes.) Serve at once; stuffed mushrooms don't reheat very well.

Note: *If you are using shiitake, buy an extra couple of large mushrooms or half a dozen small ones to substitute for the chopped stems in the stuffing.*

Don't use white champignon mushrooms for this recipe, even the ones sold as "stuffers"—their flavor is too mild and dull to stand up to the stuffing.

If you want to serve the mushrooms as a cocktail party pickup food, the recipe doubles beautifully. If you double it, only increase the butter by half.

PECANS

Pecans (*Carya olivaeformis*) are indigenous to the South. They are actually a variety of hickory (the Latin name means olive-shaped hickory). They were well known to many Native Americans, who relished them and even used their extracted oil as a seasoning. This fondness was passed on to the early European settlers, and wild pecans were used in the South as an inexpensive substitute for walnuts and imported almonds. During this century, pecans have been widely cultivated as a commercial crop in the Deep South. Shady pecan groves dot Georgia, Alabama, Mississippi, and Louisiana. In these areas, where the nuts are cheap and plentiful, were born some of the South's most famous confections—pecan pie, Creole pralines, and butter pecan ice cream, to name a few. Unfortunately, the trees cannot survive a really severe winter, so their growing area is limited, and outside it pecans can be an expensive luxury.

Not so in my family. I grew up in borrowed houses. My father was (and is) a minister, and those were the days when churches still provided a residence for their pastor. We were lucky—those pastoriums were all wonderful old houses with lots of character and, best of all, a humongous pecan tree in the backyard (one of them had six!). So for our family, pecans weren't a luxury—they were free. Then my father retired and bought his first house. The place has many assets. It is peacefully secluded on an old farm road and yet they have good neighbors who are not too far away; from the back porch and kitchen there is a spectacular view of the Blue Ridge Mountains; the garden spot is ideal. But for the first time in my living memory there was no pecan tree in the yard.

He wasted no time planting one.

Roasted Pecans   MAKES 1 POUND

When it came to entertaining at our house, roasted pecans were pretty much taken for granted. We ate and served them in prodigal quantities, and I was grown before I knew that many people considered them a luxury. I've never tired of them. To this day, they're my favorite snack food, and the one sure given when company comes to my house.

A pound of toasted nuts will serve four to six people through about two rounds of drinks. If you are serving other things along with them, allow 1 pound of nuts for eight people. The quantity in this recipe is only a pound, but you can actually toast up to 4 pounds at one time. Choose a large, deep-rimmed pan that will hold the nuts in no more than two layers. A 9 x 13-inch sheet-cake pan is perfect for up to 2 pounds of nuts. For larger quantities, choose a large rimmed baking sheet or use two smaller pans side by side.

1 pound whole pecan halves (or other nuts; see note)
2 tablespoons unsalted butter (no substitutes)
Salt

1. Position a rack in the center of the oven and preheat to 275°F. Spread the pecans on a wide, deep-rimmed pan. Roast them in the center of the oven, stirring occasionally until they begin to color, about 45 minutes to an hour. The nuts will continue to darken and crisp as they cool, so don't let them get too dark.

2. Cut the butter in bits, and add it to the pecans. Stir until it has just melted and the nuts are evenly coated. Return them to the oven and toast for about 10 minutes more.

3. Salt the pecans to taste while they are still hot and toss them until they are uniformly coated. Usually, the pecans are allowed to cool completely before serving, but in the winter, I serve them still toasty-warm from the oven. To store them (assuming you have very strange company and actually have leftovers), make sure the pecans are completely cool and place them in a tightly sealed container, such as a glass jar, a plastic storage bowl, or a tin box.

Note: *You can follow this recipe to toast almost any nut—almonds, cashews, filberts, and walnuts all work well. The cooking time is the same for all of them.*

CURRIED PECANS: Curry spices are a popular seasoning for toasted pecans in the South, especially during the holiday season. Allow 1 tablespoon of Curry Powder (page 28) for a pound of pecans. Add it with the butter in step 2, before the final toasting, which will help the curry flavor develop. Serve warm.

Sheri's Spiced Pecans   MAKES 4 CUPS

Most every cook in the South makes some version of spiced, glazed pecans, usually involving curry powder (see the variation of the previous recipe). This is Sheri Castle's, which she brightens with the woodsy flavor of fresh rosemary. Sheri uses them prodigally in salads (see Sheri's Pear and Pomegranate Salad on page 227) and recommends them as the ideal cocktail nibble for two of the South's favorite libations: bourbon and champagne.

3 tablespoons unsalted butter

2 teaspoons salt

¾ teaspoon freshly ground pepper

¼ teaspoon cayenne

½ teaspoon ground cinnamon

2 tablespoons (firmly packed) light brown sugar

1 tablespoon finely chopped fresh rosemary (not dried)

4 cups pecan halves (about 1 pound)

1. Position a rack in the center of the oven and preheat to 350°F. Melt the butter in a large saucepan over medium heat. Whisk in the salt, pepper, cayenne, cinnamon, sugar, and rosemary. Add the nuts and stir until well coated.

2. Spread the pecans on a large, rimmed baking sheet and roast until fragrant, about 10–15 minutes, stirring every 5 minutes. Pour into a serving bowl and serve warm or at room temperature.

Bacon (or Sausage), Pecan, and Herb Cornbread Dressing

MAKES ABOUT 7 CUPS, SERVING 12

In the South, just like the rest of the country, autumn is crowned by Thanksgiving, that ultimate all-American cook's feast. We have the usual turkey, cranberries, and pumpkin pie, but just like our drawling speech, we give those things our own lilting accent. Not surprisingly, pecans usually figure heavily in that accent, and mixing them into the dressing is quite popular.

Now, if you're not from the South, you should know that "dressing" here doesn't mean a sauce for salad—it's the savory bread pudding that accompanies the holiday bird—which in other places is stuffed inside it. Historically, we loved to fill turkeys with all kinds of savory stuffings just like everyone else, but by the middle of the twentieth century, most of us had come to call it dressing, and preferred it cooked in a separate pan. My family's dressing contained only stale crumbled cornbread and biscuits, sage, onion, celery, and of course salt and pepper, all bound together by homemade turkey broth. We never added things like bacon, sausage, oysters, or pecans. But over the years I've tried all those things and have even put them inside the turkey. But the core of cornbread, sage, and onion, stayed the same, so it was still comfortingly familiar.

If you want to use this as stuffing, hold back a little on the broth, loosely fill the bird's cavity, then moisten the remaining dressing as needed and put it in a smaller casserole dish in which it will be at least 1½ inches deep. Bake the casserole separately as directed below. Make sure that the stuffing inside the bird reaches an internal temperature of 165°F. Let it stay in the bird for 15 minutes, then remove it all to a warm serving bowl.

8 slices extra-thick applewood smoked bacon, diced, or 1 pound bulk sausage, preferably seasoned with sage

2 cups chopped yellow onions (about 2 medium)

4 large ribs celery, diced

4 cups stale (day old) cornbread, roughly
    crumbled or cut into 1-inch dice

4 cups stale but not dried baguette cut into
    1-inch dice

2 tablespoons chopped fresh sage

1 tablespoon chopped fresh thyme leaves

Grated zest from 1 lemon

1 cup toasted, roughly broken pecans

Salt and whole black pepper in a peppermill

Whole nutmeg in a grater

1½–2 cups turkey broth, made as for Chicken
    Broth (page 21) from the neck and giblets of
    turkey, or chicken broth

1. If you're making this to accompany turkey, remove the turkey from its roasting pan and pour off the pan juices into a fat separator. Rub a 9 x 13-inch baking dish with a spoonful of turkey fat skimmed from the pan juices or softened butter. Position a rack in the center of the oven and preheat to 350°F. Put the bacon in a large, heavy-bottomed skillet and sauté, stirring often, until it's golden brown and its fat is rendered. If using sausage, crumble it into the pan and cook until lightly browned and its fat is rendered. Remove the bacon or sausage from the pan and spoon off all but 3 tablespoons fat. If the sausage is lean and doesn't produce enough rendered fat, supplement it as needed with butter. Add the onion and celery and sauté until soft and transparent, but not browned. Turn off the heat.

2. Put both breads in a large bowl. Add the bacon or sausage, onions, celery, sage, thyme, lemon zest, and pecans; season with salt, pepper, and nutmeg to taste, and toss until well mixed. Moisten with a few spoonfuls of pan juices (if you have any) and then add enough broth to make the dressing wet but still loose and slightly crumbly, and not soggy.

3. Pour into the prepared dish and loosely flatten (it should still look a bit crumbly). Bake until golden brown and set in the center, about 45 minutes. Let rest 5–10 minutes before serving.

Bourbon-Cream Pecan Pralines

MAKES ABOUT 18 TO 20 PRALINES

This classic pecan confection is nothing like the hard, crisp pralines of French confectionary, and can be a bit tricky. But when you know your way around their tricks, they're really not difficult. There are three simple secrets. First, pralines (indeed most candy) should be made only when the humidity is low. Second, use a reliable candy thermometer. Experienced cooks often do without one, testing the candy by dropping a little into a cup of cold water (it's ready when the drop forms a soft, cohesive ball), but a temperature reading is more reliable, especially if you're a novice. Finally, don't let the candy thicken too much as you are stirring it or it will begin to form large instead of very fine crystals, then work quickly to get the candy out of the pot. The longer it sits in the warm pot, the more it crystallizes. For that reason, it's better to make this candy in small batches. If you want to double the batch, recruit someone to help you spoon it at the end.

1 cup firmly packed light brown sugar

1 cup granulated sugar

½ cup heavy cream (minimum 36 percent milk fat)

1 tablespoon unsalted butter

1½ cups roughly broken pecan pieces

1 teaspoon bourbon

1. If you have a polished stone countertop or marble pastry board, it's ideal for making pralines. Lightly butter an 18-inch square surface of the stone. Otherwise, lightly butter a piece of heavy-duty aluminum foil and have it ready on a flat surface.

2. Stir together both sugars, the cream, and the butter in a heavy-bottomed stainless-steel or enameled saucepan. Stir until smooth and put the pan over medium-high heat. If using a candy thermometer, insert it now, making sure that the probe doesn't touch the side or bottom of the pan. When the sugars are melted, stir in the butter and pecans. Bring to a boil and boil, without stirring or scraping the sides, until it reaches the soft ball stage, or 235°F on the thermometer. Remove it from the heat and let stand, undisturbed, for 4 minutes.

3. Add the bourbon and begin vigorously beating the candy with a clean wooden spoon (don't use the spoon you used to stir it earlier). As soon as it's creamy and beginning to thicken (less than a minute), drop it by the tablespoonfuls onto the buttered stone or foil. Let cool until the candy is hardened, about 15–30 minutes depending on the temperature in your kitchen. Store in an airtight container in a cool, dry place.

Cousin Tillie's Pecan Pie

MAKES TWO 9-INCH PIES

Most versions of this famous Southern pastry are corn syrup-based custards. They're good, but corn syrup is intensely sweet and can make the pie a bit cloying. For years I have looked for a pecan pie without that drawback, but which still had the satisfying balance of flavors that had made it a classic. Unfortunately, I met with little success.

Then, on what was probably the saddest day of my life, I discovered such a pie. We had just laid my sweet grandmother to rest beside my grandfather and watched as the dirt was piled onto the end of an era. The family retired to the homeplace over in Hartwell, beautifully refurbished by Ma Ma's cousin Dorothy Marrett, a soothing place to heal our wounds, surrounded by lovely memories, and by Aunt Fanny Lou's fragrant old rose bushes. And there, in the midst of it all, was the best pecan pie I had ever tasted, courtesy of my cousin Tillie Bannister.

As is typical of the best cooks when they are confronted with compliments, Cousin Tillie was mildly surprised and even a little embarrassed by my enthusiasm. It was just a plain old thing, nothing fancy, which was of course why it was so perfect. Luckily, Tillie was not so embarrassed that she wouldn't share the recipe.

1 recipe Basic Pastry (page 39)
¼ pound (1 stick or ½ cup) unsalted butter
6 eggs
3 cups (tightly packed) light brown sugar
½ teaspoon salt
2 cups pecans, roughly broken (not chopped)

1. Roll out the pastry to a thickness of about ⅛ inch and line two 9-inch pie plates with it. Prick it well, flute or decorate the edges, and chill the pastry for 30 minutes to allow it to relax.

2. Position a rack in the center of the oven and preheat to 425°F. Melt the butter in a saucepan over low heat, then turn off the heat and let it cool. Break the eggs into a mixing bowl and beat them until smooth. Add the sugar and stir until it is dissolved. Stir in the butter and salt, and stir (don't beat it) until smooth. Fold in the pecans and then pour the mixture into the prepared pastry.

3. Put the pies on the center rack of the oven, not touching, and bake 10 minutes. Reduce the heat to 325°F and bake until set and the tops are nicely browned, about 45 minutes. Cool completely on wire racks before serving.

Wilted Salad   SERVES 4

When the weather finally begins to cool across the Deep South, the late crop of lettuce, which withered in the blistering summer heat, revives and flourishes again. But since cooler weather has also stimulated heartier appetites, autumn is the season when one of our best-loved dishes of greens—a wilted salad—is especially popular.

Wilted salads are traditionally made by pouring sizzling red-eye gravy over the greens, or by wilting the greens in a pan with rendered fat and vinegar. Here is a modern version in which the traditional idea remains intact, but the wilting hot fat is a fruity extra-virgin olive oil. The taste is very different, but still satisfyingly familiar.

Choose tender, leafy salad greens—Bibb, Boston, or red-tipped leaf lettuces. Romaine is rather too sturdy for this salad, and iceberg lettuce is too watery and loses what little flavor it has when heated.

½ pound leaf lettuce (see headnote)

4 green onions

¼ cup fresh herb leaves, such as basil, oregano, tarragon, or mint (torn into small pieces if large)

⅓ cup extra-virgin olive oil

⅓ cup red wine or cider vinegar

Salt and whole black pepper in a mill

1 recipe Corn Sticks (page 34)

1. Wash and thoroughly dry the lettuce. Put it in a heatproof glass or wooden salad bowl. Trim the roots and any yellowed leaves from the onions and thinly slice them. Add them to the greens along with the herbs and toss to mix.

2. Put the oil and vinegar in a small, heavy-bottomed pan and bring them to a boil. Season with a liberal pinch of salt, a few grindings of black pepper, and turn off the heat.

3. Pour the hot dressing over the greens and toss rapidly until they're coated and beginning to wilt. Taste and adjust the seasonings, toss again, and serve at once with hot corn sticks.

SWEET POTATOES VS. POTATOES VS. YAMS

Now, here's a real mess—a history of confused inter-relations that is more convoluted than that of any first family of Virginia. First, we have sweet potatoes, *Ipomoea batatas*—the root of a tropical vine in the morning-glory family. Apparently native to Central America, it spread to South America, the Caribbean, and probably Asia. This vegetable was "discovered" by the Spanish and introduced to continental Europe early in the sixteenth century. Eventually, the name *batatas* was corrupted to "potatoes"—they were sometimes even referred to as "Spanish potatoes"—and were certainly the first tuber to be called a "potato."

Fine, that's simple enough. But then the Spanish ran across South American *pappus* (*Solanum tuberosum*), a tuber in the nightshade family that is not even remotely related to *Ipomoea batatas*. They introduced this vegetable to Europe sometime later in the sixteenth century, at which point the words *pappus* and *batatas* somehow got hopelessly mashed together and both vegetables came to be known as "potatoes."

Enter the African slave trade and the plot thickens. Africans and those Europeans who were trading with Africa knew another edible tuber—yams, of the family *Dioscoreaceae*, which is probably native to tropical Asia—but nevermind. Now, yams and sweet potatoes are not remotely related to one another, but both the early *batatas* (not as orange nor as sweet as modern hybrids) and yams had a not-dissimilar color and texture. Africans began calling sweet potatoes "yams" and, unfortunately, the name stuck. By the late 1930s it was so common-place that a hybrid deep orange sweet potato introduced in Louisiana was officially called a "yam." Add to that Margaret Mitchell's constant references to "yams" in her novel *Gone with the Wind*, which for some reason is constantly being referenced as history, throw in the sweet potato's reputation for "procuring bodily lust," stir in the fact that real yams were introduced to the Caribbean in the seventeenth century—and are still sold in West Indian markets—and you have a story so steamy, confused, and convoluted that it would make even a romance novelist's head spin.

In any case, the sweet potatoes that nearly everyone expects on the Thanksgiving table, the ones that we Southerners continue—stubbornly—to call yams, are all hybrids of those ancient *batatas*. Sweet potatoes are not nearly as starchy as true yams, and their flavor is much sweeter. Their skin is very smooth and their color, a deep hue of the inner flesh, ranges from yellow to deep orange (almost red), and they weigh from 8–10 ounces each. Real yams have a rough skin, a mildly sweet, starchy pale-yellow to white flesh, and can weigh up to 5 pounds. In other words, the two vegetables are not at all alike.

In Florida, *boniatos*, a variety of sweet potato that is close to the older types, is being grown. Available in Latino markets and specialty groceries in many parts of the country, *boniatos* can be used in any of these recipes, as can any variety of Southern orange sweet potatoes, even the ones called "yams." Avoid real yams—and I'll try to avoid the Southern habit of calling sweet potatoes by that name. (Aren't you glad?)

Sweet Potato and Leek Soup

SERVES 6

The simple substitution of sweet potatoes turns this reliable old workhorse of the French kitchen into something at once both refreshingly new and yet comfortingly familiar. While I am reluctant to call a recipe "Southern" just because it contains a "Southern" ingredient, this one does have a distinct drawl.

2 pounds sweet potatoes

3 large leeks

2 tablespoons unsalted butter

1 medium yellow onion, peeled and chopped

2 cups Chicken Broth (page 21) or 1 cup canned chicken broth mixed with 1 cup water (even if the label says "use full strength")

1 Bouquet Garni (page 32), made with 1 sprig each parsley, sage, and thyme, and 1 bay leaf

Salt and whole white peppercorns in a peppermill

1 cup light cream

1 tablespoon chopped fresh sage or parsley

1. Scrub the potatoes well, peel them with a vegetable peeler, and cut them into small dice. Split the leeks and wash them under cold running water until all dirt and grit have been removed. Trim off the roots and any tough or discolored leaves. Separate the green tops from the white parts of the leeks and set aside 1 cup of them. Slice the white parts thinly.

2. Put the butter, leeks, and onion in a heavy-bottomed 3- to 4-quart pot over medium-low heat. Sweat the vegetables until wilted and soft, but don't let them brown, about 5–8 minutes. Add the potatoes and toss until warm. Add the broth, bouquet garni, a healthy pinch of salt, and a liberal grinding of pepper. Raise the heat to medium high and bring to a boil, then reduce the heat to a slow simmer and cook until the potatoes are tender, about 12 minutes. Turn off the heat.

3. Take up and set aside 1 cup of the potatoes, then puree the soup through a food mill or in batches in a blender or food processor. The soup can be made several hours ahead up to this point. Let it cool, cover, and if making it more than 4 hours ahead, refrigerate it.

4. When you're ready to finish and serve it, return it to the pot, add the cream and bring it back to a simmer over medium heat. Meanwhile, thinly slice the reserved leek greens.

When the soup is simmering once more, add the reserved potatoes and leek and simmer until the greens are tender but still bright green—about 4 minutes. Taste and adjust the salt and pepper. Pour it into a heated tureen or divide it among heated soup plates, and serve at once with chopped sage or parsley sprinkled over the top of each serving.

Note: *For a meatless version, substitute Vegetable Broth (page 22) for the chicken broth. If you want to avoid dairy products, use peanut or olive oil for sautéing the leeks and onion, and substitute another cup of broth for the cream. The flavor will be very different, but it is still pretty dog-gone good.*

SWEET POTATO VICHYSSOISE: My friend Dean Owens made this into a superb summer soup by pureeing the entire soup. He chilled and served it exactly like vichyssoise, topped with a dollop of heavy cream, a sprinkling of white pepper, and some chopped fresh chives.

Oven-Roasted Sweet Potatoes

SERVES 4

Originally, sweet potatoes were roasted in the hot ash of the kitchen hearth. This gave them a smoky, earthy flavor that cannot be imitated in a modern oven. This was still going on later than you might think: When my father was growing up in the 1930s, he vividly remembers how he and his brothers would bank the fires for the night and shove sweet potatoes into the ashes so they'd be ready for breakfast the next morning. When I've got the grill fired up, I'll roast the sweet potatoes on the back of the grill (see page 164 for the method), which comes close to giving them that ash-roasted flavor. However, when roasted in a cast-iron Dutch oven or an unglazed

clay baking dish, as directed here, they can still taste awfully good.

4 medium sweet potatoes (about 2 pounds)
Unsalted butter, softened
Salt and black pepper in a peppermill

1. Position a rack in the center of the oven and preheat to 400°F. Scrub the potatoes well under cold running water, removing any root tendrils that may still be attached, and pat dry.

2. Prick them in several places with a fork and lightly grease them with butter. Put the potatoes in a cast-iron Dutch oven or Romertopf that will hold them in one layer (it's okay if they touch slightly, but don't crowd them). Put on the lid and roast on the center rack of the oven, turning the potatoes occasionally so that the bottoms don't get too brown, until they yield easily when pressed with your finger, about 1 hour.

3. To serve, slit each one lengthwise with a sharp knife, wrap it with a kitchen towel, and gently press until it splits and puckers. Serve at once with butter, salt, and pepper passed separately, or fill them with peppers and onions (see next recipe).

Dori's Oven-Roasted Sweet Potatoes with Peppers and Onions

SERVES 4

The most sublime topping of all for an oven-roasted sweet potato is an unapologetically large lump of butter. But in the fall, when the last of the bell peppers are sweet and ripe, novelist Dori Sanders keeps alive an old tradition by making this savory filling, which she recorded in her lovely book *Dori Sanders' Country Cooking.*

Dori modernized her version by using olive oil, but wrote: "If you want to make it like the old-timers did, substitute rendered pork fat for the olive oil." Well, Miss Dori, I do, and I did: The smell of onions and peppers simmering in bacon drippings is one of the world's great gastronomical sensations. However, if you want, you can omit the bacon and use 2 tablespoons of extra-virgin olive oil instead.

4 medium Oven-Roasted Sweet Potatoes (page 215)

4 slices bacon

1 medium yellow onion, thinly sliced

1 medium ripe (red or yellow) bell pepper, seeded as directed on page 114, and thinly sliced

Salt and black pepper in a peppermill

6 tablespoons homemade Crème Fraîche (page 18) or sour cream

2 tablespoons chopped fresh chives or scallion tops

1. While the potatoes are roasting, put the bacon in a 10-inch skillet, preferably of cast iron, over medium heat. Fry, turning it occasionally, until it's browned and crisp, about 8–10 minutes. Turn off the heat.

2. Remove and drain the bacon on absorbent paper, crumble, and set it aside. Drain off all but 2 tablespoons of the fat, and return the pan to medium heat. Add the onion and bell pepper and sauté, tossing often, until the vegetables are tender, about 8–10 minutes. Turn off the heat. Season with salt and a liberal grinding of pepper, and toss to mix.

3. Meanwhile, mix the crème fraîche or sour cream with the chive or green onion. When the potatoes are tender, remove them from the oven, slit each one lengthwise, and wrap a kitchen towel around it, pressing gently until it splits and "puckers." Gently reheat the onion-and-pepper mixture over medium heat, spoon them into the potatoes, and serve at once, with the chive cream and crumbled bacon passed separately.

Bubber's Stuffed Sweet Potatoes

SERVES 4

This is my kind of sweet potato dish. It isn't so sweet that it hurts your teeth, and the fine flavor of the potatoes isn't smothered with a lot of spices. The nutmeg and sherry enhance rather than mask the flavor, and the cheese lends a welcome savory contrast to the natural sweetness.

For those who aren't from the South, let me explain the name. To say Southerners are a bit "family proud" would be the understatement of the century. That pride has generated a long-standing tradition of naming the firstborn son after his proud daddy. Naturally, proud Daddy was named for *his* proud daddy, who had been in turn named for *his*—and so on. The result is half a dozen men in the same family with *exactly* the same name, the only difference being a number at the end. To distinguish them from one another, each gets tagged with a boyhood nickname that he never outgrows. That's why the South is populated with grown men called "Sonny," "Bud," "Red," "Skip," "Rip," "Tiny" (even when he's six-foot-two) and the now infamous "Bubba." "Bubber," in this case, was Adam Howard of McClellanville (a fishing village near Charleston) who single-handedly added a whole paragraph to the dictionary definition of eccentric. Adam was a slap-wonderful cook, as this recipe clearly demonstrates. Now that he's gone, I don't know which I miss the most—his cooking or his irreverent sense of humor.

4 Oven-Roasted Sweet Potatoes (page 215)

Salt and whole white peppercorns in a peppermill

1 blade of mace, crushed, or ¼ teaspoon ground mace, or whole nutmeg in a grater

¾ cup grated sharp cheddar

¼ cup heavy cream (minimum 36 percent milk fat)

3 tablespoons melted unsalted butter

1 tablespoon dry sherry (such as amontillado)

Sweet paprika

1. After you take the potatoes from the oven, preheat the broiler. Allow the potatoes to cool enough to handle comfortably, but don't let them get cold. Cut a slice from the top of each potato, and with a spoon or melon baller, scoop out the insides, leaving a shell about ¼-inch thick. Set the shells aside.

2. Mash the scooped-out pulp smooth and season it with a healthy pinch of salt, a liberal grinding of white pepper, and the mace or a liberal grinding of nutmeg. Beat into it ½ cup of the cheese, the cream, butter, and sherry. Taste and adjust the seasonings to suit, and continue beating until the potatoes are fluffy. Spoon the whipped potatoes back into the shells, mounding them up on top. Sprinkle the tops with the remaining cheese and paprika.

3. Place the shells on a shallow pan or cookie sheet and broil until the tops are lightly browned, about 5 minutes.

Note: *You can also make the potatoes completely ahead and reheat them in the oven. Position a rack in the center of the oven and preheat the oven to 400°F. Put the potatoes on a shallow baking dish or cookie sheet, and bake them in the center of the oven until they are heated through and the tops are lightly browned, about 20 minutes.*

If you can't find whole-blade mace, you can use the ground variety, but it won't have nearly as much flavor. I would encourage you to use freshly grated nutmeg instead. The two spices are actually parts of the same fruit, and their flavor is similar. In my opinion, freshly grated nutmeg always has a finer flavor than powdered mace.

Old-Fashioned Candied Sweet Potatoes   SERVES 6 TO 8

For more than a century in the part of the South where I grew up, candied sweet potatoes have been the standard accompaniment for baked ham and the Thanksgiving turkey, and they remain a favorite with many Georgia and Carolina families. They are sweet—REALLY sweet. But try to get over it: They're also really good.

4–6 medium sweet potatoes
1 cup sugar
½ cup (well-packed) light brown sugar
Salt
Ground cinnamon, to taste (optional)
3–4 tablespoons unsalted butter

1. Scrub the potatoes under cold water. Put them in a large, heavy-bottomed pot and cover by 1 inch with cold water. Bring to a boil over medium-high heat, reduce the heat to a steady rolling simmer, and cook until about half done (still firm at the center). Drain, reserving ½ cup of the cooking liquid (keep this hot).

2. Position a rack in the center of the oven and preheat to 350°F. Peel and slice the potatoes ½-inch thick and layer them in a 9 x 13-inch casserole dish. Mix the two sugars and a pinch of salt together. Sprinkle this over the potatoes and, if liked, sprinkle liberally with cinnamon to taste. Dot the top with bits of butter and pour the reserved cooking liquid around the potatoes.

3. Bake the potatoes, uncovered, until they are tender and the syrup is thick, about ½ hour. Let them stand 5–10 minutes before serving.

Nathalie Dupree's Sweet Potato and Turnip Gratin SERVES 10 TO 12

2–3 pounds white turnips, peeled and sliced ¼-inch thick

2–3 pounds sweet potatoes, peeled and sliced ¼-inch thick

½ cup (1 stick) butter

1–2 tablespoons finely chopped fresh thyme or marjoram

Salt and whole black pepper in a mill

¾ cup grated imported Parmesan cheese

¾ cup grated Gruyère cheese, preferably Comté

2 cups heavy cream

1 cup bread crumbs or panko

1. Position a rack in the center of the oven and preheat to 350°F. Butter a 3-quart casserole or gratin dish. Put the turnips in a large pot, cover them with water by 1 inch, then remove them. Bring the water to a boil, put the turnips back into it, and cook 5 minutes. Drain thoroughly.

2. Gently combine the turnips and sweet potatoes. Cover the bottom of the casserole with a layer of them and dot with butter. Sprinkle generously with the herbs, salt, and pepper, and cover with a portion of the Parmesan and Gruyère. Repeat until all the ingredients are used. Pour the cream around the sides, top with the crumbs, and dot with the remaining butter.

3. Bake until the vegetables are soft but not mushy, 1–1½ hours. This can be made several days ahead, or frozen for up to 3 months. Defrost it in the refrigerator and reheat for half an hour to 45 minutes in an oven heated to 350°F.

Myrtice's Crunchy Sweet Potato Soufflé SERVES 6

Don't put me in the same room with marshmallows and sweet potatoes. If I never saw another one of those syrupy so-called soufflés with rows of brown mush on top, it would not be a moment too soon. All that goop just covers up the lovely flavor of the potatoes.

Well, my prejudice aside, sweet potato soufflé is a Southern standard on Thanksgiving and Christmas tables. Not to include one in a book on Southern vegetables would be like leaving fried chicken out of a book on Southern poultry. Happily, my friend Myrtice Lewis, for years a fellow parishioner at St. John's Church, made a stellar sweet potato soufflé topped with pecans and coconut, without a single marshmallow in sight.

Myrtice is heir to a long tradition of fine cooks by way of her mother, Nianza Freeman James. With wonderful food always around, Myrtice didn't spend much time in the kitchen as a girl, and claims that she was grown before she prepared her first complete meal. That may be so, but today she's one of the best home cooks I know.

2 pounds sweet potatoes

1½ cups sugar

¼ teaspoon salt

3 large eggs, slightly beaten

¼ pound (1 stick) unsalted butter

6 ounces evaporated milk

1 teaspoon vanilla extract

1 teaspoon freshly grated nutmeg

½ teaspoon cinnamon

FOR THE PECAN CRUNCH TOPPING:

¼ pound (1 stick) unsalted butter

1 cup brown sugar

1 cup chopped pecans

1 cup grated unsweetened coconut

1. Position a rack in the center of the oven and preheat to 350°F. Wash the sweet potatoes and put them in a deep pot. Completely cover with water and then lift out the potatoes. Cover the pot and bring to a boil over high heat. Carefully add the potatoes, cover, and let the liquid return to a full boil. Reduce the heat to medium and simmer until the potatoes are tender, about 20–30 minutes, depending on the size and age of the potatoes. Drain them well, let them cool enough to handle, and peel them. Put them into a mixing bowl and mash them to a pulp.

2. Add the sugar, salt, eggs, butter, evaporated milk, vanilla, and spices to the potatoes, and mix well. Lightly butter a 2-quart glass or pottery baking dish and fill it with the potatoes, smoothing the top with a spatula or wooden spoon.

3. To make the topping, melt the butter in a saucepan that will comfortably hold all the ingredients over low heat. Turn off the heat and mix in the brown sugar, pecans, and coconut until all the ingredients are moistened with the butter. Spread or sprinkle this mixture evenly over the potatoes.

4. Bake until the topping is nicely browned and the filling is set, about 35–40 minutes.

Old-Fashioned Grated Sweet Potato Pudding   SERVES 6

This simple pudding, made with grated raw sweet potatoes bound by a vanilla-scented milk and egg custard, may be plain and homey, but for many Southerners of a certain age, it remains a tremendously comforting reminder of childhood, especially when the weather is cold and life's many trials are pressing a little too close for comfort.

2–3 large, orange-fleshed sweet potatoes (see step one)

2 large eggs

1 cup sugar

Salt

1½ cups whole milk

4 ounces (½ cup or 1 stick) melted unsalted butter

1 tablespoon Bourbon Vanilla (page 29) or 2 teaspoons vanilla extract

1 teaspoon ground cinnamon

Whole nutmeg in a grater

1. Position a rack in the center of the oven and preheat to 350°F. Lightly butter a 2-quart ceramic or glass casserole. Peel and coarsely grate enough sweet potatoes to make 3 cups, lightly packed.

2. Break the eggs into a mixing bowl and lightly whisk until smooth. Whisk in the sugar, a small pinch of salt, milk, melted butter, vanilla, cinnamon, and grate in about half a teaspoon of nutmeg (or to taste). Fold in the grated sweet potato. To give the pudding a crunchy topping, some cooks used to hold back a cup of the potato to sprinkle over the top.

3. Pour it into the prepared casserole and smooth the top with a spatula. If you've held back the cup of potatoes, sprinkle them over the top. Bake in the center of the oven until the pudding is set, about 25 minutes.

Ma Ma's Sweet Potato Custard Pies
MAKES TWO 9-INCH PIES

When my first book, *Classical Southern Cooking*, came out, I tried to be very careful about staying within the known traditions of antebellum Southern kitchens, and was braced for the inevitable "That's not the way *my* grandmother did it" with a ready answer: "Well, it's not the way *my* grandmother did it, either." What I wasn't prepared for was a complaint from Ma Ma herself.

My sweet potato pies, she informed me, both while I was stirring them up for Christmas dinner and while we were eating them, were nothing like hers. They were perfectly good, she said, but then promptly launched into a long list of what was the matter with them. Well, she was right: I had gotten so caught up with historical accuracy that my grandmother's recipe—the one I truly loved—had completely disappeared. I knew then that I'd have to do something about it. But sadly, I never got to cook with her again. Still, she is always nearby whenever I make this pie.

Get ready for a religious experience.

1 recipe Basic Pastry (page 39)

3 pounds (5–6 medium) Oven-Roasted Sweet Potatoes (page 215)

1 cup sugar

Salt

2 ounces (4 tablespoons or ½ stick) unsalted butter

4 large eggs

1 tablespoon Bourbon Vanilla (page 29), or ½ teaspoon vanilla extract, or 1 tablespoon bourbon (optional)

Whole nutmeg in a grater (optional)

Lightly sweetened whipped cream

1. Position a rack in the center of the oven and preheat to 375°F. Line two 9-inch pie dishes (preferably ceramic or glass) with the pastry and prick it all over with a fork. Chill the pastry in the refrigerator while you make the filling.

2. Peel the potatoes while still hot (they're easier to peel) and puree them with a potato ricer into a large mixing bowl, or cut them in chunks, put them in the bowl, and mash them with a fork as my grandmother did.

3. Add the sugar, a pinch of salt, and the butter, and stir until they are dissolved into the potatoes. In a separate bowl, lightly beat the eggs until well mixed and stir them into the potatoes. Stir in the vanilla and, if you like, add a generous grating of nutmeg.

4. Pour the custard into the prepared pastry and bake in the center of the oven, not touching each other, until they're set and the pastry is nicely browned, about 40 minutes. Let them cool completely on a wire cooling rack (at least 2 hours) before serving them. You may also chill them before serving.

5. Serve at room temperature or cold with a healthy dollop of lightly sweetened whipped cream.

Note: *I do like to flavor the pie with my own homemade bourbon vanilla extract or a bit of plain bourbon (I don't use commercial vanilla extract), but Ma Ma used a commercial extract and, good Baptist that she was, never used whiskey. She always cast a rather disapproving eye my way when I added it. It did not, however, stop her from eating it.*

TURNIPS

This common root vegetable is thought to be native to northern Europe, from whence it gradually migrated south and later was imported into North America, apparently with the earliest of the European settlers. As do so many other root vegetables, turnips have two seasons in the South—spring and fall.

The uninitiated often accuse Southerners of having an underdeveloped appreciation for this vegetable, claiming that we eat the part of it that everyone else throws away (the greens) and throw out the part that everyone else eats. Yes, we Southerners do love our greens, and the leafy top of this vegetable is a particular favorite, so much so that many Southerners loosely refer to all leafy greens as "turnip greens" even when the leaf in question is really mustard, kale, or collards. But it's simply not true that we cut those greens away from the root and toss it to the pigs. (The pigs should be so lucky.) The truth is the root is almost as popular with Southerners as its leafy green top.

The simplest way that we prepare this vegetable is to peel and cut them into small dice, then mix them

with their greens in a single pot. But in early autumn, when new turnips are at their crispest and most fragrant, we like them best prepared like mashed potatoes, with a little cream and butter for richness and a dusting of black pepper for added spice.

Here is how to do it, followed by some of the other lovely traditional ways that turnips are enjoyed here in the South. They are also delightful gratinéed: See Nathalie Dupree's Sweet Potato and Turnip Gratin on page 218 and the variation of Scalloped Jerusalem Artichokes on page 256. More recipes can also be found in the spring chapter (pages 84–85).

Creamed Turnips   SERVES 6

From long before I can remember until he died after my freshman year in college, my grandfather made sure that creamed turnips accompanied our Thanksgiving turkey. I never make them without missing him.

Granddaddy was not alone in his affection for pairing turnips and poultry: This is a longtime Southern favorite with any roasted fowl, and once was a fixture on Thanksgiving tables all over the South.

2 pounds fresh medium-size turnips, as much of the same size as is possible

2 tablespoons unsalted butter

½ cup heavy cream

Salt and whole black pepper in a peppermill

1. Scrub the turnips with a vegetable brush under cold running water. Trim off the taproot and most of the green top, but leave some of each attached. Put them in a large, heavy-bottomed pot that will hold them comfortably, add enough water to cover them by an inch, and lift them out.

2. Cover and bring the water to a rolling boil over a medium-high heat. Add the turnips, cover until it starts boiling again, and skew the lid slightly. Lower the heat to medium and cook until the turnips are very tender and are easily

pierced with a fork, about 20–30 minutes. Drain and let cool enough to handle.

3. Trim off all the top and taproot, then lightly skin the turnips with a vegetable peeler and slice ½-inch thick. Wipe out the pot in which the turnips were cooked and return them to it. Add the butter and turn on the heat to low. Mash the turnips with a potato masher until they are roughly pureed and the butter is absorbed. Gradually add the cream a little at a time, mashing and mixing until it is also absorbed and the turnips are velvety, but still slightly lumpy. Season with a pinch or so of salt and mix it in.

4. Pour the turnips into a serving bowl, dust with a few grindings of black pepper, and serve hot.

Turnips Stuffed with Winter Greens   SERVES 4

The late Joan Cobitz was an accomplished artist who supplemented her income by baking lovely sourdough breads for Brighter Day, Savannah's premier natural-food store, and by occasionally cooking for the private parties of a few select friends. Joan was a Yankee from Chicago, so

when one of those friends asked for an autumnal Southern buffet, she immediately called me in to help. I can't remember when I've laughed more in the kitchen. Afterwards, the hostess of that party said we had more fun than the guests.

Joan wanted to do something with turnips and greens that would be self-contained. Filling the hollowed-out turnips with their own greens seemed logical, since Southerners often cook turnip roots with their greens in the same pot. To our surprise, the greens as stuffing tasted flat and dull, but kale, another hearty fall green, turned out to be the perfect pairing. Collards, which are really just a broad-leaved variety of kale, also work well so long as they are very young and tender.

4 large turnips (about 2 pounds)

4 tablespoons unsalted butter (plus more for greasing)

1 pound kale or young collards

Grated zest of 1 lemon

½ cup dry bread crumbs

4 green onions, thinly sliced

Salt and black pepper in a peppermill

1. Position a rack in the upper third of the oven and preheat to 400°F. Trim off most of the taproots and green tops of the turnips, but leave a little of both attached. Scrub them well under cold running water and pat dry. Rub them with a little butter, wrap tightly in foil, and put them on a rimmed baking sheet. Bake in the upper third of the oven until they yield slightly when pressed with a finger, about 1 hour.

2. Meanwhile, stem and cut the greens into 1-inch-wide strips. Wash thoroughly and drain, leaving some moisture clinging to the leaves. Put them in a large, lidded skillet over medium-high heat. Cover and cook until the greens are wilted but still bright green, about 4 minutes. Turn off the heat and spread the greens on a platter to cool.

3. Warm 2 tablespoons of the butter in a small pan over medium-low heat. When it's melted, add the lemon zest and crumbs and mix until the butter is evenly absorbed. Turn off the heat.

4. When the turnips are done, unwrap and let them cool enough to handle. Slice off the tops and with a melon baller or small spoon, scoop out the inner flesh, leaving a ½-inch-thick shell. Set aside the inner flesh for another use. Put the shells on a lightly greased baking sheet or dish. (Note: You can make it to this point up to a day ahead; cover and refrigerate everything if it's prepared more than 2 hours ahead.)

5. In the skillet in which the greens cooked, sauté the onions in the remaining 2 tablespoons of butter over medium-high heat until wilted, about 2 minutes. Return the greens to the pan and season with salt to taste and a few grindings of black pepper. Toss well and turn off the heat. Fill the turnips with the greens, sprinkle the buttered crumbs over them, and bake until the crumbs are golden and the turnips and greens are heated through, about 20 minutes.

Roasted Turnips SERVES 4

Even people who claim to hate turnips will put them away with enthusiasm when they are cooked this way. Roasting brings out the natural sweetness in any root vegetable, but particularly in this one. Though they're at their best cooked in the drippings of roasted lamb, pork, or turkey and served as an accompaniment to the meat, they are powerfully good cooked in other fats and savored all by themselves.

2 pounds fresh young turnips

2 tablespoons lard, bacon or roast drippings, or unsalted butter

1 tablespoon chopped fresh sage or winter savory

Salt and black pepper in a peppermill

1. Position a rack in the center of the oven and preheat to 400°F. Trim away the taproots and tops of the turnips and scrub well under cold running water. If the turnips are very young and tender, they shouldn't require peeling (in fact, the skin lends its own distinctive flavor), but if the turnips are older and the skin appears to be especially tough, go ahead and peel them. Cut large turnips into quarters but leave the small ones whole.

2. Put the fat in a cast-iron pan or heavy casserole that will hold the turnips comfortably in one layer. Put the pan in the oven until the fat is melted and hot. Add the turnips to the pan and sprinkle with the chopped herbs and a liberal grinding of pepper. Return the pan to the oven and roast, turning the turnips frequently, until they are uniformly golden brown, about 45 minutes to an hour. If they stick, slip a metal spatula under them and gently work them loose. Drain briefly on absorbent paper, sprinkle with a healthy pinch of salt, and serve at once.

Note: *Though animal fats, especially drippings or lard, are best here because they help the turnips brown and lend the best flavor, vegans can substitute peanut or olive oil with reasonably good results.*

Glazed Turnips Monticello SERVES 4

When the first edition of this book was under construction, the version of this recipe included in the Hammond-Harwood House cookbook, *Maryland's Way,* caught my attention. Though I knew it to be a classic French dish, at the time, I credited its introduction to Southern cookery to Maryland cooks. Years later, while working on *Dining at Monticello,* I realized that the real source was probably the kitchens at Thomas Jefferson's beloved home. While no usable recipe has survived in the family manuscripts (the one attempt to recall the method was, to put it politely, unintelligible), fortunately Cousin

Mary Randolph thought enough of it to include a lovely and lucid rendition in *The Virginia House-wife* titled "Ragout of Turnips."

But never mind historical attributions. What matters to us now is that this is a lovely way to cook small, sweet young turnips. Go to the extra trouble of trimming them into uniform rounds or ovals: It's not merely for appearances. They need to be round so that they'll roll in the pan to brown evenly, and of the same size so that they're all done at the same time.

Adding a little of sugar to almost every vegetable pot became an ominous trend in Southern cooking during the late nineteenth and early twentieth centuries, but here its function is not so much to sweeten as it is to facilitate the caramelizing.

2 pounds fresh young turnips

3 tablespoons unsalted butter

1 tablespoon sugar

1 cup Meat Broth, page 20

Salt and black pepper in a peppermill

1 tablespoon chopped parsley

1. Wash the turnips and lightly peel them. If they're small and even, simply trim them into uniform ovals. If they're larger, cut each turnip into quarters or thick wedges, and then trim them into uniform ovals.

2. Put 2 tablespoons of the butter in a large lidded skillet or sauté pan that will comfortably hold the turnips in one layer. Let it melt over medium-high heat. When it's hot but not browning, add the turnips and sprinkle the sugar over them and shake the pan to make the turnips roll around until they're evenly coated. Sauté, shaking the pan frequently and occasionally tossing or turning the turnips until they're an even golden brown, about 5 minutes.

3. Add the broth, bring it to a boil, again shaking the pan, then loosely cover and lower the heat to a gentle simmer. Cook, giving the pan

an occasional shake, until the turnips are tender, about 10 minutes more. The liquid should be considerably reduced. Remove the lid, raise the heat, and let it reduce to a glaze, again shaking the pan often so that the turnips remain an even color. Season to taste with a pinch or so of salt and a few grindings of black pepper. Off the heat, swirl in the remaining butter and transfer to a warm serving bowl. Sprinkle with parsley and serve at once.

Note: *There's no real substitute for butter in this dish. You can use olive oil, but it won't be at all the same.*

LATE FIGS

For most of the South, figs are seasonal in mid-to-late summer (our season in Savannah is usually over by the beginning of August), but inland and further north, figs often hit their peak as summer is slipping into early autumn—right about the time the early migrating birds stop in to refuel on their way south for the winter. Those lucky enough to have fig trees in their gardens go to great lengths to keep the birds from stealing their crop, covering the trees with protective nets and decorating its branches with reflective aluminum pie plates and strips of foil.

When we've had our fill of them right off the tree, juicy-sweet and still warm from the sun, or wrapped in thin slivers of country ham or prosciutto, the surplus is simmered with sugar and lemon into a thick conserve to slather on hot biscuits, top baked soft-ripened cheese, and fold into cake batter or ice cream.

Rebecca's Fig Preserves   MAKES ABOUT 7 HALF PINTS

When Southerners go to visit, no matter what the occasion, they always bring a gift. These gifts may be whimsical or practical—or just plain odd depending on the level of eccentricity of its giver. If you're lucky, it will be some kind of homemade conserve. The first time my lovely friend and colleague Rebecca Lang came to Savannah to teach a class, she arrived offering a festively ribboned jar of these preserves—and a handmade bowl to serve them in. Most every Southern cook who has a fig tree (or knows someone who is easily sweet-talked out of a peck or two of fruit) has her own version, varying from this only in detail.

3 pounds fresh, ripe figs, preferably
  Brown Turkey figs

4 cups sugar

1 small lemon, cut lengthwise into quarters, seeded, and thinly sliced

¼ cup freshly squeezed lemon juice
  (about 1 large lemon)

1. Stem the figs and, if they're large, cut them into quarters; if small, simply cut them in half. Layer them with sugar and sliced lemon in a heavy-bottomed, 6-quart stainless-steel or enameled iron Dutch oven. Add the lemon juice and 2 cups of water and, without stirring, bring it to a boil over medium heat.

2. Remove the pot from the heat, transfer the figs to a large glass or ceramic bowl, and let cool 30 minutes. Cut a piece of parchment or

wax paper to fit and lay it directly on top of the figs. Refrigerate for at least 8 or up to 12 hours.

3. Put the figs back into the pot in which they cooked and bring them to a boil over medium heat. Boil, stirring occasionally, until both the figs and lemon are translucent and the syrup has thickened slightly, about 45 minutes, carefully skimming and discarding any foam that forms on the surface.

4. Using a clean stainless-steel spoon and wide-mouthed canning funnel, transfer the preserves to sterilized half-pint canning jars. Cover with sterilized new lids, seal with clean rings, and process 10 minutes in a water bath as directed on page 11. Let them completely cool on clean, double-folded towels, not touching, before storing in a cool, dark pantry or cupboard. Rebecca recommends letting the preserves ripen for at least 1 week before consuming them.

Rebecca's Baked Brie with Fig Preserves and Pecans   SERVES 8

Brie cheese skinned of its top rind, slathered with chutney, and baked has become a favorite warm winter appetizer all over the South. Friend and fellow cookbook author Rebecca Lang gives it a personal touch by covering the cheese with her own homemade fig preserves and local pecans.

1 (8-ounce) wheel brie cheese

¼ cup Rebecca's Fig Preserves (this page), or your
  own favorite fig preserves

1 teaspoon chopped fresh rosemary (don't use dried)

8 pecan halves

Crackers or French bread, for serving

1. Position a rack in the center of the oven and preheat to 350°F. Trim the rind off the top of the brie, leaving a ¼-inch-wide border of rind around the edge. Line a baking sheet with parchment and put the cheese on it.

2. Stir together the fig preserves and rosemary in a small mixing bowl. Spread this over the skinned top of the cheese. Bake in the center of the oven for 8 minutes.

3. Remove it from the oven and arrange the pecans over the preserves. Return it to the oven and bake 5 minutes longer, or until the pecans are lightly toasted. Serve immediately with crackers or French bread.

Cinnamon Fig Ice Cream   MAKES 1½ QUARTS, SERVING ABOUT 6

Ice cream made with fresh figs (Fresh Fig Ice Cream, page 174) is a luxury that has an all-too-brief window of opportunity for just a few precious weeks in late summer. But fortunately fig preserves make an equally lovely and indulgent ice cream that can be enjoyed all year round.

1¼ cups fig jam or 1½ cups Rebecca's Fig Preserves (page 225), or your favorite fig preserves (see note)

2 cups whole milk

2 whole cinnamon sticks

6 large egg yolks

¾ cup sugar

2 cups heavy cream (minimum 36 percent milk fat)

Salt

2 tablespoons ruby port

1. If using jam, put it into a bowl and stir to loosen it. If using preserves, put them in a food processor fitted with a steel blade and pulse until finely chopped. Choose a saucepan with a really thick, heavy bottom, or prepare the bottom of a double boiler with at least 1 inch of water and bring it to a simmer over medium heat. Either in the saucepan or top pan of the double boiler, bring the milk and cinnamon to a simmer over direct medium heat.

2. Whisk the egg yolks lightly in a heatproof bowl and whisk in the sugar until smooth. Gradually beat in a cup of the hot milk. If using a double boiler, transfer the top pan to the bottom half with the simmering water. Stir in the egg yolk mixture into the remaining milk in a steady stream. Cook, stirring constantly, until the custard thickly coats the back of the spoon. Remove it from the heat and stir until it's somewhat cooled.

3. Add the cream and a small pinch of salt. Stir a ladleful of the custard into the jam or preserves to loosen them, then stir it and the port into the remaining custard. Stir until cooled, remove the cinnamon (it can be rinsed, dried, and reused once), then cover and chill the custard for at least 2 hours or overnight.

4. Prepare an ice cream churn following the manufacturer's instructions. Pour in the custard and freeze until it is the consistency of commercial soft-serve ice cream. Transfer it to a deep freezable container and freeze for at least 2, and as many as 8 hours, to let it harden and ripen.

Note: *The figs in jam are already mashed or chopped. The fruit in fig preserves is usually whole or at most halved or quartered. Preserves will need to be chopped as directed in step 1 or the ice cream will be too chunky.*

PEARS

When I was growing up, the pears that we could get in our rural community were too hard to eat raw, so most of them were put up in preserves, relishes, and spicy chutneys. The only pears we had to eat whole came from a can, and most often arrived at the table in a "fancy company" salad that consisted of half a canned pear lying on an iceberg lettuce leaf, its core cavity filled with a spoonful of mayonnaise topped by a sprinkling of coarsely grated cheddar.

Fortunately, good eating pears are now commonplace in our markets, and so are better pear salads. But the salad and fruit bowl are not the only place this luscious fruit turns up. They're also cooked in any way that we prepare apples (especially Apple Butter, page 193). Here are a few other deeply Southern ways to enjoy them.

Sheri's Pear and Pomegranate Salad

SERVES 6 TO 8

North Carolina cookbook author and cooking teacher Sheri Castle has spent most of her career championing the rebirth of local farmers' markets across the region. Her *The New Southern Garden Cookbook* celebrates the new diversity that these markets have brought back to Southern kitchens. When I asked her to share a recipe for this book, we agreed that this one handsomely demonstrated how she has honored tradition while embracing some of the new things that the South's energetic young farmers are introducing (and in some cases, reintroducing) to Southern tables.

Besides, it has bacon in it—which Sheri and I firmly believe to be a major food group all on its own.

2 ripe but firm pears

1 tart, crisp green apple

1 recipe Late-Harvest Riesling Vinaigrette (recipe follows)

4 cups lightly packed baby arugula, frisée, Belgian endive, mesclun, and/or thinly sliced radicchio

Arils (fleshy pink seeds) from 1 pomegranate (about ½ cup)

6–8 strips candied bacon, cut into bite-size pieces

½ cup crumbled blue cheese

1 cup Sheri's Spiced Pecans (page 209)

¼ cup beet micro greens (optional)

1. Unless the skins are especially tough or blemished, don't peel the pears and apple. Core and cut them into thin slices or julienne (matchstick-size strips). Put them in a glass bowl and toss gently with ¼ cup of the vinaigrette.

2. Toss the salad greens with enough vinaigrette to moisten and spread them on a large serving platter or divide them among individual salad plates.

3. Arrange the pears, apple, pomegranate arils, candied bacon, cheese, and spiced pecans over the greens, drizzle with the remaining vinaigrette and sprinkle with micro greens, if using. Serve immediately.

Note: *Removing the arils from a pomegranate is not as much of a challenge as keeping their staining juice contained while you're doing it. Sheri recommends submerging the opened pomegranate in a basin of cold water to keep the juice contained while you separate the arils from their connective membranes and skin.*

Late-Harvest Riesling Vinaigrette

MAKES ABOUT ¾ CUP

This dressing is lovely not only for the preceding recipe, but just about any green or fruit salad, and is especially beautiful drizzled over sliced vine-ripened tomatoes. Late-harvest Riesling is a wine made from the grapes that are left on the vines to the end of the season. Their sugars are very concentrated, so the resulting wine and the vinegar that's made from it are intensely sweet. I make this dressing with a light, fruity olive oil, but when the salad it will dress contains nuts, Sheri Castle likes to use the oil from that nut. Since nut oils can be strong, she tones them down with a milder-flavored grapeseed or olive oil.

Nut oils also go rancid more quickly than others, so store them in the refrigerator once the bottle or tin is opened, and take a good sniff of it before using. If you're still not sure, taste a drop for good measure.

¼ cup late-harvest Riesling vinegar (available at specialty groceries)

2 tablespoons finely chopped shallot

½ teaspoon salt, plus more, to taste

1 teaspoon Dijon mustard

6 tablespoons grapeseed oil or mild, fruity extra-virgin olive oil

2 tablespoons pecan or walnut oil

Whole black pepper in a mill

1. Put the vinegar, shallot, salt, and mustard in a pint-size glass jar with a tight-fitting lid. Let sit 5 minutes. Add both oils and black pepper to taste, close tightly, and vigorously shake the jar until the dressing is completely blended. Taste and adjust the seasonings.

2. Use this dressing as soon as possible. Leftovers will keep, well covered and refrigerated, for up to a week. Let it come to room temperature, and always taste and adjust the seasonings.

Candied Bacon

MAKES 12–16 SLICES, DEPENDING ON THE THICKNESS OF THE BACON, SERVING 1 TO 8 PEOPLE, DEPENDING ON *THEIR* THICKNESS AND LEVEL OF DISCRETION

Bacon glazed with brown sugar is an old brunch staple that has been around for decades, but it got a new life when it was sensationalized as "pig candy" by my friend Jill Conner Browne, Boss Queen of the Sweet Potato Queens of Jackson, Mississippi. It covers two of the four SPQ food groups (salty and sweet), and gets a special dispensation for not being deep-fried or gratinéed with cheese because it's bacon (the main reason

I could never be a vegetarian). This is Sheri Castle's version, which is the one she uses for her Pear and Pomegranate Salad (page 227). She has also been known to cut it into small bite-size pieces, pile it into a serving bowl, and put it out as a cocktail nibble.

What a gal.

Vegetable oil cooking spray

1 cup (firmly packed) light brown sugar

¾ teaspoon cayenne pepper

¼ teaspoon dry mustard

1 pound thick-cut best-quality bacon (I like applewood smoked)

1. Position a rack in the center of the oven and preheat to 350°F. Line a large rimmed baking sheet with foil and fit it with a wire cooling rack. Mist the rack with the cooking spray. Mix together the sugar, cayenne, and mustard and spread it on a plate.

2. Press one side of each slice of bacon into the spiced sugar and lay it, sugared-side down, on the wire rack. Sprinkle the tops of the bacon evenly with the remaining sugar, being careful not to scatter it onto the pan below (where it will burn and smoke up your oven).

3. Bake until the bacon is crisp and the sugar is bubbly, about 15 minutes. Let it cool on the rack until the glaze hardens, Store it in an airtight tin. If, that is, you have any left to store.

Baked Pears in White Wine   SERVES 4

Some of the best fruit desserts in Lettice Bryan's wonderful book *The Kentucky Housewife* (1839) were hidden as afterthoughts in a chapter on fruit sauces intended as a condiment for meat. This is one of them.

Look for small pears: The ones that Mrs. Bryan used would have been much smaller than the behemoth hybrid fruit that is available to most of us these days. The pears make a showier

presentation when cooked whole and presented standing upright. If you can find only the larger pears, don't despair: You can still use them in the recipe, but they'll need to be split. Refer to the note at the end of the recipe for cooking larger fruit.

4 small Bosc or firm Bartlett pears (about 1½ pounds, see note)

1 cup dry white wine or vermouth

1 lemon

Sugar

Whole nutmeg in a grater

½ cup heavy cream (minimum 36 percent milk fat) or Bourbon Custard Sauce (page 47)

1. Position a rack in the center of the oven and preheat to 350°F. Wash the pears under cold running water and peel them. Cut out the blossom end (at the bottom of the fruit) with a paring knife and then scoop out the core with small melon baller, leaving the fruit whole.

2. Lightly butter a deep, lidded casserole (preferably flameproof) that will just hold the pears upright with the lid on. Put in the fruit and pour the wine over it. Cover and bake the pears in the center of the oven until tender, about 1 hour, basting them occasionally with the wine.

3. Meanwhile, cut the zest from the lemon with a vegetable peeler and cut it into fine julienne. When the pears are tender, remove them to a serving platter or individual dishes. Halve the lemon and squeeze a few drops of its juice over each pear.

4. If the casserole in which the pears cooked isn't flameproof, transfer their pan juices to a saucepan. Sweeten to taste with a tablespoon or so of sugar and bring it to a boil over medium-high heat. Boil until it is reduced to a thick, syrupy glaze. Freshen it with a squeeze or two of lemon juice and pour it over the pears. Garnish with the lemon zest, a grating or so of nutmeg, to taste, and serve warm, with a pitcher of the heavy cream or custard passed separately.

Note: *If the pears are large (weighing more than 6 ounces each), you will need only two for this recipe. Split them lengthwise after peeling them, scoop out the core with a melon baller, and bake them lying cut-side down in one layer. If you don't have a large enough lidded baking dish, use an open casserole and cover the pears with a sheet of buttered parchment paper or foil.*

Pear Chips   MAKES ABOUT 6 HALF PINTS

The name of this conserve may seem a little confusing to those for whom "chips" are a crisp snack food, since there's nothing crisp about this. The pears are cut up into small chips, then simmered with lemon in spiced syrup until the fruit is clear and tender and the syrup is thick and spreadable. It's an ideal filling for hot biscuits or spread for breakfast toast, but it's also a nice relish for roast pork or game birds.

2 pounds (4 cups) sugar

2 cups water

1 large lemon, sliced as thin as possible

1 cinnamon stick

2 pounds firm but ripe pears, peeled, cored, sliced thin, and then cut into small chips

1. Stir the sugar and water in a large, heavy-bottomed stainless-steel or enameled pot until the sugar is mostly dissolved. Bring it to a boil over medium heat.

2. Add the lemon, cinnamon stick, and pear chips, bring it back to a boil, and cook over medium heat until the pears are translucent and tender and the syrup is thick. (To test the syrup, let a drop or so drip onto a cool saucer. It's ready when it jells as it cools.)

3. Remove and discard the cinnamon, and using a clean stainless-steel spoon and canning funnel, transfer the conserve to sterilized half-pint canning jars. Cover with sterilized new lids, seal with rings, and process for 10 minutes in a water bath (page 11). Cool the jars on clean, double-folded towels and store in a cool, dark cupboard. Refrigerate any conserve that does not seal and consume it within 4–6 weeks.

PERSIMMONS

Persimmons are native to our continent and were once plentiful in the wild, a free and delectable late-autumn treat after the frost had nipped most of the other, less hardy fruits. In fact, a frosty nip helps this fruit ripen and render it edible. Nothing can equal the meltingly sweet flavor of a ripe persimmon, but when not perfectly ripe, its pulp is so astringent that it will turn your mouth inside out.

Today, as rural areas give way to urban development, wild persimmons are becoming rarer. Both domestic (developed from imported hybrids) and large Japanese persimmons are available in the markets from autumn through late spring. These commercial fruits do not have the distinctive flavor of wild fruit, in part because they're not allowed to ripen on the tree. Consequently, they're often hard and a little green. Pastry chef Karen Barker says that this can be remedied by freezing the fruit overnight, thereby simulating the frost that helps break down the persimmons in the wild. Let them thaw completely

before using. They'll collapse and look shriveled and wrinkly, but that's the way they're supposed to be.

Persimmon Pudding Magnolia Grill

SERVES 8 TO 10

A favorite way of using persimmons in the South used to be the brewing of persimmon beer. That art, however, like the wild fruit, is fast disappearing. Old-time persimmon pudding is still popular in our region, even in upscale restaurants like the celebrated Magnolia Grill in Durham, North Carolina, a now-closed legend that was known for the innovative yet traditional elegance of its menu. This old-fashioned pudding was one of the restaurant's seasonal favorites. The recipe came from Karen Barker, who, with her husband, Ben, was co-proprietor of the Grill and the restaurant's pastry chef. Karen is originally from Brooklyn, yet both her pastries and her tongue have long since developed a distinctly Southern accent.

When selecting persimmons for this recipe, Karen advises, "Be sure the persimmons are perfectly ripe (i.e., ugly, mushy, and shriveled) or else they will provide you with one of the world's worst taste sensations." A mild understatement. If you are using the large commercial Japanese persimmons found in supermarkets, see above for Karen's tips on using this fruit.

1¼ cups flour

¾ teaspoon baking soda

¾ teaspoon baking powder, preferably single-acting

½ teaspoon powdered ginger

½ teaspoon powdered cinnamon

⅛ teaspoon freshly grated nutmeg

⅛ teaspoon powdered cloves

⅓ teaspoon salt

3½ ounces (7 tablespoons) butter

¾ cup plus 1½ tablespoon sugar

3 large eggs

1½ cups plus 1 tablespoon half-and-half

1½ cups strained persimmon puree (see note)

2 tablespoons apricot jam

1 recipe Bourbon Custard Sauce (page 47) or vanilla ice cream

1. Position a rack in the center of the oven and preheat to 350°F. Fill a teakettle with water and put it on to boil. Butter a 10-inch round, 1-inch deep cake pan, line the bottom with parchment or wax paper, and butter the paper. Set aside.

2. Sift together the flour, soda, baking powder, ginger, cinnamon, nutmeg, cloves, and salt and set aside. In a separate mixing bowl, cream the butter and sugar until fluffy. One at a time, break the eggs into a separate bowl and incorporate them into the butter and sugar mixture, beating well after each addition.

3. Alternating, gradually add the sifted dry ingredients and the half-and-half. When both are incorporated, stir in the persimmon puree and the apricot jam. Pour the batter into the prepared cake pan and put the pan in a larger sheet-cake pan or roasting pan.

4. Put the pan on the center rack of the oven and carefully pour boiling water into the larger pan until it comes halfway up the sides of the smaller one. Bake until the pudding is golden brown and firm, but still moist, about 1 hour and 10 minutes. The center should be moist but not wet and runny. Serve warm, with custard sauce or with your favorite vanilla ice cream.

Note: *To puree persimmons, stem and cut them in half lengthwise. Remove the seeds and scrape the flesh from the skins. Discard the skins and place the flesh in a food processor fitted with a steel blade. Process until smooth. If you don't have a processor, you can puree them with a food mill or force them through a wire strainer.*

Winter

BEANS, GREENS, AND SWEET FLORIDA CITRUS

A Southern winter is perhaps the most difficult season of all to pin down with any accuracy. A Southern summer is hot and humid—and just how hot and humid is only a matter of degrees. Winter, on the other hand, can be just about anything, depending on where you are—from brisk snow-skiing temperatures to balmy sunbathing weather. Among the factors that play into this are the vast differences in our geography. From the blustery, snowy crests of the Great Smoky Mountains to the palm-edged beaches of Key West and delta bayous of Louisiana, the South has just about every imaginable terrain except desert. It isn't so much a single region as it is a collection of many regions. Each meets the winter months in its own way, and even within a given region, there are wild fluctuations in weather patterns and temperatures. Perhaps it isn't surprising, then, that winter cooking is the most varied in our repertory.

Still, cold is relative, and even areas with the mildest of winters experience at least a few weeks of chilling weather. Midwinter visitors to Savannah are unpleasantly shocked to find that we can have weeks of subfreezing temperatures as they scramble to locate long trousers and an extra sweater.

At any rate, even if the dip in temperature is only a drop from bikini to sweater weather,

something on the table that warms both the insides and the imagination can be a welcome thing indeed, and all Southern kitchens respond accordingly.

Before rapid air freight made possible the mass distribution of produce from other parts of the globe, the winter selection of vegetables was limited to hefty winter squashes and root vegetables, the sturdier greens of the cabbage family, dried beans, fruits, and vegetables, and our ever-present hominy. Yet, traditional winter vegetable cookery is our most varied and imaginative—in part because of the limited variety, and in part because the season is punctuated by exuberant religious festivals where feasting (and therefore elaborate cooking) figure prominently.

Whether it is Thanksgiving, Chanukah, Christmas, the relatively new festival of Kwan-zaa, a ritual celebration of the crowning of the year, or Mardi Gras, that last hurrah before Lent, throughout the winter season Southerners are busy cooking and eating as at no other time. Regardless of the cook's tradition, the object is a celebration, and we are not about to let the tri-fling fact of limited resources get in our way.

DRIED BEANS AND PEAS

Dried beans and peas have long been an important winter staple for much of the world, since they are cheap and easy both to grow and store. In the South, certain varieties are so common to a given region—red beans in New Orleans and cowpeas in the Carolina Lowcountry, for example—that they have become an identifying element of the region's cuisine. But regardless of the variety, most of the ways of preparing them have hints of African cookery about them. It's interesting and probably instructive that the most "Southern" of all peas—cowpeas and black-eyes—are actually native to Africa.

On the other hand, not all our beans are African imports. Most of them are native to this country, members of the extensive kidney-bean family, which includes such well-known varieties as black beans, navy beans, great northerns, pintos, and those famous Creole red beans. Aside from these familiar types, there are dozens more, some of which are slipping sadly into obscurity, while others are being planted again. At Seabrook Village Museum, an early free-black community south of Savannah, there has been a valiant effort not only to preserve the homes and one-room school of this Lowcountry farming community, but also one of its crops—the Seminole pea. Only a few years ago, this little red pea faced almost certain extinction, and even though Seminoles are once again being cultivated, their future is still by no means secure.

Presoaking and Parboiling Dried Beans and Peas SERVES 8

Dried beans are traditionally soaked and parboiled before they're used in most recipes. While modern science dictates that there is no reason to do it, and nowadays many cooks don't take this extra step, it does help prevent the skins of the beans from splitting. Some argue that soaking and parboiling takes away flavor and nutrients, but this isn't a problem if you cook them in their soaking liquid and then use their cooking liquid in the finished dish. Many cooks don't use the soaking liquid because it's supposed to cause more gas, but in that department, I can't tell the difference, so I opt for the route with more flavor.

1 pound dried beans or peas

1. Pick over the beans and remove any stones and blemished beans. Place them in a colander and rinse them under cold running water. Transfer the washed beans to a glass or stainless-steel bowl that will hold three times their volume. Add enough cold, preferably soft water (see note) to cover them by 2 inches. Let soak for at least 6 hours or overnight.

2. Transfer the beans with their soaking water to a large, heavy-bottomed stainless-steel or enameled pot and add enough soft water to cover them by 2 inches. Or you can pour off the soaking water, rinse the beans, and put them in the pot with enough fresh soft water to cover by 2 inches. Bring slowly to a boil over medium heat, carefully skimming away the scum as it rises. Reduce the heat to medium low and simmer until the beans are tender,

about 1 hour. They're now ready to use in any of the following recipes.

Note: *Dried beans cook best in soft water (water that is low in minerals) that hasn't been salted; both hard minerals and salt inhibit the beans' ability to soften. If your tap water is especially hard, use filtered or distilled water.*

Stewed Black-Eyed Peas   SERVES 6

This basic recipe can be used for finishing any dried beans or peas that have been prepared by the previous recipe. Salt pork is essential for a traditional flavor, but you can omit it and substitute 2 tablespoons of butter or olive oil for the rendered fat—though the flavor will not be remotely the same, it'll still be very good.

¼ pound lean salt pork

1 medium yellow onion, peeled and chopped

1 large clove garlic, lightly crushed, peeled, and minced

1 pound dried black-eyed peas, soaked and precooked as directed on previous page, with their cooking liquid

1 Bouquet Garni (page 32), made of 1 bay leaf, 2 healthy sprigs thyme, and 1 sprig parsley

1 whole pod fresh or dried cayenne pepper

Salt

1 tablespoon chopped parsley or fresh mint

1. Cut the salt pork into thin slices and rinse well under cold running water. Pat it dry and put it into a heavy-bottomed enameled or stainless-steel 4-quart pot over medium heat. Cook, turning it occasionally, until it's crisp and its fat is rendered. Remove it from the pan and spoon off all but 2 tablespoons of the fat. Add the onion and sauté until translucent and softened but not browned, about 4–5 minutes. Add the garlic and sauté until fragrant, about half a minute longer.

2. Return the pork to the pan. Add the peas with their cooking liquid, the bouquet garni, and the pod of cayenne. Bring it to a boil, reduce the heat to a slow simmer, and gently cook until the peas are tender and the liquid is somewhat reduced and lightly thickened, about 45 minutes to an hour.

3. Taste and adjust the salt as needed, then let it simmer for a couple of minutes more. Remove and discard the whole pepper pod, and transfer the peas to a warm serving dish. Sprinkle with the parsley or mint and serve at once.

Note: *If you are cooking the peas without meat, a dash (and only a dash) of Thai fish sauce or soy sauce can be added to give the subtle meaty flavor that the pork lends. Vegans can get a similar flavor by adding a dash of soy sauce. For a leaner broth, substitute half a pound of lean country ham in one or two large pieces. Omit step 1 and put the ham, onion, garlic, bouquet garni, and pepper pod in the pot with enough water to cover. Simmer at least 30 minutes (1 hour is better), then add the peas and their cooking liquid.*

Black-Eyed Pea Fritters   SERVES 6

Wherever an African cook has touched the cuisines of the Americas, there are pea fritters. In South America and the Caribbean, the fritters are known by various derivations of the African name *akkra*—akaras, aklas, and acarajés, and even calas. In the South, they are usually called "fritters" or "croquettes," and in New Orleans, calas are rice fritters. Classic African akkras are made from a paste of raw dried peas that have been soaked, skinned, and ground up but not precooked. Southern pea fritters deviate in that they are always made from leftover cooked peas. The paste tends to fall apart in the hot fat, so they must be bound together with egg and covered with crumbs.

Black-eyed peas are most frequently used for these fritters, but any leftover beans will do; in Creole New Orleans, they are made with red beans. Regardless of what kinds of beans or peas were used, traditional recipes called for the skins to be removed before the peas were mashed. Peeling cooked peas is a royal pain, and you know me—lazy to the bone—so I've never bothered. If you use the food processor, it purees the skins so well that you don't even know they are there.

2 cups stewed dried black-eyed peas (previous page), drained

1 small yellow onion, minced fine

1 teaspoon Pepper Vinegar (page 25) or cider vinegar mixed with a dash of hot sauce or pinch of cayenne

Salt

1 large egg, lightly beaten

1 cup dry bread crumbs

Lard or peanut oil (for frying, see step 4)

1. Puree the beans in a food processor fitted with a steel blade. Transfer them to the mixing bowl. If you don't have a processor, you can puree them in small batches in a blender, or put them through a food mill. Add the onion, vinegar, and a healthy pinch or so of salt. Mix well, then taste and adjust the seasonings.

2. Add the egg and thoroughly work it in. Let stand for at least 10–15 minutes. The peas will absorb some of the egg, making the mixture a little stiffer.

3. Spread the crumbs on a wide pie plate. Drop a rounded tablespoon of the pea puree onto them, then roll it until all sides are lightly coated and it forms a 1-inch ball. Repeat until all the croquettes are formed. They can be made to this point several hours ahead. Set aside, uncovered, on a platter or cookie sheet.

4. Preheat the oven to 150°F (or the "warm" setting). Put enough oil or lard in a deep skillet or deep-fat fryer to come halfway up the side of the pan. Turn on the heat to medium high, and when the oil is hot but not quite smoking (375°F), put in enough fritters to fill the pan without crowding. Cook until they are uniformly browned, about 4 or 5 minutes, turning them halfway through if they are not completely covered by the fat. Handle them as little as possible; they tend to break up. Lift them out with a slotted spoon, drain them briefly on absorbent paper, and keep them in the warm oven while the rest of the croquettes cook. Repeat until all the croquettes are fried and serve at once with more pepper vinegar passed separately.

Note: *An important aspect of any frying is getting the fat hot enough, but it's particularly critical for pea fritters. There's no vegan equivalent for this: Without the egg and breading, the little critters just disintegrate in the fat, especially if it isn't hot enough. A few may fall apart anyway, but don't panic: Just lift out the bits, drain well, and eat them as a cook's treat.*

Any cooked, leftover beans can be used. You can also dress them up with a tablespoon of chopped fresh herbs (or a teaspoon of dried herbs). Thyme and sage are good with any variety; mint is especially lovely with black-eyed peas. You could also substitute four green onions, finely minced, for the yellow onion or add a minced clove of garlic.

Lima Bean Soup   SERVES 8 AS A FIRST COURSE, OR 4 AS A MAIN COURSE

The Southern variety of lima beans, a legume native to America, is called butterbeans (see page 129). They're small and have a distinctive buttery taste—hence the name. They're indispensable in Southern vegetable soup, but their large, yellow cousins, while common outside the South, don't often turn up in our pots, which is too bad. Their creamy, yellow flesh and delicate, distinctive flavor make an especially fine soup that'll persuade even the most hardened winter-hater that cold weather does have its benefits and that life, even in January, may be worth living after all.

1 pound dried large lima beans, washed, soaked, and parboiled as directed on page 234, with their cooking liquid

1 quart Chicken Broth (page 21)

2 medium yellow onions, peeled and chopped

2 sprigs parsley, plus 2 tablespoons chopped parsley

Salt and whole white peppercorns in a peppermill

1 cup heavy cream (minimum 36 percent milk fat) (optional)

½ cup finely julienned, uncooked, dry-cured (country) ham (optional)

1. Put the cooked beans, their liquid, and the broth in a heavy-bottomed, 4-quart stainless-steel or enameled pot and bring slowly to a boil over medium heat.

2. Add the onions, parsley sprigs, salt to taste, and a liberal grinding of white pepper. Let it return to a boil, then reduce the heat to medium low and simmer until everything is very tender, about 1–1½ hours.

3. Puree half the beans through a food mill, or in a blender or food processor. Stir the puree back into the soup, thinning it a little with water if it's too thick, and bring it back to a simmer. Remove and discard the parsley. Stir in the optional cream and/or ham, let it just heat through, and serve at once, sprinkling each serving with the chopped parsley.

Maryland White Bean Soup   SERVES 6

This handsome, warming soup has been a winter staple all along the Eastern Seaboard for more than two centuries. It even turned up at Monticello, and is credited in the Jefferson family manuscripts to Gouverneur Morris, a diplomat of the early American republic who was a close relative of the Jefferson/Randolph clan.

Onion is not mentioned in the oldest recipes, and the entire soup was rubbed through a sieve to make a smooth, elegant puree, but later recipes always include the onion and today only a few of the beans are pureed as a light thickener. The older, elegant versions all garnished the soup with parsley and buttered croutons, but for a hearty family meal, omit the croutons and parsley and serve it with Corn Sticks (page 34).

The same recipe was used in Savannah for its famed soup made with black beans (sometimes called "turtle" beans). Garnished with sieved hard-cooked egg, thinly sliced lemons, and minced parsley, it was outranked in elegance only by real turtle soup. To make it, simply see the variation at the end of the recipe.

1½ pounds (4 cups) dried great northern or navy beans, soaked

2 tablespoons unsalted butter

1 large yellow onion, trimmed, split lengthwise, peeled, and diced small

3 large ribs celery with leafy green tops, chopped

2 large carrots, trimmed, peeled, and diced

2 small turnips, trimmed, peeled, and diced

1 large parsnip, trimmed, peeled, and diced

6 cups Ham Broth, page 22

1 Bouquet Garni (page 32), made with 1 bay leaf and 1 sprig each of parsley, sage, and thyme

Salt and whole black pepper in a peppermill

2 tablespoons finely minced flat leaf parsley

1½ cups Buttered Croutons, page 37

1. Using a 6-quart, heavy-bottomed, stainless-steel or enameled iron Dutch oven, sort, soak, and precook the beans as directed on page 234. Drain off but reserve with their cooking liquid. Wipe out the pot in which they cooked and return it to medium heat. Put in the butter, onion, and celery, and simmer until they are softened and translucent but not colored, about 5 minutes. Add the carrots, turnips, and parsnips and simmer until softened, about 5 minutes more.

2. Add the broth, bring it to a simmer, and cook 5 minutes. Add the beans and 2 cups of reserved liquid, the bouquet garni, and taste and season well with salt and pepper. Bring to a simmer and cook gently for at least 30 minutes or as long as 1 hour.

3. Puree a cup of the beans with some of the liquid in a blender, or with a stick blender partially puree just enough of them to thicken the soup. Let it simmer a few minutes more. If it's too thick, thin it with more of the reserved bean cooking liquid.

The soup can be made ahead up to this point. Reserve the rest of the bean cooking liquid to thin the soup with later, since it thickens when it is cooled and reheated. Taste and adjust the seasonings one last time.

4. To serve, ladle the hot soup into heated bowls and garnish each serving with parsley and a few croutons, or sprinkle with parsley and pass the croutons separately.

VARIATION: Savannah Black Bean Soup— Simply substitute black beans in the above recipe and substitute marjoram or oregano for the sage in the bouquet garni. Omit the croutons and garnish each serving with a thin slice of lemon, a sprinkle of the minced parsley, and a spoonful of hard-cooked egg forced through a wire-mesh sieve.

PEAS (OR BEANS) AND RICE

If I had to choose a single dish that summarized the African influence on Southern tables, it would be peas and rice. Whether it's our lowly Hoppin' John, served on New Year's Day for luck (or any day when our luck has not been so good), South Florida's Cuban black beans, or Creole red beans (both of which are cooked without rice but always served over it), the soul-satisfying combination of peas and rice is directly descended from West African cooking. As slaves from that region were brought to the Caribbean and rice-growing regions of South Carolina and Georgia, they made a distinct and lasting impression on the cooking of these areas. Many elements of Southern cooking are a part of this legacy, but the rice and peas combination is perhaps the most enduring of all.

My Hoppin' John   SERVES 4 TO 6

Every Lowcountry cook has his own version of this classic African dish of peas and rice, ranging from the starkly simple to the painfully elaborate. When I am teaching it as a historical recipe, I feel bound to stay within traditions, but here's how I make it for myself.

Hoppin' John differs from other pea and rice dishes in that the rice and peas cook together. It's really a pilau—a dish in which rice cooks in a rich, aromatic broth—in this case, the flavorful cooking liquid from the peas.

Folk etymologists and pop historians like to tell cute stories about the origins of the name "Hoppin' John," and they can keep right on telling them for all I care. I adhere to culinary historian and author Jessica Harris's theory that it's probably an Anglicized corruption of an old West African name.

2 cups dried cowpeas, black-eyed peas, or crowder peas
½ pound lean salt-cured pork or 1 country ham hock
Vegetable oil (if needed, see step 3)
1 large onion, peeled and finely chopped

2 ribs celery, strung and diced

2 large garlic cloves, peeled and minced

1 whole pod red pepper, preferably cayenne

1 Bouquet Garni (page 32), made with a healthy
   sprig each of fresh parsley, mint, thyme, a leafy
   celery top, and 2 bay leaves (see note)

Whole black pepper in a peppermill

Salt

1 cup raw rice, washed and rinsed as directed on
   page 37 (Carolina-Style Rice)

10–12 fresh mint leaves

1. Sort the peas to remove any stones and blemished peas, wash and drain them, and put them in a nonreactive bowl that will hold more than twice their volume. Add enough cold (preferably soft) water to cover them by 2 inches and soak the peas for 6 hours or overnight.

2. Put the peas into a large pot with their soaking liquid and enough water to completely cover them by at least an inch. Do not add salt. Bring it slowly to a boil over medium heat, carefully skimming off the scum as it rises. Reduce the heat to a slow simmer, cover, and simmer for half an hour.

3. Put the salt pork or ham hock in an iron skillet over medium-high heat. Cook, turning frequently, until 2 tablespoons of fat are rendered from it. (If it's lean and not much fat comes out of it right away, add a little vegetable oil to help it brown and keep it from sticking, then supplement the rendered fat with more oil as needed.) Remove the pork, add the onion and celery, and sauté them until softened, about 5 minutes. Add the garlic and sauté until fragrant but not colored, about half a minute. Add this to the peas along with the pork, hot pepper pod, bouquet garni, and a liberal grinding of pepper. Raise the heat to medium high and bring it back to a boil, then reduce the heat to a simmer, cover, and cook gently until the peas are tender, about 1 hour.

4. Taste the peas and correct for salt. If the pork is very salty, they may not need any. But keep in mind that the broth must be highly seasoned in order to flavor the rice. Take up 2 cups of the broth into a separate pot and bring it to a boil over medium heat. Add the rice, bring it back to a boil, and reduce the heat to a slow simmer. Cover loosely and simmer for 12 minutes. Fluff the rice with a fork, cover it tightly, and let it sit for a minute to build steam inside the pot. Then turn off the heat and move the pot to a warm spot to let it steam for another 12–15 minutes.

5. When the rice is ready, remove and discard the pepper pod and bouquet garni and drain the remaining broth from the peas, but don't discard it. Fluff the rice with a fork and gently mix in the peas, tossing them with the fork rather than stirring. If the hoppin' John is too dry, add a little of the reserved broth.

6. If you like, you can remove the lean meat from the salt pork or ham hock, chop it, and stir it into the hoppin' John. Just before serving, cut the mint leaves into fine slivers and sprinkle them over the hoppin' John. Don't do this ahead, or the residual heat will turn it brown.

Note: *You can omit the meat altogether and sauté the onion and garlic in 2 tablespoons olive or peanut oil, or in vegetable oil mixed with 1 teaspoon sesame oil for a touch of Africa. You must use a certain amount of fat in the dish to have an authentic pilau.*

If you don't have fresh thyme or oregano, substitute ½ teaspoon each of the dried herbs. If fresh mint isn't available, add ½ teaspoon of crumbled dried mint in step 3 and garnish the finished hoppin' John with 1 tablespoon of chopped parsley.

Creole Red Beans and Rice

SERVES 4 TO 6

Here come the letters from New Orleans saying that my red beans are all wrong—even though I have faithfully followed traditional recipes. Every New Orleanian, Creole and otherwise, has his/her own version of this, the Big Easy's staple Monday fare—and few of them agree with one another, so it's for sure they won't agree with somebody from Georgia. But here goes nothing.

1 pound red beans (see note)

1 tablespoon olive oil

½ pound andouille sausage (see note), sliced ¼-inch thick, or diced country ham

1 large yellow onion, split, peeled, and chopped

1 medium green bell pepper, stemmed, seeded, and chopped

1 large carrot, peeled and diced

1 rib celery, strung and diced

2 cloves garlic, peeled and minced

1 Bouquet Garni (page 32) made from 1 bay leaf, 1 large fresh sprig each of parsley, thyme, and sage or oregano

1 whole pod fresh hot pepper (omit if using andouille sausage)

½ cup dry red wine

Black pepper in a peppermill and salt

2 cups Carolina-Style Rice (page 37)

3–4 small scallions or green onions, thinly sliced, optional

1. Wash, soak overnight, and parboil the beans as directed on page 234, until they are nearly tender, about 30–45 minutes. While the beans simmer, keep a teakettle of simmering water handy. There should always be enough liquid to cover the beans completely. If the liquid gets low, supplement it with the simmering water.

2. Meanwhile, put the olive oil and sausage or ham in a large skillet or sauté pan and over medium-high heat. Sauté until lightly browned

on all sides and remove it from the pan. Pour off all but 2 tablespoons of fat (if there's less than 2 tablespoons, supplement it with more olive oil). Add the onion, bell pepper, carrot, and celery and sauté over medium heat until they are softened but not browned, about 5 minutes. Add the garlic and sauté until fragrant, about half a minute more.

3. Add the vegetables and sausage or ham to the beans along with the bouquet garni, hot pod pepper (left whole, if using), wine, and a liberal grinding of black pepper. Raise the heat and bring the liquid back to a boil, then reduce the heat to low and simmer until the beans are very tender and thick, about 1½–2 hours. Taste and correct the salt, remove and discard the hot pepper and bouquet garni. Serve over rice, garnishing each serving, if liked, with the scallions.

Note: *To make authentic Creole red beans and rice au maigre, omit the meat and increase the olive oil to 2 tablespoons, or use 1 tablespoon each of oil and unsalted butter.*

Creole red beans are not remotely the same as red kidney beans. They're smaller, milder in flavor, and more of a ruddy red-brown than the burgundy red of the kidney beans. You can find them in specialty groceries and some natural-food stores. However, if you can't find true red beans, you may substitute light red kidney beans. Dried beans that you've cooked yourself are preferable, but you can make reasonably good red beans using canned beans, provided that they don't have any added spices or other flavorings.

Andouille is a spicy smoked pork sausage that is a specialty of Louisiana cookery. It can sometimes be found in specialty groceries or can be mail-ordered from specialty food vendors. Kielbasa can also be substituted for it, though I prefer to use country ham when I don't have the right sausage for this dish.

White Beans with Brown Onion Sauce Monticello SERVES 6

Though founding father Thomas Jefferson had a lifelong habit of copying out recipes for the cooks at Monticello, only a handful have survived in his hand, of which this recipe is one. The original document was simply titled "dried beans" but what it lacks in catchy nomenclature it more than makes up for in its perfect balance. The cooking directions as Jefferson copied them were simply to "boil them till done but not mashed," so for clarity I looked to his cousin Mary Randolph's *The Virginia House-wife*. Period cookbooks do not mention presoaking dried beans as directed on page 234. While modern chemistry says that there is no real reason to presoak them, keep in mind that beans that have not been presoaked must be brought to a boil slowly, otherwise they swell too quickly and their skins will split.

1 pound (about 2½ cups) dried white beans, such as great northern or cannellini
1 ounce (2 tablespoons) unsalted butter
½ medium white onion, trimmed, peeled and minced
1 rounded teaspoon unbleached all-purpose flour
About 2–2½ cups beef broth or cooking liquid from the beans
Salt and whole black pepper in a pepper mill

1. Sort through the beans to remove any blemished ones and small stones, wash well, drain, and put them in a tin or stainless steel–lined pot with enough water to cover them by 2 inches. Bring slowly to a boil over medium heat, carefully skimming the scum as it rises. Reduce the heat to low, and simmer steadily until the beans are tender, about 1½–2 hours. Have a simmering teakettle of water at hand to replenish the water as needed to keep the beans completely covered. When they're tender, drain the beans, reserving their cooking liquid.

2. Put the butter and onion in a pot that will hold all the beans over medium-high heat. Sauté, stirring frequently, until deep gold in color. Stir in the flour and cook until bubbly and smooth, about half a minute more. Slowly stir in 1 cup of broth (or bean cooking liquid), and cook, stirring constantly, until thickened and smooth, about 4 minutes.

3. Add the beans to the gravy, adding enough broth (or reserved cooking liquid) to just cover the beans, and bring it back to a simmer. Season well with salt and pepper, and simmer for about 5 minutes, to allow the seasonings to be absorbed. Serve hot.

Walter Dasher's Black-Eyed Pea Salad SERVES 6

Black-eyed pea salads and salsas, often inelegantly called "redneck caviar," are two popular and refreshing ways of serving an old Southern favorite. This version, which can be served either way, comes from one of Savannah's premier chefs, Walter Dasher.

Walter apprenticed with Chef Gerry Klaskala in the kitchen of Savannah's legendary 45 South. When Gerry left the restaurant to open the celebrated Buckhead Diner in Atlanta, Walter was invited to fill his mentor's shoes, which he did beautifully for 8 years. After he retired, he remained a lively influence on Savannah's culinary scene by way of cooking classes that he taught in tandem with his wife, Alice. Though he is no longer cooking or teaching professionally, his cooking remains legendary, and the rare invitation to dinner at his house is not to be refused.

Once you taste this salad, you'll know why.

2 cups (12 ounces) dried black-eyed peas
3 ham hocks
½ medium red bell pepper, diced
½ medium yellow bell pepper, diced

1 shallot, chopped

¼ small Vidalia or other sweet onion, chopped

1 tablespoon chives, chopped

1 recipe Balsamic-Ginger Vinaigrette (recipe follows)

8–10 fresh basil leaves

1. Soak the beans overnight as directed on page 234. Drain and set them aside. Put the ham hocks in a 4-quart pot. Add 2 quarts water and bring the liquid to a boil over medium heat, reduce the heat to a simmer, cover, and cook for 1 hour.

2. Add the peas to the pot, raise the heat, and bring it back to the boiling point. Reduce the heat to low and simmer until the peas are tender, about 1–1½ hours. The peas should remain covered by the liquid, so keep a teakettle of simmering water handy in case more water is needed.

3. Drain the peas, discarding the ham hocks. Allow the peas to cool, then mix them with the red and yellow peppers, shallot, onion, and chives. Pour the dressing over the salad and toss until well mixed. It can be made a day or two ahead of time. Cover and refrigerate until you are ready to serve it.

4. Just before serving, cut the basil into fine chiffonade and strew it over the top of the salad. Serve cold.

Note: *Walter likes this as an accompaniment to duck or quail, but it's also wonderful with almost any grilled meat or poultry, or served as a salsa with a basket of tortilla chips on the side for dipping.*

Balsamic-Ginger Vinaigrette

MAKES ABOUT 1 CUP

This dressing is great not only in the Black-Eyed Pea Salad (previous page), but on just about any fresh green salad, and also makes a fine marinade for pork tenderloins or any poultry destined for the grill.

⅛ cup (2 tablespoons) balsamic vinegar

⅛ cup (2 tablespoons) red wine vinegar

½ tablespoon finely minced fresh ginger root

2 tablespoons Dijon mustard

1 teaspoon sugar

Salt

¾ cup extra-virgin olive oil

Black pepper in a peppermill

Combine the two vinegars, ginger, mustard, and sugar in a glass or stainless mixing bowl. Add a small pinch of salt (to help the oil emulsify). Whisk until smooth. Gradually whisk in the olive oil, a few drops at a time, until it is all incorporated and emulsified. Season to taste with more salt, if needed, and a few liberal grindings of black pepper.

CABBAGE

Cabbage was once a winter staple, not only in the South, but everywhere it was grown. Packed in straw and stored in a cool, dark cellar, the tight heads kept through the winter, providing a reliable source of vitamins when other green vegetables weren't available. Another common method of preserving cabbage was to make sauerkraut—shredded cabbage pickled in salt. It was a tedious job, and Mother used to share the work with our neighbor from across the field. They shredded the cabbage with an old wood mandoline and layered it with salt in a heavy stoneware crock. They weighted it and covered it tightly with a clean cotton cloth, since the cabbage had to be kept completely submerged in brine and away from light and air—a tall order with curious little fingers like mine around.

The uninitiated may think it odd that this "German" dish was so popular in the South, but there were pockets of German settlers across the region, especially in the Carolina hills where I grew up, and after all, salt-pickling cabbage was a means of preservation that had been used by almost all Europeans, including the English, for millennia. Regardless of how it is kept, cabbage is still a winter favorite in the South.

In choosing a cabbage for the following recipes, look for heads with plenty of crisp, healthy-looking, dark green leaves. If the outer leaves have been stripped away from the cabbage, it is usually because the leaves have wilted, so cabbage heads that are stripped down to the tight, white inner leaves are usually not fresh.

Nita's Stewed Cabbage SERVES 4 TO 6

People who profess to hate stewed cabbage marvel at Nita Dixon's version of this commonplace dish. The secrets to its success are several. First, she never puts salt pork or bacon in the pot, explaining that there are other ways to make things taste good than to always put meat in them. Second, she says you must be careful not to overcook it; the cabbage should still be quite green and, though tender, have a pleasing firmness to the bite. Most important of all, the cabbage must be as fresh as possible. Says Nita, "Baby, if you want them vegetables to taste good,

they better be fresh." Choose a cabbage with plenty of healthy, dark green leaves.

1 small, fresh green cabbage (about 2 pounds)
1 medium green bell pepper
1 medium yellow onion
2 tablespoons fat left over from frying chicken, or unsalted butter
1 clove garlic, crushed and peeled
Salt, sugar, and ground cayenne
2 tablespoons unsalted butter

1. Strip off any discolored or withered leaves from the cabbage, but don't discard any of the healthy-looking, dark green leaves. Remove the dark green leaves, wash them thoroughly, roll them together, and cut them into thin strips. Set aside. Quarter the cabbage and cut out the core from each quarter. Sliver each quarter lengthwise into the thinnest possible strips. Set aside separately from the dark green leaves.

2. Stem, core, and seed the pepper and cut it into the thinnest strips you can manage. Cut off the root and stem ends of the onion, split it lengthwise, peel, and slice it into thin strips.

3. Choose a kettle that will comfortably hold all the cabbage. Put the 2 tablespoons of fat or butter into the kettle with the dark green cabbage leaves, bell pepper, and onion. Turn on the heat to medium and sauté until the vegetables are wilted. Add the garlic, give it a stir, and add just enough water to barely cover the cabbage. Cover and steam until crisp-tender, but still a little underdone, about 5 minutes. Add the remaining cabbage, a couple of healthy pinches of salt, a large pinch of sugar, and a pinch of cayenne, and cover the kettle. Cook until the cabbage is tender but firm to the bite, about 15 minutes more. It should still be bright green and not army-fatigue brown. Stir in the butter, taste and adjust the seasonings, and serve hot.

Note: *As to seasonings, Nita cautions that you have to let your mouth guide you here. Keep tasting and play with them; some bell peppers can have a bitter edge and you'll want to use a little less. Some will be very mild and you may want to add more. She has given you free rein with the cayenne, but use discretion. Don't add so much that you can't taste anything else.*

Mary Randolph's Cabbage Pudding (Stuffed Cabbage) SERVES 4

Here's an early nineteenth-century recipe, from a time when no household, rich or poor, ever wasted anything. This sturdy but lovely dish was one of many that provided a tasty and economical way of giving new life to leftovers. In more well-to-do households, it would have been considered a side dish and shared the table with other meat, but it makes a delightful winter supper on its own.

Variations on this dish survive in modern Southern cookbooks, though usually they follow the more common method of stuffing and rolling individual leaves. Stuffing the whole cabbage is a bit more troublesome, but it does make a spectacular presentation.

This recipe probably came to Mrs. Randolph from her cousin, Thomas Jefferson, who copied out a similar one for the cooks at Monticello.

1 large, whole cabbage (about 3 pounds)

1 medium onion, peeled

½ pound cooked meat or poultry, or ¾ pound ground beef or bulk sausage

2 tablespoons dry bread crumbs

1 tablespoon chopped fresh parsley

1 tablespoon chopped fresh herbs, such as thyme or marjoram, or 1 teaspoon crumbled dried herbs

Grated zest of 1 lemon

Salt and black pepper in a peppermill

1 large egg

1 quart Meat Broth (page 20), optional (see step 9)

2 tablespoons unsalted butter, softened

1. Fill a large kettle that will easily hold the cabbage half-full of water and bring it to a boil over high heat. Meanwhile, strip off the outer green leaves of the cabbage, saving two or three if they are unblemished, and discarding any that are wilted or scarred. Wash everything well under cold running water.

2. Slip in the cabbage and any reserved outer leaves into the boiling water and let it come back to a boil. Cook until the outer leaves of the head begin to wilt and can be pulled back easily, about 15 minutes. Remove the cabbage and drain well.

3. Without detaching them from the stem, carefully pull back three layers of leaves. Make a cross-shaped incision in the center of the cabbage, being careful not to cut through the bottom stem or to puncture any of the outer leaves. Pull back a few layers of the cut leaves, like the petals of a flower, and cut out the heart of the cabbage, leaving all the outer leaves attached to the stem.

4. Chop the heart and the onion fine, and put them in a large mixing bowl that will comfortably hold the next seven ingredients.

5. If you are using fresh ground beef or sausage meat, put it into a skillet and brown it over medium-high heat, stirring until it just loses its raw, red color. Drain off the excess fat and add the meat to the mixing bowl. Otherwise, chop the leftover meat or poultry fine and add it to the cabbage. Add the crumbs, parsley, herbs, and grated lemon zest. Season with a liberal pinch of salt and a few grindings of black pepper. Toss until all ingredients are thoroughly mixed.

6. Break the egg in a separate bowl and beat it until it is light. Add the egg to the stuffing mixture and mix it in.

7. Spread a large, double-layered square of cheesecloth on a work surface and put the cabbage in its center. Lay open the leaves and fill it with the stuffing mixture, packing gently so as not to break the outer leaves. Now carefully fold the leaves back over the stuffing as much like their original position as possible. If there is any leftover stuffing, work it into the layers of leaves.

8. Wrap the reserved outer leaves around the cabbage, then pick up the corners of the cheesecloth and pull them up around the whole. Tie it securely with twine, making it as tight as possible, then wrap several lengths of twine around it and knot it tightly.

9. If you are using broth, drain off the blanching liquid from the kettle and add the broth (or you may simply poach the cabbage in the blanching water; add a small handful of salt to it). Over a medium-high fire, bring the liquid to a boil and add the stuffed cabbage, gently lowering it into the liquid. Let it return to a boil, skim it well, and lower the heat to the slowest simmer you can manage, and let it simmer for 1 hour.

10. Lift the cabbage out of the kettle, drain it, and lay it on a warm platter. Cut the twine, unwrap the cheesecloth, and carefully slip both twine and cloth out from under the cabbage. Spread the softened butter over the cabbage and serve at once.

Stuffed Cabbage Leaves in Sweet-Sour Tomato Sauce   SERVES 4

Today, few Southern cooks are inclined to undertake stuffing a whole head of cabbage as outlined in the previous recipe, but stuffed individual leaves remain popular. You may make the filling richer by substituting bulk sausage for the ground meat, or vary it by substituting chopped leftover cooked meat, chicken, or turkey. If you're using cooked meat, decrease the cooking time to about 30 minutes and moisten the filling with a beaten egg or two egg yolks. You may also substitute marinara or sour cream for the sweet-sour sauce. If you use sour cream, dust the top with paprika before baking.

1 medium green cabbage

About 3 cups Sweet-Sour Tomato Sauce (recipe follows)

2 tablespoons bacon drippings, unsalted butter, or olive oil

1 small yellow onion, peeled and chopped

1 large clove garlic, crushed, peeled, and minced

1 pound ground beef, pork, or lamb

1 tablespoon chopped fresh or 1 teaspoon crumbled dried thyme

2 tablespoons chopped flat-leaf parsley

1 cup cooked rice

Salt and whole black pepper in a mill

Ground cayenne or hot sauce, optional

1. Bring 4 quarts of water to a boil in an 8-quart pot. Meanwhile, trim any discolored leaves from the cabbage and rinse it well under cold running water. Add a small handful of salt to the boiling water and, using a fryer basket or pasta insert, carefully lower the cabbage into the water Let it cook until outer leaves are wilted, about 2–4 minutes. Lift out the whole cabbage, cut off wilted off outer leaves, and then return it to boiling water. Repeat until 8 large leaves have been wilted and removed. Set the remaining cabbage aside for another use (but cook it within two days). Pat the leaves dry and trim the thick part of the stem.

2. Position a rack in the center of the oven and preheat to 350°F. Smear a 9-inch square or shallow 2-quart oval casserole with a little of the tomato sauce.

3. Put the fat and onion in a small skillet over medium heat and sauté until the onion is softened and beginning to color, about 5 minutes. Add the garlic and sauté until fragrant, about half a minute more. Turn off the heat. Lightly mix the onion and garlic with the beef, herbs, and rice, and season well with salt, pepper, and cayenne or hot sauce.

4. Spread the cabbage leaves on a flat work surface. Divide the stuffing among them, placing it loosely in a sausage shape near base of leaf. Roll the leaves as follows: First, fold the base up and over stuffing, then fold sides inward over it, and roll it up in a fairly tight cylinder. Put the filled leaves, seam-side down, into the prepared casserole as you finish rolling them.

5. When all the leaves are in the casserole, cover them with remaining sauce and bake until the filling is cooked through and the leaves are tender, about 45–50 minutes. If the sauce begins to get too dry, add a spoonful of water and cover the casserole. Serve warm.

Sweet-Sour Tomato Sauce   SERVES 4

This is not only a lovely sauce for the preceding recipe but for simmering meatballs and for dipping vegetable fritters of almost any kind.

2 tablespoons bacon drippings or olive oil
1 medium onion, peeled and finely chopped
2 cloves garlic, crushed and minced
1 (28-ounce) can tomato puree
½ cup red wine or cider vinegar
⅔ cup light brown sugar
1 tablespoon chopped fresh or 1 teaspoon crumbled dried thyme
Salt and whole black pepper in a mill

1. Put the drippings and onion in a wide saucepan over medium heat. Sauté, tossing often, until the onion is softened and beginning to color, about 5 minutes. Add the garlic and sauté until fragrant, about half a minute.

2. Add the tomato puree, vinegar, sugar, and thyme and season well with salt and pepper. Bring to a simmer, then reduce the heat to medium low and let simmer 20 minutes. Taste and adjust the vinegar, sugar, salt, and pepper as needed, then let it simmer at least 10 minutes longer. The sauce can be made ahead, pour it into a clean quart jar or storage container, let it cool completely, then cover and refrigerate until needed. It will keep for a couple of weeks.

Braised Cabbage and Onions

SERVES 4

This is my favorite way of cooking cabbage. The old recipes invariably called it "fried cabbage," and at the end of cooking the liquid does indeed boil away and the cabbage and onions do fry, lightly caramelizing and taking on a lovely golden color and marvelously concentrated sweetness.

Braised cabbage is a fine accompaniment for any roasted meat or poultry, but it is wonderful on its own, with cornbread and a dash or so of Pepper Vinegar (page 25).

2 cups (tightly packed) shredded fresh cabbage (about ½ an average head of cabbage)
2 cups thinly sliced yellow onion (about 2 medium onions)
2 tablespoons lard (preferred) or unsalted butter
¼ cup Meat Broth (page 20) or water
1 tablespoon chopped parsley
Salt and black pepper in a peppermill

1. Put the cabbage, onion, fat, and broth or water into a large, heavy skillet fitted with a lid and cover it tightly. Turn on the heat to low. Cook slowly, stirring from time to time, until the vegetables are very tender, about 45 minutes to 1 hour. If the pan gets too dry, add a few spoonfuls of water—don't add more broth—but no more than is absolutely necessary to keep the vegetables moist.

2. When the vegetables are very tender, remove the lid and raise the heat to medium high. Cook, stirring constantly, until all the moisture in the skillet is evaporated and the cabbage and onions are both colored a rich gold. Be careful; they should brown but not scorch. Turn off the heat, stir in the parsley, and season to taste with salt and a few liberal grindings of pepper. Serve warm.

Note: *Lard is an important element of this dish—both for flavor and color; no other fat (not even bacon drippings) allows the cabbage to brown as nicely. If you prefer not to use lard, however, butter can be substituted. If you wish to avoid animal fat altogether, the only plausible choices are olive or peanut oil.*

Coleslaw   SERVES 6 TO 8

The essential accompaniment for any fish fry or barbecue in the South, and the salad for any covered-dish supper, is coleslaw. We love it as a side dish for fried fish and chicken, and often treat it like a condiment, slathering it thickly over barbecue sandwiches, hot dogs, and even hamburgers.

There are more Southern recipes for slaw than there are Southerners, but all of them fall into two basic categories. One is almost like a cabbage pickle, based on a thin, sweet-sour vinegar and oil dressing that is heated to the boiling point and poured hot over shredded cabbage; the other is creamy, dressed with mayonnaise or boiled dressing. This version is of the creamy persuasion.

1 medium green cabbage (about 2 pounds)
1 small yellow onion
1 medium carrot
1 recipe Boiled Dressing (recipe follows)
1 teaspoon celery seeds
1 teaspoon dry mustard
Salt and black pepper in a peppermill

1. Strip off the tough outer leaves of the cabbage, quarter it, and cut out the core. Discard the core or, if it's not bitter, set it aside and munch on it yourself while you make the slaw—it's delicious. Shred the cabbage, either by hand with a small paring knife (preferable) or with a food processor.

2. Put the cabbage in a large mixing or serving bowl. Peel the onion and coarsely grate it into the cabbage or chop it fine and add it. Peel the carrot and shred it through the large holes of the grater or in the food processor. Add it to the cabbage.

3. In a separate bowl, combined the boiled dressing, celery seeds, dry mustard, a large pinch of salt, and a few liberal grindings of black pepper. Mix well and pour the dressing

over the slaw. Stir until the cabbage is uniformly coated. If the salad isn't creamy enough, stir in a little more boiled dressing. Let the salad stand for half an hour to allow the flavors to meld, and serve cold.

Boiled Dressing   MAKES 1½ CUPS

Since olive oil was always imported and expensive, Southerners long ago adopted this cream-and-egg-based dressing for salads. Though nowadays it's considered a bit old-fashioned and olive oil is no longer so scarce, this dressing remains popular. Aside from coleslaw, it makes a good dressing for chicken or potato salads, especially if you are cooking for someone who for health reasons cannot eat uncooked eggs.

The name, of course, is an oxymoron: It doesn't really boil and will curdle if it is ever allowed to do so.

1 tablespoon sugar

1 teaspoon dry mustard

2 tablespoons all-purpose flour

Salt

½ cup water

¼ cup vinegar

2 large egg yolks

1 tablespoon unsalted butter

¼ cup heavy cream

1. Prepare the bottom half of a double boiler with water and bring to a simmer over medium heat. Mix the sugar, dry mustard, flour, and a small pinch of salt in the top boiler. In a separate bowl, combine the water, vinegar, and egg yolks, and beat with a whisk until smooth. Slowly whisk this into the dry ingredients.

2. Put the top boiler over the simmering water, and cook, whisking constantly, until the dressing is thick, about 5 minutes. Don't stop whisking or take your attention away from it, because it thickens suddenly. As soon as the dressing is thick, immediately take the top boiler off the heat and beat in the butter and cream. Stir until cool and chill before using.

COLLARD GREENS

Collards are a variety of kale, a member of the extensive cabbage family (their name is thought to be a corruption of colewort, an old name for kale). They are native to Europe and not, as is often supposed, Africa. Yet collards have long been part of the diet of all Southerners, most especially those of African descent, maybe because collards bear a resemblance to a green that had been a staple of the cookery of their African homeland.

Once they're cut from their roots, collards don't keep well, but the plants are hearty enough to survive a mild frost and last well into the winter, even in the colder regions of the South, and fresh greens are almost always available through New Year's Day—at which time they are eaten throughout the South for good luck. In the Deep South, they often survive the entire winter, providing fresh greens when little else may be available.

Good collards are widely available in the South—at greengrocers, farmers' markets, and even supermarkets. Outside the region, they can often be found at West Indian markets or grocers in African-American or Portuguese communities. Collards are usually sold in whole plants (or heads) like a cabbage. A single plant weighs 1–2 pounds, depending on size, and will produce three to five servings. If you have trouble finding collards, move to a civilized part of the country—or, failing that, substitute either of their cousins, curly or flat-leafed kale.

Nowadays, fresh collards are turning up in many markets already washed and cut and allegedly ready for the pot. I wish I could recommend them, but they're rarely fresh, and worse, are always full of hunks of stem, which are too tough to eat, so you end up spending just as much time picking them out as you would washing and cutting the greens yourself.

To prepare collards and other kale for the pot, separate the leaves from the main stem. Fill the sink with cold water and put in the greens a few at a time, swishing them around to loosen any dirt. Repeat this until the greens are clean and free of sand and grit (you may have to change the water several times). Cut or strip the greens from their tough center stem. The old way of "pulling" collards is to put your fore- and middle fingers on either side of the stem at the base of the leaf, then pull upward, stripping the greens from the stem. The stem will break at the point where it's tender enough to cook.

If the recipe calls for the greens to be cut, stack several leaves together, then roll them into a cylinder like a cigar, and cut crosswise into ½- to 1-inch-wide ribbons (depending on what the recipe requires).

Traditional Stewed Collards

SERVES 4 TO 6

These are the collards that are traditional New Year's Day fare in most Southern households, usually paired with black-eyed peas or hoppin' John (page 238) for luck and prosperity. But they're also traditional for many families at Thanksgiving and are welcome throughout the fall and winter months when more delicate greens may be scarce. The exact cooking time will vary depending on the age and freshness of the greens, and on whether they have been nipped by frost, which makes them tender and especially sweet.

In the South, many markets sell "seasoning ham"—usually large chunks of country ham that are left at the ends after the raw ham is sliced. They're leaner than hocks and are what I use for seasoning both collards and dried peas. If you can't get them, use the same amount of trimmed ham slices or see if your deli will sell you a scrap chunk of prosciutto.

1 pound lean country ham in 1–2 large pieces, or a country ham hock

1 tablespoon vegetable oil

1 medium yellow onion, trimmed, split lengthwise, peeled and thinly sliced

1 whole hot pepper

2 large heads collards

Salt and whole black pepper in a peppermill

Turbinado "raw" sugar, optional

Pepper Vinegar (page 25)

Cornbread (page 34)

1. Brown the ham or hock in the oil in a large, heavy-bottomed Dutch oven (preferably enameled iron) over medium heat. Remove it, add the onion, and sauté until it is golden, about 5 minutes. Add 2 quarts water and the hot pepper (left whole) and bring slowly to a boil. Cover, reduce the heat as low as possible, and let simmer for at least half an hour—1 hour will only improve it.

2. While that simmers, wash, stem, and cut the greens as directed on pages 248–49. Raise the heat under the broth to medium high and bring it back to a rolling boil. Drop in the greens by large handfuls, bring it back to a boil, and reduce the heat to a bare simmer. Cover and cook until the greens are tender, about 20 minutes for young, tender collards or those that have been frost-nipped, as much as an hour for mature greens. Taste, adjust the salt, and add a

few grindings of pepper. If they're not naturally sweet, you may also add a spoonful or so of turbinado sugar. Simmer a few more minutes to allow the flavor to blend. Remove and discard the pepper pod and serve with Pepper Vinegar and Cornbread passed separately.

Note: *Stewed greens hold up well to being made ahead and may be made several days before and reheated. They also freeze well and will keep for up to 6 months. If you are making them specifically for freezing, stop the cooking before the greens are quite tender. If you happen to have ham broth on hand, you can omit the ham called for here. Sauté the onion in the oil, then add the broth and pepper pod, bring it to a boil, and simmer about 10 minutes before adding the greens.*

Two Classic Wilted Winter Greens

Slow stewing is the most traditional way of preparing collards and other winter greens in the South, but it isn't the only one. Slow cooking produces a distinctive (and strong) smell that many find objectionable. However, even Southerners who hate the smell will have their greens, and for them, braising (or wilting) is the traditional method of choice. The cooking time is considerably shortened and circumvents the permeating odor of a slow simmer. Out of the hundreds of variations, since practically every Southern cook has one, here are two from solidly traditional cooks who begin with the same idea and take it in two different directions. Both are served with Cornbread (page 34) and Pepper Vinegar (page 25), and in the Florida Keys, they pass a bottle of Old Sour (page 273). Either of these recipes makes an excellent accompaniment for pork, veal, chicken, or rice dishes.

Bonnie Carter's Wilted Winter Greens   SERVES 4

Bonnie Carter is a traditional Southern cook in the best sense of both adjectives, as comfortable and accomplished on an open hearth as she is in a modern kitchen. Her pound cakes are still the standard by which I measure my own.

Bonnie developed this recipe from old cookbooks especially for the hearth-cooking classes she occasionally teaches at the conservatory on Oatland Island. It's at its best when cooked over fragrant hardwood coals but even tastes wonderful when the best fire you can manage is electric, so long as you use a well-seasoned iron skillet or Dutch oven.

2 pounds collards (1 large or 2 small plants) or kale
¼ pound thin-sliced bacon, cut into 1-inch pieces
1 medium yellow onion, peeled and sliced ¼-inch thick
Salt and black pepper in a peppermill
Pepper Vinegar (page 25) and/or Old Sour (page 273)

1. Wash, stem, and cut the greens into 1-inch-wide strips as directed on pages 248–49. Pile them into a bowl and set aside.

2. Put the bacon in a deep, lidded skillet (preferably cast iron) or Dutch oven. Turn on the heat to medium high and cook, uncovered, until most of the fat has been rendered and it's lightly browned but not crisp, about 5 minutes. Add the onion and sauté until softened, about 3 minutes. Add a big handful of greens with the water that's still clinging to them and stir until they're wilted. Repeat this until all the greens are in the pan. Season lightly salt and generously with pepper, cover tightly, and cook until the greens are nearly tender, about 8–10 minutes.

3. Remove the lid and continue cooking, stirring almost constantly, until the liquid is evaporated and the greens and onion are nearly dry and tender, about 5 minutes more. Turn off the heat and serve at once with pepper vinegar or Old Sour.

John Taylor's Wilted Greens

SERVES 6 TO 8

Cookbook author and culinary historian John Martin Taylor is best known for his work in reviving true Carolina Lowcountry cooking. His cookbook, *Hoppin' John's Lowcountry Cooking*, set a new standard for regional American cookbooks. But when I met John, I discovered that we shared a passion for a cuisine other than that of our native South—specifically, the herb-scented cooking of Genoa and the Ligurian coast known as the Italian Riviera.

Consequently, while John's kitchen is solidly Southern, it always has a hint of the Riviera about it. Says he: "My cooking will be forever influenced by my years in Italy, but nothing so marks it as my use of olive oil. I love the way it tastes and smells—and the way it looks on food, too." Here, he uses olive oil the way Bonnie Carter uses bacon grease in the previous recipe.

This is a deceptively simple dish; its ingredients are few and its method virtually artless. Like most simple dishes, its strength lies in the quality of its ingredients. John advises: "You don't have to spend a fortune on a premium extra-virgin oil for dishes like this one where the taste of the greens is paramount, but the better the oil, the better it'll taste." More important than good oil are good greens, as fresh as possible, preferably obtained from a local grower.

3 pounds collards (3 small plants or 2 large ones)
¼ cup (4 tablespoons) olive oil
2 teaspoons salt
Pepper Vinegar (page 25) or Old Sour (page 273), optional

1. Wash, strip, and cut the greens into 1-inch strips as directed on pages 248–49. Pile them into a large bowl.

2. In a large, heavy-bottomed stockpot or Dutch oven, heat half the olive oil over high heat until it is just at the point of smoking. Pick up a large handful of the trimmed collards and add it to the pot, with the water that is clinging to the greens. Stir vigorously with a large wooden spoon until they're all wilted, then continue adding them by handfuls until all of them are in the pot.

3. Add the salt and the remaining olive oil, and stir well one last time. Immediately reduce the heat to low, cover, and braise for 15 minutes. Taste the greens, and if they need to cook a little more, replace the cover and continue cooking over low heat until they are done to your liking. Serve hot, passing pepper vinegar and/or Old Sour separately if you like.

CRESS, WATERCRESS, AND CREASIE GREENS

In the moist bottomland around the countless streams and rivers that ribbon the South, watercress grows in wild abundance. Most of us are familiar with the common hothouse variety, but don't realize that it's just one of many varieties of cress, including the common land cress, which down South is often called "creasie greens" or "peppergrass." Though today found mostly in the wild, land cress was once cultivated in early gardens and was enjoyed both as a salad green and cooked vegetable, especially in African-American families, not just as food, but also as a tonic for the ailing.

The late Edna Lewis, the celebrated Southern chef and cookbook author, fondly recalled that whenever one of her many brothers and sisters was ill, her mother would send the healthy children out into the snow-blanketed fields around their home in Freetown, Virginia, to gather the ground-hugging land cress that flourished beneath the snow.

Though Mrs. Lewis preferred wild cress above the hothouse variety, she cautioned against gathering it from commercially farmed fields, maintained roadsides, or even your own lawn, where chemical plant control has often been used. Unless you are sure, it is safer to stick to the cultivated variety.

Steamed Watercress or Creasie Greens   SERVES 4

In *The Taste of Country Cooking*, Mrs. Lewis suggests wilting cultivated cress in olive oil, like John Taylor's Wilted Greens (page 251). Here, the greens simmer luxuriously in ham broth, a very traditional way of cooking them, especially when they are the wild variety.

2 cups water

¼ pound smoked pork or country ham

4 bunches watercress (about 1½–2 pounds) or freshly gathered creasie greens

Salt

Pepper Vinegar (page 25)

1. Put the water and pork or ham in a lidded heavy-bottomed pot that will comfortably hold all the cress at one time. Bring it to a boil, uncovered, over medium-high heat, then reduce the heat to a slow simmer, cover, and cook until the pork or ham is falling apart tender, about 1 hour.

2. Wash the cress thoroughly (if it is wild cress, wash it in several changes of water, since it is usually very gritty). Drain it well, trim off any roots or tough stems, and add the cress to the pot. The liquid won't cover it

at first, but as the cress wilts, it will throw off more liquid and also lose volume. Steam until the cress is completely tender, about 45 minutes for wild greens; cultivated cress will take less time. Taste and adjust the salt, if it needs any more, and simmer a minute or so longer.

3. You can drain it or serve it in small bowls with its pot liquor. Pass pepper vinegar with the greens.

Nathalie's Grits and Greens   SERVES 8

My dear friend and mentor Nathalie Dupree, the renowned cookbook author and television cooking teacher, is perhaps best known and loved by her fans for what one critic calls her "endearing klutziness." That trait stemmed partly from the fact that she's hopelessly nearsighted and had trouble reading the teleprompter, but mainly it was because she wanted her students to see that she's no more perfect than they, so she rarely let them tape over her mistakes.

When I asked for a recipe for this book, my first choice was a squash casserole that she invented when she grabbed a bag of coconut out of the freezer, thinking it was bread crumbs; it was classic klutzy Nathalie. But after poring over her two Southern classics, *New Southern Cooking* and *Southern Memories*, we settled on this one because you don't get more innovative, yet more solidly Southern, than cooking grits and greens in the same pot.

3 cups whole milk

1 cup heavy cream (minimum 36 percent milk fat)

1 cup quick grits (not instant)

6 tablespoons (3 ounces or ¾ stick) unsalted butter

1 pound greens (turnip, spinach, poke sallet, or chard), deveined and stemmed

1½ cups freshly grated Parmesan (preferably Parmigiano-Reggiano)

Salt and black pepper in a peppermill

1. Combine the milk and cream in a 3-quart heavy-bottomed pot (preferably nonstick). Bring it almost to a boil over medium heat. Stirring constantly, pour in the grits in a thin, steady stream. Let it return to a simmer and cook, stirring often, until the grits are thick and tender, about 15–20 minutes. Remove from the heat, stir in 2 tablespoons of the butter, and set aside in a warm place (a basin of hot water is ideal).

2. Wash the greens in a basin of cold water, changing the water if necessary, until all the sand and soil are removed from them. Lift them out into a colander and drain briefly but not thoroughly—there should still be plenty of water clinging to the leaves. Put the wet greens in a large, lidded frying pan. Cover and cook over medium-high heat until the greens wilt, about 5 minutes. Quickly drain and refresh under cold running water. Drain well and gently squeeze to remove all excess moisture.

3. Melt the remaining 4 tablespoons of butter in the frying pan in which the greens cooked over medium heat. When the butter is melted, add the greens and sauté until heated through, about 2 minutes. Turn off the heat.

4. Stir the greens and Parmesan into the grits until the cheese is melted. Add a healthy pinch or so of salt and a few liberal grindings of pepper, both to taste. Pour the grits and greens into a warm serving dish and serve at once.

Note: *This dish can be made ahead and reheated over low heat or in a microwave oven, but wait until after reheating it to add the Parmesan. Nathalie sometimes garnishes the dish with poke shoots, the tender stalks of new poke plants that are no bigger than asparagus. If you have such wonders, blanch them in salted boiling water for about 5 minutes.*

You may also substitute, as Nathalie nowadays does, stone-ground whole-corn grits, but allow at least an hour for them to cook, since they take a good deal longer than processed hominy grits.

JERUSALEM ARTICHOKES

When I first started teaching Southern cooking, I went around waving this little root vegetable like a Confederate flag. It became my symbol and example for the traditional Southern cooking that I had come to champion: a native American vegetable, once very popular on Southern tables, all but forgotten (except as an ingredient for pickles and relishes) in recent times. Even now, as it is beginning to be rediscovered, it is being treated mostly as an Italian vegetable.

Jerusalem artichokes are, of course, neither artichokes nor from Jerusalem. They are the tuber of a native American sunflower (*Helianthus tuberosus*), one of several sunflower varieties that were cultivated by Native Americans for food. The charming and picturesque name, which goes almost all the way back to the vegetable's introduction to Europe, most likely derives in part from a corruption of an Italian name—*girasoli*. Though the usual explanation for why it was called an artichoke is that its flavor vaguely resembles that of artichokes, it may have a more curious derivation. According to some historians, the unopened flower buds, which look a bit like an artichoke, were once eaten by Native Americans in much the same way that we eat artichokes hearts today.

Nowadays, American growers are marketing these tubers as "sunchokes." Old crank that I am, I prefer the older, more picturesque name, but "sunchoke" is probably what you will have to ask for. This root is harvested after the plant blooms out. That happens at different times of the year throughout the country. In the South, Jerusalem artichokes begin to come into season in early autumn. In colder regions, they show up around Christmas and are available until spring. California sunchokes, a hybrid variety, are available almost year round, though they are sometimes hard to come by in late summer and early fall.

In spite of the vegetable's native origins, most of the old recipes for Jerusalem artichokes have a European lineage, which is betrayed by ingredients unknown to pre-Columbian America—butter, cream, bread crumbs, citrus juice, wine vinegar, and the like.

Boiled Jerusalem Artichokes

SERVES 4

This is the basic recipe for preparing Jerusalem artichokes. Once they are cooked, they can be scalloped, sauced with cream, breaded and fried, dressed as salad, or served just as they are—with perhaps a bit of melted butter. In selecting artichokes for boiling, remember that they should all be roughly the same size so that they cook evenly.

You can peel the artichokes after they're boiled or when they're cooked another way, but never peel them before boiling: The skins not only help keep the flavor in, they also prevent the flesh from turning dark and getting soggy.

2 pounds Jerusalem artichokes, as much
  the same size as possible
Salt

1. Scrub the artichokes under cold running water and pat dry. Don't let them stand in water or they'll start to turn black. Put them in a large, heavy-bottomed pot with enough water to cover them by an inch. Lift out the artichokes, cover the pot, and bring it to a boil over high heat.

2. Add a small handful of salt and the artichokes. Let it return to a boil, then loosely cover, reduce the heat to medium, and simmer until just tender, 12-20 minutes (the exact timing will depend on their size). Watch them carefully, overcooking will make them turn dark and sodden. Drain quickly and, if you like, peel them. Serve hot, tossed with butter, a liberal pinch of salt, and a few grindings of black pepper to taste, or use them in one of the following recipes.

Maryland Jerusalem Artichoke Soup   SERVES 6

This luscious, velvety soup is a perfect vehicle for the subtle but distinctive flavor of Jerusalem artichokes. The other ingredients are kept to a minimum and deliberately understated so that their flavor will predominate, so while the recipe may look plain, and it is, the resulting flavor is anything but simple.

You can lighten the soup by substituting milk for the cream, but don't be tempted to enrich it by substituting cream for the milk. The cooked and pureed artichokes have a creamy richness that neither needs—nor benefits from—added fat.

Bet you thought you'd never hear me say that.

1 lemon
2 pounds Jerusalem artichokes
1 medium yellow onion, peeled and minced
2 tablespoons unsalted butter
2 cups Chicken Broth (page 21) or 1 cup canned broth mixed with 1 cup water

1 Bouquet Garni (page 32), made with a healthy sprig each thyme and parsley, 1 leafy celery rib, and 1 bay leaf
Salt and whole white peppercorns in a peppermill
1 cup whole milk
½ cup light cream
1 tablespoon minced parsley

1. Have ready a basin of cold water that will comfortably hold all the artichokes. Cut the lemon in half. Set aside one of the halves. Squeeze the juice from the other half into the water and drop in the spent peel. Scrub the artichokes under cold running water and, one at a time, peel them with a vegetable peeler and cut them into ¼-inch slices. Put each one in the acidulated water as soon as it is sliced (this prevents discoloring).

2. Put the onion and butter in a large, heavy-bottomed pot over medium heat. Sauté, tossing frequently, until the onion is softened but not colored, about 5 minutes. Add the broth and bouquet garni, raise the heat, and bring it to a boil. Reduce the heat to medium low, cover, and simmer 30 minutes.

3. Drain the artichokes and add them to the pot, raise the heat to medium high, and bring it back to a boil. Reduce it once more to a steady simmer, cover, and simmer until the artichokes are soft, about 25 minutes. Remove and discard the bouquet garni. Take up a cup of the artichokes and cut them into small cubes.

4. Puree the soup in batches with a food mill, blender, or food processor. Season well with salt and a liberal grinding of pepper, return it to the pot, and add the reserved cubed artichoke. (The soup can be made several hours or a day ahead up to this point. If making more than 4 hours ahead, or if the day is warm, transfer it to a storage container, cover, and refrigerate.)

5. When you're ready to finish and serve the soup, add the milk and cream and reheat gently

over medium heat, stirring frequently to prevent it from sticking and scorching. Take it from the heat and squeeze in the juice from the remaining lemon half. Stir, taste, and adjust the seasonings, and pour the soup into a heated tureen or divide it among warmed soup plates. Sprinkle each serving with the minced parsley.

Note: *This soup needs the substance of meat broth to give it the necessary body. If you are cooking without meat, however, you can substitute Vegetable Broth (page 22).*

Scalloped Jerusalem Artichokes

SERVES 4 TO 6

This sumptuous side dish is a fine companion for just about any meat, poultry, or fish that doesn't contain cream, but is substantial enough to stand on its own as a main dish.

The cream must have a fat content of at least 36 percent or it may never thicken properly. If you are unable to get cream that is rich enough, sprinkle each layer of artichokes with a tablespoon of soft bread crumbs. This will thicken the cream without giving it that disagreeable pasty quality that flour sometimes imparts.

2 pounds Boiled Jerusalem Artichokes (page 254)
Salt and black pepper in a peppermill
1 cup heavy cream (minimum 36 percent milk fat)
2 tablespoons unsalted butter
¾ cup dry bread crumbs

1. Position a rack in the upper third of the oven and preheat to 400°F. While the artichokes are still warm, peel them if you like (the skins should slip right off) and slice ¼-inch thick. (It isn't necessary to peel them; I rarely do.)

2. Lightly grease a 2-quart gratin or shallow casserole with butter. Add the artichokes in overlapping rows in no more than two layers, lightly seasoning each layer with salt and a few grindings of pepper. When all the artichokes are in the dish, pour the cream evenly over them.

3. Melt the butter in a small skillet over medium heat and turn off the heat. Add the crumbs and toss until the butter is evenly absorbed. Sprinkle the crumbs over the casserole and bake in the upper third of the oven until the cream is thick and bubbly and the crumbs are nicely browned, about half an hour.

VARIATION: Scalloped Turnips: This recipe is also a lovely way to prepare turnips. Simply substitute small white or purple turnips for the Jerusalem artichokes, first simmering them whole following the method for boiling artichokes above.

Jerusalem Artichoke Salad SERVES 4

While Jerusalem artichokes can be sliced paper thin and used raw in salads, old Southern cooks used to make salads with boiled artichokes, much like potato salad. It makes an interesting twist on that old picnic and dinner-on-the-grounds standard.

You can prepare the entire salad ahead of time, but don't cook the artichokes ahead of assembling the salad or they'll turn dark. Besides, they should still be a little warm when they are dressed so that they absorb some of the dressing.

2 large hard-cooked eggs
½ teaspoon dry mustard
¼ cup red wine vinegar
2 tablespoons olive oil
2 pounds Boiled Jerusalem Artichokes (page 254)

Salt and black pepper in a peppermill

2 green onions, washed and trimmed of roots and discolored leaves, and thinly sliced

1 tablespoon capers, rinsed and drained

2 tablespoons minced parsley

4–6 fresh lettuce leaves, washed and drained

1. Slice the eggs crosswise into rings and separate the yolks from the whites. Set the whites aside. Put the yolks in the bottom of a salad bowl, add the mustard, and mash them smooth with a fork. Gradually add the vinegar, beating with the fork, until it forms a smooth paste. Add the oil, a drop at a time, beating until it is emulsified. The dressing can also be made in a blender or food processor (see note).

2. While the artichokes are still warm, slice them ¼-inch thick. Don't peel them unless you dislike the skins. Add them to the dressing and toss until they are well coated. Season well with salt and a liberal grinding of pepper, and toss well.

3. Add the green onions, capers, and 1 tablespoon of the parsley to the salad and lightly toss. Taste and correct the seasonings and give it a final toss. Let it cool completely before serving.

4. When you are ready to serve, arrange the lettuce on a platter and turn the salad out onto it. Sprinkle with the remaining parsley, lay the reserved egg white rings decoratively around the edges, and serve at room temperature.

Note: *To make the dressing in a blender or food processor, put all the ingredients except the oil in the bowl of the machine and blend. With the machine running, gradually add the oil through the feed tube (or hole in the blender lid) in a very thin stream and blend until it is emulsified. If you want to make this salad without eggs, it will of course be thinner. Put the ingredients in a jar, put on a tight lid, and shake the jar until the dressing is well mixed, or blend the*

mustard, vinegar, a pinch of salt and grinding of pepper together in a blender, then, with the motor running, add the oil in a thin stream.

POTATOES

Potatoes are so central to the average American diet that we forget that they have not always been so commonplace. They are not even native to our continent, but to South America. Just how this South American member of the nightshade family ended up in the north is a matter of some colorful debate, with historians disagreeing almost violently on the point. The most common theory is that they were introduced to North America by way of Europe. The fact that they're to this day often called "Irish" potatoes by many Southerners is suggestive and has led a few careless historians to jump to the conclusion that they were imported to our continent by way of Ireland, a scenario that's not very likely. A few older sources and historians (including Thomas Jefferson) believed that potatoes had already migrated to North America by the time the Europeans arrived, and this theory can't be completely discounted. Well, however the potato got here, what is certain is that it didn't figure prominently in the Southern diet until the eighteenth century, and even then was overshadowed by sweet potatoes.

Though sweet potatoes have traditionally outdistanced regular potatoes in popularity down South, the proliferation of fast-food fries and chips has long since tipped the balance of their consumption down here. That isn't to suggest that we haven't always enjoyed them, however. There are many potato dishes that are of course pretty much universal—those fries and chips, for example—not to mention mashed, scalloped, and baked potatoes. Good recipes for those dishes are commonplace and were included in two of my other books, *Classical Southern Cooking* and *Essentials of Southern Cooking*, so I haven't repeated them here. Instead, I offer a few that you might not have expected to find on Southern tables.

Potatoes are usually stored in a cool, dark place where air can circulate freely, so when my northern editor saw "if they have been refrigerated" in a recipe, she questioned why anyone would do that. In the Deep South, if we buy potatoes in quantity, the refrigerator may not be ideal, but it's the only place to keep them without having them sprout and rot prematurely.

Mary Randolph's Potatoes and Onions SERVES 6

This is mashed potatoes with an old Virginia twist. Mrs. Randolph left the proportion of potatoes to onions up to the cook's individual taste, but I've imposed mine here—a 2-to-1 ratio. You needn't feel bound by it. If you prefer the onion flavor to be more subtle or robust, simply adjust the proportions to suit your own taste.

2 pounds mature boiling potatoes of a uniform size
1 pound medium yellow onion
2 tablespoons unsalted butter
¼ cup heavy cream (minimum 36 percent milk fat)
Salt
Black pepper in a peppermill (optional)
1 tablespoon chopped parsley or chives (optional)

1. If you store your potatoes and onions in the refrigerator, take them out at least half an hour before you cook them. Wash the potatoes under cold running water, scrubbing off any dirt without breaking the skin. Wash the onions briefly, trim off the roots, and cut a deep "X" in the root ends. Don't peel them. Put the vegetables in a stockpot that will hold them and leave at least 2 inches of room at the top. Add enough water to cover them by about an inch, remove the vegetables, cover the pot, and bring the water almost to a boil over medium-high heat.

2. Add the potatoes and onions, let it come to a full, rolling boil, then reduce the heat to a slow simmer and cook until both are tender and easily pierced with a fork—15–30 minutes, depending on the size and age of the vegetables. Also, one of them may take longer than the other to

cook, so watch carefully. If either is done before the other, remove it and keep warm until the other is done.

3. Drain and let the potatoes and onions sit in the pot, uncovered, for about 5 minutes. Peel the potatoes with your hands; the skins will slip right off. Trim off the stems and roots of the onions and peel them. Force the potatoes through a coarse sieve or potato ricer into the pot in which they cooked. Mrs. Randolph rubbed the onions through a sieve, but you may puree them in a blender (they won't go through a ricer). Mix them into the potatoes along with the butter, cream, and a healthy pinch of salt.

4. Return the pot to low heat, stirring and mashing until it's smooth and the liquid is incorporated. If it appears a bit dry, add a spoonful or so more cream but don't overdo it. Taste and adjust the seasoning, and transfer to a warmed serving bowl. If you like, dust the top with a generous grinding of pepper and one of the chopped herbs—or a little of both—and serve hot.

Ilda's Scalloped Potatoes with Ham
SERVES 4 TO 6

It was my first night in Italy. Our class had spent the day sketching in the picturesque port towns of Portofino and San Fruttuoso. Soaked with Riviera sunshine and salty Ligurian air, we were very hungry, as only active young people can be. Already, I'd had my first espresso, focaccia, and spaghetti alla carbonara, and was game for anything our cook, Ilda, fed to us. She had long since gone home but had left a casserole for us to bake for our supper. She called it *casseruola al forno*, which only means "baked casserole"—not much of a clue. We popped it into the oven and made a salad. The aroma filled the house, rich and tantalizingly Italian; something very familiar about it kept teasing my imagination. At last we sat down to supper, the spoon pierced the crusty cheese and the creamy filling oozed out. I tasted it—and was enveloped by the memory of a dozen covered-dish suppers back home. Our exotic Italian casserole was only scalloped potatoes with ham, a dish I'd cut my teeth on.

Ilda's recipe came home with me and has become a tradition in my own family. Ilda made it with prosciutto cotto (boiled ham), so I usually use a good quality cooked ham in my own version, but will often make it with country ham (our own cousin of prosciutto), especially for a special occasion like one of those covered-dish suppers.

2 pounds boiling potatoes

3 tablespoons unsalted butter

2 tablespoons minced yellow onion

2 tablespoons unbleached all-purpose flour

2 cups milk

Salt and whole white peppercorns in a peppermill

Whole nutmeg in a grater

1 cup diced cooked ham or raw country ham
   (or prosciutto)

1 cup freshly grated Gruyère

¼ cup freshly grated Parmigiano-Reggiano
   (no substitutes)

1. Wash the potatoes under cold running water and put them in a stockpot with enough water to cover them by 1 inch. Remove the potatoes, cover the pot, and bring the water to a rapid boil over high heat. Add the potatoes, cover, and let it return to a boil, then reduce the heat to a steady simmer and cook until the potatoes are easily pierced with a fork. Drain and set them aside until they are cool enough to handle. Position a rack in the upper third of the oven and preheat to 375°F.

2. Put the butter and onion in a saucepan over medium heat. Sauté until the onion is softened but not colored, about 5 minutes. Sprinkle in the flour and whisk until it is smoothly blended.

Whisking constantly, slowly add the milk and continue whisking until it begins to thicken. Reduce the heat to low and simmer, stirring frequently, until thick, about 10 minutes. Season to taste with a pinch or so of salt, a grinding of white pepper, and a generous grating of nutmeg. Turn off the heat.

3. Peel the potatoes and slice ¼-inch thick. Lightly butter a 2-quart gratin or shallow casserole and cover the bottom with a layer of potatoes. Scatter a third of the ham over them and spoon a third of the sauce over all. Scatter a third of the Gruyère over the sauce, then add another layer of potatoes, ham, sauce, and Gruyère, repeat with a third layer, finishing with sauce and Gruyère. Sprinkle the Parmesan over the top and bake in the upper third of the oven until golden brown and bubbly, about half an hour. This can also be assembled ahead of time and cooked later, but it can also be baked completely ahead as it reheats beautifully. Serve hot.

Bailee's Latkes

MAKES ABOUT 30 LATKES, OR 6 TO 8 SERVINGS

Until recently, many Southerners wouldn't have known a latke from a bagel. Yet potato pancakes have long been a standard in Southern cooking; it's just that they didn't generally come to the table accompanied by their Jewish name. That's never been the case in Savannah, where there has been a continuous and highly respected Jewish presence since the city's beginning. The first Jews arrived here barely five months after the colony's founding, and though their numbers have always been small, their influence on the cultural and social life of Savannah has been anything but insignificant.

Only one of Savannah's three congregations is orthodox and keeps kosher year round, but recently there's been a renewed interest in Jewish culinary traditions even among Reform congregations, tempered though those traditions have been by a Southern accent. (When Congregation K. K. Mickve Israel holds its annual food festival, the Hard Lox Cafe, in Forsyth Park, its telling slogan is "Shalom, y'all.")

For years, artist and cooking teacher Bailee Kronowitz brought the best of those traditions

to the rest of us in Savannah with her intelligent and lively teaching. Her potato latkes were exemplary—traditional-tasting but a bit unorthodox in method. (I can't tell you how many rolled eyes I've gotten from Jewish cooks when I share this recipe.) Usually latkes are made with hand-grated potatoes and onions, but Bailee preferred to chop them in the blender—a technique that is about as orthodox as would be cooking them in bacon fat. Though the texture of the potato batter is finer than when hand-grated, there's still plenty of it—and needless to say the latkes are a snap to make.

1½ pounds (2–3 medium) mature baking potatoes

½ pound (about 1 large to 2 medium) yellow onions

1 large egg, well beaten

1–2 tablespoons flour

Salt and black pepper in a peppermill

Vegetable oil for frying

1 cup applesauce (preferably homemade)

1 cup homemade Crème Fraîche (page 18) or sour cream

1. Position a rack in the upper third of the oven and preheat the oven to 150°F (the "warm" setting). Prepare a basin of cold water that will hold all the potatoes without overflowing. Wash and peel the potatoes, cut them into 1-inch chunks, and drop them into the basin of water. Peel and quarter the onions and set them aside.

2. Lift a potato chunk out of the water, pat dry, and put it in a blender. Cover and process at medium speed until it's finely chopped. Drain and add the remaining potatoes, one at a time, until they are all chopped fine, and transfer them to a glass or ceramic bowl. Process the onions in the same way, then add the potatoes back to the blender along with the beaten egg, cover, and pulse until well mixed. Add 1 tablespoon of flour, and pulse until it is well mixed and slightly thickened. If necessary (some potatoes have more water than others), add another spoonful of flour. Season with a healthy pinch of salt and a few grindings of pepper.

3. Film the bottom of a frying pan (preferably cast iron) with oil about ⅛-inch deep. Turn on the heat to medium high and heat until it is sizzling hot (375°F). Drop the potato batter by heaping tablespoonfuls into the pan until it's full but not crowded. Fry the latkes until they are nicely browned on the bottom, about 3–5 minutes. Turn and cook until the other side is evenly browned, about 3 minutes more. Drain the cooked latkes briefly on absorbent paper and transfer them to a cookie sheet. Keep them in the warm oven while the remaining latkes cook. Repeat until all the batter is cooked, and serve at once, passing applesauce and sour cream separately.

Note: *The potatoes and onions should be finely chopped, but they shouldn't be a smooth puree, so don't overprocess them. The easiest way to keep this from happening is to pulse the blender rather than letting it run continuously.*

Bailee often made latkes ahead and refrigerated them. After they've completely cooled, cover well and refrigerate until half an hour before you're ready to serve them. Take them out of the refrigerator, position a rack in the upper third of the oven, and preheat the oven to 350°F. Transfer the latkes to a cookie sheet and bake until hot, about 5 minutes.

Funeral Salad

SERVES A LOT OF PEOPLE (AT LEAST 12)

When somebody dies down South, the bereaved family is swamped with food. Will D. Campbell gives the best explanation for this phenom-enon in his novel *Brother to a Dragonfly* (1977): "Somehow in rural Southern culture, food is always the first thought of neighbors when there is trouble. That is something they can do

and not feel uncomfortable. . . . 'Here, I brought you some fresh eggs for your breakfast. And here's a cake. And some potato salad.' It means, 'I love you. And I am sorry for what you are going through, and I will share as much of your burden as I can.' And maybe potato salad is a better way of saying it."

Maybe it is.

I really don't know why it's always potato salad, so don't ask—I don't make the rules. Every cook I ever knew has his own particular potato salad for such an occasion—and rarely is the recipe written down. You just make a big bowl of the stuff, throwing in things until it tastes right and looks as if it will feed a crowd. When my friend Adam Howard was growing up, his mother's version was called "Forest Home Salad" in polite company, but "Funeral Potato Salad" at home, because the only time she made it was for somebody's funeral. This is my own Funeral Salad.

4 pounds red-skinned potatoes

Salt

Dry white vermouth

1 cup chopped (1 small) sweet onion, preferably Vidalia

½ cup chopped (about 4) green onions

1 cup finely chopped celery

2 tablespoons finely chopped parsley

½ cup pitted Greek black olives, cut into thin strips

½ cup pitted green olives, cut into thin strips

2 tablespoons small whole (or coarsely chopped large) capers

4 hard-cooked eggs, peeled and chopped

1 cup Homemade Mayonnaise (page 44)

2 tablespoons Dijon mustard

¼ cup wine vinegar

Black pepper in a peppermill

1. Scrub the potatoes under cold running water and put them into a stockpot with enough water to cover them by an inch. Remove the potatoes, cover the pot, and bring the water to a boil over high heat. Add a small handful of salt and the potatoes. Let it come back to a boil, reduce the heat to medium, and cook until the potatoes are barely tender, about 20 minutes. Exact times will depend on the size and age of the potatoes—some will take longer, some less—so keep an eye on the pot and don't overcook them. Drain and let them sit in the pot until they're cool enough to handle. Peel and cut them into large dice, and transfer them to a large bowl. Sprinkle generously with vermouth and a pinch or so of salt. Let cool.

2. Add the two onions, celery, parsley, black and green olives, capers, and hard-cooked eggs. Lightly toss and add the mayonnaise, mustard, vinegar, and a few liberal grindings of pepper. Mix well until the dressing evenly coats everything. Taste and correct the seasonings and let stand for half an hour before serving.

Note: *Don't let a salad with homemade mayonnaise sit out at room temperature for more than an hour, and promptly refrigerate any leftovers, or you could have bacteria tap-dancing on top of it.*

Potatoes vary in density and absorptive capacity; the vermouth helps keep them from absorbing too much dressing, but even so, you may find that the salad is too thick if the potatoes are especially thirsty. If this happens, make a simple dressing of two parts vinegar to one part olive oil, mix it well, and add it by spoonfuls until the salad is the consistency that suits you. Taste and correct the seasonings. The added vinegar will naturally make the salad more tart, so you may need to tone it down a bit with a touch more salt or even vermouth.

Baked Potato Salad   SERVES 6 TO 8

The dilemma is all too familiar—you had a barbecue last Saturday or there was a death in your family on Monday. It's now midweek, the visitors are gone, and you have 40 pounds of potato salad in the refrigerator. You can't face another ounce of the stuff on your plate. Hating the idea of throwing it out, and unable to give it away no matter how much I bribed and pleaded, I'd guiltily stow it in the back of the refrigerator until its top had sprouted a nice junior-high science project and it started to attack anyone who opened the door.

That was before my late friend Jim King served me his solution to the problem, which involves neither mold, nor bribery, nor secret burials at midnight. Undisturbed by the surplus, Jim slapped it into a casserole, strewed a few buttered crumbs over the top, and popped it into the oven.

I know what you are thinking, but just wait until you taste it.

8 cups Funeral Salad (page 261) or any mayonnaise-based potato salad you happen to be swimming in

4 tablespoons unsalted butter

1 cup dry bread crumbs

1. Position a rack in the upper third of the oven and preheat to 400°F. Press the potato salad into a casserole that will hold it in a layer about an inch deep (a 9 x 13-inch dish).

2. Melt the butter in a small skillet or sauté pan over medium heat. When it's just melted, turn off the heat and add the crumbs. Stir until the butter is evenly absorbed into them and sprinkle them over the potato salad. Bake in the upper third of the oven until the potatoes are bubbly and hot and the crumbs are nicely browned, about 25–30 minutes. Serve hot.

WINTER SQUASH

There is probably no more confusing botanical history than that of edible gourds, which is of course what all squash are. They are part of a larger botanical family that includes pumpkins, cucumbers, and all types of melons, and have been cultivated and highly prized throughout the world since time immemorial. As to their origin, though, no one is really sure. There are theories placing their beginnings in both Asia and the Americas. Most botanists and historians agree that the varieties common in our country are either natives or hybrids developed from native stock. But weighty issues of origin matter only to historians and are of little consequence to us when we sit down at the table.

Though winter squash have been grown and eaten all along in the South, there was a time when they were thought of almost as a kind of Northern vegetable. For a Southerner, "squash" meant the yellow crooknecks or the odd, flying-saucer-shaped cymlings or pattypan squash. Winter squash had come to be treated more as a sweetmeat than a vegetable, and when I was growing up, they were mostly made into pies or baked with brown sugar and spices, much like candied sweet potatoes. Both were popular dishes and I utterly loathed them. It was only after I was grown and had been introduced to savory dishes like the ones that follow that I began to like winter squash at all. Now they are one of my very favorite winter vegetables—and these recipes, some of my favorite dishes.

Winter Squash Bisque with Seafood Confit   SERVES 6

About the same time that the first edition of this book premiered, truffle oil burst on the culinary scene as the hot ingredient of the day. Inevitably, cheap, artificially flavored truffle oils flooded the commercial market to meet the demand, and were sloshed around with abandon, turning up in numbing doses and with equally numbing frequency in dishes where it had no business being. This lovely soup was one of them. The flesh of

winter squash may be dense, sweet, and rich, but there's a delicacy about it, too. A few shavings of fresh truffle might enhance that flavor, but those wanton doses of cheap oil just obliterated it. Where more level heads have prevailed, the garnish is a drizzle of pumpkin-seed oil or just a splash of heavy cream and minced herbs.

And along the coast, it's paired with the season's late seafood harvest—a far more logical, not to mention delectable, option.

1 large butternut squash

1 small yellow onion, split, peeled, and thinly sliced

1 medium leek, trimmed, split lengthwise, cleaned, and thinly sliced (both white and tender green parts)

2 tablespoons unsalted butter

3 cups chicken broth

1 bouquet garni made with 1 large sprig each leafy celery top, flat-leaf parsley, sage, and thyme

Salt and whole white pepper in a mill

2 cups whole milk

½ cup heavy cream

Winter Seafood Confit (recipe follows), optional

2 tablespoons thinly sliced fresh chives or green onion tops

1. Peel the squash and cut off the long neck where it begins to flare. Split the fatter section in half and remove and discard the seeds. Cut the squash into 1-inch chunks. You should have about 5 cups.

2. Warm the onion, leek, and butter in a large, heavy-bottomed saucepan over medium-high heat. Sauté, tossing often, until translucent, about 4 minutes. Add the squash and toss until heated through, about a minute more. Add the broth and bouquet garni and season with salt and a grinding of white pepper. Bring to a boil, loosely cover, and reduce the heat to low. Simmer until the squash is tender, about 10–15 minutes. Turn off the heat. Remove and discard the bouquet garni. Puree the soup in batches

in a blender or food processor. It can be made several hours or a day ahead to this point. Cool, cover, and refrigerate if making more than 2 hours ahead.

3. When you are ready to serve the soup, return it to the pot, bring it to a simmer over medium heat, and stir in the milk. Bring it back to the simmer, taste, adjust the salt and pepper, and simmer 3–5 minutes longer. Ladle the soup into warmed soup bowls, drizzle a tablespoon of cream into each serving, and, if using, top with a spoonful of seafood confit. Garnish with a sprinkle of chives and serve at once.

Winter Seafood Confit   SERVES 4 AS AN
APPETIZER, 6 TO 8 AS A GARNISH FOR THE SOUP

When French cookery is mentioned as an influence on the cooking of the South, most people (even Southerners) tend to think immediately of New Orleans, but the cuisines of each of the South's old coastal cities, from Baltimore to St. Augustine, Mobile to Galveston, have always had a continental flair. This cold seafood confit whispers of classic haute cuisine, but it does so with a drawl—y'all.

It needn't be confined to garnishing the previous recipe: It makes a delicious first course appetizer served forth in chilled cocktail glasses, scallop shells, or lettuce cups.

½ cup dry white vermouth

3 large cloves garlic, lightly crushed, peeled, and minced

2 teaspoons chopped fresh oregano, stripped stems reserved

1 tablespoon chopped fresh parsley, 2–3 stripped stems reserved

2 teaspoons chopped fresh thyme, stripped stems reserved

2 dozen large mussels, scrubbed under cold running water and "bearded"

3 tablespoons extra-virgin olive oil

½ pound small shrimp, peeled and (if you must) deveined

½ pound small bay scallops

½ pound lump crabmeat

½ teaspoon hot pepper flakes, or to taste

1 lemon, halved

Salt

1. Bring the vermouth, ⅓ of the garlic, and herb stems to a boil in large saucepan over medium heat. Cover, lower the heat, and simmer 5 minutes. Raise the heat once more and add the mussels, cover tightly, and steam until they just pop open, about 2 minutes. Remove the mussels and shuck them. Boil the pan juices until reduced by half and syrupy. Turn off the heat. Remove and discard the herb stems. Pour the cooking liquid over the mussels.

2. Put 2 tablespoons of the oil and remaining garlic in a 10-inch skillet over medium heat. When it is sizzling and fragrant, add the shrimp, scallops, oregano, parsley, and thyme. Toss until the shrimp are just curled and pink. Add the mussels and their reduced liquid, crabmeat, and hot pepper flakes to taste, let it warm through, and turn off the heat. Transfer to a glass bowl, add the remaining oil and a squeeze or two of lemon juice, to taste. Toss, then taste and adjust the salt and lemon juice. Cool, cover, and refrigerate until needed. Serve cold.

Baked Sausage-Stuffed Winter Squash   SERVES 4

Cold weather in Savannah may not be as severe or as lasting as in more northerly regions, but when our weather turns nasty, it's really nasty. The high humidity creates an icy dampness that seeps right through your clothes and sticks to your skin like a sheet of wet plastic. Nothing throws off that damp, icy mantle—except possibly a shot of bourbon—any better than this spicy dish. Like a well-worn pair of flannel long johns, it envelops with its warmth and fills one with a lingering sense of well-being.

2 small winter squash (about 1 pound each), such as acorn, butternut, or kabocha

Salt

2 pounds bulk sausage or 1 pound ground veal or pork

2 tablespoons butter (only if using veal or pork)

1 medium onion, peeled and chopped

3 cloves garlic, lightly crushed, peeled, and minced

2 cups cooked Carolina-Style Rice (page 37)

10–12 fresh sage leaves or 1 teaspoon crumbled dried sage (omit if using sausage with sage already in it)

Nutmeg in a grater

Ground cayenne, and black pepper in a peppermill

1 lemon

1 large egg, beaten

2 tablespoons butter (4 tablespoons if using veal or pork)

½ cup dry bread crumbs

1. Position a rack in the center of the oven and preheat to 375°F. Meanwhile, wash the squash, halve them lengthwise, and scoop out and discard the seeds. Lightly butter a baking dish that will comfortably hold the squash in one layer and put them on it split-side up. Sprinkle lightly with a little salt and set aside.

2. Crumble the sausage into a large skillet or sauté pan and over medium heat. Brown it well, stirring often, remove it from the pan, and drain briefly on several layers of absorbent paper. Spoon off all but 2 tablespoons of fat from the pan. (If using veal or pork, brown it over medium heat in 2 tablespoons of butter.) Add the onion to the pan and sauté until translucent and colored pale gold, about 5–8 minutes. Add the garlic and sauté until fragrant, about a half a minute more. Turn off the heat.

3. Return the sausage or meat to the pan, add the rice, sage (if the sausage doesn't already contain it), a liberal grating of nutmeg, and salt to taste. If you're using veal or pork, add a pinch of cayenne and a liberal grinding of pepper. Grate in the zest from the lemon, then cut it in half and squeeze in the juice from one of the halves. Toss until uniformly mixed, then taste and correct the seasoning. Add the beaten egg and mix well.

4. Divide the filling equally among the squash halves, mounding it in the center if necessary. Melt the butter in a skillet over low heat. Turn off the heat, add the crumbs, and mix until the butter is evenly absorbed. Sprinkle the crumbs over the filling and bake the squash in the center of the oven until tender and cooked through, about 1 hour.

Braised Winter Squash   SERVES 4

Winter squash take to braising like a duck to water. It brings out and enhances their savory-sweet flavor better than any other way of preparing them. Though traditionally served with a sturdy meat dish, such as roasted pork or grilled chops, this is substantial enough to stand on its own as a main course.

2 small (about ¾ pound each) or 1 large (about 2 pounds) winter squash, such as acorn, butternut, cashaw, or kabocha

3 tablespoons bacon drippings (preferable) or unsalted butter

1 large onion, peeled and chopped

1 clove garlic, crushed and peeled

8–10 fresh (or 5–6 dried) sage leaves

Salt and black pepper in a peppermill

½ cup Chicken Broth (page 21) or water

1 tablespoon chopped fresh sage or parsley

1. Peel the squash. If you're using butternuts, cut off the long neck where it begins to flare. Split the squash in half, remove and discard the seeds, and cut into 1-inch chunks.

2. Put the fat and onion in a large, lidded skillet (preferably cast iron) or heavy sauté pan that will hold the squash in a single layer. Put it over medium heat and sauté until the onion is transparent but not browned, about 5 minutes. Add the squash and raise the heat. Toss until it is glossy and hot, about a minute, then add the garlic, sage, a healthy pinch of salt, and a liberal grinding of pepper. Toss well and add the broth. Bring it to a boil, cover, and reduce the heat to a bare simmer. Cook until the squash is nearly tender, about half an hour.

3. Remove the lid and raise the heat to medium high. Reduce the liquid, shaking the pan and turning the squash frequently to prevent it from sticking, until the liquid is evaporated and thick, and the squash is just beginning to brown. Turn off the heat. Taste and correct the seasonings, transfer the squash to a warm bowl, sprinkle with the chopped herbs, and serve at once.

Winter Squash Country Captain

SERVES 4

Country Captain is a spicy tomato-based curry that came into the South by way of England's East Indian trade. It isn't really an Indian dish, but an English adaptation of one. Since the early nineteenth century, Country Captain has been popular all along the Atlantic Seaboard in every major Southern port from Baltimore to Savannah.

The traditional main ingredient of Country Captain is chicken, but Charlestonians and Savannahians also like to make it with shrimp. It's also an excellent way to cook winter squash, since they take well to curry and develop a rich, meaty flavor that makes this substantial enough to serve as a meatless main dish.

1 medium (about 2 pounds) winter squash, such as acorn, butternut, or kabocha

3 tablespoons unsalted butter or olive oil

1 large onion, peeled and chopped

1 large green bell pepper, seeded and chopped

2 large cloves garlic, crushed, peeled, and minced

2 tablespoons Curry Powder (page 28) or 1 tablespoon commercial curry powder

1 tart apple (such as Granny Smith), peeled, cored, and diced

2 pounds ripe tomatoes, scalded, peeled, seeded, and chopped as directed on page 101, or 2 cups seeded and chopped canned Italian tomatoes with their juices

1 teaspoon sugar

Salt

1 cup currants or raisins

1 tablespoon chopped parsley

4 cups cooks Carolina-Style Rice (page 37)

½ cup grated unsweetened coconut

½ cup toasted peanuts

1. Peel the squash. If you're using butternuts, cut off the long neck where it begins to flare. Split the squash in half, remove and discard the seeds, and cut into 1-inch chunks. Put the fat, onion, and bell pepper in a large, lidded skillet or heavy sauté pan over medium heat. Sauté, tossing often, until they're softened but not browned, about 5 minutes. Add the garlic and curry, and sauté until fragrant, about half a minute more.

2. Add the squash and apple and toss until they're hot and evenly coated. Add the tomatoes, sugar, a large pinch of salt, and currants. Bring to a boil, reduce the heat to a gentle simmer, and cover. Simmer, stirring occasionally, until the squash is tender, about 1 hour. If, when the squash is done, there's too much liquid in the pan, raise the heat briefly and let it boil away. Turn off the heat and stir in the parsley. Serve hot over rice, with the coconut and peanuts passed separately.

Note: *Traditionally, this would be called a "two-boy" curry because there are only two condiments. The condiment tray can have as many as ten "boys" and include such things as chutney, Bombay duck, diced cucumber, mango, oranges, and bananas. Add any of these if you like, though in Savannah anything more than a five-boy curry is considered pretentious.*

FLORIDA CITRUS FRUITS

Just as the days become their shortest and darkest, Indian River oranges and grapefruits arrive in the market, bringing a bit of Florida sunshine to breakfast tables all over the country. It should be no surprise, then, that Floridians, just as we Georgians sport that ubiquitous peach, emblazon everything with an orange. It's the symbol not only of the state's best-known industry, but of the sun, which is always supposed to be shining overhead. Actually, it rains a lot in the Sunshine State (which is why citrus trees flourish there), and the trees only bear fruit in the winter, but the carefree notion of endless oranges and sunshine endures.

In Florida's semitropical climate, citrus fruit has flourished since the Spanish introduced it in the sixteenth century. But it wasn't until the War Between the States that the fledgling industry began to develop in a big way. It actually got a boost from something that was designed to bring the South to its knees: Union blockades. With the South's supply of imported fruit effectively cut off, Floridians scrambled to fill the gap. The Florida citrus industry was on its way, but it was another century before it really took off. The development of frozen concentrated orange juice created a year-round market for what had previously been a seasonal product, and the citrus boom was on.

Today, the state, particularly the Indian River region, is known throughout the country for its citrus fruits, which are considered by many (and certainly by proud Floridians) to be the finest in the world. Though Florida is not the only major producer of citrus fruits in the country, whenever freezing temperatures dip south of the Georgia state line, threatening the ripening crop, the whole country holds its collective breath.

Dozens of varieties of citrus fruits are grown in the region, from juice oranges, which mainly supply the

frozen concentrate industry, to exotics like honeybells, tangelos, pomelos, and ugli fruit. While many of these citrus fruits are marketed nationally, some are produced only for the local market, and others are not marketed at all. The fruits most commonly available to us and the rest of the country are Valencia, navel, blood, and honeybell oranges; tangelos and tangerines; pink, white, and red grapefruit; and lemons and limes. Unless a recipe states that a specific citrus fruit be used, you can use differing varieties of each type interchangeably.

For those of us who are a certain age, one of the most fragrant memories of childhood is the fat orange that bulged the toe of our Christmas stocking. To this day, the bright, pungent aroma released when an orange is peeled whispers of all the good things about our Christmases past.

That holiday fragrance lingered long after the holly in our house. My mother's baby sister, who for most of her life lived in South Florida, always sent a crate of citrus fruit to remind us that warm sunshine would come again—and that she was enjoying it year round (ha, ha).

Well, nowadays children feel cheated if all they get in their stocking is an orange, and the rest of us are no better. We take this sunny fruit for granted, relegating it to a juice glass at breakfast, forgetting that this little bit of sunshine can brighten many a meal at winter's table.

Of course, the best way to experience citrus fruit is firsthand. If you've never eaten a tree-ripened grapefruit, naturally chilled by a cool February night, then you have missed one of the world's great delights. But you don't have to be in Florida to enjoy this bit of Florida sunshine; just look for the Indian River label on the grapefruit in your market.

Citrus Fruit Facts

My aunt had her own grapefruit tree in her backyard. When perfectly ripened, grapefruit will just fall right off the tree, so all she had to do for a perfect, naturally chilled breakfast on those chilly February mornings during peak season was go out to the yard and pick one up. While most of us can't have that kind of tree-ripened freshness, with care, we can come close.

- Citrus are tropical fruits, and in general, they don't tolerate cold well. Conventional wisdom is that they shouldn't be refrigerated, but while it's true that unripe citrus fruit won't ripen well under refrigeration, it's actually the best way to store it once it is ripe. A good alternative to refrigeration, preferred by aficionados, is a cool, dry place.

- Don't stack or crowd unrefrigerated fruit, and check it regularly for rot. You know the expression about one bad apple . . .

- If you've been sent a gift box of citrus fruit, don't store it in the box. Unpack and store it as suggested above.

- Ripen citrus fruits at room temperature, laid out in one layer, with no single piece of fruit touching another.

Ambrosia   SERVES 6 TO 8

Appropriately named, this luscious fruit salad has been a traditional Christmas dish all over the South at least since the days of Sarah Rutledge's *The Carolina Housewife* (1847). The essential ingredients are oranges and freshly grated coconut, and it must have them both to be authentic, but depending on where you are in the South, other citrus fruits, and often pineapple, are added to the bowl.

Today, in the interest of novelty (at least, that's all I can figure), ambrosia has been subjected to all sorts of indignities, including sugar, which it does not need; packaged sweetened coconut, which it does not want; or worse, canned pineapple and lurid maraschino cherries; and—God help us—gelatin and nondairy topping. The fresh, clean flavor and spirited finesse that made real ambrosia's name so appropriate gets literally buried alive.

What follows is Annabella Hill's classic recipe. The critical ingredient is fresh coconut juice, so when selecting a coconut for this recipe, hold it near your ear and shake it: It should slosh happily with plenty of juice.

1 small, fresh coconut with juice
1 fresh, ripe pineapple
6 large, sweet oranges, such as navels or honeybells

1. Fit a fine-meshed wire strainer over a bowl. Using a skewer, ice pick, or Phillips-head screwdriver, punch out the stem scars that make the little monkey face on one side of the coconut. Invert the coconut over the strainer and drain all the juice into the bowl. It should smell of fresh coconut. If it smells musty, the coconut is old; discard the whole thing. Lay the nut sideways on an unbreakable surface (the patio, a bare concrete floor, the front walk—whatever). Tap it firmly with a hammer around the middle, rotating the nut, until it cracks and splits. Turn each half rounded-end up, and tap until the shell breaks apart. Pry the white flesh from the shell, peel off its brown hull with a paring knife or vegetable peeler, and shred the nutmeat with a grater.

2. Cut off the stem and sprout ends of the pineapple, and holding it over a bowl to catch the juices, peel it. Cut out the core and slice the pineapple in ¼-inch-thick pieces. The easiest way to do this is to cut the pineapple flesh from the core in vertical wedge-shaped sections. You can also use a special gadget that is designed for the purpose (it looks like a corkscrew on steroids), or if you're lucky, some grocers will actually peel and core pineapples for you. Cut the sliced pineapple into bite-size chunks and add it to the bowl containing its juice.

3. To peel the oranges: Cut off the stem and blossom ends by cutting all the way through to the flesh of the orange. Holding the fruit over a bowl to catch the juices, peel them with a paring knife, just barely cutting through the outer membranes of each section. Cut the oranges crosswise into ¼-inch-thick slices, remove the seeds, and put them in the bowl with their juice.

4. Cover the bottom of a glass serving bowl with a layer of oranges, sprinkle with a handful of the coconut, and cover with a layer of pineapple. Sprinkle the pineapple with another handful of coconut. Repeat with the oranges, coconut, and pineapple until all the fruit is in the dish, finishing with a thick layer of coconut. Pour the reserved coconut juice slowly over the ambrosia and let it stand for an hour or so before serving.

5. Combine the reserved pineapple and orange juice and drink it yourself—cook's treat.

Grapefruit and Avocado Salad

SERVES 4

Grapefruit would seem to have an odd name if you've never seen it growing on the tree, since there's very little about this large, yellow-to-pink fruit that would suggest grapes. But after you've seen it on the tree, all is clear: The fruit actually grows in grape-like clusters.

The tart-sweet flavor of this fruit is ideal for savory cooking and for salads like this Florida classic, which is a great first course for any fish dinner. You can also turn it into a fine luncheon main course by adding cooked and peeled shrimp. Allow about 1½ pounds of large shrimp.

If the grapefruit isn't very sweet, you can add a little sugar to the juice when you make the dressing, but go easy; the idea here is salad, not dessert.

2 large pink grapefruit

2 medium avocados

2 tablespoons reserved grapefruit juice (see step 1)

2 tablespoons lemon juice

Salt

Sugar (optional, see step 2)

½ cup extra-virgin olive oil

4–8 romaine or Boston lettuce leaves, washed and drained

2 tablespoons chopped fresh mint leaves

1. Cut the tops and bottoms from the grapefruit and, holding the fruit over a bowl to catch the juice, peel it with a paring knife, cutting all the way through the connective membranes to the inner flesh. With a sharp knife, separate the sections from their membrane and add them to their collected juices. Peel the avocados, then split lengthwise, pit, and cut them into thin wedges.

2. Combine 2 tablespoons of the reserved grapefruit juice, the lemon juice, a large pinch of salt, and sugar to taste (taste the grapefruit juice; if it's already sweet, it won't need sugar). Slowly whisk in the olive oil, beating until emulsified.

3. Arrange the lettuce leaves on individual salad plates. Lift the grapefruit sections from their juice, pat dry, and arrange on the lettuce with the avocados, alternating in a fan pattern.

4. Pour the dressing over the salad, sprinkle with chopped mint, and serve at once.

Note: *The salad can be made an hour ahead up through step 2. Don't make it too far ahead or the avocado will begin to oxidize and discolor.*

Sherried Grapefruit   SERVES 4

Here is another old, forgotten classic that makes an exquisitely simple and lovely first course for brunch, lunch, or a light dinner. It also makes a refreshingly light dessert for the end of a fish dinner or heavy winter meal.

4 large, ripe pink or red grapefruit

Medium-dry sherry such as amontillado

Sugar

4 mint sprigs

1. Cut each grapefruit crosswise in half. Cut out the sections with a citrus knife or serrated utility knife and transfer them to a glass bowl. Add just

Broiled Grapefruit   SERVES 4

This nearly forgotten but lovely standard is past due for rediscovery. It's an elegant, delicious way to begin a winter breakfast, brunch, or luncheon. Old cooks often added a spoonful of brandy or bourbon to each serving. Southern food guru John Egerton (see John Egerton's Lemon Curd, page 272) added a dusting of cinnamon and drizzled the center cavity with a bit of honey.

2 large grapefruit (white, pink, or red, your choice)
Demerara, turbinado, or light brown sugar
4 teaspoons bourbon or brandy, optional
2 tablespoons butter, cut into 4 equal chunks
4 fresh strawberries and mint sprigs, or, for nostalgia, pitted maraschino cherries

1. Split each grapefruit crosswise in half and loosen the sections from their connective membranes with a citrus knife or serrated utility knife. Sprinkle the cut surface of each with sugar to taste, but so that the surface is well covered. If liked, sprinkle each with a spoonful of bourbon and let it stand 15–30 minutes.

2. Position a rack 6 inches from the heat source and preheat the broiler for at least 15 minutes. It should be very hot. Put the grapefruit cut-side up on a rimmed baking sheet and top each with butter. Broil until the sugar melts and the tops are lightly brown and glazed, about 5 minutes.

3. Garnish with strawberries (or cherries) and mint and serve warm.

Pompano or Snapper Palm Beach
SERVES 4

Another old Florida classic, this might well have been served at Whitehall, Henry Flagler's serenely elegant mansion that was one of Palm Beach's crowning jewels. Though once expanded

enough sherry to barely cover them. Let sit 15–30 minutes, taste, and add sugar as needed. Gently stir until the sugar is dissolved, then cover and refrigerate until thoroughly chilled. You may make it to this point up to 8 hours ahead (if you're serving it for brunch, make it up the night before).

2. Meanwhile, scoop the membrane from the grapefruit rinds, being careful not to tear or puncture the shells so that they form natural cups. Cover and refrigerate them until needed. (If you prefer, you can omit this step and simply serve the fruit in small glass dessert bowls.)

3. To serve, put 4 of the grapefruit cups into glass dessert bowls (or trim them so that they'll sit flat on a glass plate, or omit them altogether). Divide the fruit evenly among the grapefruit cups or dessert bowls, garnish with mint, and serve cold.

into the pan. Fry, turning once, until golden and just cooked through, about 1–2 minutes per side, depending on the thickness of the fillets.

3. Remove the fish to warm serving plates and alternately arrange the grapefruit and orange sections on top.

4. Return the pan to the heat, add the reserved grapefruit juice, stirring and scraping to loosen any cooking residue and bring it to a boil. Let it reduce slightly, then turn off the heat. Stir in the parsley and whisk in the remaining butter. Pour the sauce over the fish and serve at once.

John Egerton's Lemon Curd

MAKES ABOUT 2½ CUPS

John Egerton was a journalist, historian, and dyed-in-the-wool Southern cooking advocate from Nashville, Tennessee. Through his columns for *Southern Living* magazine and his two excellent books—*Southern Food* and *Side Orders*—he did much to preserve and advance the cause of traditional Southern cooking.

When I asked him for a recipe to include in the first edition of this book, I told him that it didn't matter what it was so long as it was Southern and a vegetable or fruit. With characteristic promptness, he sent three recipes. The surprise was that all three were for lemon curd, to which he was incurably addicted. When I reminded him that my book was about vegetables and fruit, he reminded me that lemons are fruit. When I said that perhaps I might want something a bit more, well green, John shot back that I could make it with limes.

Clearly, lemon curd was what I was going to get.

And why not? There's nothing better or more Southern, for though its roots are English, lemon curd has been a staple on Southern tables since the late eighteenth century. It's the nicest and

into a resort hotel that rivaled The Breakers, the mansion's modern additions were later removed and it has been carefully restored as a proud reminder of the city's Gilded Age heyday.

1 large pink grapefruit

1 large navel orange

4 tablespoons clarified butter

4 (5-ounce) pompano or snapper fillets

Salt and whole white pepper in a mill

Instant blending flour or all-purpose flour in a shaker

2 tablespoons minced flat-leaf parsley

2 tablespoons unsalted butter, chilled and cut into bits

1. Peel and section the grapefruit as directed in step 1 of Grapefruit and Avocado Salad (page 270), being sure to peel and section the fruit over a bowl to collect the juice. Over a separate bowl, peel and section the orange in the same way. Set the orange juice aside for another use.

2. Melt the clarified butter in a nonstick pan over medium-high heat. Pat the fish fillets dry and season lightly with salt and a liberal grinding of pepper. When the butter is hot, lightly dust both sides with instant flour and slip them most traditional of fillings for lemon pies and tarts, and is singularly wonderful slathered over breakfast toast.

¼ pound (1 stick) unsalted butter
½ cup freshly squeezed lemon juice (4–5 lemons)
3–4 teaspoons (or more, to taste) grated lemon zest
1 cup sugar
3 whole large eggs and 3 large egg yolks

1. Prepare a double-boiler bottom with water and bring it to a boil over medium heat. Reduce the heat to a slow simmer and put the top pan over it. It should not touch the water. Add the butter to the pan and let it just melt, then add the lemon juice, grated zest, and sugar. Stir until the sugar dissolves.

2. In a separate bowl, beat together the whole eggs and yolks until smooth. Slowly stir them into the pan and continue stirring until it is smooth. Cook, stirring constantly, until the curd is very thick and the spoon leaves a distinct path in it, about 10 minutes. Turn off the heat and take the top boiler off the bottom.

3. Continue stirring until the curd has cooled somewhat, then pour it into a glass storage container and let it cool completely. Cover and refrigerate until thoroughly chilled before using. It keeps well in the refrigerator for up to a month, though it is unlikely you will have it that long.

Note: *This amount will fill a 9-inch prebaked pie shell. You may use the leftover whites to make a meringue topping for it. It will also fill a dozen prebaked tartlet shells or provide three layers of filling for a 9-inch round layer cake.*

Working with a butter and egg custard can be tricky. Don't let the butter get too hot before the eggs are added or they could curdle, and keep the heat low. The custard continues to thicken as it cools, so don't try to cook it to the stiff consistency of a bottled curd.

KEY LIMES

The southernmost point in the South is, ironically, sometimes not considered to be a part of "The South" at all. But while the trail of islands off the tip of the Florida peninsula, known to us as the Florida Keys, is much influenced by its Caribbean neighbors, Key West nonetheless maintains a distinctly Southern place. Perhaps that's due in part to the fact that it has long been a favorite winter hideaway for some of the South's great eccentrics such as Tennessee Williams and everybody's strange uncle.

Throughout those Keys and across the southern part of the Florida peninsula grows the famed Key lime, a small, round, fluorescent yellow citrus fruit about the size of a golf ball. This lovely but intensely sour fruit has long been a distinctive element of Floridian and Deep South cookery. Unhappily, it has a unique flavor that is miles from common Persian limes and has no real equivalent. If you can't get Key limes, the closest you can come to their juice is to mix 2 parts Persian lime to 1 part lemon juice.

Old Sour   MAKES ABOUT 2 CUPS

Key limes unfortunately don't have a long season nor do they keep well, so the cooks of Key West long ago devised Old Sour as a means of preserving the juice to use out of season. Like its cousins, the pickled lemons of the Mediterranean and the lemon catsups of northern Europe, it has become a distinctive and essential flavoring on its own.

This is the late Jeanne Voltz's recipe from *The Florida Cookbook*. Jeanne insisted that it should never be refrigerated and knew of Key West cooks whose Old Sour was from a starter they got as a wedding present more than 50 years ago; sitting on the dining-room sideboard in an old whiskey bottle, it has never, in those 50 years, seen the inside of a refrigerator. And it has never spoiled.

Use Old Sour to add tartness to greens or as a condiment with any fish or shellfish. A few drops are all you will need—as one old cookbook, put it, "it ain't called 'Old Sour' for nothing."

16–18 Key limes, or about 8 regular limes
and 8 lemons

1 tablespoon sea salt

1. Roll the fruit well to release the juice, split them, and squeeze out the juice. Strain it into a measuring cup. You should have 2 cups, depending on the juiciness of the fruit. Put the juice into a pottery crock or glass jar.

2. Add the salt and stir with a clean stainless spoon until the salt is completely dissolved. Cover the container with a double layer of cheesecloth or thin muslin, and secure the cloth with a tight rubber band. Set the container aside at room temperature and let it mature, undisturbed, for no less than 2 weeks. Jeanne recommended at least 6–8 weeks for proper fermentation.

3. When the aging is complete, the sauce is ready for use. Pour it into a bottle, seal it tightly with a cork or screw cap, and store it in a cool, dark cupboard.

Note: *While bottled Key lime juice is available at some groceries and supermarkets, it won't work for Old Sour, since it's been pasteurized and therefore won't ferment. To make this without fresh Key limes, instead of the proportions given on page 273, mix equal parts freshly squeezed Persian lime and lemon juice.*

Marion's Key Lime Pie

MAKES ONE 9-INCH PIE, SERVING 6

The most famous of all dishes made with this iconic fruit, Key lime pie has become standard fare all over the Southeast: Almost every seafood restaurant from the Keys to the Outer Banks of North Carolina serves some version of it, usually the one popularized in the second half of the century that's made with sweetened condensed milk clotted with highly acidic Key lime juice. While that version is good, it's frankly rather heavy and cloyingly sweet for my taste. Charleston-based food writer Marion Sullivan makes a subtler and altogether more satisfying one that is closer to the original pie, filled with buttery lime curd.

FOR THE CRUST

¾ cup graham cracker crumbs

¼ cup light brown sugar

3 tablespoons unsalted butter, melted

FOR THE FILLING

4 eggs

1 cup sugar

6 tablespoons freshly squeezed Key lime juice (not bottled) or 4 tablespoons Persian lime juice mixed with 2 tablespoons lemon juice

2 tablespoons finely chopped or grated Key Lime or lemon rind

Salt

¼ pound (½ cup or 1 stick) unsalted butter, melted

1 cup lightly sweetened whipped cream

1 lime, sliced (optional)

1. To make the crust, mix together the crumbs and sugar, add the melted butter, and blend until evenly moistened. Press this into a 9-inch pie pan and refrigerate 30 minutes. Position a rack in the center of the oven and preheat to 300°F. Prepare the bottom half of a double boiler with 1 inch of water and bring it to a simmer over medium heat.

2. Whisk together the eggs, sugar, juice, rind, and salt in the top pot of the double boiler. Put it over but not touching the simmering water and cook, stirring constantly, until thickened. Slowly whisk in the butter and cook, stirring constantly, until thickened. Remove from the heat and stir until cooled slightly, then pour into the prepared crust. Bake in the center of the oven until set, about 20 minutes.

3. Remove the pie to a wire cooling rack and let cool to room temperature, then refrigerate until chilled and firm. Just before serving, cover the pie with the whipped cream or garnish each slice with a piped rosette of it and a slice of lime.

Confederate Breakfast SERVES 4

This will give your morning orange juice a lift it's never had before. An old-time Southern remedy for the morning after, it's also pretty good the morning before. It gives the hungover something to live for, and the still-sober something to hope for. Think of it as a mimosa with a kick like a mule.

1 cup bourbon
3 cups orange juice, preferably freshly squeezed
4 sprigs fresh mint
Thin orange slices

1. Combine the bourbon and orange juice in a pitcher, and stir well.

2. Fill four old-fashioned glasses with ice. Pour the mixture over it. Garnish with the mint sprigs and orange slices, and serve cold.

Note: *One of Savannah's celebrated hosts, the late Dean Owens, always made this with frozen orange juice concentrate, using the concentrate can as a measure. Put equal parts undiluted concentrate, bourbon, water, and ice in a blender. For the really hungover, add a raw egg. Blend until smooth and serve in chilled cocktail or old-fashioned glasses.*

Calamondin Orange Marmalade

MAKES ABOUT 2 PINTS

Calamondin oranges have become very popular in gardens across the Deep South, though unlike most other citrus trees, they're grown more as an ornamental plant than for table fruit. Calamondin oranges are lovely, looking exactly like miniature tangerines, with the same thin, delicate skin, but there the resemblance ends: The pulp and juice are as sour as a Key lime. That's not to say that this fruit isn't at all useful in the kitchen. The juice makes a fine tenderizing marinade

and can be substituted for bitter orange, lemon, or lime juice, and the fruit makes a superlative marmalade.

Calamondins are not sold commercially, so if you have neither a tree nor a generous neighbor who does, you may substitute kumquats here.

2 pounds calamondin oranges
2 pounds (4 cups) granulated sugar
Kosher or pickling salt (not table salt)

1. Wash the fruit under cold running water and drain. Carefully twist off the stems (don't pull them or the skins will tear). Halve, seed, and thinly slice the oranges, conserving all their juices (if possible, do this on a cutting board with a juice well). Put the fruit and its juices into a heavy-bottomed stainless-steel or enameled pot as it is cut.

2. Add the sugar, 1¾ cups water, and a small pinch of salt. Stir until the sugar has mostly dissolved, then bring to boil over medium heat, stirring often. Adjust the heat to maintain a steady but not a hard boil and cook until the skins are transparent and tender and the syrup is thickened and jellies when dropped from the spoon onto a saucer

(210–220°F on a candy thermometer). It will take about half an hour or a little more.

3. Let the marmalade cool slightly, then, using a sterilized stainless-steel ladle and wide-mouthed funnel, transfer it to sterilized half-pint jars. Cover with new canning lids, cool, and refrigerate or, for prolonged storage, process in water bath for 5 minutes (see page 11 for the method).

Crystallized Citrus Peel

MAKES ABOUT 2 POUNDS

Since citrus fruit was, until recently, a luxury for most people, nothing about it got wasted. Its colorful and fragrant peelings were made into a conserve that is one of the loveliest candies ever devised.

In the South, crystallized citrus peels are indispensable during the holiday season, not only as a candy, but as an important component of holiday baking (such as the Fruitcake Cookies on page 280). Though commercially candied peel is widely available today, most of it is unfortunately made with high-fructose syrup and has very little flavor. Luckily, the process of making your own is not difficult or time-consuming and is an excellent way to use leftover citrus peelings that we otherwise toss out. The old recipes called for the peel to be blanched three to four times to remove the bitterness, but doing so with our hybrid fruit removes an important element of the flavor. I find that twice is usually enough.

To use leftover rinds left from making juice (or from fruit used for breakfast or ambrosia), cut them into quarters and scoop out any remaining pulp and membrane. Wash well under cold water and store in an airtight container, such as a plastic storage bag, refrigerated, for up to 3 days, until you have enough rinds for a batch. If you are taking the rinds from whole fruit, cut them into quarters and pull out the sections with their outer membranes. The fruit can be used in fruit salad, or sectioned and served as is.

1 pound whole orange, grapefruit or lemon rinds, scraped clean of any pulp and connective membrane, but with the white pith left intact

1½ pounds (3 cups) sugar

1. Scrub the rinds under cold water and pat dry.

2. Put enough water in a heavy-bottomed stainless or enameled pot to completely cover the rinds. Bring it to a boil over medium-high heat and add the rinds. Let the water return to a boil and cook briskly for 5 minutes. Drain, refresh under cold running water, then cover with cold water once more. Return the pot to the heat and bring the water to a boil. Allow to boil for 3–5 minutes and drain thoroughly. When the rind is cool enough to handle, cut it into ¼-inch-wide strips. Return it to the pot and sprinkle 1 cup of the sugar over it. Bring it to a simmer over medium-low heat, stirring often. A syrup will form as the sugar melts into the moisture remaining in the rinds. Cook, stirring occasionally, until most of this syrup is absorbed by the rinds, about 10 minutes. Turn off the heat.

3. Spread the candied rinds on a wire cooling rack set over a baking sheet to catch drips, and let it dry at room temperature until it is firm and only a little sticky—about 8 hours. You may also do this in an oven set on the "warm" setting; it should take 2–4 hours. Check it frequently after the first hour to make sure the candy does not dry too much.

4. Spread the remaining 2 cups of sugar on a wax paper or parchment-lined cookie sheet and roll the rinds in it until they are coated. Wipe the rack clean and return them to it until they are dry to the touch. Store the candy in an airtight tin or plastic container. If it gets sticky and wet, roll it in more sugar and let it air-dry once more.

CRANBERRIES

Cranberries are a native American fruit, indigenous to the northeastern part of the United States. They aren't especially Southern, but they've been showing up on our holiday tables for centuries. Recipes for them were commonplace in old Southern cookbooks. Most of those recipes follow traditional English practice, substituting cranberries for gooseberries. Modern Southern cooks still use this fruit mostly as a condiment for the holiday turkey or as a relish for game, often pairing it with Florida oranges—a refreshing, and classic, combination.

Purefoy Cranberry Orange Relish

MAKES ABOUT 8 CUPS

The dining room of the old Purefoy Hotel in Talladega, Alabama, once had a national reputation for its fine table. Its Sunday dinners were practically a social institution. Though the hotel is long gone, Talladegans still talk of those dinners as if they had just been to one last Sunday. Much of the Purefoy's lovely cooking is alive and well in Talladega and frequently appears in the dining rooms of the city's many graceful antebellum houses, thanks to a cookbook written by Eva Purefoy, who for many years supervised the hotel dining room and the kitchen.

This is Miss Eva's recipe for the cranberry relish that used to appear on the holiday menu at the hotel. Its light, fresh taste has made it a holiday standard not only in Talladega, but all over the Southeast.

Lillie King, who gave me this recipe, always chopped the relish with an old-fashioned hand-cranked meat grinder, but you can use a food processor—just be careful not to overprocess it.

1½ pounds (two 12-ounce packages) fresh cranberries

3 whole oranges

3 small, tart apples, such as Winesaps or Arkansas Blacks, or 2 large, tart apples, such as Granny Smiths

2½ cups sugar

1. Wash all the fruit and dry well. Pick over the cranberries and discard any that are soft or blemished. Peel the oranges, reserving the peel. Cut the oranges crosswise into ¼-inch slices and remove the seeds. You can peel the apples if you like, but it isn't necessary. Cut them into quarters and remove the cores.

2. Put the cranberries, oranges, orange peel, and apples through a meat grinder into a glass or stainless mixing bowl. Stir in the sugar, cover, and refrigerate for at least 24 hours. Stir again before serving, and serve it cold.

Food Processor Method:

Cut the orange peel, oranges, and apples into chunks roughly the same size as the cranberries. Put them with the berries into a processor bowl fitted with a steel blade. Pulse the machine until the fruit is uniformly chopped fine. Transfer to a glass or stainless-steel bowl, and stir in the sugar. Cover and refrigerate for at least 24 hours. Stir again and serve it cold.

Note: *This keeps for up to a month refrigerated. Don't leave the storage bowl sitting out; scoop only as much relish as you need into a separate*

serving bowl, using a clean, stainless-steel or silver spoon. Be sure that the storage bowl is kept well covered.

DRIED FRUIT

Though Southerners have long stored apples in the root cellar or cold front bedroom to be enjoyed all winter, and today have ready access to Florida and Texas citrus fruit, which appear in the market around Thanksgiving and remain in season until the first strawberries begin to ripen, drying has long been a favorite way of keeping out-of-season fruit to enjoy all year round, and they remain popular on Southern tables to this day.

Stewed Figs in Wine   SERVES 4

What dried fruit loses in succulence is more than made up for in the rich concentration of its flavor. Here, that flavor is further enriched by stewing the figs in a sweet dessert wine. Once, this was a standard winter dessert, but nowadays it's considered to be somewhat plebeian. Mind you, that misguided attitude does not prevent it from being a deeply satisfying thing to eat on a cold winter night.

1 pound dried figs
1 lemon
1 cup Madeira, tawny port, or dry sherry
1 cup Bourbon Custard Sauce (page 47)

1. Wash the figs under cold, running water and drain well. Pare a 1 x 3-inch piece of zest from the lemon, and set the fruit aside.

2. Put the figs, piece of lemon zest, and wine in a porcelain-lined or stainless-steel saucepan. Add enough water to cover the figs, and bring it slowly to a boil over medium heat. Reduce the heat to a simmer, loosely cover, and gently stew until the figs are plump and tender, about an hour.

3. Raise the heat to medium high, and let the cooking liquid boil to a syrup. Turn off the heat. Remove the figs to a glass serving dish or divide them among individual serving plates. Cut the lemon in half and squeeze the juice from one of the halves through a strainer into the syrup. Stir well, taste, and adjust the lemon juice, then pour the syrup over the figs. Serve them warm or at room temperature with the sauce passed separately.

Martha Nesbit's Fried Pies

MAKES 12 PIES

For more than a decade, from the mid-1970s until the late '80s, the weekly food section of the *Savannah Morning News* was distinguished for its stylish writing and good regional cooking. Those were the years that my friend Martha Giddens Nesbit was at the helm as food editor.

Martha left the paper to write her first cookbook, *A Savannah Collection*, containing recipes gathered during her years at the newspaper. Though privately published and only distributed locally, the book became a standard for local cooks, and visitors by the hundreds have carried it home to all corners of the country. Her second book, *Savannah Entertains*, has reached an even larger audience.

Martha grew up in Valdosta, Georgia. When I asked her for a taste that characterized her childhood, without hesitation she answered, "fried pies," a homey pastry that was a standard sympathy offering in her hometown. She explained, "Whenever there's sadness in a small Southern town, there are sure to be fried fruit pies. These crescent-shaped pastries are filled with stewed dried fruit and fried with love, often delivered on a cracked flowered serving platter with a gentle smile, to help the grieving keep up their strength." Martha says that they almost made you look forward to somebody dying.

FOR THE FRUIT FILLING:

8 ounces dried fruit (peaches, apples, or
  a mixture of both)

⅓ cup sugar

FOR THE PASTRY:

3 cups (about 14 ounces) all-purpose flour

2 teaspoons baking powder, preferably single-acting

1 teaspoon salt

1 tablespoon sugar

⅓ cup shortening (see note)

1 large egg, lightly beaten

Peanut oil, for frying

Confectioners' sugar (optional)

1. Put the fruit in a heavy-bottomed, stainless-steel or enameled pan. Add the sugar and enough water to cover the fruit. Bring it to a simmer over low heat, and simmer until the fruit is tender, about 45 minutes to 1 hour. Drain any remaining liquid and mash the fruit well with a potato masher or fork.

2. Sift together the flour, baking powder, salt, and sugar into a large mixing bowl (or put it in the bowl and whisk to mix it). Add the shortening and cut it in with a pastry blender or fork until the mixture resembles coarse meal. Make a well in the center and add ½ cup of cold water and the beaten egg. Stir together with a fork until it forms a soft dough.

3. Lightly flour your hands and divide the dough into 12 equal balls. Roll out each ball on a light floured surface with a floured rolling pin into a circle about ⅛-inch thick. Spoon a tablespoon of the fruit into the center of each, then brush the edges of the dough with a little water. Fold the dough over the fruit to form a half-circle, gently pressing the moistened edges together with the tines of a fork to make sure they're well sealed. If the edges are a little ragged, you can trim them with a sharp knife.

4. Put enough oil in a deep, heavy skillet or deep fryer to cover the bottom by an inch. Turn on the heat to medium high. When the fat is hot but not smoking (around 365°F), put in enough pies to fill the pan without crowding. Fry until the bottoms are nicely browned, about 4 minutes, turn, and fry until uniformly browned, about 4 minutes more. Drain briefly on paper towels and, if you like, dust lightly with confectioners' sugar. Serve hot or at room temperature.

Note: *Martha and I have a running debate on shortening for the pastry. She uses only vegetable shortening, claiming that it is healthier than lard, but I use lard, claiming the reverse. Either one works fine. So will unsalted butter.*

It may take a batch or two for you to perfect making fried pies. Biscuit dough requires a certain knack that only experience can teach, as does perfect frying. I nearly burned half of my first batch, so don't get discouraged if your first pies aren't perfect.

If the prospect of frying sends you into a fat panic, you can bake them instead, as my grandmother and mother often did. Position a rack in the upper third of the oven and preheat it to 350°F. Put the pies on an ungreased cookie sheet, brush with melted butter, and bake until lightly browned, about 12 minutes.

As to serving them, Martha says that they should go on the table "between the layer cake with caramel icing and the fresh coconut cake." Well, we should all be so lucky.

Fruitcake Cookies

MAKES BETWEEN 8 AND 9 DOZEN

These rich morsels are a holiday staple all across the South, and people who profess to hate actual fruitcake will put them away with gusto. They're descended from old-fashioned English "rock cakes"—so-called because of their shape rather than their texture (although some cooks have been known to take that name a bit too literally). For all intents and purposes, they're drop cookies made with a thick fruitcake batter. Today they're most often made with commercially candied fruit, but this recipe is based on the older versions, which contained only dried fruit, homemade candied citrus peel, and nuts. Good quality glacéed cherries do make more colorful cookies, and can be substituted for the dried cherries if you like.

This batter is stiff, so use a 2-teaspoon cookie scoop to drop it, or push it from a shallow teaspoon with the back of a second spoon.

1 cup pitted dried cherries, halved

1 cup currants

1 cup chopped dates

1 cup chopped Crystallized Citrus Peel, page 277, made with oranges

1 cup golden raisins

1 cup dark raisins

¼ cup plus 2 tablespoons bourbon

¼ cup plus 2 tablespoons medium dry sherry

1 cup roughly chopped walnuts, preferably black walnuts, or pecans

2 cups all-purpose flour

½ teaspoon ground cinnamon

½ teaspoon freshly grated nutmeg

1 teaspoon baking powder

4 ounces (½ cup) unsalted butter, softened

1 cup sugar

2 large eggs

1. Lightly mix the cherries, currants, dates, crystallized peel, and raisins in a large bowl. Add ¼ cup each of bourbon and sherry, toss well, cover with plastic wrap, and macerate at least 8 hours or overnight.

2. Position a rack in the center of the oven and preheat to 325°F. Line two or three large baking sheets with parchment or lightly butter them and set aside. Add the nuts and 1 cup of flour to the fruit and toss until everything is evenly coated. Sift or whisk together the remaining flour, cinnamon, nutmeg, and baking powder.

3. Cream the butter and sugar until light and fluffy. Beat in the eggs one at a time and, alternating between them, add the flour and remaining bourbon and sherry. Fold in the nuts and fruit.

4. Drop the batter in heaped teaspoonfuls onto the prepared pans 1 inch apart. Bake until lightly browned, about 12 minutes. Cool on the pans on wire racks and then transfer the cookies to airtight tins. Wait at least 48 hours before serving.

Resources

The most reassuring thing about good Southern cooking is that it doesn't require a lot of specialty ingredients that you need to move heaven and earth to find. Most of the ingredients called for in this book are available at just about any local market in America. I've suggested substitutes where appropriate for the few products that tend to be strictly regional, and many of them are readily available by mail order. Here are a few key sources.

Southern Soft-Wheat Flour

Daisy Organic Flour
PO Box 299
Lancaster, Pennsylvania 17608
Tel.: (800) 624-3279
www.daisyflour.com

King Arthur Flour
PO Box 876
Norwich, Vermont 05055
Tel.: (800) 827-6836
www.kingarthurflour.com

Martha White Foods
PO Box 751030
Memphis, Tennessee 38175
Tel.: (800) 663-6317
www.marthawhite.com

White Lily Foods
4740 Burbank Road
Memphis, Tennessee 38118
Tel.: (800) 595-1380
www.whitelily.com

Grits and Cornmeal

Freeman's Mill
518 Country Club Road
Statesboro, Georgia 30458
Tel.: (912) 852-9381
www.freemansmill.com

Hoppin' John's
(Online only)
www.hoppinjohns.com

Logan Turnpike Mill
3485 Gainesville Highway
Blairsville, Georgia 30512
Tel.: (800) 844-7487
www.loganturnpikemill.com

Old Mill of Guilford
1340 NC Highway 68 North
Oak Ridge, North Carolina 27310
Tel.: (336) 643-4783
www.oldmillofguilford.com

For Cornmeal Only

Fowler's Milling Company
[No relation]
12500 Fowlers Mill Road
Chardon, Ohio 44024
Tel.: (800) 321-2024
www.fowlermill.com

Carolina Gold Rice

Anson Mills
1922 C Gervais Street
Columbia, South Carolina 29201
Tel.: (803) 467-4122
www.ansonmills.com

Anson Mills also offers organic whole-corn grits, cornmeal, soft-wheat flour, other specialty grain products, and Sea Island red peas, the pea originally used for authentic hoppin' John.

Southern Dry-Cured (Country) Hams and Other Cured Pork Products

Benton's Country Hams
2603 Highway 411
North Madisonville,
Tennessee 37354
Tel.: (423) 442-5003
www.bentonscountryhams2
.com

S. Wallace Edwards & Sons, Inc.
PO Box 25
Surrey, Virginia 23883
Tel.: (800) 222-4267
www.virginiatraditions.com

W.G. White & Company
2119 Highway 601 North
Mocksville, North Carolina
27028
Tel.: (866) 600-4267
www.wgwhite.com

Pecans

Pearson Farms
5575 Zenith Mill Road
Fort Valley, Georgia 31030
Tel.: (888) 423-4374
www.pearsonfarm.com

Pearson Farms also grows and sells quality Georgia peaches in season. Tell Al and Mary that Damon sent you.

Ellis Brothers Pecans, Inc.
1315 Tippettville Road
Vienna, Georgia 31092
Tel.: (800) 635-0616
www.werenuts.com

Sunnyland Farms, Inc.
Jane Wilson
PO Box 8200
Albany, Georgia 31706
www.sunnylandfarms.com

Young Pecan Company
1831 West Evans Street
Florence, South Carolina
29501
Tel.: (800) 829-6864
www.youngpecans.com

Sourwood Honey

Blue Ridge Honey Company
Bob & Suzette Binnie
PO Box 15
Lakemont, Georgia 30552
www.blueridgehoneycompany
.com

Savannah Bee Company
Ted Dennard, Beekeeper
211 Johnny Mercer Boulevard
Savannah, Georgia 31410
Tel.: (800) 955-5080
www.savannahbee.com

Index

About the Author

Damon Lee Fowler is a culinary historian, a food writer, and the author of numerous cookbooks, including *Savannah Chef's Table* (Lyons Press), *Classical Southern Cooking*, *Fried Chicken: The World's Best Recipes*, and *The Savannah Cookbook*. His work has appeared in national publications, including *Bon Appétit*, *Food & Wine*, and *Relish*. He lives, eats, and writes in Savannah, Georgia, where he is the featured food writer for the *Savannah Morning News*.

PHOTO BY TIMOTHY HALL